BABEL IN ZION

BABEL
IN ZION

JEWS, NATIONALISM, AND

LANGUAGE DIVERSITY

IN PALESTINE, 1920–1948

Liora R. Halperin

Yale

UNIVERSITY PRESS

New Haven & London

Published with assistance from the Louis Stern Memorial Fund.

Yale University Press books may be purchased in quantity for
educational, business, or promotional use. For information, please
e-mail sales.press@yale.edu (U.S. office) or sales@yaleup.co.uk
(U.K. office).

Set in Baskerville type by IDS Infotech Ltd., Chandigarh, India.
Printed in the United States of America.

Library of Congress Cataloging-in-Publication Data
Halperin, Liora.

Babel in Zion : Jews, nationalism, and language diversity in Palestine,
1920–1948 / Liora R. Halperin.
pages cm
Includes bibliographical references and index.
ISBN 978-0-300-19748-8 (hardcover : alk. paper)
1. Multilingualism—Palestine—History—20th century. 2. Jews—
Palestine—Languages—History—20th century. 3. Hebrew language—
Palestine—History—20th century. 4. Jews—Identity. I. Title.
PII5.5.I75H35 2014
404'.20956940904—dc23

2014016767

A catalogue record for this book is available from the British Library.

This paper meets the requirements of ANSI/NISO Z39.48–1992
(Permanence of Paper).

10 9 8 7 6 5 4 3 2 1

To Sasha,

my partner on this journey

CONTENTS

Note on Transliteration and Translation, ix

Acknowledgments, xi

INTRODUCTION
Babel in Zion, 1

CHAPTER ONE
Languages of Leisure in the Home,
the Coffeehouse, and the Cinema, 26

CHAPTER TWO
Peddlers, Traders, and the Languages of Commerce, 62

CHAPTER THREE
Clerks, Translators, and
the Languages of Bureaucracy, 99

CHAPTER FOUR

Zion in Babel: The Yishuv in
Its Arabic-Speaking Context, 142

CHAPTER FIVE

Hebrew Education between East and West:
Foreign-Language Instruction in Zionist Schools, 181

CONCLUSION

The Persistence of Babel, 222

Notes, 231

Bibliography, 275

Index, 303

NOTE ON TRANSLITERATION AND TRANSLATION

Throughout this book I have followed the Library of Congress transliteration system for Hebrew, with a few modifications. I use "tz" rather than "ts" for tzadi, and I omit most diacritical marks and dots. On occasion, an additional apostrophe is used to remove ambiguity (e.g., *mis'har* rather than *mishar*). In cases where a person's name is conventionally spelled differently from how my transliteration would suggest, I retain the conventional spelling. I use English terms for Zionist institutions such as the Jewish Agency (Ha-sokhnut ha-Yehudit), the Jewish National Council (Ha-Va'ad Ha-Le'umi), and the Central Council for the Enforcement of Hebrew (Ha-mo'atzah ha-merkazit le-hashlatat ha-'Ivrit). In a few cases, institutions that have well-known Hebrew names, such as the Histadrut, are referred to by that name. When transliterating words that came to Hebrew from English, I often maintain spellings closer to English even when the standard transliteration system would indicate otherwise (e.g., Briti rather than Beriti).

During the British mandate period, Jews, Arabs, and foreigners all used the term "Palestine" when they were writing in English about the political unit they were living in. When Jews prepared Hebrew and English versions of the same bureaucratic document, they used "Eretz Yisra'el" (Land of Israel) in Hebrew and "Palestine" in the English translation. In this book, I use "Palestine" as the English translation of "Eretz Yisra'el" when the political unit is at issue, but "Land of Israel" in cases where the Jewish resonance of the term is central to the source.

ACKNOWLEDGMENTS

While writing about Jews coming to terms with unfamiliar surroundings, I myself was on the move. I wrote the first version of this book as my PhD dissertation while a graduate student at UCLA but living in Somerville, Massachusetts, as a visiting fellow at Harvard. I was fortunate to be able to continue work on my book manuscript in several excellent institutions and academic communities: Yale University, Princeton University, and the University of Colorado Boulder.

The journey that led to this book began in an act of displacement when David Myers convinced me that some of the most exciting work in Jewish studies was happening on the West Coast. And indeed, I found at UCLA a remarkable community of scholars and students and a vibrant history department and Jewish studies program that inspired me and pushed me to grow personally and intellectually. David's support and generosity, along with his tough questions, have remained a constant, and he has continued to inspire me as I move forward in my own career.

Sarah Stein, though she joined the UCLA faculty midway through my graduate years, took me on as a student and impressed me with the meaningful feedback, support, and mentorship she has provided. Naomi

Seidman, with her love of language, close readings of texts, and sharp eye offered me innumerable insights. Arieh Saposnik's deep knowledge of all things related to the Yishuv and Zionism helped me hone my presentation of historical context. Derek Penslar was one of the first people I spoke with about my scholarly interests—when I was a sophomore in college—and he has been enormously generous over the many years since with professional guidance and incisive scholarly feedback. Arnold Band, Ra'anan Boustan, Michael Cooperson, and James Gelvin, all at UCLA and John Efron at the University of California, Berkeley, were central to my graduate training and have provided important mentorship and assistance over the years.

Over the years as this project came to fruition, I received invaluable support, assistance, and feedback from scholars, many of whom are also friends, at several institutions. Thanks to Amos Bitzan, Leena Dallasheh, Hilary Falb, Peter Gordon, Jonathan Gribetz, Shaun Halper, Anat Helman, Susanna Heschel, Sara Hirschhorn, Adriana Jacobs, Abigail Jacobson, Nathan Kurz, Rena Lauer, Lital Levy, Jessica Marglin, Anita Norich, Shachar Pinsker, Orit Rozin, Eliyahu Stern, Rephael Stern, and Mir Yarfitz. William Friedman, Rena Lauer, Sarah Potvin, and Nadira Mansour provided me with invaluable editing and research help.

Some of the costs associated with the research for and publication of this project were supported by a Jacob K. Javits Fellowship, a Foundation for Jewish Culture Maurice and Marilyn Cohen Dissertation Fellowship, a Schusterman Israel Studies graduate fellowship, the Princeton Department of Near Eastern Studies, and a Eugene M. Kayden Award from the University of Colorado Boulder. I completed much of my work on the manuscript as a Jacob and Hilda Blaustein Postdoctoral Associate in Judaic Studies at Yale University and an Assistant Professor of Near Eastern Studies and Judaic Studies at Princeton. I am grateful for the communities of scholars and academic resources that I found at those two institutions, and to Steven Fraade and Paula Hyman (*z"l*) at Yale and Martha Himmelfarb, Peter Schaefer, and Sukru Hanioglu at Princeton for their roles in bringing me to, and supporting me at, those two positions. For their help in arranging formal and informal visiting affiliations over the course of work on this project, as well as for giving me important insights, I would like to thank Hagit Lavsky and Uzi Rebhun at the

Hebrew University, Ruth Wisse and Mark Kishlansky at Harvard, and Ilan Troen and Eugene Sheppard at Brandeis. Elana Shohamy was an enormous source of both academic guidance and gracious hospitality during my multiple stays in Tel Aviv, and Galit Hasan-Rokem and Freddy Rokem were wonderful hosts in both Berkeley and Jerusalem. Thanks also to Vivian Holenbeck, Rachel Rockenmacher, Renee Reed, Karen Chirik, Angela Bryant, Sarah Boyce, Baru Saul, Kellie Matthews, and Jamie Polliard for their administrative support. Special thanks to David Shneer at the University of Colorado Boulder as well as to the enormously generous and supportive members of the CU history department and Jewish studies program for bringing me out to Colorado and providing me the ongoing mentorship to bring this project to completion.

As I gathered the sources for this book, I was helped along by many talented archivists, including Nava Eisen and the staff of the Education Archives at Tel Aviv University; Tziona Raz, Nellie Varzarevsky, and the staff of the Tel Aviv Municipal Archives; Helena Vilensky at the Israel State Archives; Rochelle Rubenstein at the Central Zionist Archives; Gabriel Mordoch at the Oral History Division of the Center for Contemporary Jewry; Aharon Azati at Yad Tabenkin; Vardit Samuels at the Harvard University Judaica Division; and the staffs at Yad Ya'ari, Beit Berl, the Lavon Institute, the Jabotinsky Archives, the National Library of Israel, the Haifa Municipal Archives, and the Jerusalem Municipal Archives. A special thanks to Meira Henis for sharing the marvelous photograph of her mother that I discuss in the introduction and to Ruti Herman at Kibbutz Ha-Zore'a for granting permission to share photos from her father, Eliezer Be'eri.

I presented pieces of this project at a wide range of conferences and workshops. I am thankful to the participants and attendees at those gatherings for feedback that helped shape the iterations of this project. Particular thanks to participants at the Yale Writing History and Modern Jewish Studies Workshops, the Frankel Center at the University of Michigan, Schusterman Center for Israel Studies at Brandeis, the Harvard Modern Jewish Worlds Workshop, and the Princeton Judaic Studies Workshop.

Michael Gordin, Anat Helman, Derek Penslar, Shachar Pinsker, and Lital Levy read versions of the manuscript and gave wonderful feedback. I am thankful also to the two incisive anonymous reviewers for Yale University Press; to my editors at Yale, Jennifer Banks, Heather Gold, and

Jeffrey Schier, for patiently shepherding me through the publishing process; and to freelance copy editor Kip Keller. Errors in content are of course mine alone.

My friends and family never ceased to provide me support and guidance as I confronted the range of professional and personal uncertainties that come with bringing an academic project to completion. I have been fortunate to have great, supportive relatives in my various places of residence: Los Angeles, Berkeley, Massachusetts, Connecticut, New Jersey, and Israel. The steadfast friendship of Ilana Sichel, David Schlitt, Shira Kieval, and Mihaela Pacurar has helped me navigate through the ups and downs of these past years. A special thank-you to my parents and sister for their love and unconditional support. And, finally, to Sasha Senderovich, who has supported me enthusiastically, lovingly, and patiently from the very beginnings of this project until its completion.

INTRODUCTION

BABEL IN ZION

Learn Hebrew! Every Jew in Palestine, whether he has just come or whether he is a longstanding resident, must speak and conduct all his business in the old-new language of the Jewish people: Hebrew. Our education, our press, and our theater are Hebrew. Just as in public life, likewise also in private and family life, Hebrew is heard among us!!!
—*Yiddish passage from a flier advertising Hebrew courses,*
late 1930s or early 1940s

On the occasion of the one-hundredth anniversary of the city of Tel Aviv, in 2009, the Tel Aviv Municipality collected family photographs from longtime residents of the city and displayed them prominently in its streets. A certain photo caught my eye. It depicts a woman in her twenties, dressed in an unusual and elaborate costume constructed of national flags labeled with names of world languages: German, Romanian, Polish, Russian, Yiddish, Greek, and English. She holds a sign in her hand in the shape of the Star of David that reads: "I am a Hebrew woman and Hebrew is my language." Emblazoned on her chest is the purported description of the costume: "the Hebrew language and its attackers." The caption of the photo, attached by the curators of the series, entitled "The City Revealed," tells us that the woman in the photo is Paula Gottlieb Sutker, and the time is the festival of Purim in 1925.

Paula Gottlieb (Sutker), Purim 1925.
Courtesy of Meira Henis.

The photograph comports with a popular narrative of the Hebrew revival in which young people, particularly in the Tel Aviv area, took it upon themselves to defend the Hebrew language against abuse and neglect, often resorting to brash tactics and public pageantry to impress on their fellow Hebrews the need to speak Hebrew. Paula's costume appears to be a passionate statement of the pro-Hebrew consensus that "united left and right, religious and secular Jews" at a moment when the Zionist movement was well-established in the Yishuv, the Jewish community of prestate Palestine, and Tel Aviv, the new, Jewish city founded in 1909, already had scores of Zionist cultural institutions, an autonomous Hebrew-language school system, and an established tradition of public rituals.[1] It would seem that Paula had taken advantage of the holiday of Purim, a traditional feast devoted to public revelry and costumes, to display this normative message. The costume was indeed a hit. Paula wore it to the Agadati Ball—a popular pageant that attracted particularly the young with promises of good food, wine, and prizes—and took home second prize, a set of silver pitchers and cups, which she brought to the studio of the photographer who staged the picture.

But as I investigated the photo, through a series of telephone calls that eventually landed me in the living room of Paula's daughter, Meira, the story behind the photo turned out to be somewhat different. Paula, it turns out, wasn't exactly a Hebrew activist. She had immigrated to Palestine from Warsaw in 1924, a seamstress's daughter who had learned from her mother how to sew linens and nightgowns. She struggled with the Hebrew language all her life; that Purim, less than a year after immigrating, she almost certainly knew little more than a few words. Meira suggested that Paula might have been encouraged to don the costume by her older brother, Ben-Zion, a Hebrew cultural activist and journalist who had changed his surname to Yedidyah upon immigrating to Palestine a decade earlier, in 1914. Such an interaction, too, would reflect certain commonplaces about the Zionist Hebrew promotion project: it might seem that there unfolded an interaction between two classic types of individuals: a nonpolitical immigrant woman who had trouble adjusting to Hebrew, and a confident, cultured man devoted to promoting a pro-Hebrew agenda. In this reading, Ben-Zion was the clear victor, who quite physically projected onto his sister an image of youthful civic activism that would become a photographic symbol of Tel Aviv, the First Hebrew City.[2]

Yet neither the type represented by Paula, the voiceless immigrant with a linguistic agenda mapped onto her body, nor that by Ben-Zion, the proud Hebraist, fully captures the dynamic personal and institutional interactions around language that defined the 1920s, 1930s, and 1940s in Palestine. Language diversity and multilingualism, this book argues, were more than atavistic remnants slated for correction by Hebrew activists and the advancing force of Hebrew culture. Likewise, the rejection of other languages was more complex and more incomplete than blustery rhetoric—or dogmatic costumes—would allow. Purim is traditionally a time of mockery and carnival, a time not only to celebrate the victory of the weak over the strong but also to poke fun at the ideological orthodoxies that demand stark oppositions.[3] The costume's assertion of a dichotomy between Hebrew and "its adversaries" thus could be read not as a statement of ideological commitment but instead as caricature of a society negotiating between an ideal of language exclusivity and the evident persistence, even importance of those "adversarial" languages whose names were carefully sewn onto Paula's dress.

We cannot know Paula's intentions for certain, but her dress offers us a portal into the field of linguistic practice and discourse in a society where individuals and institutions used languages other than Hebrew for personal, commercial, professional, and political reasons. How can we understand the society in which Paula chose to don a costume attesting to the threat of language practices marked as foreign? How does her stark representation of Hebrew's struggles and other languages' incursions match up with the linguistic reality that she, her family, and her friends encountered—and created—in a Jewish immigrant society, operating semiautonomously under British rule in the heart of the Arabic-speaking Middle East?

While considering the scope of the Zionist movement's promotion of Hebrew in the years before Israel gained independence in 1948, the following study demonstrates and clarifies Jews' proficiency in, concern for, exposure to, and discussion of languages other than Hebrew. Using archival sources in tandem with visual sources, oral histories, and journalistic pieces, among other sources, it charts the contours of Hebrew's hegemony and the limits of that hegemony in negative relief, that is, it focuses not primarily on the rise and formation of Hebrew and Hebrew culture but on the intersections and interactions of that culture with linguistic others in a variety of settings.

Chronologically, this study is focused primarily on the years between 1920, when the British, then the military occupiers of Palestine, first declared Hebrew an official language of that country, and 1948, when Israel declared independence and began to formalize language policies in the context of statehood. With fin de siècle Zionist Hebrew promotion efforts as its backdrop, and taking the growth of Hebrew institutions as a matter of fact, it considers the stakes of language diversity in both urban and rural settings in Palestine, across social groups who differed in their assessment of Hebrew's role, and in both official discourse and lived practice. Through a consideration of language practices and discourses about language in several social spheres—commercial settings, leisure-time spaces, bureaucratic offices, neighborhoods, propaganda offices, and schools—it recasts the Jewish community of mandate Palestine in light of its persistent contacts with Jewish and non-Jewish world communities, global markets, the British administrative apparatus, and the local Palestinian Arab population. Attitudes toward and perceptions of language practice lend insight into the dynamic and ambivalent processes by which Zionists effectively defined "Hebrew society" as a society that, in many settings and to many people, could not be Hebrew-only.

Beyond identifying a chasm between official rhetoric and lived practice, this book seeks to understand the complexity of Zionist official discourse itself, which, aside from moments of activism or rejection of other tongues, exhibited two other significant modalities in its responses to language diversity: acquiescence in the practical realities of language diversity and explicit acceptance of certain forms of language proficiency as a means of furthering the Zionist project. Such a realization reflects the fact that a Hebrew cultural community was constrained and shaped by external and internal contexts. Rather than assume a dichotomy between ideology and practice, and between official and popular discourse, the investigation of everyday linguistic negotiations suggests that it would be inappropriate to view elite actors as ultranationalist ideologues, and "ordinary people" as primarily resisters or counterhegemonic actors. Jews of multiple professions and origins, and of differing relationships to the Zionist movement, found themselves in a society where the reality of multilingualism and language contact was persistent, inescapable, and in need of negotiation.

Reviving Hebrew

Hebrew, long used in a limited set of mostly religious and scholarly Jewish contexts, was the subject of a literary revival beginning in mid-nineteenth century Europe; the Zionist movement in Palestine, through a far-reaching educational and cultural program, promoted it as a spoken language beginning in the late nineteenth century. The program of Hebrew promotion drew strength from a longer Jewish tradition of adulation for Hebrew, which had been afforded the respect and special status of a ritual object as far back as antiquity.[4] Eliezer Ben-Yehuda, whose Hebrew Language Committee and lexicon of the Hebrew language helped create a full linguistic corpus for Hebrew beginning in the last decade of the nineteenth century, had spoken of the national tongue as the strongest bond between members of the nation: "That which a person imbibes along with his mother's milk, that which he sucks from her nipples, that which accompanies him all the days of his life regardless of the circumstances, those spiritual phrases in which he thinks his dearest thoughts." Such rhetoric marks Zionism as a fairly typical late-nineteenth-century linguistic nationalist movement, one appealing to cultural and ethnic bonds through the strongly romantic and gendered rhetoric of the mother tongue, lamenting dependency on larger nations, and seeking independence from a larger national body or multinational empire. These were movements that Hannah Arendt described as "the nationalism of those people who had not participated in national emancipation and had not achieved the sovereignty of a nation-state."[5]

Indeed, Zionist language promotion bears the markers of modern language-promotion efforts more broadly, moving through the stages of development adumbrated by Miroslav Hroch: a literary revival by a small number of committed intellectuals; a lexicographic effort to expand and modernize the language; and finally, a mass program to disseminate the language through education.[6] While features of the Hebrew language revival are sui generis, the focus of this study is not to set the Zionist experience apart from others, but rather to understand the specific ways that its language ideologies developed in a particular set of circumstances, and to draw transnational comparisons where relevant, both with other national groups and with Jews in other settings.

Scholars have emphasized that cultural Zionist rhetoric of national authenticity presupposed linguistic unity. That unity, in turn, compelled the jettisoning of linguistic alternatives. In his 1917 memoir, *A Dream Come True*, Ben-Yehuda likened the prerevival linguistic condition of Jewish Palestine—as a metonym for the Jewish world more generally—to the Tower of Babel:

> There were not more than thirty thousand Jews in the whole country . . . and these thirty thousand were not a community united by a common language. They were a veritable generation of the Tower of Babel [*dor ha-palgah*]. The communities spoke various languages, each one the language of its country of origin, so they felt themselves to be almost foreigners to one another.[7]

This chaotic linguistic situation was corrected, according to this discourse, by the imposition of a hegemonic Hebrew ideology. For Israel Bartal, Eliezer Ben-Yehuda's program of language consolidation captured "the new totalizing identity of the New Jew." As Arieh Saposnik writes, "If in Europe, non-Jewish languages were inevitably dominant, Palestine seemed to offer a unique setting that would be largely free of such temptations—a culturally virgin soil on which a new national culture could become the definitive, ultimately hegemonic cultural force of a new metropole." For it to succeed, in this view, the triumph of Hebrew required the sidelining or suppression of other tongues, even at the cost of pain, repression, and oppression: "The success of the new creation depended on the suppression of the old one," writes Yael Chaver. "In Eretz Israel they sought totality, exclusivity, and total dominance of Hebrew culture, both in the public sphere and in the private sphere," writes Zohar Shavit.[8]

The transformation was impressive—the dominant wave of historical scholarship until recently has focused on accounting for Hebrew's rise to dominance.[9] But the success of Hebrew has had an obscuring function. Shavit states that the official rhetoric obscures a real multilingual reality but downplays the general significance of this multilingual space, especially those aspects of multilingualism that were not products of imported Jewish culture: "Those cultures were imported to Eretz Israel and existed in it alongside the official culture, but like illegitimate children, they were ignored and excluded."[10] Because of the grandiose rhetoric and ultimately successful outcome of this cultural project, along with the perception that other languages, when they existed, were ignored, we know more about individuals' and institutions' pro-Hebrew efforts than we do about their and their society's layers of language competencies in speaking, understanding, reading, and writing several languages; the settings in which those competencies were deployed; and the range of attitudes expressed toward those languages alongside and despite pro-Hebrew efforts.

As we consider the stakes of language use in a multilingual space, we should remember the sociolinguist Jan Blommaert's reminder that multilingualism "should not be seen as a collection of 'languages' that a speaker controls, but rather as a complex of specific semiotic resources" useful for specific functions.[11] Speakers often use bits and pieces of language to accomplish specific social functions without having full competence (or fluency), without using other languages to replace Hebrew, or without attaching deep ideological weight to every choice. The language politics of Palestine, in other words, not only concerned which languages would be spoken natively or fluently, but also included beliefs and opinions about languages that people could hear or see around them but did not understand well or at all.

A caveat at this point is necessary: in a setting where multiple languages were discussed abstractly and symbolically as much as concretely, the actual evolving vocabulary and syntax of language was not normally at issue and is thus not the focus of this study. Though linguists have commented incisively on the mechanisms of language creation and change, particularly the deliberate shaping of Hebrew in light of its language contacts,[12] this study deliberately lends credence to the broader and vaguer concepts of "Yiddish," "Arabic," "English," and so forth, noting that such categories had discursive relevance to those who were discussing language issues, even if, and often precisely because, they were imprecise and could refer to a range of linguistic behaviors.

Because Hebrew had not been a spoken language and because its advocates struggled mightily to establish its status in the first years of the Zionist movement, the historical narrative of Hebrew's success has long been concerned with charting and explaining its rise to dominance or encouraging further advocacy on behalf of a still-nascent language.[13] As battles were won and institutions consecrated, and as existential threats to Hebrew waned, the story of language revival reached a denouement. The story of the Hebrew revival itself normally ends around 1914, by which point a series of organizational victories had ensured that the main institutional structures of the Yishuv would be Hebrew-speaking. These institutional milestones included the establishment of the Hebrew Language Committee in 1890, oriented mainly toward the coining and dissemination of vocabulary and grammatical regulations; the formation of the Hebrew Teachers' Federation in 1903; the 1910–11 decision of the leftist labor organization Po'ale Zion to publish its journal in Hebrew rather than Yiddish; and the 1914 capitulation of a German-financed technical school in Haifa, called the Technikum (later the Technion), to demands that it teach all subjects in Hebrew rather than German. "By the time [World War I] broke out," writes Saposnik in his excellent study of the formation of Hebrew culture in the late Ottoman period, "a set of initially haphazard and somewhat disparate cultural endeavors had become sufficiently harmonized to constitute the infrastructure of a new (albeit still small) Jewish national society in Palestine with its own distinct way of life." With a Hebrew-language school system, political institutions, culture-making organizations, and literature, the Yishuv after World War I was, in most respects, a Hebrew society. These institutional victories coincided with an overall monolingualization of Jewish politics across eastern Europe as well, further cementing Joshua Fishman's observation that "Jews became increasingly monolingual in the [interwar period], fully in accord with the Central European Herderian romantic view of 'one people, one language.' "[14]

How, then, do we account for the evident multilingualism of Palestine's Jewish community in the interwar period? The common historical narrative focuses on language maintenance by a network of established pro-Hebrew institutions that constituted, Benjamin Harshav writes, a "full, nationwide, secular polysystem." The key moments in this history are sensational protests over instances when another language threatened to gain prominence. These include a proposal to institute a chair in Yiddish at Hebrew University in 1927, which was met with protests, and Yiddish film screenings in Tel Aviv in the 1930s, which were greeted by stink bombs. Those who have studied direct resistance to the Hebrew project during this period emphasize a rather unified support for Hebrew after World War I despite occasional resisters and agonized, personal feelings of loss. Yael Chaver speaks of "a mainstream narrative that could not concede the existence of an alternative culture—or even a subculture—marked by language because such an admission would cast doubt on the total success of the project."[15]

Multilingualism was ubiquitous in Yishuv society, scholars would agree, but it emerges both in the discourse of the time and in much of the historiography as a form of anarchy and lawlessness, following the comments of a visitor from England who remarked, "When you walk in the streets [of Tel Aviv], which are always full of people, you find a modern Tower of Babel. Every language in the world is spoken here." Babel, in the minds of Zionists, was not a neutral description; it was the marker of insufficient social controls, the disintegration of national energies into an all-consuming, incomprehensible chatter. In turn, the phenomenon of Babel was relevant insofar as it was challenged and reversed. This approach is particularly visible in Zohar Shavit's article "Tel Aviv Language Police," an overview of efforts to curb non-Hebrew language use, which argues that city officials, zealous Hebrew promoters, and ordinary city residents "were on the alert regarding the presence of Hebrew in the public sphere."[16] Several organizations arose over the course of the mandate period to enforce Hebrew. These include the Battalion of the Defenders of the Hebrew Language (Gedud megine ha-safah), active in the 1920s; the Organization for the Enforcement of Hebrew (Igud le-hashlatat ha-'Ivrit), active in the 1930s; and the Central Council for the Enforcement of Hebrew (Ha-mo'atzah ha-merkazit le-hashlatat ha-'Ivrit), active in the 1940s, along with the Culture Committee of the Jewish National Council. I revisit these organizations and explore their layered motivations, questioning both the reach and the totalizing intention of their efforts.

The success of a mainstream Hebrew-language policy required neither the total marginalization of other languages nor the end of speculations about their relevance. This book demonstrates that language dominance, though real and powerful, was not without its limits and that those limits, when viewed as more than stumbling blocks, illuminate the extent and the impact of a national group's contacts with outside entities: in this case, the Jewish Diaspora, the European powers (especially Britain), and the Arab world. To recover multilingualism—and to recast it not only as an illicit underground but also as the robust and inevitable reality of a group living in contact with other groups—is to reconsider the extent to which a small Jewish Zionist community, settling a foreign territory and undecided about its territorial, political, and cultural objectives, was intertwined with the cultures of Jews and non-Jews abroad, as well as the non-Jewish and non-Zionist populations of Palestine itself.

A Multilingual Community

Jews referred to their community in Palestine in the years before the establishment of the State of Israel as the Yishuv. The term was used to refer to the Jewish population in Palestine historically, but in the context of the history of Zionism usually refers to what Zionists called the "New Yishuv," the Zionist settlement project, as opposed to the "Old Yishuv," the populations of religious Jews who had been living in the cities of Jerusalem, Hebron, Safed, and Tiberias for centuries. The first waves of Zionist immigrants came to Palestine in 1882 as part of a movement called Love of Zion (Hibat Zion). According to British government censuses, there were approximately 83,000 Jews in Palestine in 1922 (13 percent of the total population) and 165,000 in 1929 (20 percent of the population). A wave of Jewish immigration from Nazi Germany further increased the population, from 185,000 in 1932 to 375,000 in 1935. Despite a period of severely restricted immigration during and just after the war, the Jewish population of Palestine reached around 700,000 in 1948.[17]

This community, built in stages, was linguistically diverse in two key ways even before it encountered the linguistic landscape of non-Jewish Palestine. First, the Yishuv was an amalgam of Jews from several parts of the world, the majority of whom had resettled in Palestine in the context of the Zionist project. The growth of immigration meant that over time a smaller and smaller percentage of the Jewish population was native to Palestine. According to Roberto Bachi's statistics, 58.3 percent of the immediate post–World War I Jewish population was born in Palestine, the majority of them part of the Yiddish- or Ladino-speaking "Old Yishuv," whereas 42 percent of the Jewish population in 1931 and 35 percent of the Jewish population in 1948 was born in the country—the remainder were immigrants who in all cases had another language as a first language. In 1948, just under half the population was speaking languages other than Hebrew, either exclusively (20 percent) or as a first language in addition to Hebrew (25 percent).[18] According to a survey of those speaking a language other than Hebrew in 1916, nearly 60 percent spoke Yiddish, 7 percent Ladino, and 30 percent Arabic; in 1948, 47 percent of those speaking another language spoke Yiddish, 17 percent

German, and 7 percent Arabic, with significant percentages as well for Romanian, Polish, Ladino, Hungarian, and Bulgarian.[19] Many of the languages that would come to be referred to in Zionist discourse as "foreign" were in fact mother tongues for segments of the population.

Second, in addition to their mother tongues, immigrant residents of Palestine had often learned other languages through their studies or their personal or professional lives abroad. Hebrew was one of these learned languages for many, but language politics in the Yishuv was not merely a confrontation between Hebrew and mother tongues. When asked about their language capabilities in a 1927 survey, the 430 members of the Hebrew Teachers' Federation in Palestine, founded in 1903 to promote and expand a network of Hebrew-language schools, named among them some twenty languages in which they had full or partial competence in speech, reading, or writing. The vast majority (over 80 percent) indicated that they regularly read books and newspapers in two or more languages besides Hebrew, including European tongues such as French, German, Russian, and English.[20]

Jewish immigrants to Palestine, like many other Jews, were multilingual because they were relatively well educated and mobile. That they maintained these competencies in Palestine—and used them to their benefit—indicates that a long Jewish history of multilingualism was harnessed—and not only upended—in Palestine. The scholar of nationalism Benedict Anderson speaks of the ways that shared national imagining was created in part through the distribution of printed artifacts in the national vernacular, noting that the imagined community of the nation "had an outermost stretch limited by vernacular legibilities."[21] While this linguistic "outer limit" may have indeed been limiting in geographically bounded and largely monolingual areas, it was far more expansive in most Jewish settings, where the stretch of communal imaginings was broad, where members of a community had layers of linguistic proficiency, and where communal boundaries were only imprecisely marked by language. While the Zionist movement's educational program attempted, in theory, to limit the vernacular legibilities of its children to Hebrew—a move that Yonathan Shapiro argued led to conformism in the Israeli population[22]—the social benefits conferred by multilingualism not only persisted in practice, but also widened the range of parties with whom Zionists could engage. We must think about how a tangled web of languages, language competencies, and language awareness functioned in practice, keeping in mind that the grand promises and simplistic dichotomies of national revival rarely describe the rough-and-tumble of lived experience. We must not assume either simple Hebrew hegemony or, as that visitor to Tel Aviv did in 1938, a model of chaos. As in other urban settings around the world, and in both urban and rural settings in this society, a community persistently confronted with language difference took a complex stance toward languages other than Hebrew. Though proscribed in some settings by small but vocal and effective activist groups, language difference was widespread in practice.

Layers of Linguistic Contact

The Yishuv was embedded in several overlapping circles of influence that constrained and shaped the theoretical hegemony of a Hebrew cultural and a Jewish national project. These can be conceived of, broadly, as Jewish, regional, and imperial. Jews were situated in the Yishuv, a network of Jewish settlements populated largely by immigrants and founded and managed by Zionist institutions; in Arab Palestine, a place primarily populated by an Arabic-speaking population; and in mandate Palestine, a corner of the larger British Empire. Hebrew was, at one and the same time, a dominant local or "native" language into which Jewish speakers of several other languages were pressured to integrate; a language of immigrants seeking a foothold in a territory whose majority did not wish to accommodate their presence; and a minority national language recognized as indigenous, granted official rights by a hegemonic European power, and locked in a struggle for recognition and limited autonomy within a multilingual, multiethnic, binational territory.

The Yishuv: Hebrew and the Jewish Diaspora

The Yishuv was a community increasingly populated by Jewish immigrants from across the world, primarily eastern and central Europe, as well as smaller immigrant populations from western Europe, North Africa, the Middle East, and North America. These augmented the small Ashkenazi and Sephardi populations that had resided in or come to Palestine before the advent of Zionist immigration. In the formulations of Zionist thinkers, the establishment of an ethnic national community in Palestine was the teleological end point of a Jewish history of dispersion. At the same time, this ingathering of exiles, as the quasi-messianic parlance had it, was a microcosm of Jewish diversity. Those immigrants who came to Palestine after World War I, many from Poland and Germany but some from parts of the new Soviet Union, often came not out of attachment to Zionist ideals but out of a perception that they had no other options.[23] German and Austrian refugees in the 1930s were escaping Nazi rule, sometimes after having explicitly opposed Zionism.[24] Once in Palestine, immigrants tended to integrate into the dominant ethos (though some demonstrably did not). Their motley ideological origins, however, meant that their commitment to self-refashioning was frequently in question. National commitments could blend more readily with individualistic and economic motives, unrepressed nostalgia for and connection to European cultural forms, and a lighthearted disdain for official strictures.

The field of scholarship on Hebrew and its linguistic others has been particularly enhanced by scholarship on Hebrew and Yiddish. This particular language pairing represented the earliest linguistic conflict in the history of the Zionist movement—dating back to ideological clashes in eastern Europe in the mid-nineteenth century in which Jewish nationalists negotiated which of the two languages—one a vernacular, the other used primarily for ritual purposes—might be the better vehicle for Jewish self-determination. The early-twentieth-century relationship between Hebrew and Yiddish is thus a later chapter in a longer phenomenon of diglossia—or in Max Weinreich's term, "internal bilingualism"—involving two languages that demarcated the confines of Jewish communal life. The story of Yiddish in Palestine is the story of the Yishuv's reception of—and frequent repression of—eastern European Jewish immigrants, who were coerced, ridiculed, and repressed.[25] Telling the linguistic history of the Yishuv through the lens of Jewish immigrant language diversity highlights the persistence of diasporic attachments in the homeland, and the struggles of Hebrew enforcers to affirm and reinforce the ideological preeminence of Hebrew and its hegemony within the space of the national project.

Arab Palestine

The formulation of Hebrew as the indigenous tongue capable of neutralizing foreign mother tongues becomes problematic, however, when the Yishuv is repositioned in a regional or local spatial setting. The Yishuv—with its internal Jewish complexity—was physically embedded in Palestine, a country populated (at the beginning of the mandate period, overwhelmingly) by Arabic speakers. Mythologies of national return aside, Zionists and Hebrew were a demonstrably foreign and minority presence in Palestine. Immigrants coped, as Donna Divine puts it, with an acute sense of alienation in the homeland.[26] Their foreignness, however, was even more palpable to the indigenous non-Jewish residents. Palestinian Arabs' widespread trepidation about and opposition to the Zionist project slowly but surely prompted an organized, though largely ineffective, Palestinian political movement to advocate for restrictions on land sales and Jewish immigration. These developments, in turn, were an object of concern for Zionist organizations such as the Histadrut (General Federation of Labor), the Jewish Agency, and Jewish National Council (a nonpartisan council of the Jews of Palestine). The Zionist concern with the negation of exile (*galut*), though explicitly tied only to the intentional estrangement from diasporic Jewish experience, was implemented and realized through a negation—or better put, foreignizing—of the native communities of Palestine itself.

The Arabic language became a chief means of negotiating the newfound territory. The earliest Zionist settlers freely romanticized forms of Arab and Bedouin life, and Arabic learning was often tied to these activities. Meanwhile, a set of Jewish orientalists, some Zionist, came to Palestine over the course of the early twentieth century and became involved in founding the Hebrew University School of Oriental Studies, a major center for the study and exegesis of classical Islamic texts. Other activists turned to Arabic over the course of the mandate period for what they termed more practical and utilitarian purposes, seeing school and community Arabic study as simultaneously a means of making contact between Jewish and Arab groups, illuminating the culture and politics of the Arab world, and distributing pro-Zionist propaganda, including socialist propaganda, to Palestinian Arab communities. Arabic study and associated conversations about the language became part and parcel of the Zionist attempt to understand, coerce, and control a native population increasingly opposed to Zionist immigration and settlement. The post-1948 years have received the lion's share of attention regarding this subject, although some forays into the prestate period have sought to establish context and background for a set of emergent language relations that expressed the largely coercive linguistic treatment of Arabic in the state period.[27] Reconsidering Zionist discussions about Arabic in the mandate period on their own terms reflects a persistent, evolving concern about the place of Arabic knowledge—and thus of Palestinian Arabs—in the collective understanding of the Yishuv.

Mandate Palestine: Hebrew Culture under British Rule

The Zionist movement envisioned the Yishuv as a wholly Jewish space in which Hebrew was posited as a hegemonic language bombarded by foreign imports, immigrants, and cultural forms. Arab Palestine, meanwhile, was seen as a wholly non-Jewish space, the firmament on, around, and within which the Yishuv would develop. Hebrew also developed, however, in a further sphere of power relations: mandate Palestine, ruled by the British. The British placed the Yishuv in a version of a role that had become ubiquitous by the twentieth century in other settings: Jews were neither the ruling power nor the powerless natives. Rather, they were a small but elite nationalist group constituting itself under European imperial rule and exercising a notable degree of leverage over the ruling power.[28] Though the British mandate, unlike a true colony, was structured to allow the greatest possible autonomy for Palestine's national groups, in anticipation of national independence, the British controlled post and telegraph offices, sanitation, and policing. Thus, the relative autonomy of schools and protostate institutions met with a variety of linguistic pressures that spoke to the lack of overall Hebrew hegemony in Palestine. With the British conquest of Palestine, English competed with French and German as the clear European language of choice for the Yishuv; English also increasingly became the portal for international diplomacy, science, and commerce. Moreover, the specific linguistic policies of British rule, in particular its official trilingualism, shaped and constrained the linguistic policies of the Zionist movement, which had to accommodate itself to the demands and official status of English. These accommodations, though marked by certain particularities, were not entirely different from those occurring in other parts of the British Empire.[29]

Taken together, the discourses and anxieties attached to language diversity indicate shifting power relations both within the Yishuv and between the Yishuv and external entities. Even after Hebrew became institutionally dominant, its proponents were never sure of its strength as a compelling symbol of global Jewish unity, its political power in relation to the British Empire and the native Arab population, and its ability to serve as a language of economic power. Indeed, the particular linguistic pressures just recounted were not simply other or foreign; they over time came to refer to the looming specters or past, present, and future tragedy—the incompleteness and perhaps eventual demise of the Jewish nation. Yiddish evoked for many Zionists the historical threat of national subservice and decline; Arabic, the past, present, and future resistance to Zionism in the homeland; German, assimilation and later the Holocaust; and English, like German before it, the prospect that national identity would be swept away by global forces. Language marked moments of contact within the community and between members of the community and other communities, both locally and overseas. In negotiating the purview of German, Yiddish, English, Arabic, and other languages, Hebrew's promoters considered the scope and limits of Hebrew itself.

Language and Nation

Critics have pointed out the fractured and incomplete nature of nationalism, suggesting that nationalism is both a less concerted force than that suggested by modernist theorists of nationalism and an ideology that conditions collective behavior in certain ways and contexts but not others. This critique has invited a study of the nationalist everyday: scholars have explored how, particularly in multicultural societies or in colonial settings, top-down dictates are negotiated, subverted, or fitfully accommodated on the level of practice. Tara Zahra charts the significance of "national indifference," which "appears most clearly at the moments that nationalists mobilized to eliminate it" but which is most often buried by official records that "obscure bilingualism and national ambiguity." Monica Heller, a sociolinguist focusing on Quebec, writes that people regularly transgress known or expected categories of usage, fail to do what researchers might expect of them, and contest language in ways that challenge assumptions about nation and language. My study, in part a beneficiary of this scholarly turn in several disciplinary fields, describes a situation wherein elites and masses alike—many of immigrant backgrounds and possessing various configurations of multilingual abilities—contended with the difficulty they found in speaking Hebrew, the greater ease of using more familiar tongues, and a number of personal, symbolic, or instrumental justifications for the use of other languages.[30]

Nonetheless, globalizing currents, interethnic contacts, and national indifference do not always weaken the nation. Rather, in this particular setting, those contacts shaped and defined the nation and its rhetoric in discernible ways.[31] The figures and communities in the Yishuv that tolerated or promoted other languages were by and large interested not in undermining Hebrew or promoting an alternative project but rather in promoting the Hebrew project by way of and in reference to the other languages they remembered, knew, or encountered. Hebrew needed cultivation, but its promotion could occur only in the context of a politically and economically strong society, one that might gain or preserve its strength by effectively managing relationships with outside groups, whether British, Arab, Jewish, or something else. Rather than a search for alternatives, for a marginal underground that resisted the mainstream, we find much meaning in a search for disjunctures and accommodations even within social spheres and communities that were undeniably part of the mainstream.

This inquiry is founded on an appeal to bring the study of language—long a focus for sociolinguists and scholars of literature—into the historical field and, specifically, into the expanding realm of cultural history. Peter Burke noted in 2008 that while the new cultural history of the late 1980s and 1990s might be reaching its methodological end point, "Some domains, such as the cultural history of language, are only now opening up to historical research." The field of sociolinguistics, so keenly attuned to the link between language and social structures, traditionally had a decisively nonhistorical bent. Though individual scholars retained an interest in history, the emphasis on fieldwork and structural analysis—a turn to synchronic study from the diachronic historical linguistics or philology of the nineteenth century—largely precluded engagement with the past in works about language ideology, though studies of language ideology in the present abound. Social historians, meanwhile, have called attention to the structure of discourse and the construction of collective attitudes, but have rarely addressed historical discussions about language itself—they have been oriented toward "ideology in language" but not "ideology about language," to use Ursula Schaefer's useful distinction. More recently, though, scholars have become engaged in what Peter Burke has called "socio-historical linguistics," with an emphasis on rein-serting human history into the field of linguistics or, more germane to this project, on "the social history of language," which places the study of language, its use, and its social symbolism more firmly in the realm of historical studies.[32]

This trend of integrating the study of history with the study of language has not made significant inroads in the study of Israel and Palestine, though cultural histories of Tel Aviv have included sections on language practice and ideology, and I draw extensively from them in parts of this study. The great majority of work on language remains clustered in two rich fields. Sociolinguists of Israel (and the few who deal with prestate Palestine) have been concerned with the analysis of language practice, language change, and contemporary language attitudes. Scholars of liter-ature, meanwhile, have explored ambivalences about the techniques and possibilities of Hebrew literature, the persistence of non-Hebrew prose, and reflections on language diversity and loss as they appear in novels and poems by a limited number of writers. The study of literature has been a particularly fruitful realm in which to explore questions of language, to such an extent that it might occasionally appear that literature was the sole space in which a society under pro-Hebrew dictates had the freedom to negotiate or reflect upon linguistic alternatives.[33]

This project understands cultural history broadly, incorporating a wide range of archival and published sources in order to capture the often-nameless actors whose practices, decisions, and behaviors, often on a local level, collectively constituted the linguistic landscape and discourse of the Yishuv. The approach aims to reconstruct a cultural depth and complexity that is effaced by focusing on elites and emphasizing these elites' nationalist bona fides, and to reveal the lasting connections felt by

Zionists, including supporters of Hebrew, to those languages and cultures that lay outside the communal boundaries of the Yishuv.

The five chapters of this book trace Jewish anxieties about Hebrew's dominance and awareness of Hebrew's multilingual context across several overlapping social, institutional, and geographic spaces. It seeks evidence of quotidian responses to these concerns both in official documents and between the lines of the archival sources often created and preserved to document the spread and promotion of Hebrew. Some of the material that arises, seemingly incongruously, in the historical record takes the form of anecdotes—a letter to protest or praise a person or decision; an official conversation about an individual incident; a journalistic account of something seen or heard; a memory plucked from the recesses of experience and recorded in a memoir. The anecdote, Stephen Greenblatt and Catherine Gallagher have written, following Roland Barthes, "exposes history by momentarily betray[ing] the incompleteness and formality of the historical narrative." For the cultural historian, anecdotes reflect the voices of those not ordinarily represented in the archive. Greenblatt and Gallagher, summarizing Michel Foucault, call anecdotes "residue of the struggle between unruly persons and the power that would subjugate or expel them."[34] In this case, power rested not with a state, but with a network of semiautonomous protostate organizations operating to promote a political and cultural program. These structures, like those of a state, actively (even if not always consciously) suppressed alternative narratives, which nonetheless survived in residual form in the historical record.

The most evident and widely publicized realm of contest over Hebrew hegemony was in the leisure-time space of the Yishuv, the spaces people inhabited when they were neither working nor participating in organized political activities and in which immigrants tended to use more familiar spoken tongues and to consume imported culture in languages other than Hebrew. The first chapter considers the mix of censure and license that users of other languages confronted around their practices in three key leisure-time spaces: the home, the coffeehouse, and the cinema. These settings, precisely because they were characterized by a great deal of social and linguistic license, became primary targets for citizen bodies and organizations concerned with broadening and cementing the purview of Hebrew within an immigrant population and combating what they saw as laziness and insufficient devotion to Hebrew. At the same time, to use Erving Goffman's phrase, these were "off-stage spaces" where Hebrew did not have to be used.[35] The city of Tel Aviv, which tended to be populated by less ideological immigrants than those in agricultural settlements, was the chief site for such discourses, but the association between non-Hebrew language and leisure pervaded rural settings as well.

The quest to make Hebrew the dominant language of the Yishuv was complicated, however, not only by seemingly lazy or excessively fun-loving immigrants. The second chapter demonstrates that the conditions for defending Hebrew and promoting its hegemony were shaped also by material and economic relations, which become clearer when we consider the marketplace and the commercial sphere as spaces of linguistic contact and contestation. To construct a Zionist economy, according to the prevailing labor conception, was to exclude foreign labor and non-Jewish products from the marketplace. In expressing fear about language mixing in the marketplace, Zionists referred to a long historical association between Jewish commerce, multilingualism, and a raft of derogatory valuations ranging from parasitism to cosmopolitanism and from poverty to excessive wealth. The Zionist movement aimed to reverse course, restoring Jews to a state of economic productivity, rootedness, and language consolidation. But global and local realities restricted this vision. As a consequence, forms of commerce regarded as typically diasporic—both international trade and street peddling—persisted in the Yishuv, and they were marked by the use of languages other than Hebrew.

The rhetoric surrounding leisure-time activities and commercial goods was, by and large, the rhetoric of import, infiltration, or incursion. That is, it presumed the disruption of a dominant and supposedly hegemonic Hebrew system by people, practices, goods, and services from elsewhere that brought in foreign languages and influences. But as the final three chapters show, this story is also about the self-understanding of a community that, within frameworks of local and regional power, was distinctly limited and not hegemonic. Real and anticipated linguistic encounters within Palestine functioned as sites for the negotiation of amorphous and shifting power relationships between the Yishuv and local and regional counterparts: namely, the British mandate government, the Arab population of Palestine, and the Arab world.

Chapter 3 reconsiders the status of Hebrew in light of British control. Though the Yishuv enjoyed a great deal of autonomy in running its affairs, and though the laws of the mandate ensured an official status for Hebrew and Jewish communal autonomy, English knowledge was nonetheless beneficial in advancing Zionist aims within a British-ruled territory. A small but significant number of Jews found these skills useful either as employees of the British government or within Zionist institutions, which needed staff members proficient enough in English to engage in written communication. Though such arrangements were never flaunted, they were pervasive and help explain the prominence of English after Israel's independence.

The Palestinian Arab community also exerted its power over the Yishuv. It did so both through its capacity to shake the community through violent acts and, more abstractly, through its implicit ability to prove or disprove the legitimacy of particularly Labor Zionist promises by showing or not showing evidence of cooperation with the Zionist project. The fourth chapter outlines the scope of Jewish engagement with Arabic in Jewish communities and organizations, calling attention to the multiple, often conflicting ways that individuals and groups conceived of their practical relationship to the language of their neighbors. Arabic, when foreign, could be learned either organically or in structured settings, and when learned fluently by Ashkenazi Jews or known natively by Mizrahi or Sephardi Jews, could be deployed for interpersonal contacts, propaganda work, and military-like intelligence. Whether used by those who anticipated peaceful relations with Palestinian Arabs or those who anticipated conflict, Arabic came to symbolize both linguistic access to the local environment and the means of neutralizing a potential threat.

If English- and Arabic-language learning, as discussed in chapters 3 and 4, were on one level the products of practical exigencies, it would be wrong to frame Jewish language acquisition as purely a pragmatic or instrumental response. The fifth chapter delves into the space widely regarded as the sanctum of the monolingual Hebrew society—the Hebrew educational system—and looks at justifications offered for the teaching of both English and Arabic to children at various levels. While practically oriented curricula sought to limit language acquisition to the minimum required for instrumental competence, other voices passionately argued that English and Arabic, in different ways, could be conduits to a stronger Hebrew nation, either by drawing this underdeveloped nation closer to Europe or, in the case of Arabic, by connecting a fundamentally European population with a source of Semitic authenticity.

Neither the five loosely defined spaces discussed nor the body of primary sources presented in this book represents the sum total of discussions about Hebrew and other languages in the Yishuv. The body of sources about language in mandate Palestine is vast and diverse. Indeed, where a rich trove of material in this study illuminates a particular type or field of experience, it also may suggest research questions—about the interplay of language, identity, and nationalism in the social, cultural, and intellectual history of the Yishuv—that lay beyond the scope of this project. My sources, from a range of urban municipalities, agricultural communities, ideological movements, and central Zionist political institutions, as well as the periodical press, tended to emerge from and comment on either urban or kibbutz life. Deeper archival work in some of the scores of local and municipal archives around Israel might illuminate the experiences of denizens of First Aliyah Zionist colonies such as Rishon LeZion or Rehovot, which predated the socialist Zionist settlements and the city of Tel Aviv, or the particular perspectives of religious Jews living in Jerusalem, Hebron, Tiberias, or Safed. What questions did these communities ask about language and how did they respond to the trends that they were observing? Moreover, deeper inquiries into the correspondence, memoirs, and journalistic production of those writing in Palestine in languages other than Hebrew might offer other complementary or unique perspectives. How, for example, did the non-Hebrew-language press within Palestine, whether the Arabic press based in Jaffa or Haifa, or immigrant publications in German, Polish, Yiddish, or other languages, respond to discourses emerging from or connected to Zionist institutions? Such further research would likely augment and give further texture to my claim that the Zionist program to adopt Hebrew was complicated by a range of personal, communal, and collective considerations.

The layered sets of linguistic pressures uncovered here, products and reflections of extralinguistic trends and forces, did not signal a new condition. On the contrary, they evoked for denizens of the Yishuv a long history of Jewish exile that, despite Zionist rhetoric, was not entirely effaced in the homeland. Persistent exposure to linguistic mixing evoked a classic Jewish symbol, Bavel (in its Hebrew spelling), the site of both the mythic language mixing of Genesis 9 (Babel) and the site of exile whence, in the sixth century BCE, "Israel and Judah were carried away for their transgressions" (Babylon), according to 1 Chronicles 9:1. A legendary space of both linguistic and cultural mixing, and one repeatedly invoked by Zionists, Bavel did not dissipate in the newly configured Zion. Jewish residents pondered whether their social relations, political dealings, and economic activity bore traces of *galutiyut*, the exilic condition, and instinctively deployed references to Babel and to exile when they wanted to criticize others for acting cowardly, weak, selfish, or otherwise inappropriately.[36] The ambivalence about *galutiyut*—both about maintaining excessive links to other cultures and about constructing a society in Palestine that was overly dependent on relations with non-Jewish groups—found particular expression in rhetoric about linguistic multiplicity.

The Tower of Babel, in the discourse of many Zionist leaders, was both the starting point for a teleological history that would and should culminate in linguistic consolidation and also the dystopian end point for Zionist society if it erred on this journey; language mixing had no explicit place in the idealized Zionist project, notwithstanding Herzl's early, rejected proposal that the Jewish state would be a "federation of tongues" where a single common language would not be necessary. In practice, the vaunted Jewish homeland, far from allowing a complete break with the pre- or non-Zionist Jewish condition, was subject to many of the same disaggregating—and creative—forces, products of shifting power relations and intersecting and conflicting ideological, political, and economic pressures. The divide between diasporic disorder and consolidation in the homeland was far from clear—indeed, national consolidation spelled the structuring and negotiation of diversity, not its elimination. As James Clifford writes, "The nation-state, as common territory and time, is traversed and, to varying degrees, subverted by diasporic attachments."[37] Babel would persist in Zion, and Zion's residents would not entirely reject it.

Let us return, then, to the curious Purim costume with which we opened. Whatever the circumstances surrounding Paula Gottlieb's initial choice to put this stunning costume together, the judges of the costume contest awarded her the second-place prize, recorded by the photographer's flash. The family, in turn, kept the photograph in their records as a meaningful memento, and the "City Revealed" exhibition selected this photo as one that lent particular insight into the early years of Tel Aviv. The fight against the Yishuv's linguistic multiplicity has had notable cultural staying power. But critically assessing the multilingual reality the photo implies offers us a window into not only a past of national dogmatism and its present commemoration, but also another story embedded, possibly from its moment of inception, in the costume itself: a far more layered and ultimately deeply telling story of the dynamics of linguistic diversity in a society officially committed to the promotion of a single tongue.

CHAPTER ONE

LANGUAGES OF LEISURE IN THE HOME, THE COFFEEHOUSE, AND THE CINEMA

There is no urban culture without coffeehouses, without idlers.

—*A. S. Lirik (Aaron Levi Riklis)*

Labor, exertion, and sacrifice stood at the center of the Zionist move-ment's self-conception, and linguistic sacrifice in particular proved a potent symbol of nationalist commitments. To cast off the detritus of the Diaspora, according to mainstream ideology, Zionists were to engage in pioneering (*halutziyut*), a task defined both by cultivating the land and by building institutions to support the national project. The ideal of the pio-neer was developed in the period of the Third Aliyah (wave of Zionist immigration to Palestine) in the years between 1919 and 1923 and was also applied retroactively to members of the Second Aliyah, who came between 1904 and 1914. Immigrants of these two waves of immigration, mainly from the Pale of Settlement within the Russian Empire and the Soviet Union, often deliberately chose Palestine over America or internal-migration options and tended to be particularly ideologically committed.[1]

The volitional quality of pioneering extended to the realm of language as well. Hebrew, both the chosen national language and a language that in practice required a degree of self-sacrifice, symbolized the laborious process of building a nation. Using one's mother tongue, in contrast, appeared to embody a form of laziness. In a tract from 1921, Aharon Moshe Wizansky, a Zionist activist in Zurich who would soon after move to Palestine and teach at the elite Herzliya Gymnasium in Tel Aviv, argued against the claim, then widespread in Europe, that Yiddish should be supported over Hebrew as a national language because it was less burdensome. Easiness and comfort were not the goals, insisted Wizansky: "Not every unloading [of a burden] is liberation, just as not every loading [of a burden] is subjugation."[2] Members of the two major waves of immigration before World War II, known as the Fourth and Fifth Aliyot, were frequently cited as lazy for their continuing use of mother tongues (mainly Yiddish, Polish, or German). Such rhetoric had existed earlier, too. An article from 1936 spoke of the "inertia of adhering to Yiddish," saying that new immigrants were not taking up "the heavy burden of national values" but instead "the lighter rubbish."[3] These words capture a common pro-Hebrew perspective about the nature of cultural revival: relaxation—particularly relaxation that involved the casting off of hard-to-enact nationalist conventions—was not a form of freedom but a dangerous retreat into chaos. These poles of meaning—structure versus laziness, construction versus chaos—defined the sphere of leisure in the Yishuv, and became particularly apparent when leisure-time practices visibly (or audibly) defied a central tenet of Zionist material and cultural construction: that it be always conducted in Hebrew. Leisure was thus both a central realm for the use of languages other than Hebrew and a primary site of contest over the purview of Hebrew.

The three sites of leisure-time language use considered in this chapter demonstrate a fundamental tension surrounding the presumption that leisure was to take place in Hebrew, a language that required exertion, rather than in languages that provided spaces away from the strictures and rhetoric of the Zionist movement. The home was the perceived bastion of the mother tongue and the enervating domestic influences that would, in official rhetoric, be supplanted through education and national culture. The coffeehouse marked the importation of European street culture and the appearance of private conversation in a semipublic space. Finally, the cinema housed the imported cultural products of western Europe and the United States. In all cases, the use or consumption of languages other than Hebrew was attractive because it was natural, but by re-creating or evoking leisure-time patterns that had existed outside the Yishuv, these practices cast into question the capability of Hebrew to be hegemonic.

This chapter, like the one that follows, focuses in large part on Tel Aviv as an epicenter of encounter between an officially Hebrew Yishuv and people, products, or pressures coming from outside its confines. Together, they present Tel Aviv, the "First Hebrew City," as a paradoxical space where ideological norms, including linguistic norms, were both enforced and systematically discarded. In the growing literature on Tel Aviv, the city has been regarded as an anomaly, a place shaped both by collectivism and by cosmopolitanism and ideological diversity: "the most national, but at the same time—paradoxical though it may sound—the most international city of its size in the world." But the features that defined Tel Aviv, its leisure, and its commerce, while overwhelmingly concentrated in and associated with this urban space, were not limited to it. The tensions visible in the cinemas, coffeehouses, and marketplaces of Tel Aviv did not dissipate at its municipal boundaries into a state of national purity in the rural realm. As Louis Wirth wrote in his famous tract on urbanism, urbanization denotes not only life within the city, but also the proliferation of urban modes of life that "are apparent among people, wherever they may be, who have come under the spell of influences which the city exerts."[4] And indeed rural denizens, nearly all originating from the cities of Europe, also partook of Tel Aviv, its products, culture, and cultural forms, and encountered there, though in less intense form than in the countryside, the dynamics of linguistic and cultural encounter typical of the urban center.

Negotiating the Purview of Hebrew

The supposition that the exertion associated with Hebrew maintenance would suffuse both work and leisure—in other words, that leisure would express a pioneering ethos—rested on a radical reorientation of Hebrew's purview and a repositioning of its relationship within the traditional dichotomy of sacred and profane languages. Hebrew, the language of the sacred, was set apart, associated with spatially or temporally limited activities such as prayer and study. But in the Yishuv, the situation of Hebrew had theoretically been transformed. Refashioned as a vernacular, the language was tied not primarily to delimited ritual but to the ostensibly perennial work of building municipal, political, and educational institutions. The concept of labor, *'avodah*, was resignified in the Zionist context to refer not only to one's occupation or physical effort but also to the collective, often metaphorical work of building a country, whether in agricultural fields and industrial factories or in cultural clubs and the home, and in both times of work and times of leisure. The word *'avodah*, which was used in rabbinic discourse to refer to Temple worship, was used frequently to describe culture and literature, for example, in Hayim Nachman Bialik's mention of "the labor of literature" in his speech to the Twelfth Zionist Congress in 1921 or in the author Abraham Levinson's references to the "labor of [Hebrew] culture" at the Eighteenth Zionist Congress in 1933. Carnivals, sports, books, theater, and newspapers were all part of the Hebrew culture-building activities of the Yishuv. As Hebrew became, in the estimation of one scholar, "the language of entire lives: in theater and song, in literature and politics, in the sciences and in private reflections, in poetry and in signs on the street," and the "language that does all the labor [*melakhah*] demanded of it," as Nathan Alterman wrote, those tongues that had formerly functioned as profane vernaculars were nominally eliminated and deemed irrelevant.[5] In practice, however, the sanctity and set-apart quality of Hebrew was less stripped away than transformed. That which was in danger of defilement now was not the divine but the nation, construed as sacred and therefore requiring constant maintenance and oversight by its caretakers, the members of the nation.

Hebrew between Sacred and Profane

In this new national orthodoxy, Hebrew was to be a perennial tongue extended to the realms of both work and leisure. In practice, however, the notion that leisure was to be construed as a time of Hebrew language use was not intuitively acceptable. The exceptions made for other language use during leisure time highlight both the constraints on Hebrew hegemony and the persistent effort to brand non-Hebrew mother tongues as foreign imports.

One temporal site particularly associated with the nonuse of Hebrew was the Sabbath, the primary day of leisure in the Yishuv. Ironically, in the traditional Jewish experience, the Sabbath was also linguistically marked, but in reverse. Hebrew, the quintessential sacred tongue, was associated with the special ritual requirements of the Sabbath, the day on which Jews were enjoined to desist from quotidian labor, known biblically as *melakhah*, hear the Torah read, and recite a mostly Hebrew liturgy. Noting this ritual place of Hebrew, some rabbis went further, recommending Hebrew speech on the Sabbath. The custom, apparently most widespread in early modern central Europe, was also practiced by some religious women in Ottoman Jerusalem.[6] The work week, it went without saying, was the time for profane languages, whether local tongues or Jewish languages such as Ladino and Yiddish; the Sabbath, in contrast, would contain a flash of the sacred language amidst and against the profane.

The Sabbath continued to be marked as a day apart by many modern, Hebrew-speaking Jews, but now in a linguistically opposite way: it was in practice a day for languages other than Hebrew. A newspaper feature in the mid-1940s recounted the story of "a professor from among the German immigrants": "He learned Hebrew, lectures in this language, and speaks it every day of the week. But on the Sabbath he speaks German. His friends asked him why. He said, 'It says in our holy book, "Do not do any sort of labor [on the Sabbath]," and I strictly observe this commandment.' "[7] The story is a clear adaptation of a better-known anecdote about the writer Hayim Nachman Bialik, who had died several years earlier, in 1934: "Once Bialik was caught in the act [*be-kalkalato*], speaking Yiddish on the Sabbath and they asked him 'How can it be?' He replied: 'Yiddish speaks itself but speaking Hebrew is labor [*melakhah*], and labor is forbidden on the Sabbath.' "[8]

We would be incorrect to assume that anyone, Bialik included, made a rigid distinction between Sabbath and weekday language use; the absurd strictness of the distinction is part of what makes these anecdotes function as jokes. But a joke, based on rigid oppositions or absurd juxtapositions, functions as a mirror in which societies see themselves.[9] Indeed, the Zionist Sabbath, the day of rest and leisure in the new national context, became a setting for negotiating the limits of Hebrew dominance, in this case among immigrants who knew a variety of other languages and enjoyed using or hearing them during their free time.

Bialik's friends respond to his linguistic deviance with a mix of condemnation and laughter—a double move of license and control. When the friends enter, they deem Bialik to be committing a transgression and act surprised. Bialik's response, however, elicits a form of empathetic laughter from the reading audience and, implicitly, from those who visited him— his transgression was familiar; moreover, it fit within the unwritten rules dictating the boundaries of language use in the Yishuv. Bialik had a particular role in the imagination of the Yishuv. As Miryam Segal points out, he was the emblematic Hebrew writer who never entirely learned Hebrew and who did not cease speaking other languages.[10] This contradiction was familiar to many, who despite their interest in and commitment to Hebrew in theory, were not interested in using it exclusively. Speaking Yiddish (or German, in the professor's case) could be construed as both an unforgivable breach and an entirely unremarkable activity specifically characteristic of the Sabbath, the day of rest. This combination of shock and acquiescence, of damning scowls and knowing winks, is laced through the sources on language and leisure in the Yishuv.

The shock, on the one hand, was palpable. "The profane has overpowered the holy," wrote a proponent of Socialist Zionist Hebrew culture in 1936. "Newspapers, meetings, and official business [take place] in Hebrew but profane life [*haye hulin*] [takes place] in the language of inertia and routine." Zionist work, he implied, was regularly taking place in Hebrew; the real threat to the language was arising during times away from work, times marked by the traditional Jewish notion of "profaneness" and defined by inertia and laziness. Bialik himself criticized the distinction between "Hebrew, which is the language of holidays and demonstrations in the schools, and other languages, which are the languages of ordinary (profane) days and regular use."[11]

Were these practices—whether Bialik's individual "relapse" into Yiddish or the general practice of using other languages outside school and ceremonies—basically acceptable or basically unacceptable? On the face of it and from an official perspective, these manifestations were clearly unacceptable and thus subject to policing. Leisure is a sphere in which social norms are enacted and national ideals performed, and in which elites can exert control over the masses by encouraging or requiring certain collective pursuits. Official interest in leisure derives precisely from its independent nature; leisure invites concern "because it ostensibly represents the area of activity in which people can most be themselves." Controls on leisure, ultimately, are designed to shape "the kind of people that citizens are supposed to be when they are being themselves."[12] In the case of the Yishuv, many of these controls—incomplete by their nature—focused on language.

Policing the Boundaries of Language Usage

The interplay of license and control, central to scholars' descriptions of the paradox of modern leisure, was pervasive in Zionist authorities' dealings with language transgression. The contestation over Sabbath language practices captured in the Bialik joke resonated in a society negotiating the terms of Sabbath observance, which, along with Hebrew language, constituted the "Hebrew" quality of the Yishuv.[13] Religious Jews were interested in seeing traveling, cooking, and the use of money, electricity, and music curtailed on the Sabbath. Community committees, in Haifa, for example, worked hard to prevent such desecrations.[14] Secularly oriented members of the Yishuv, on the other hand, attached a different kind of importance to the Sabbath: they did not tend to observe traditional Sabbath restrictions, which they pejoratively associated with diasporic societies, but saw the Sabbath instead as time for secular nationalist activities.[15] Bialik's transgression, then, was not a nationalist rejoinder to and reinterpretation of traditional structures, but a snub to new nationalist "laws" and cultural orthodoxies.

Zionists had not so much cast off the bonds of Sabbath restriction as recast them in secular-nationalist terms of Hebrew piety; those who disregarded these terms were impious in a national sense. The Labor Zionist leader Yitzhak Tabenkin felt that there was no place in the world where the Sabbath was as truly experienced as in Tel Aviv, the secular kibbutzim, and moshavot. Israel Kolatt suggests that Tabenkin was promoting "a new mode of Sabbath observance," one closely bound up with a new orthodoxy.[16] Leisure in this new mode would be structured by—and would serve—the demands of a Hebrew nationalist project. The Sabbath, like other holidays, was reconstructed as a secular festival in which Zionist ideals could be performed through communal rituals that replicated a sense of separateness and transcendence traditionally associated with religious ritual. These activities, which were particularly prominent in Labor

Zionist institutions, have led Anita Shapira to write: "Basically the Palestine labor movement was a religious movement."[17] Schools created ceremonies for the Sabbath, usually performed on Fridays, some involving a ritual donation to the Jewish National Fund box and a "sermon" on the political issues of the day.[18] Sabbath was also a time for organized cultural activities in Hebrew. In 1928, the American financier Samuel Simon Bloom funded the construction of Ohel Shem, a community center that Bialik hoped would provide cultural and educational programming on the Sabbath. Raphael Patai recalls lecture series on Sabbath mornings at the Bet Ha-'Am in Tel Aviv and the Edison Cinema in Jerusalem.[19] Such rituals and undertakings gave expression to "festive time," a lifestyle that existed beyond profane time and bound the group together. Significantly, the glue that bound them was their Hebrew-language substrate: the Zionist Sabbath was a Hebrew Sabbath, not a Jewish Sabbath.

A high degree of collective commitment, intimidation, and mutual censure could surround these Hebrew leisure practices. Scholars have noted that totalitarian regimes are particularly distinguished by their attempts to intervene fully in leisure practices.[20] Stephen Kotkin uses a specifically linguistic metaphor to describe such a process in the Soviet state: "Publically expressing loyalty by knowing how to 'speak Bolshevik,' " he writes, "became an overriding concern."[21] While the kind of state coercion in the Soviet Union was notably absent in the Yishuv, a softer version of coercion existed, one characterized by "a voluntary collectivism manifest in the willful recruitment of contemporaries to build a shared society and establish a shared identity."[22] Literary figures, leaders, and organizations collaborated in a shared cultural and linguistic project that largely transcended political divisions and that saw intimidation tactics as a way to cultivate fellow citizens' true and authentic selves. This kind of ideological volunteerism correlated with strong collective censure of individual behaviors that seemed to transgress social norms. In the absence of an enforcement apparatus, the consequences of misbehavior, including linguistic misbehavior, were entirely in the realm of mutual critique and did not, for example, engage the legal or police system. Such organizations and individuals, lacking real powers of enforcement, have been referred to as the "informal state," a term particularly relevant in this stateless context.[23] Nonetheless, the fantasy of social control—expressed in part as linguistic control—was palpable. A society committed to a radical revision of community life and the individual saw it as absolutely reasonable to control not only what its members did on the job, but also what they did during times of leisure.

While debauchery—or "deviant leisure"—tends normally to be associated with young people and their presumably deficient self-control, the discourse on deviant linguistic leisure in the Yishuv for the most part pertained to adults, who were labeled as petty criminals—*portze geder* (transgressors); promoters of *hefkerut* (lawlessness); and *hotrim* (saboteurs)—for their tendency to use or access their mother tongues in leisure-time spaces. Children, schooled in Hebrew classrooms and indoctrinated while young about the value of Hebrew, tended not to be linguistic offenders in this regard.[24] Much of the subtext of public debates about Hebrew leisure implies a generational conflict between children and their parents, whose leisure was seen as deviant and who were subject to policing. To the extent that most adults tried to perform a Hebrew identity in official or work settings, they seem to have fulfilled Erving Goffman's notion of acting, in which "the surface of agreement, the veneer of consensus, [is] facilitated by each participant concealing his own wants behind statements which assert values to which everyone present feels obliged to give lip service."[25] The relationship between wants and values was by no means wholly antagonistic: the desire to embody a set of ideals and to fit in could be as strong as the desire to indulge in the familiar, to be part of a subculture in another language. Leisure became a space in which to navigate the intersection of personal wants and national values. Language became a central marker in this process.

Granting Indulgence for Linguistic Deviance

The Yiddish writer Yehoash was expressing a common ideological consensus when he wrote, speaking of language practice in the Zionist settlements of the Second Aliyah: "Yiddish here is as impure as pork. To speak Yiddish in the street a person must have tremendous courage."[26] Anat Helman outlines the sanctions imposed against such speakers throughout the mandate period, including "social pressure, cultural exclusion, derogatory jokes, and even discrimination."[27] But the intense and real censure of language diversity by members of the Yishuv coexisted with a great deal of license, license that made visible the limits of Hebrew hegemony and challenged its proclaimed status as the indigenous language. Many were demonstrably nonchalant about instances when languages other than Hebrew were used during leisure time—in many cases, even lip service to the ideal of Hebrew was not necessary.

Time off, in the scholarly literature on leisure, can be conceived of as time in which social norms can be discarded or even mocked. To adopt again the language of Goffman, leisure-time activities have the potential to occur "backstage," away from the viewing and judging eyes of a social audience. The backstage is the "place, relative to a given performance, where the impression fostered by the performance is knowingly contradicted as a matter of course." While Goffman, concerned with nonverbal performance, does not consider the possibility that using a dominant language can itself be a social performance, he does note that the backstage can be a space for "dialect or substandard speech."[28] In a society characterized by programmatic social expectations, leisure time offered a way not only to relax into alternative linguistic practices but also to poke fun at official strictures. Even the most heavily monitored societies maintain "backstage" spaces of linguistic deviance. In the controlled environment of Soviet Magnitogorsk, where workers could be fired for lack of loyalty, "a person could 'speak Bolshevik' one moment, 'innocent peasant' the next, begging indulgence for a professed inability to master fully the demanding new language and behavior."[29] As we shall see, public censure of multilingual leisure was combined with a repeated tendency to beg— and to be granted—indulgence for linguistic deviance.

The Home

Leisure is defined by the absence of labor. But in a setting where labor was construed to include cultural as well as industrial production, leisure was not a unique, separate space but rather a set of contested spaces where pro-Hebrew social expectations ran up against multilingual lived realities. The domestic sphere was particularly charged in this respect as the space most fully "backstage" but also most associated with corrupting influences, particularly on children. Critics of home language practices, seeking to root out non-Hebrew languages, conducted a symbolic alchemy, revaluing the most familiar native tongues, German, Yiddish, or Arabic, as imported foreign products, to be stamped out in favor of "native" Hebrew.

Rivka Avrahmson, whose family came to Palestine from Odessa in 1922, was asked in an interview with the Hebrew University's Oral History Division, "What language did your parents speak between them at home?" She answered: "I remember the slogan 'Hebrew man, speak Hebrew.' That was the slogan. But my mother couldn't restrain herself, so Russian words would come out, Yiddish words, too."[30] Avrahmson's comments, spoken years after the fact, present mother tongues, Russian and Yiddish in this case, as libidinal forces that "slipped out" because of a lack of self-discipline. But while Israelis, in retrospective interviews, sometimes display embarrassment about past multilingual behavior, feelings were more mixed at the time.

The degree of non-Hebrew use at home is captured in census data that, even considering likely overreporting of Hebrew use, shows enormous use of other languages.[31] According to the 1916–18 census conducted by the Palestine Office of the Zionist Organization, 77 percent of children in Tel Aviv and the agricultural settlements spoke any amount of Hebrew, while only 36 percent of parents did. The proportion of Hebrew speakers in the older Jewish settlements of Hebron, Tiberias, and Safed was only 3 to 5 percent. Thirty years later, in the 1948 census, about 54 percent of respondents claimed to use Hebrew as their sole language, but just under 20 percent, likely those who had immigrated immediately after the war, did not use any Hebrew at all.[32] From the perspective of Hebrew advocacy, these numbers indicate remarkable strides in Hebrew promotion; nonetheless, they also show that nearly half of the Yishuv was using other languages always or sometimes. And the home was a space where languages other than Hebrew were most likely to be spoken. A 1939 newspaper article confirms that "even many who don't have trouble speaking Hebrew will speak foreign languages [*lo'azit*] with their families and frequently switch to a foreign language when they want to express their opinions more deeply."[33]

The home occupied a complex place in relation to the dictates of public life. In the perception of some, the interests of central Zionist organizations did not really extend to the home. Writing derisively about the failure of Zionist society to promote Hebrew, a writer in *Haaretz* spoke of the "no-man's-land" (*shetah hefker*) of the Yishuv, saying, "If you want to learn and teach Hebrew to your family, you can; if you don't want to, rest assured that no institution will force you to."[34] Expressing her concern about the tendencies of the Histadrut, the organization of Jewish labor unions in Palestine, Rachel Katznelson wrote: "Laws and obligations are valid for the group, the moshav, the neighborhood, the union. They are the subject of public discussion, of criticism, and of demands, but the movement has no interest in what happens inside the comrade's home."[35] This trend of institutional uninterest is evident in the fears of Abba Houshi, of the Haifa Workers Council, that in the absence of proper institutional intervention, women appeared to be developing bourgeois attitudes inconsistent with the goals of the labor movement.[36]

Discourses about language in the home had a clearly gendered aspect. Male immigrants were more likely than immigrant women to speak Hebrew at home, to such an extent that many children grew up hearing their mother tongues literally from their mothers, while their fathers insisted upon Hebrew—this trend has been identified in other national contexts as well.[37] In one case, Yitzhak Bitansky, another Hebrew University interviewee, remembers learning Yiddish from his grand-mother, while the others in the house spoke Hebrew. His wife, Rachel Bitansky, interviewed at the same time, recalls her mother speaking to her mainly in Yiddish ("She wanted me to know Yiddish," she reports), while her father spoke to her in Hebrew.[38] Yiddish was not the only Jewish mother tongue recalled in this way; a mother's words to her Tripolitanian Jewish son evoke a similar affinity with Arabic. Zion Falah came to Palestine in 1922 with a group of Zionist Jews from Libya who settled in the Montefiore neighborhood of Tel Aviv. He recalled that his family spoke Arabic at home, which his mother called "our Yiddish," suggesting a certain parallelism between two homey yet officially rejected Jewish mother tongues, Yiddish and Arabic.[39]

But if in practice the home was a space removed from the Hebrew public life, it was by no means construed as outside the norms of Hebrew society, as Houshi's concern implies. The home was at once the space most logically "foreign," owing to its status as first bastion for new immi-grants and the space that Hebrew, functionally foreign, needed to capture if it were to make claims to mother-tongue status. Thus, the home could be construed as the place of women's "work" not only in the economic sense but also in the cultural or national sense: women were to cultivate the "new Hebrew man" in his childhood years, in large part by using Hebrew in the home. Naomi Seidman has explored the process by which the paradigmatic mother tongue, Yiddish, was silenced under such logic, and the figure of the Jewish mother transformed: "the mother's silence, self-sacrifice, and absence (or, alternatively, her transgression) are built into the mythical structure" of the Hebrew revival.[40]

Educators paid close attention to the perceived ability or inability, willingness or unwillingness, of women to socialize their young children into Hebrew. Israel Rubin Rivkai, an expert in pedagogy, expressed concern that Hebrew, the "mother tongue" of the collective, was not the mother tongue of many mothers. Because of children's tendency to imitate what they hear, a mother speaking "bastardized" Hebrew would produce a child with malformed speech. Luckily, thought Rivkai, most children in Palestine were being educated not by their families but by schools acting in loco parentis to ensure proper language acquisition.[41] Above and beyond the problem of "bastardized Hebrew," Rivkai touched on the diversity of languages that the child hears "not only in the streets, not only in the cities, where one can hear tens of different languages, but also in the house."[42] The "not only . . . but also" construction implies that while language diversity might be expected in public leisure-time practices, the truly private space of the home should be fully steeped in Hebrew rather than sharing features with the classic city leisure spaces.

If the cultural work of women lay squarely in the interaction between mother and child, then the home could not in fact be characterized as a leisure space free from public pressure. More likely, the practice of foreign-language speaking in the home would be considered a deviation from established "work" norms, akin to employees speaking their native languages while working on the factory floor. Women, traditionally associated with the private sphere, did not naturally have a division between work and leisure and thus had no clear way to escape from the dictates of Hebrew "work." Indeed, much of the early scholarship on leisure "assumes that leisure is *public* and *male*—the world of extra familial institutions and places, a world inhabited and acted upon primarily by men"; by contrast, "few have asked what women were doing while men attended the saloon or lodge." In fact, what they were doing was often a mix of work and fragmented leisure: "Workplaces do not convert easily into places for leisure."[43] The conflation of work and home for women makes it easy to conceive of women's language-related activities in the Yishuv either as all-out subversions of Hebrew norms or, conversely, as heroic attempts to overcome linguistic inclinations by turning the home into a Hebrew Zionist sphere.[44] As we might expect, this condemnation of improper language use in the home arose from women's tendency to carve out a sphere of leisure, usually spaces away from their children where they could engage in "women's talk" while cooking or doing housework.[45] This sort of speech took place in a space apart from social norms and authority, in "a liminal moment in an otherwise structured and regulated day."[46]

The home was a space for multilingual relaxation in another way as well: it was a space of reading and writing that did not always occur in Hebrew. Writing—in both letters and journals—was an important home activity for many women in the Yishuv at a time when journaling was a mark of cultural achievement in Europe. Because it was so common for young members of a family to come to Palestine while leaving parents or grandparents behind, letter writing became a primary means of communication across long distances. Through this activity, those in Palestine maintained contact not only with the people they loved but also, by extension, with the languages that reminded them of home.

Others kept diaries and journals chronicling their experiences, many of which were written in native languages. Memoir writing, often based on journal entries, was also common. Frieda Hirsch, whose memoir Guy Miron studies, wrote in German peppered with Hebrew words that represented features of daily life. In this German text, Hebrew "represents not her link to Jewish tradition, but, rather, her encounter with the new daily reality"; it reflects not a deep set of Hebrew commitments, but the practical place that this language played in her life.[47] Analysis of such journals reveals substantive differences between those kept in Hebrew often intended for eventual publication and those kept in other languages. Deborah Bernstein and Musia Lipman's comparison of two journals written in the 1920s and 1930s makes this clear. The diary of a woman called Anya, written in her native language of Russian, was "often fragmented, confused, or written in private code, which makes it often inaccessible to the reader." The diary by a woman they call "R.," on the other hand, was written in awkward, nonnative Hebrew and in an "epigrammatic" style, "strewn with capitalized words and stock pieties." The authors note that this second style was typical of pioneering women, for whom "the public took over the private, even in the diary." This comparison may indicate that for nonnative speakers, ideologically charged Hebrew produced a different kind of prose from that written in other, more familiar languages. When Hebrew penetrated even the most private of spaces, the result was increased ideological conformity; when it did not, as in Anya's case, an individual space remained that avoided official pieties not only in its "inaccessible" syntax, but also in the initial choice of language.[48]

Reading was also a particularly important leisure activity at home. Reading patterns in Yiddish were often clearly gendered, since women indulged in lighter reading in Yiddish and men were more likely to read in Hebrew. Sarah Rafaelovich reminisced in an interview that her mother never really learned Hebrew, but continued to take great pleasure in Yiddish literature, which her father would read to her mother: "She would work and he would read to her, so that she would enjoy it." Rafaelovich emphasizes the light nature of her mother's favorite books, juxtaposed against the serious nature of her father's Torah learning. She also indicates that her mother's enjoyment of Yiddish literature came not during periods of rest, but periods of work, presumably housework. The home was also a space of reading for men, Yitzhak Bitansky remembers in an interview: "My uncle was very intelligent. He would come over from time to time and they would read Yiddish poetry." Tzvi Elpeleg remembers his father, a simple man who was nonetheless a connoisseur of literature: "There wasn't a book, in Yiddish of course, of Mendele or Zalman Shneur or Sholem Aleichem that he didn't know by heart. He had read every one of them more than once. He would tell the stories of these books to anyone who would lend him an ear."[49]

In a society remembered for its activism against foreign languages, the widespread acceptance of foreign-language reading was notable. Much attention has been paid to the rise of Hebrew book publishing and the importance of translations into Hebrew during the period of growth in

Hebrew literature.[50] No Hebrew literary figure expected original Hebrew literature to fulfill the cultural needs of the emerging society. At least until the 1940s, most agreed that "culture in Hebrew," that is, translated culture, could supplement original "Hebrew culture"; expressed no problem with translations; and indeed encouraged a robust commitment to translated literature. As Heinrich Loewe, director of the National and University Library, wrote, speaking of the appropriateness of translation: "If Israel maintained its hold on its independent ancient culture through the Hebrew language; it also had a connection with other people's cultures."[51] Modern Hebrew literature could be enriched by taking in European literature through translation.[52]

The focus on the relationship between original and translated literature, however, obscures a more basic point: untranslated foreign books did not stay outside Zionists' homes; many works of literature, even if a translation existed, were still read in the original. For the most part, access to foreign and Hebrew books alike was gained through libraries, though there was also a market in imported books. To note that people were checking out foreign-language books and reading them at home is also to note that libraries were stocking such books. According to statistics from Tel Aviv in the late 1930s, of 15,587 books in the Sha'ar Zion Library, 61 percent were in languages other than Hebrew. In Bet Ahad Ha-'Am, a center for secular Hebrew culture opened in early 1928, 43 percent of its 13,964 books were in foreign languages. The labor movement appears to have been less interested in acquiring foreign books. According to a 1938 survey, 37 percent of the books in the Barzilai Library, founded in 1922, were in foreign languages.[53] In total, of the 29,551 books in public libraries in Tel Aviv, 59 percent were in languages other than Hebrew in 1934, when a survey was done.[54]

Multilingual collections were a feature of not only Tel Aviv libraries. Kibbutzim, too, generally more ideologically orthodox and understood to be particularly devoted to Hebrew use, also held foreign-language collections. An article by Y. Edelshteyn about the kibbutz library at En Harod described several types of Jewish books at the library: classics in Hebrew, foreign classics translated to Hebrew, Jewish journals, and Modern Hebrew books. Yet this collection of Hebrew books and texts of various kinds did not seem to satisfy the kibbutz readership fully. The article described a demand for more technical books and foreign works: "The interest in new Russian literature is great and strong and the Palestinian reader does not have access to them." In other words, noted the writer, "The disparity between the library's contents and the demands of the readers is becoming clearer every day."[55] Statistics show that 15 percent of the 172 library users on that kibbutz of 200 were reading Russian, 8 percent Yiddish, and 2 percent German. The writer points out as "interesting" the fact that 12–15 percent of the readers of Russian were young people, taking in Dostoevsky, Lenin, and Kropotkin, among others.[56] Meanwhile, students complained in the bulletin of the Balfour School that some of their friends were reading in French and Russian.[57] Many of the Russian authors had been translated into Hebrew—*Crime and Punishment* in 1924, *The Brothers Karamazov* in 1928 (both by Shtibl), and Kropotkin's book on the French revolution in 1930 (by Ha-Po'el Ha-Tza'ir)—and some might have read them in translation. Nonetheless, most of these books had been translated into Yiddish also, and this fact, combined with our knowledge that many had reading proficiency in Russian, suggests that many immigrants were reading these books in languages other than Hebrew.

Reading in other languages was by no means limited to Jews on the margins; it was widespread and acceptable among the Hebrew cultural elite. One of the most extensive sets of survey data that we have of reading habits comes from the 1927 survey of teachers in the Yishuv administered by the Hebrew Teachers' Federation as part of the publication of a twenty-fifth-anniversary volume.[58] Seeking to understand the makeup of its teaching force, the organization asked an extremely wide range of questions about education, political affiliations, and community activities, as well as several questions about language practice.[59] The 430 surveys, collected from 311 men and 119 women (77.8 percent of the teachers' union at the time), reveal a group that had been influenced by foreign literature and continued to read in foreign languages in Palestine.

The teachers, like their cohort of Zionist immigrants as a whole, were a multilingual group who prided themselves on their cultural attainments even as they promoted Hebrew study. According to the officially reported statistics in the anniversary volume, the majority of teachers, 63.7 percent, listed Yiddish as their mother tongue, followed by Hebrew (9.5 percent), Spanish/Ladino (4.7 percent), and Russian (3.5 percent).[60] Their reading abilities were even more diverse: nearly all were able to read at least two languages besides Hebrew, and many listed three, four, or more (one listed eight languages: Hebrew, Russian, Polish, Danish, German, English, French, and Yiddish). They freely noted that they were influenced by what they read in foreign languages. Eighty-four percent explicitly mentioned Hebrew as a language that influenced them, 45.6 percent mentioned Russian, 29.5 percent mentioned German, 10.5 percent mentioned French, and 7.9 percent mentioned Yiddish.[61] Among those teachers born in Palestine, 30 percent mentioned German as the most influential language, and 18.1 percent mentioned French.[62] These figures make clear that teachers, those entrusted with the project of educating children in Hebrew, had no compunction about stating that Russian and German literatures had an effect on them, likely seeing these foundational reading experiences (many in their home countries) as building blocks for the worldly culture they hoped to bring to their teaching in Palestine.

Teachers made clear that their diverse reading practices did not cease when they arrived in Palestine: only 11.4 percent noted that they did not read in any languages other than Hebrew at present. The vast majority read in multiple languages: more than a third mentioned one language besides Hebrew, more than 20 percent mentioned two, and a few mentioned five, six, or even seven languages.[63] The large numbers reading in French and German are consistent with the teachers' claims to have been influenced by these literatures, likely in their primary and secondary education. The large English numbers are more striking—they may indicate a high level of English proficiency among teachers, the spread of English education in the first decade of British rule, or the availability of English books thanks to the British.[64] Yaakov Meir Yakhna wrote, "The Hebrew Bible influenced me greatly" but noted, "Even today I keep . . . Shakespeare, Byron, Tolstoy . . . in my room." With respect to newspapers, reading in other languages was dependent on availability. This conjecture is borne out by the response of Shmuel Berles, a reader of Yiddish, Hebrew, Russian, German, and French, who claimed to read newspapers in Hebrew and those "in the rest of the languages when I have the opportunity."[65]

Where foreign speech was contested and commented on by enforcers, foreign-language reading in private spaces did not appear to earn this disapproval. Despite the great emphasis of historians on the spread of Hebrew publishing, foreign-language reading (usually done at home) was a common immigrant leisure-time activity in the Yishuv—and because the majority of the population at every point during the British mandate period was made up of immigrants, the trend continued even as the sheer numbers of native Hebrew speakers increased. Reading was a way for immigrants to use the languages they considered their mother tongues during time away from work and to connect with literature written in languages that they had learned in school or at university and that they considered portals into world culture. Thus, foreign-language reading was not only a retreat into the comfortable but, in many cases, also a sphere in which people with already broad horizons could expand their minds and be connected with the world beyond the Yishuv.

The Coffeehouse

Multilingual leisure activities were not confined to the home. Edward Ullendorff is incorrect in his conclusion that "whatever the predominant means of communication in the privacy of the home may have been, in public, in the street or on the bus, Hebrew alone prevailed."[66] One of the most important gathering places for some was the coffeehouse, which, Shachar Pinsker writes, was a "replacement for the home, for the community"; a variety of memoirs recall the coffee shop as a space of gathering.[67] The coffeehouse, an intermediate, or "third," space between the private space of the home and the visible sphere of public life, became a principal point of contest, an intracommunal, intergenerational struggle over the purview of Hebrew and, concurrently, the place of the "foreign" in the heart of the Yishuv.

An anecdote published in the early 1940s reflects the linguistically charged environment of the coffeehouse, both a space of linguistic lenience and a potential site for activism.

> In a coffeehouse in Tel Aviv. A mother and her small son by a table. They have a good relationship but they have an old argument: the son is embarrassed because his mother doesn't understand a single word in Hebrew

even though they've been in the country for six years (three quarters of the boy's life!). On the counter that functions as the contact point between the café and the kitchen there is a sign written in large letters [*otiyot shel kidush levanah*]: "Speak Hebrew!" The son reads it and explains to his mother in German: "Mama, it says here that you need to speak Hebrew, that you are obligated to speak Hebrew." "That's for the waiters," says the mother.[68]

The anecdote—constructed as a joke and published in a humor compilation published by the Jewish National Council's Culture Committee—helps us understand the coffeehouse as a site of contest over leisure-time language practice, a space occupied by activists, café goers, and servers.

Some saw the coffeehouse as a place for Hebrew activism, a site inhabited by those who would not abide by linguistic dictates in general. The activists were likely to be members of the eastern European pro-Hebrew cultural intelligentsia, or young people, perhaps students at the local gymnasium. The presence of the sign, with its large letters, marks not only the presence of Hebrew activists but also calls attention to the absence of Hebrew. Like a smoker lighting up next to a No Smoking sign, linguistic behavior in the café could become inherently subversive because of the explicit prohibition. The story suggests that the young son is a member of this pro-Hebrew set and depicts a generational divide in which the young son is in the position to enforce social norms. In this tale, the mother is the delinquent who has failed to learn the language despite six years in the country and who, moreover, forces her son to defy the sign by explaining to her (in German) the rules of the land.

The anecdote was likely funny to those who read it because the woman's leisure activities evoked a culture of coffeehouse going with deep resonance in the imagination, bringing to mind an ambivalent Jewish society theoretically but not actually leaving "exilic" culture behind. The mother in this anecdote represents a culture of German-speaking Jewish immigrants, who, according to one account, "imported" to Palestine "coffeehouse life."[69] Exhibiting a stereotypical distaste for those of inferior social stature, the mother equates her linguistic deviance with exceptionalism; she implies that people "like her," in other words, German immigrant coffeehouse goers, can thumb their noses at Zionist cultural conventions.

In the early to mid-1930s, the influx of German-speaking Jews to Palestine—one-third of whom moved to Tel Aviv—created what Batia Carmiel called "the coffeehouse revolution." One of the "most visible changes" brought about by the influx of German speakers, wrote Sylvia Gelber in her memoirs, was the "espresso coffee machines . . . installed in new, European-style cafes."[70] A 1946 assessment of Yishuv commerce noted that "the primitiveness that characterized culinary establishments among the pioneering people has largely disappeared (at least in the cities) and in their place have appeared networks of sophisticated restaurants and coffeehouses built according to European standards."[71] At least thirty coffeehouses were founded in the period between 1932 and 1947, many in the new northern areas of Tel Aviv around Ben-Yehuda and Dizengoff Streets. It was, Carmiel writes, "a small celebration of familiar tastes and sounds of the German language—an echo of a destroyed world." In the 1920s, the coffeehouses had been truly multilingual spaces, but in the 1930s and beyond they were overwhelmingly marked by the sound of German. Arabic, incidentally, was less heard, as business and social interactions between Jews and Palestinian Arabs declined in the wake of intercommunal violence, particularly the Arab revolt of 1936–39 but also as early as the 1921 Nabi Musa riots, which provoked a wave of Jewish displacement from Jaffa to Tel Aviv. Elite coffeehouses, we should remember, had already been places of extravagance, elegantly clad waiters, and fancy foods—but in the 1930s these decadent features came to be specifically associated with the German type, the German language, and the leisure practice of those who "spent every Sabbath afternoon at one of the German coffeehouses," as Hilda Hoffman described her family's practice.[72]

Despite the close association of Germans with the coffeehouse, the site, as we have mentioned, had been marked as a multilingual space before the German-speaking immigration of the 1930s. The elite coffeehouses of the 1920s—Galei Aviv, Ginat Ha-Sharon, and Palatin (which also functioned as a hotel)—were the site of linguistic mixing on several levels. Immaculately appointed and architecturally stunning, these establishments were sites of contact between British dignitaries, Arab elites, and Jewish intellectuals. The writer Binyamin Tammuz remembered both leisurely encounters and business meetings involving Arab citrus growers and Jewish clients, as well as rendezvous between British soldiers and local Jewish women. Other official business was also carried out in the coffeehouse. Zachary Lockman discusses Histadrut meetings in the mid-1930s that convened in Arab coffeehouses in Haifa with the intention of organizing Arab railway workers.[73] The intermingling of "Yiddish, Russian, Hebrew, and Arabic," in Tammuz's memory, evokes a space that enabled connections between Jews and others in Palestine.[74] Meanwhile, older, Arab coffeehouses in Jaffa attracted mixed groupings of Jews, Palestinian Arabs, and foreigners, those who did not want or were not able to go to the upscale establishments farther north.[75]

Urban coffeehouses and clubs could serve as a structured setting for discussing literature and ideology in Hebrew as well as in other languages.[76] Shachar Pinsker has extensively explored the literary coffeehouse culture in Vienna, Warsaw, Lvov, and Odessa. These spaces were both symbols and incubators of modernist writing. Crucially, these intellectual meeting spots were multilingual, with Hebrew writers mixing with Yiddish, Polish, German, or Russian writers.[77] Yiddish literary salons emerged in the Yishuv, for example, the one hosted by Mordechai Narkiss in Jerusalem and attended by the Yiddish poet Rikuda Potash. The Yiddish Journalists and Writers Club, founded in 1928 by Avrom Rivess, was a gathering place for serious Yiddish writers.[78] Hebrew students at the Herzliya Gymnasium were up in arms when, in 1914, the Yiddish writer Chaim Zhitlowsky was invited to speak at a coffeehouse in Jaffa.

Members of the Sephardi community in the Yishuv also sought out coffeehouses and used them to converse in their native tongues, whether Greek, Bulgarian, or Ladino: "If you want to see how much the commercial center has attracted the Sephardi community," wrote a (presumably Ashkenazi) writer for *Davar*, "listen to the spoken languages" in places where Sephardim "look for a meeting place in their native language." In that case, this writer felt, the deviant coffeehouse culture was a direct product of unemployment—during waves of higher unemployment, new coffeehouses opened—but it was also a place where workers would come after a day of labor. The escapist function of the space was clear in either case. When asked why the coffeehouse was so important to him, one man replied to the reporter: "In these difficult days there are many thoughts that bother us. During a conversation with friends in the coffeehouse we forget our difficult situation." To the writer, the solution to this degenerate mix of foreign languages, deviance, and unemployment was employment: "Save these forces for labor and creativity!" he proclaimed.[79]

Coffeehouse "transgressions" appear to have come both in speech and in print. Newspaper articles frequently commented on the German sounds of the coffeehouses, for example, Café Snir: "Around us the crowd hums like a beehive. The bees are not making honey here, but their mouths are dripping German."[80] To a self-proclaimed Zionist tourist from Warsaw, the sound of German meant that "exile has been inserted into our life of revival"—it was as though he were sitting not in Tel Aviv but in Berlin.[81] Language—in this case German—was the dominant sign of the outside having been let in; the reference to a particularly exilic mode of leisure was an indication to him that Hebrew cultural work was not being sufficiently completed. The central place of foreign newspapers in the coffeehouses further incensed activists. In 1938, twelve organizations, including the Union of Coffeehouse Owners and the Union of Hotel and Restaurant Owners, drafted a letter to Haifa businesses letting them know that Tel Aviv coffeehouse and hotel owners were insisting upon making only Hebrew newspapers available and that it was time for Haifa businesses to do likewise.[82] Apparently, though, such insistence made little difference in either city. In 1946, the Culture Committee of the Jewish National Council was still writing letters to coffeehouse owners about "numerous complaints" from visitors to coffeehouses who found "daily, weekly, and monthly newspapers in various foreign languages rather than periodicals in Hebrew, the language of the Land of Israel."[83] The evidence makes clear, though, that customers' desire was not only for Hebrew. One café even explicitly advertised to customers that one would "always find a collection of the newspapers and journals in all the languages present in the country."[84]

Besides Hebrew activists and coffeehouse patrons, a third group was also suggested by the mother-and-son anecdote that begins this section. We should not assume that the Speak Hebrew! sign was intended only for bourgeois coffee drinkers or that the only axis of linguistic tension was between two classes of elites, the pro-Hebrew zealots and the German-speaking immigrants. The German mother was not entirely wrong to assume that the message was "for the waiters." Some of the coffeehouses in Tel Aviv had huge staffs—a picture of the staff from Galei Aviv shows thirty employees: waiters, kitchen staff, and members of the orchestra, dressed in European costumes with suit coats and bowties.[85] They, too, might have been overlooking their own "linguistic obligations," either while in the back room preparing the food or on the café floor itself.

Goffman assumes that actors perform on the front stage according to social norms, but relax from these modes in backstage areas (the kitchen or back room of a restaurant is in fact his central example). In this case, however, employees may have spoken in German specifically in the front-stage space in order to more attentively serve the needs of the clientele or to present a more cultured appearance. After 1933, it appears that even those who weren't fluent in the language tried to speak some German in such settings. Menahem Brinker of the Central Council for the Enforcement of Hebrew (CCEH), a Hebrew enforcement organization in the 1940s, remarked that "even Sephardi Jews try to speak German to the German Jew who addresses them," concluding: "We have an upside down world," for "in every land of immigration the immigrant tries to speak the language of the resident but among us the opposite is true: the resident learns the language of the immigrant and imposes it on himself."[86]

Other waiters may have been Germans themselves who appeared to eastern European immigrants to be upper class and snobbish, despite their service jobs. Such a sentiment is present in a 1937 article in the journal *Tesha‘ Ba-Erev* that described the large coffeehouse on Pinsker Street as "100-percent German-speaking and German-singing," and as characterized by both arrogance and laziness. "You get the impression," the writer said, "that they are doing you a favor and that you should thank them for taking the trouble to come from Berlin to serve you on Pinsker Street."[87] In this article, the strong link between German language and laziness does not apply only to diners and coffee drinkers, but also to those who worked at the coffeehouse. The German-speaking atmosphere of the café became not merely a synonym for bourgeois leisure, but for the incursion of deviant leisure into spheres of employment.

The Cinema

If immigration patterns shaped the politics of spoken, written, and read language, developments in technology also changed the role of foreign languages in the Yishuv's leisure-time pursuits. More passive forms of leisure-time foreign-language consumption such as movie watching were particularly tenacious, for their popularity was not necessarily the result of a spate of immigration or a dearth of Hebrew knowledge. The appeal of film—audibly foreign but translated in sub- or intertitles—was in part its exoticness. Those who enjoyed it were not necessarily holding onto old practices linked to their past lives. Rather, movies offered viewers the possibility of experiencing a world larger than the ones that they inhabited. The premise of all-Hebrew cultural construction thus pushed against not only the perceived residue of the past but also against the always-novel commodities offered by foreign cultures.

The Yishuv fits two paradigms often used to discuss media consumption. One body of literature on colonial and postcolonial states concerns the passive reception of foreign (usually Western) media and explores the effects of cultural imperialism on local identities.[88] A second body of literature considers an inverse phenomenon: the importation of non-Western immigrants' own cultural commodities to Diaspora communities, usually in the West. This second group of works—nearly all focused on the past twenty to thirty years—consider how immigrants—from South Korea or India, for example—maintain communal networks through media and create, in the words of James Curran and Myung-Jin Park, a "global-local connexion that is eroding the national." Curran and Park contrast this present hyperconnectivity with a prior state of affairs: "The identity of diasporic communities can now be sustained not through treasured postcards and the fading memories of grandparents, but through daily cultural feeds."[89] This "new" development is not so new, however. Jews in the Yishuv indeed treasured personal postcards and memories, but also expressed their connection to their past homes through foreign-language cultural consumption in a way that, many Zionists felt, eroded the Hebrew and the national. In the Yishuv's case, the two causes of cultural importation—Western cultural imperialism and nostalgia for home— sometimes overlapped. The West was alluring, but it was also, for many, home. The "retreat" into the comfortable or the nostalgic could at one and the same time be an aspiration to cosmopolitanism, progress, and modernity in its manifold forms.

The period of the British mandate saw the meteoric rise of movies as a preferred leisure activity in Palestine. In 1913, Mayor Dizengoff had traveled to Alexandria to learn how to run a city and saw that European and American films were in wide distribution there. The Eden Cinema, which opened in 1914, had a monopoly over films for thirteen years in exchange for a 1,000-franc annual payment to the municipality. As David Shalit writes, at first the theater was looked down upon for several reasons not directly connected to the languages of the films: it seemed too bourgeois, a sentiment that persisted into the 1950s.[90] When the Eden Cinema opened, film was "perceived by the standard bearers of the Zionist-Hebrew cultural revolution as a dangerous factor, which with its low values, its frivolousness and its escapism constituted a threat to the demanding values of Zionism."[91] Letters to the Tel Aviv Municipality decried the cinema as a center of thievery and prostitution, perhaps in part because it was known that movie halls in Russia were used for prostitution and that in the United States special sections of some theaters were set aside for women who came alone to films, so as to prevent harassment.[92] Overall, film appeared to be an importation of the decadent culture that Jews had supposedly left behind in Europe.

The Eden's monopoly ended with the opening of the Ophir Theater in 1927 by Moshe Caraso, a Jew from Greece. A huge burst of theater building followed—within the next five years, at least five other cinemas were opened: Mograbi (1930), Migdalor (1931), Ramon (1932), the open-air Gan Rina, and Bet Ha-'Am. By the end of the 1930s there were twelve.[93] Jerusalem saw the opening of Zion (1912), Orion (c. 1920), Regent (c. 1928), and Edison. The first movie house for sound films in Haifa was the 'En Dor near Jaffa Street in the German colony, which appears to have attracted both Jewish and Arab audiences. Ami Yuval remembers that the Haifa audience would "participate actively in the films": "When the evil robber sneaked onto the screen behind the good hero, they would be sure to warn him about the danger by shouting '*aharekha!*' or '*wara'ak!*'" (behind you!—Hebrew, Arabic).[94] Such anecdotes offer some indication that Palestine audiences approached movies not in "reverential silence," as would become the norm in Europe, but as an involved community of spectators.[95]

Much scholarly work on film in Palestine is concerned with the emergence of a Hebrew film industry oriented toward reflecting Zionist ideals on-screen. The films produced in Palestine in the 1930s, indeed, show rather orthodox Zionist conceptions of the land, hide instances of regret or uncertainty, and "show life in the land, the emerging culture, and construction as the correct and only way of life." Nonetheless, the highly filtered message of a small number of Zionist films does not speak to an overall saturation of Hebrew film, for the number of Hebrew films was dwarfed by the quantity of imported films. Movie distributors, even if they were Zionists, were entrepreneurs and not cultural purists, and they were more than happy to bring in films that would sell tickets. These films came to Palestine through a well-developed distribution network relying on agents like Yitzhak Molcho from Salonika, who worked for both the Gaumont Company (Paris) and Metro-Goldwyn-Mayer (Hollywood) distributing films between Jerusalem and Tehran. In the 1920s, Cairo was the film distribution center for the entire Middle East and the site of American and European company offices. Many of the early links between Cairo and Palestine were made by a man named Krichevsky, a Palestinian-born Jew who, after spending some years in Egypt, returned to Palestine. Krichevsky, "who spoke Hebrew but not fluently," quickly became the "movie king" in Palestine, meeting with distributors in the Shor Brothers Café, on the corner of Herzl and Lilienblum Streets in Tel Aviv. The first film that Krichevsky gave to Yerushalayim Segal, a famous translator of Hebrew films whose autobiography provides important insights into the Palestine film industry, to promote was an American film, *The Kid*, starring Charlie Chaplin. Segal brought it to the Eden "with great success."[96] The appeal of such imported films was clearly higher than that of the films first produced by the Zionist movement, which tended to offer more propaganda than entertainment and displayed low-quality production values. For all their national appeal and despite the economic success of Hebrew Zionist films such as *Oded the Wanderer* and *This Is the Land*, Hebrew films lend insight more into the values that ideological filmmakers wanted the Yishuv to embody than into the viewing practices of Jewish audiences.

Languages went from visual markers—intertitles in the silent cinema (*re'ino'a*)—to audible output in the sound era. In the early years of imported silent films, Hebrew was not regularly inserted into intertitles. When it was used, the language was often riddled with errors. Segal recounts that because most films came from Egypt, which was at the time culturally influenced by French, all the titles on the films were in French.

"My wife, Esther, didn't know French," he wrote later, "so I would trans-late the titles for her."[97] He continued: "When I was explaining the titles to my wife, others sitting nearby also leaned over and as the number of listeners grew I had to raise my voice to explain." When there were Hebrew translations, he added, they often arrived a day later than the movie itself. Eventually, Segal realized that it would be more logical to do the translations himself, and he became the main producer of Hebrew intertitles, and later subtitles, for foreign films.[98]

The creation of sound film in the United States changed the dynamics both of foreign-language exposure in the Yishuv and of the contours of language activism. The auditory quality of the *kolnoʻa* ("moving voice"), the new word for "cinema" supposedly coined by Bialik, had clear impli-cations for those concerned about linguistic purity.[99] If the film medium was threatening to the Hebrew ethos, broadly construed, the emergence of the talking film exacerbated the perception of threat. The Battalion of the Defenders of the Hebrew Language, founded in the late 1920s to combat linguistic infractions, was quick to respond with concerns that talking films would serve as "an instrument for the dissemination of for-eign languages in the land" and "interfere with our own language's rise to dominance." The influence of foreign speech and song, if disseminated through the cinemas, would have a particularly deleterious effect on youth, and so the battalion insisted that these conduits, foreign films and songs, not be allowed into the Yishuv.[100] Educators as well noted the cor-rupting effects of movies, stating the danger in part in linguistic terms. In a 1940 essay, Eliezer Rieger, the former inspector for the General Zionist schools and later a professor of education, expressed concern that movies were escapist and didn't provoke introspection. But more than this, "the cinema projects foreign languages into the ears of thousands of Hebrew listeners in Palestine on a nightly basis at a time when the Hebrew lan-guage still is in such dire need of cultivation and zealous love."[101]

These appeals had little effect, as Rieger himself knew; the cinema houses quickly filled with foreign sound films, and the lack of government oversight meant that little could be done (cinema, Rieger pointed out, was distinct from radio, which the government operated). The first sound film to show in Palestine, in 1930, was *The Jazz Singer*, the 1927 American film that was itself the first full-length picture with synchronized dialogue.[102] The vast majority of the films shown in the Yishuv were foreign: of the 118 films screened in Tel Aviv in 1930, 38 were American, 26 were German, and 25 were Russian. Of the 400 films shown between 1935 and 1939, 50 percent were American or British, 15 percent were German, and 5 percent were Russian.[103]

Eden Cinema program, 1934. Courtesy of the Department of Special Collections and University Archives, Stanford University Libraries.

Contemporary movie playbills demonstrate the full range of films shown in the 1930s, which included Spanish, Austrian, Czech, Polish, French, German, British, and American films.[104] Researchers can analyze many of these films at greater length and speculate about how particular themes might have been received by members of the Yishuv. We can only assume that, as in other non-Western settings, viewers made their own meanings of the Western societies they saw depicted, and conjured imaginative thoughts, or possibly nostalgic memories, about geographic and political alternatives.[105] The smorgasbord of international fare was the context in which Zionist film developed and a foil against which Hebrew cultural production could be pitted.

The Migdalor and other theaters, we should emphasize, did not exclusively show foreign films; they also screened Hebrew films as they were released. Judah Leman's landmark Hebrew film *Land of Promise* (*Le-hayim hadashim*), for example, screened at the Migdalor on 26 October 1935, according to an advertisement: a Carmel Newsreels labeled "Winter 1935" shows children lining up to see it.[106] When Jews saw such Hebrew films, they were exposed to a compelling display of Zionist propaganda that tended to highlight the heroism of the pioneer, the renewed connection with nature enabled by Zionist settlement, and the total distinction between old and new Jewish life. *Land of Promise*, the film scholar Ariel Feldestein has written, "emphasizes freedom, building, and the joy of creativity for the pioneers who paved the way for the whole people."[107] Used in this way, the movie screen became one of several stages for the performance of Zionist ideology, along with theater, song, and art. In practice, though, cinemas were not, on the whole, spaces for the projection of Hebrew orthodoxy, but a space away from that orthodoxy.

Protest against Western films was vociferous, but particular opposition emerged to Yiddish films, most of them imported from the United States. Until the mid-1930s, Yiddish appeared to be the greatest on-screen threat. In part, opposition derived from a perception that Yiddish was still vying with Hebrew to be the Jewish national language. In part, the concern about Yiddish stemmed from a fear that the British, who had granted Hebrew official status, would renege on this commitment if they came to believe that Hebrew was not the real mother tongue of many Jews. In 1930, Shoshana Persitz, a member of the Tel Aviv city council who had emigrated from Kiev in 1925, wrote a letter to Colonel Frederick Herman Kisch, chairman of the Palestine Zionist Executive, about the danger of "Zhargon cinema," using a common pejorative term for Yiddish, and asked him to "prevent scandals."[108] "The matter is fairly simple," she wrote. "It is forbidden for us politically to arouse a debate between the Yiddish and Hebrew languages in Palestine because this could harm the relationship of the Government to the Hebrew language." Foreign languages, she appears to suggest, are not dangerous per se; what is dangerous is to allow a visible battle between rival Jewish national languages. Therefore, she continues, "in the war for Hebrew it is not English, German, etc. that are dangerous (though I am opposed to any foreign-language in the country), but rather this language [Yiddish] alone." Persitz points here to a blanket discomfort with all foreign-language films as well as a special concern about Yiddish, which, she says, "was rooted in our exilic days" and offers the risk that "we copy our bitter exile to this place as well."[109] Exile, it seemed to her, could be imported to Palestine in the form of film, and the danger had the potential to be far-reaching.

Yosef Luria from the Department of Education wrote a letter on 15 September 1930 to cinema managers in Jerusalem, appealing to their national consciousness and asking them with all forcefulness to desist from showing Yiddish films. The letter was published in *Haaretz* on 26 September. Theatrical performances, he wrote, constitute "propaganda for the Yiddish language." The films would "afford a certain amount of satisfaction to some section of the common people who know no language but Yiddish ['*Ivri taytsh*'] but what they will certainly do is play into the hands of the faithless sons of the nation, the enemies of her revival." Like Persitz, Luria expressed his belief that while all languages are harmful to Hebrew, Yiddish is the most harmful: "It is doubtless true that non-Hebrew performances in general do more harm than good from the national point of view; but that cannot be helped so long as there is no production of talking films in Hebrew in Palestine and at any rate the other foreign languages do not threaten the position of Hebrew as Yiddish does."[110]

Not all Jews joined in the consensus against Yiddish films, and many Zionists in Palestine were not convinced that censuring imported Jewish culture was good either for Diaspora-Yishuv relations or the promotion of Jewish culture in the Yishuv itself. Indeed, the new availability of Yiddish language in talkies appeared to reopen uncertainties about the place of diasporic Jewish culture in Palestine and about the relationship between Yiddish and Hebrew more specifically. Some were unsatisfied with the strong language that members of the Education Department used to denounce Yiddish. The Jewish Agency, which acted as a representative to Jews around the world, was particularly concerned with the offense that Jews outside Palestine might take. Werner Senator at the Jewish Agency expressed concern about Luria's letter, saying that "the Jewish agency should offer an example of tolerance and respect for the feelings of large masses of the Jewish people outside Palestine." Moreover, he suggested that Luria's letter would provoke anti-Jewish propaganda, particularly in Poland, by "confirm[ing] the negative attitudes of ardent antisemitic governments in their endeavors to extinguish the Jewish language."[111] Many ordinary Jews may have felt like Senator: there seemed to be something off about wholly barring the consumption of foreign Jewish culture in the old-new Jewish homeland: though it might be officially unacceptable, surely society could accommodate its presence.

The best-known film-related controversy in the Yishuv surrounded the screening of *Mayne yidishe mame* (*My Jewish Mother*) in 1930. This film, directed by Sidney Goldin and produced by the Judea Film Company in New York, was screened at the Mograbi Theater in Tel Aviv on 27 September 1930, only four months after its New York premiere.[112] The Jewish National Council turned to the Tel Aviv city council and asked the Mograbi to cancel the performance so as to prevent "public scandals." Members of the Battalion of the Defenders of the Hebrew Language also asked the theater to cancel the film and wrote to the Tel Aviv Municipality on 8 September asking it to "take a stance against those who want to change the Hebrew ways of the city."[113] One day earlier, Aviezer Yellin and Asher Erlich of the Hebrew Teachers' Federation had written to the Eden Cinema to express concern about a rumor that that venue, too, was planning to show a film in Yiddish; they called attention to "the great danger" that such a move would pose to the Hebrew language and Hebrew culture.[114] Later that month they wrote again to the Jewish Agency in Jerusalem, pointing out that the showing of Yiddish films would represent a retreat in a long-standing battle against Yiddish, a battle in which Hebrew now held the upper hand: After decades of efforts "the Yiddish language has been cast aside. Hebrew now occupies its place. Nonetheless, many viewing eyes are waiting for any opportunity to increase the prestige of the Yiddish language."[115]

Dozens of city residents signed a petition asking that the showings of *Mayne yidishe mame* be canceled, but to no avail: a showdown was set to unfold.[116] At its opening, members of the Battalion of the Defenders of the Hebrew Language, on guard against public displays of a foreign language, bought tickets and entered the theater, and as the film began they started making so much noise that it was impossible to continue the screening. The police came, but the screening had to be canceled.[117] The *Jewish Daily Bulletin* in New York reported on "a number of hot-headed defenders of Hebrew [who] spattered ink and hurled foul smelling objects at the screen as the audible part of the picture began."[118] As crowds gathered to protest the first screening, Mayor Dizengoff issued an order to the police to prevent the second screening.[119] Eventually, a compromise was reached: all the talking and singing parts of the film would be excised, and the show would go on.[120]

Anat Helman analyzes the event by suggesting that immigrant habit and recalcitrance made Yiddish appear to be a threat: "In a city of immigrants there was still a temptation to use mother tongues."[121] This discussion of primal urges and insufficient self-control suggests an opposition between a series of pro-Hebrew organizations that maintained order and a population that gave in easily to temptation. Though instinct may have played a role in the persistence of foreign films, the importation of films was a more conscious coordination between movie distributors, theater owners, and the population itself, all of which were broadly committed to the promotion of a Zionist society but welcomed foreign options on the screen nonetheless.

On 16 September 1930, Josef Rivlin, an agent working in Palestine for the Judea Film Company, wrote back to the Jewish Agency administration regarding their requests to cancel film screenings. "Despite the fact that we agree with the Battalion on these matters," he wrote, "at a time when offering talking films and cabaret songs in all sorts of other languages is permissible, we can't allow that Jewish talking films, performed by the best Jewish actors in the world and with Jewish content, should not be allowed to show in Palestine."[122] In the first part of his comment,

Rivlin appears to be paying lip service to a particular collective ideology, one that would prohibit Yiddish films. His further comments, however, indicate that his worldview differs from that of the battalion as he points out the hypocrisy of limiting Jewish access to Jewish art, which he believed was more important to the Zionist movement than a commitment to Hebrew. Nonetheless, he conceded: "If public opinion and the national institutions continue in their insistent opposition to the showing of these films of course we won't want to be a transgressor [*poretz geder*] and it is quite possible that we will agree as agents of the company to not bring Jewish talking films."[123] If Hebrew hegemony is hegemonic enough, he seems resigned to admit, we will bow and follow. But by casting doubt on the power of the pro-Hebrew effort and offering concrete objections to its politics, Rivlin effectively shows that small groups of Hebrew advocates were not nearly strong enough to impose a monolingual standard for film screenings. Public pressure in support of Hebrew and in opposition to Yiddish on-screen, real as it was, functioned more on the level of suggestion than enforcement. The "informal state," as it were, was in the position to dictate norms and to shift public discourse to support these norms, but not to change the way people lived.

Rivlin's concerns were not primarily principled; they were financial. He insisted that if a film that had been sent to the movie houses was not screened, the agency stood to lose eight hundred Palestine pounds (£P800).[124] Other theaters, too, were worried that if they abandoned a film on ideological grounds, their competitors would step in, fill the demand, and reap the profits. A representative of the Eden Cinema wrote to the Battalion of the Defenders of the Hebrew Language on 7 September 1930, saying that he would commit to not show the film on the condition that other theaters make the same commitment.[125] The market spoke louder than ideology. Looking at Rivlin, we could conclude he was simply avaricious. But the market pressures to which he was responding were products of viewer demand: members of the Yishuv wanted to spend their leisure time watching films in multiple languages, including Yiddish, and ideology had little power to stop them.

But concerns didn't end with Yiddish. With the mass arrival of German-speaking Jews, the concern about films shifted from Yiddish to German. A letter from a committee dedicated to boycotting German goods wrote to the Tel Aviv Municipality with two complaints: cinemas were offering translations into German and were allowing mistakes in Hebrew subtitles, both indications that the institutions were inappropriately privileging German over Hebrew.[126] Over time, cinemas increasingly exhibited advertisement slides in German before the start of the movie.[127] In addition, some complained that the movie houses were advertising the films themselves in German, which they would refer to by speaking of "languages other than the official languages of Palestine."[128] Moviegoers enjoyed their (subtitled) films for the same reasons that counterparts around the world did: the drama, the action, the novelty. To commentators, the cinema, like the coffeehouse, seemed to do two objectionable things at once: it brought together foreign imports from countries far overseas and kindled latent desires within the Yishuv to luxuriate in mother tongues and leave behind Hebrew.

The protests against foreign-language cinema create an image of a population of lazy, indulgent, non-Zionist viewers pitted against heroic, single-minded enforcers. In practice, however, those who chose to spend their leisure time outside a Hebrew realm were making conscious choices that were not entirely antinationalist. These were "excellent films," wrote Yerushalayim Segal about German productions, "the comedy was entertaining, the tragedy was shocking." One day, a German film about the unfinished symphony of Schubert was shown in the Mograbi Theatre after languishing in the closet of the distributor for two years. "I don't understand why it hasn't been shown until now," Segal remarked to a friend. "It's a gem!" With the rise of Hitler to power, opposition arose to showing German films in the Yishuv. But, it took "protests, altercations, and riots before they stopped showing German-speaking films."[129] Historians remember the altercations, with all their color and ideological vigor, but not the many viewers whose insistence and interest, much of it simple and nonideological, made the protests continue. In the midst of one of many such film-related fights (in this case, about cinemas advertising in foreign languages) the CCEH intoned, as it had before and would do so again in so many other contexts: "There is no room in our lives for any foreign language. It is undermining the stability of the Yishuv."[130]

In reality, there was quite a lot of room for foreign languages in the leisure-time establishments of the Yishuv. Even the unemployed, as an article in *Ha-Tzofeh* had it, would find a shilling to visit the cinema, giving up the Hebrew language and the building of the land for "the scrap of a dream which is called a cinematic film," a space where he might "absorb the sounds of tantalizing languages" and feel himself transported far away from Palestine.[131] Some sources have assumed that the desire for foreign-language films, like foreign-language speech, reflected a fundamental uninterest in Zionism: "For [Fourth Aliyah] immigrants, *to whom the Zionist ethos was foreign*, the cinema was the most acceptable cultural consumption product," as David Tartakover's history of film has it.[132] In a sense, Tartakover is right that filmgoers were acting nonideologically; but he is wrong to assume that their nonideological behavior necessarily indicated a lack of national sentiment. In reality, film, like the other leisure-time activities discussed in this chapter, offered brief, contained respites from the burdens of building the land and the cognitive difficulties of speaking the language. Seeking out "tantalizing languages" did not mean a once-and-for-all abandonment of the Zionist project, a defiant move to cast down the shovel and cast out the language. Seeking leisure activities in other languages, the writer of the article knew, had little to do with disregard for Zionism as such but rather arose out of an implicit knowledge that Hebrew's reach was not total, that there was space outside it and beyond it.

The ardor of the "informal state" and its language-policing efforts existed in a complex relationship to the robust multilingual leisure sphere of the Yishuv and, eventually, the State of Israel. The most intimate of spaces and the most apparently nonpolitical of activities became targets for language activism; they also developed as spaces to affirm the presence and acceptability of languages other than Hebrew within and alongside Hebrew culture, whether in the form of non-Hebrew speech or the consumption of non-Hebrew culture.

CHAPTER TWO

PEDDLERS, TRADERS, AND
THE LANGUAGES OF COMMERCE

The cultural venues discussed in the last chapter constituted one small segment of the broader consumer market in the Yishuv; the far larger part of the market pertained to the buying and selling of goods and services, including foreign, or "non-Hebrew," ones. These products, too, were marked not only by their place of provenance but also by the multilingual culture that surrounded their sale and served merchants and customers as they engaged in transactions that transcended the cultural or physical boundaries of the Hebrew nation.

The journalist and educator Abraham Ludvipol, writing in the newspaper *Haaretz* in 1919, referred to a contingent of the Yishuv population critical of the fact that Hebrew schools of commerce, schools intended to prepare students for work in the capitalist market, were engaged in the teaching of non-Hebrew languages. Those schools, which offered languages deemed useful for business—namely, English, Arabic, and French—were, in the eyes of the critics, "destroying and demolishing the basic foundations"—by which they meant the agricultural foundations—on which the Zionist project needed to be founded. Ludvipol, though deeply committed to Hebrew culture, disagreed with this assessment and offered a rejoinder to the most dogmatic proponents of an all-Hebrew education. Hebrew labor and Hebrew production were centrally important, he assured his readers, but one should not forget that they were useless without markets and consumers, who tended to be diverse and concentrated in urban areas. Through urbanization, Jews might develop a sense of commercial endeavor that departed from the boundaries of petty shopkeeping and opened Jews' minds to new, modern commercial concepts.[1] The Hebrew project, he implied, could flourish only in the context of urban commercial exchange, even if that necessarily meant that some students had to acquire multilingual skills.

Ludvipol was referring here to the multilingual demands of bookkeeping, international trade, and office work. But he was calling attention to a broader context of linguistic diversity surrounding commercial activity in street markets, shops, and offices, particularly but not exclusively in the Yishuv's urban center, Tel Aviv. Tel Aviv was founded in 1909 and began a period of meteoric economic growth in the years after World War I. Imports thus were not limited to the personal or cultural (though often monetized) experiences of leisure time; instead, imports and local non-Jewish products came from a set of networks of exchange that both sustained the Yishuv and introduced a series of questions about the limits of its economic autonomy and power.

Hayim Nachman Bialik, whose leisure-time language practices we noted in the last chapter, told a 1929 gathering of Hebrew-language supporters, "The true conquest of language is not in literature or the press, but rather in the market, the factory and workshop, the bank . . . When there is denigration of the language there, all the schools and celebrations are useless."[2] The conquest of the market could not occur without the conquest of language; likewise, the conquest of language required the conquest of the market. But such coordination required not only commitment to language but also a degree of economic control over the marketplace that was not feasible. Though it was a language of ideological weight, Hebrew was by no means a language of economic power. Foreign languages flooded the marketplace not only because non-Hebrew speakers inhabited the space of the Yishuv, but also because powerful non-Hebrew economic entities inhabited the marketplace: both lower-priced Arab products and high-priced but attractive European products. The cultural and linguistic effects of international and interethnic commerce would be tolerated as part of a non-Zionist "hedonistic ethos" that coexisted and competed with the pioneering spirit.[3] But at the same time and in certain circumstances, as Ludvipol suggested, tolerance of commerce could itself be a Zionist position, since the growth of the market could promote nationalist priorities.

Commercial activity sat at a point of interface between the Yishuv and its internal and external others, and thus was inherently multilingual. This conjunction had deep and problematic roots for many Zionists. Both Jews and their anti-Semitic critics had long regarded commerce as a Jewish undertaking, and capitalism as such had ambivalent resonances in Zionist and Jewish historical memory. The biblical story of the Tower of Babel, an etiology of human linguistic diversity, is also, in some of its strands, a specific critique of Babylon, the great ancient commercial metropolis that was punished with language diversity as a consequence of the excesses of urban life.[4] But the typological Babel, over time, became a characterization and critique of Jews themselves, who, despite their esteemed Hebrew language, emerged as the epitome of commercial power, international exchange, and language diversity—the quintessential denizens of Babel.[5] Concern about degenerate Jewish economic life found a particularly accessible object in language. Operating implicitly within a paradigm that associated Hebrew with national unity, and language mixing with a dysfunctional diasporic Jewish commerce, members of the Yishuv—in Tel Aviv in particular—considered the significance of widespread foreign-language use in commercial settings and vied with one another about the necessary degree of association between Hebrew exclusivity (a cultural aim) and commercial self-sufficiency (an economic aim).

The diversity of the market reflected the diversity of Palestine more broadly: Jewish merchants were often new immigrants from a variety of settings; many suppliers and salespeople were Palestinian Arabs who ventured into Jewish communities to make sales; and many high-end products were imported from England, France, and the United States. The commercial sphere was thus both a locus of language contact and a field onto which some Zionists projected anxieties about the persistence in Palestine of diasporic commercial practices and the Yishuv's continued reliance on Western markets and foreign goods. This was true even while many tolerated a great deal of deviance from the principle of Hebrew labor and the Hebrew language, treating the market as a space not only where language acquisition and use was required but also where accommodation to the realities of exchange might seem to promote the overall growth of a Hebrew society.

Ludvipol, with his high-minded rhetoric, was not describing a theoretical urban future, but a reality unfolding before his eyes, ten years after the city of Tel Aviv was founded. During the period from 1918 until 1949, the urban population of Palestine fluctuated between 71 percent and 83 percent of the entire Jewish population, making concerns about commercial and linguistic practice in this typically urban space far from a peripheral concern. Some new immigrants had found work on kibbutzim; the majority, however, had made their way to Palestine's emerging cities, first and foremost Tel Aviv but also the Hadar Ha-Carmel area of Haifa, the newer neighborhoods in Jerusalem, and smaller urban centers elsewhere.[6] The rise of urban capitalism in Palestine was buoyed by immigration trends: the largely petit bourgeois Fourth Aliyah, a group that came mainly from Poland in the mid-1920s, gave the Yishuv a more strongly capitalist stamp and contributed to massive urbanization and industrialization, trends that proved essential for the economic vitality of the Yishuv.

Just as commerce was a main Jewish occupation abroad, it continued to be a common Jewish occupation in Palestine. In addition to those immigrants who immediately opened shops or other businesses, a number who failed in their initial attempts at agriculture moved to the cities and joined the ranks of the commercial class. By the end of the 1930s, Tel Aviv had more than 3,500 shops, or one store for every forty-four people, a higher ratio than existed in either Britain or the United States.[7] According to Yaakov Groman in his 1946 study of retail commerce, immigration brought a stream of people who did not need to change their occupations in Palestine: many of those in commerce abroad remained in that profession, drawing on both skills and networks that had served them elsewhere. Nonetheless, he pointed out, a much smaller percentage of Jews in Palestine were engaged in commerce compared with the Jewish population abroad, for some did make their way into other sectors. Only 13.3 percent of Jews in Palestine were in commerce, according to a 1931 government survey, compared with 52 percent in Germany, 31 percent in

Poland, and 47 percent in Hungary.[8] The organizational break between Europe and Palestine marked a new insistence on Hebrew language and culture, a new independence from foreign support, and a relatively larger Jewish agricultural sector than existed elsewhere; it did not, however, mean a totally new relationship to commerce.

Commerce, Jews, and Language

The apparent similarity between Palestine and the Diaspora meant that commerce in the Yishuv triggered fears about the persistence of the Diaspora and the limits of economic or cultural autonomy. Jews had a long historical affinity with commerce, and some Zionists, drawing a rich store of negative imagery from anti-Semitic portrayals of the past, intuitively bristled at those practices that evoked the stereotypes of Jewish diasporic commerce, defined in the cultural imagination by degenerate wanderers, peddlers, deal makers, and deceivers, not the new ideal of proud, nationally committed, self-sufficient laborers. Doctrinaire fears about multilingual commerce were projected in two directions: onto low or degenerate commerce, associated with Yiddish and Arabic, and onto high or international commerce—particularly the banking and import sectors—associated with English, French, and other European languages.[9] Specific pro-Hebrew citizens' organizations, the Battalion of the Defenders of the Hebrew Language, and the Central Council for the Enforcement of Hebrew (CCEH) emphasized an unassailable link between the Hebrew language and Hebrew labor, and excoriated figures who betrayed this dual principle. But practice took forms different from those that these activists might have recommended.

Anxieties about the deleterious effects of Jewish commerce had defined the Jewish experience since the Middle Ages. The medieval church branded Jews as economic outliers—and indeed enforced this status through limitations on Jewish landholding and guild membership. The stereotype of the Jew as a crooked dealer, famously represented in Shakespeare's *The Merchant of Venice*, persisted for centuries.[10] When the Zionist movement, in the broad aggregate of its political and cultural strands, strove and claimed to negate a Jewish exilic condition characterized by both abnormal commerce and multilingualism, it was responding to an imperative sketched out nearly a century before. Paired language and economic reforms were at the heart of Jewish *Verbesserung* ("improvement") efforts in the period of the German Enlightenment and onward. The Prussian bureaucrat Christian Wilhelm von Dohm, in his 1781 program for the civic improvement of Jews, suggested that Jews be forced to keep their commercial records in the language of the land, implying that a language switch would be part and parcel of a move away from an undefined set of devious practices: "Fraud and crooked dealings," he writes immediately after offering his language recommendation, "should be represented to Jews as the most heinous crime against the state which now embraces them with equal affection, and these crimes should be subjected to the harshest penalties."[11] A similar recommendation was adopted in Joseph II's Edict of Toleration less than a year later, which abolished all writing in "Hebrew and the so-called Jewish language and writing of Hebrew mixed with German."[12] A relapse of typically Jewish linguistic behavior would be thus concurrent and coextensive with a relapse of defective commercial behavior; linguistic reform was a path toward economic normalization.

In the nineteenth century, a century of movements for and promises of Jewish emancipation, the commercial essence of the Jews received yet more attention. Karl Marx famously used the word for Jews and Judaism (*Judentum*) as a synonym for commerce, a personification of the enervating effects of capitalist exchange that drew from analogies already widespread in the medieval period.[13] In 1911, Werner Sombart offered the thesis that Jews were temperamentally predisposed to succeed at capitalism and had brought this mode of economic production into the world, leading to the demise of the idyllic, feudal system that had characterized northern Europe.[14] The elevation of Jews to icons of destabilizing commerce served to mediate other populations' discomfort with the capitalist system itself. European discourse tended to associate particular types of economic activity with stigmatized Jews and to make such economic practices "vehicles for expressing widely felt anxieties about commerce in a manner that was politically safe and psychically tolerable."[15] The establishment of an urban Jewish center in Palestine therefore could not be a symbolically straightforward undertaking; despite the flourishing of Jewish commercial activity in early-twentieth-century Palestine, the Yishuv leadership, unsurprisingly, treated it with a mix of neglect and minimization as it devoted a great deal of rhetorical energy to the promotion of agriculture, manual labor, and affinity with the land.

Taking a chief marker of commercial excess to be language diversity, the Palestinian Zionist program promoted both Hebrew unity and economic reinvention as a two-pronged answer to the Babel of language and the Babylon of commerce. This labor-language synthesis represented a fusing of two distinct but overlapping trends of the late Ottoman period: a push for Hebrew labor and an appeal for the Hebrew language. Advocates of economic separation in the first years of the twentieth century adopted a rhetoric of *'Avodah 'Ivrit* (Hebrew labor), a program of market separation intended in their view to both bolster Jewish economic independence and reduce the possibility of Jewish exploitation of Palestinian Arabs. "Without Hebrew labor, there will be no Jewish economy; without Hebrew labor, there will be no homeland," said the labor leader and future prime minister David Ben-Gurion.[16] The Zionist type of the new Hebrew man took on a particularly strong cast within the labor movement, which suggested that physical vibrancy and cultural rejuvenation could stem only from economic self-sufficiency. Meanwhile, the Hebrew language, linked to the romantic spirit of the Hebrew nation, was a central plank of the labor calculus, and was strongly supported within the Labor Zionist leadership that grew in strength after World War I. But Hebrew support was by no means only a labor principle, having been originally advocated by "cultural Zionists" more directly concerned with the moral and spiritual cultivation of the Jewish people than with their economic formation. With the passage of time and the solidification of a Hebrew cultural center in Palestine, the two projects, economic investment and cultural revival, became part and parcel of a broadly shared program of Jewish self-sufficiency.

The Conquest of Labor and the Conquest of Language

Labor separation and the "conquest of labor" was one of the foundational economic strategies of the Zionist movement. In agricultural settings, this principle was marked by the exclusion of Arab farm labor; in Tel Aviv, it emerged in the city's original conception as a Jewish city and the lasting mythology and intention that "it [be] built, from the foundations to the roof-corbels, by Jewish hands."[17] The "conquest" of labor was a process contingent on the continual willingness of business owners to recruit only Jewish labor and the commitment of the Jewish marketplace to support "Hebrew" products, the common term for products made by Jews.

The fulfillment of these economic commitments was frequently measured in linguistic terms. "Hebrew" marked both language commitments and broader cultural desiderata. Marketers often make claims about the substance or value of a product through language—in packaging, advertising, or announcements. Visible and auditory linguistic markers impart specific cultural meaning to goods and play an important role in fetishizing commodities, making them seem more than their component material parts.[18] In a multilingual environment such as the Yishuv, which was acutely aware of its roots in multilingual Europe, the aesthetics of linguistic practice in the commercial sphere—on products and packaging as well as in voices spoken and heard in the marketplace—were particularly symbolic. In official rhetoric, the ideal world was a Hebrew-speaking society characterized by productive Hebrew labor, and Hebrew products became incarnations of a set of elusive ideals.

The campaigns on behalf of Hebrew goods (which were often called *totzeret ha-aretz*, "produce of the land" or "local products," in reference to both local provenance and Jewish producers) were public and marked by vigor, grassroots organizing, and occasionally intimidation. These efforts, moreover, which seem to have begun in earnest in 1924, transcended earlier tensions between Labor and non-Labor Zionists, an indication that a new cultural consensus around economic separation had emerged. That year, a mass immigration of mainly Polish Jews contributed not only to a major increase in the urbanization of Palestine but also to the expansion of industry. At just the moment when a large number of Jewish-produced industrial goods were available for display, increased imports to Palestine introduced new concerns about foreign goods and the Yishuv's ability to push the British to adopt policies protective of Jewish businesses.[19] Eliezer Rieger, notable for his efforts on behalf of Hebrew-language education, wrote in a 1924 issue of the magazine *Mis'har ve-ta'asiyah* (Commerce and industry) that the municipal council of Jewish Jaffa had adopted a resolution requiring its members to buy only Jewish-produced fruit and to cover their roofs with Jewish-produced tiles.

Concurrently, the head rabbinate of Jaffa stated that Jews were obligated to purchase Jewish goods and that transgressors would have to pay a fine to charity. "Right and left are uniting in the demand to strengthen local products (*totzeret ha-aretz*)," the ruling had it, though abuses continued.[20] The first exposition of locally produced Hebrew goods was held in Tel Aviv in 1924 with 192 displayers (30–40 percent of producers). The exhibition was intended not only to promote certain consumption patterns among Jews in Palestine, but also to attract foreign Jewish businesspeople and thus to promote export opportunities.[21]

Hebrew products were promoted in a range of places. Schools asked their students to write essays about the importance of *totzeret ha-aretz*. Shimriyah Levin wrote an essay in high school entitled "The Idea of *Totzeret ha-Aretz:* What Is It?," in which she wrote, with the optimism and naïve simplicity of a school student: "If we buy the products of our country we are providing places of work for [people] who were previously unemployed . . . And it's not just this. In fact, if industry develops, commerce will also develop, and if we trade with faraway countries, [this money] will make it possible to buy lands or increase industry. So we need to use only local products so we can build our country and achieve our goals."[22] Kibbutzim raised the issue in their local discussions. Raphael Patai remembers a debate on Kibbutz Giv'at Brenner about whether it was acceptable to sell all the dairy products produced on the kibbutz to Tnuva, the Histadrut's cooperative, and purchase products for its own consumption from Lithuania and Australia. By doing so, they would increase the cash receipts of the kibbutz, since imported milk and butter were half the price of locally produced versions. How, though, could Tnuva promote *totzeret ha-aretz* if "the producers themselves did not fulfill this duty but instead bought foreign butter?"[23]

Alongside the promotion of *totzeret ha-aretz*, this very orthodoxy was subject to parody. While Shimriyah Levin was singing the virtues of local goods in a naïve school essay, the first Hebrew comedy revue at the Matate theater in Tel Aviv in 1924 performed *An Anthem of Local Products* (*totzeret ha-aretz*). Its title song, "Zemer le-totzeret ha-aretz" (A song for local products), admonished: "You want satisfaction / and aliyah, brother? / From your shoelace to your hat / you must buy / only from the products of our land [*totzeret artzenu*] / only from the fruit of our might and our efforts."[24] While the sentiment was similar to those copied in school essays, this setting suggests a more lighthearted engagement with those strictures and a sense that perhaps a totalizing commitment to all-Hebrew consumption was somehow laughable. Interestingly enough, moreover, Shimriyah Levin did not prove to be a Hebrew purist. Her materials are preserved in the Central Zionist Archive not because of her activism on behalf of Hebrew products, but because, following her graduation from the Lämel high school in Jerusalem, she became at teacher at the Tel Aviv School of English, a private institute for the teaching of English.

The quest for the elusive Hebrew market was construed as an escape from a particular set of antimodels, dystopias. In numerous commercial spaces, the apparent replication of degenerate diasporic commercial modes was expressed as a return to Babel. In this discourse, commercial Babel was dotted with products and commercial spaces evocative of *galut:* the peddler, the used-goods wagon, the vegetable lady, the bottle of perfume, the imported soap, all of which announced their deviance by the linguistic tags that announced, marked, and symbolized their economic status. At the same time, these linguistic markers delineated the contours of economic isolationism, and its limits.

Zionist discomfort with commercial practices was focused in two directions: against peddlers selling low-quality goods, and toward marketers and sellers of desirable European products.[25] Peddlers could be Jews, suspect because of their visible dirtiness, their tendency to be seen as a public nuisance, and their (usually) Yiddish-language shouts, or Palestinian Arabs, automatically problematic because of the presumption that they were selling Arab- (rather than Jewish-) produced goods to Jews. On the other hand, foreign importers and goods raised the hackles of observers. Some opposition was directed at British goods, which were not technically foreign in a land ruled by the British.[26] In the years following 1933, opposition to foreign goods was also directed at German goods that flooded the Yishuv as part of the Ha'avarah (transfer) agreements with the Third Reich, which allowed German Jewish immigration in exchange for commitments to buy and import German goods.[27] Both of these forms of commercial practice were marked by linguistic practice. Low commerce, on the one hand, was signaled by local Palestinian Arabs, Arabic-speaking Jews, or eastern European immigrants conversing in Arabic, Yiddish, or sounds perceived as nonlinguistic grunts and screeches. High commerce was characterized by Jews using their knowledge of English, French, or German to interact with international markets and bring in foreign goods. If undesirable labor was linked in practice to undesirable language, the conquest of labor was construed as a conquest of language.

Low Commerce: *Alte Zakhen* and the Itinerant Peddler

Historically, Jews restricted from owning shops sometimes turned to peddling, which required little capital. Peddlers were controversial figures; in seventeenth- and eighteenth-century Germany, they were seen as tricksters who would wander between towns selling goods door-to-door and thus competing with local merchants. The very methods of peddling appeared intrusive: guilds in Frankfurt complained that Jewish merchants were accosting people in the streets to offer their wares, while lawmakers in Hamburg complained that Jews were making too much noise by calling out their wares with "inappropriate shouting" and "inappropriate language."[28] Some governments banned Jewish peddlers altogether in response to guild pressures to reduce competition with Christian businesses.[29] In nineteenth-century Germany, Jews began to make the upward move from peddling to shopkeeping and, at least in practice, were no longer overwhelmingly involved with peddling. Nonetheless, the stereotype of the Jewish peddler and his aberrant language attended their commercial activity. Jews were understood to speak *Mauscheln*, a hidden language closely linked to street commerce. August Lewald, a Jewish convert to Christianity, expressed doubt in his *Memoirs of a Banker* (1836) that his conversion had erased his Jewish discourse.[30]

The association between spoken language and trade is particularly apparent with respect to the traditional marketplace, where goods are promoted through speech and sales must be negotiated orally. Oral transactions, moreover, are linked to the exchange of information—the marketplace is a place where ideas are transmitted. The Hebrew term for peddling, *rokhlut*, is from the same root as *rekhilut* (gossip), and is linked closely to a form of ambulatory speech discredited by the Jewish tradition.[31] Gossip has, moreover, tended to be associated with marginal populations, including women and the lower classes, who are generally regarded as misinformed, devious, or idle. To outside observers, the speech patterns of these oral communities can seem degenerate and monotonous; the upper classes "viewed formulaic epithets and cliché ridden sayings as symptomatic of a tired and stagnant culture," part and parcel of a general disdain for the poor.[32] These rapid and stylized verbal exchanges were wrapped up in stigmatized economic practices. The shame and stigma of gossip was associated, Melanie Tebbutt found, with the stigma of pawning goods; both acts were linked to loose morals (including sexual morals).[33]

Peddling was a visible though numerically small field of commerce in Tel Aviv. A Tel Aviv Municipality survey in 1926 indicated that of 13,652 workers in Tel Aviv, 2,405 (or about 18 percent) were in commerce; of these, 1,386 were shop owners, 241 were peddlers, and 71 were milk roundsmen.[34] A British survey from 1935 indicates 85 milk roundsmen; 36 cake roundsmen; 38 fish peddlers and stands; 197 fruit shops, stands, and peddlers; 140 ice cream and soft drink stands and peddlers; and 51 stationery shops and peddlers.[35] Though the peddler population was less than 2 percent of the total according to these numbers, it aroused a disproportionate amount of attention on the side of the municipality. Peddling came to represent the link between poverty, linguistic deviance, commercial deviance, and social danger, though a list of arrests from late 1925 makes clear that peddlers were no more likely than other businesspeople to be operating without proper licenses.[36] In this context, linguistic reform served as a symbol—often a superficial one—of social engineering. "Why," griped a contributor to *Yedi'ot 'Iriyat Tel Aviv*, the municipality's bulletin, "don't they sufficiently monitor the candy peddlers who make sales by the school gates without any sanitary oversight, which certainly harms the health of our children? . . . How long will peddlers disturb the rest of residents at dawn with their guttural chants?"[37]

The distaste for peddling and other forms of low commerce was historically bound up with Yiddish. But the field of low commerce in the Yishuv had a more complex set of linguistic referents. The image of the degenerate commercial agent was projected in two directions: onto Yiddish and a set of eastern European stereotypes, and onto Arabic, Arab Jews, and a set of Oriental stereotypes. A shared vocabulary was used to refer to both types, branded at once "exilic" (*galuti*), a term with specifically European resonances, and Levantine (*levantini*), a term with Arab or Oriental references. As Abraham Yaakov Brawer wrote in a survey of Tel Aviv markets: "Two influences are afoot: Arab Jewish and Eastern European Jewish, the latter of which is dominant."[38]

The term *galuti* has generally been associated with eastern Europe, while *levantini* has, especially since the 1950s, become closely associated with Arabs and, especially, with the large Mizrahi and Sephardi populations sometimes referred to in the literature as Arab Jews.[39] The terms—and their associated referents—were intertwined in the Yishuv, however. Characterizations of European Jews as degenerates, Derek Penslar writes, mirrored contemporary assessments of Native Americans and other non-European peoples.[40] In turn, Steven Aschheim has shown, western European Jews at times saw their eastern counterparts, *Ostjuden*, as bearers of negative (even if authentic) Jewish traits that had not been effaced by assimilation.[41] Eastern European Jews in Palestine branded Arab Jews and Arab non-Jews as outsiders; by extension, eastern European Jews who were insufficiently committed to Zionist goals were branded as Arabs. Through this chain of displaced associations, to be a peddler in the Yishuv was to be, typologically, an Arab; to be an Arab, in turn, was to be a ghetto Jew still caught in premodern ways of thinking and behaving. The "Levantine marketplace," then, though classically identified with the Arab bazaar, referred in the Yishuv to both the suq and the shtetl. When the fictional Friedrich Loewenberg of Theodor Herzl's 1902 *Altneuland* first travels to Palestine, he finds that Jerusalem is characterized by "shouts, smells, tawdry colors, people in rags crowding the narrow, airless streets, beggars, cripples, starveling children, screaming women, bellowing shopkeepers." The image of unhygienic circumstances, sickness, and inarticulate utterances, writes Michael Selzer, evoked the eastern European ghetto.[42] Just as in Europe, the visual and vocal markers of commerce in Palestine could be a cause for concern and the target of social reform.

A great deal of effort was exerted to transform the outdoor oriental-ghetto marketplace of Jerusalem into western European–style shops. Some of this initiative came directly from the British, who set out in 1917 to design a hygienic marketplace, with a fountain and a large symmetric courtyard, in the area that later became the Mahane Yehudah market-place (the plan was never implemented).[43] But some Jews were also proponents of such reform. Alfred Boneh, head of the Economics Department at Hebrew University in 1938, spoke of Tel Aviv not only as a replacement for Jaffa, but also as part of a larger modernizing trend that would ultimately see "the famous Oriental market . . . departing the world" and remaining "a romantic historical relic and a reminder of a period and type of economy that has left the world."[44]

The Yishuv, or at least Tel Aviv, had seemingly fulfilled Herzl's vision that Palestine look "just like America," with modern suburbs and wide, straight streets. The presumed divide between the old and new modes of commerce, marked as Eastern and Western, appeared to be epitomized in the opposition between Tel Aviv and Jaffa. A 1946 review of retail commerce in Palestine contrasted the Jewish market with the Arab market: "[The modern commercial sector] is the fruit of the pioneering labor, devotion, self-sacrifice, and dedication of many. Go out to the alleys of the neighboring, non-Jewish city. You'll see the booths or the Oriental-style bazaars, the monotonous and unhygienic displays of merchandise, and the primitive selling techniques using stone-weights. And from there return to the Hebrew Tel Aviv and you'll see a *piece of Europe that was transplanted to the East*."[45] The transformation, however, was not complete. "Eastern" commerce persisted in the Yishuv and became marked by a mélange of commercial agents speaking Yiddish or Arabic, and sometimes a little of each. A South African traveler to Palestine remarked, "The stores by and large leave the impression of a shop in Shnipeshok [a small town near Vilnius] or any other diaspora city. They have no European taste or form."[46] The East—Arab and European—was visible in Palestine, and it seemed an imposition.

The association between Yiddish, Arabic, and low commerce persisted throughout the mandate period and appears not to have been very responsive to shifts in immigration patterns or the perception, common by the later part of the period, that German had replaced Yiddish as the greatest threat to the integrity of Hebrew culture. Perceptions of language use in homes, cafés, and theaters changed dramatically with the changing waves of aliyah, with Yiddish appearing most dangerous until the early 1930s, when widespread German use among members of the Fifth Aliyah seemed to overshadow the language practices of the many Yiddish speakers. Germans too could be peddlers. Aviva Askrov recalls a memorable character who sold hot dogs outside the Mograbi theater "in the rain, in the summer, in the winter, for years" while being treated as something of a pariah: "No one would speak with him." It appeared to be a known fact that this man was a failed performer, a man whose immigration to Palestine had interrupted his career as a legitimate producer of culture: "They said he was once an opera singer, that he was a known man," she states, introducing him as not only a cultured individual but also a particularly elite singer. "He was a Yekke, I think. He wore a white hat and a white robe. He would be there every day."[47] This failed German immigrant, called by the common slang term for German speakers in the Yishuv, returns in the memories of Tzipi Dagan, whose grandparents owned a sewing-supplies store on Allenby Street one door down from the Mograbi theater. She, too, recalled "the Mograbi, with its clock and hot-dog seller, the opera singer who stood under the clock and sold hot-dogs."[48] The specter of Levantinism haunted the Yishuv well beyond the creation of the State of Israel in 1948, though the eastern European referent of the term seems to have declined in importance and been displaced by Middle Eastern referents. "We are duty bound," wrote David Ben-Gurion in 1966 following a wave of Moroccan immigration to Israel, "to fight against the spirit of the Levant, which corrupts individuals and societies, and preserve the authentic Jewish values as they crystallized in the Diaspora."[49] The target of opprobrium in these prestate cases is a set of cultural forms associated with both eastern Europe and the Orient, that is, that which must be overcome.

The degenerate urban market had two concurrent and contradictory linguistic features: its multiplicity of languages and its absence of (proper) language. On the one hand, Eastern and eastern European cities were seen as unnaturally multilingual: Tel Aviv mayor Meir Dizengoff warned: "Every new immigrant reaching our city should remember that Tel-Aviv is not an ordinary Eastern city, with a mixture of people and tongues. Tel-Aviv is a civilized Hebrew city, with one language only, the language of the Bible, and all foreign languages brought from abroad should make room for this language."[50] The psychology that led to linguistic mixing was deemed diasporic, and specifically characteristic of the European Diaspora. Yehoshua Karni'eli accused speakers of non-Hebrew languages of continuing "the thread of their Diaspora existence."[51] On the other hand, this despised space showed deficient forms of language, nonlanguages that resembled animal noises. A letter to the Tel Aviv Municipality in 1938 complained of "those who hawk their wares in loud voices and strange yells (with clapping of hands and dances) which deafen the ears from five in the morning until after midnight)."[52] A newspaper article that same year complained of the "Levantine shrieks" of the Tel Aviv market.[53] These aberrant linguistic forms signaled for the complainants lingering inefficiencies and aberrations in an otherwise productive economy.

For Hebrew advocates, then, the regulation of language functioned symbolically as a regulation of untoward commercial behaviors and low-quality wares. When the Organization for the Enforcement of Hebrew (Irgun le-hashlatat ha-'Ivrit) wrote to Israel Rokach, the mayor of Tel Aviv, in 1939, it argued that "the calls in Yiddish by the peddlers, the fixers of primus ovens, the sellers of old clothes, etc., are injurious and embarrassing." Unfortunately, they wrote, "we haven't heard a demand from the public to put an end to this."[54] Municipalities regularly berated peddlers for causing noise and dirtiness, blocking doors, and other uncultured behaviors.[55] The secretary of the municipality attempted to respond by regulating the practice of peddling, but in light of his limited powers of regulation, resorted instead to "trying to explain to peddlers the importance of Hebrew," implying that a reform in their language practices would reduce the disruption of their commercial practices.[56]

Student language-enforcement organizations also took it into their own hands to eliminate these commercial behaviors. An anecdote from a student at the Herzliya Gymnasium in Tel Aviv recalled "a small but characteristic episode" of language regulation that occurred in the years just before World War I but, as later examples show, represented a scenario that was repeated later as well. The student recalled a peddler who sold candles, soap, and matches, hawking his wares in the form of a Yiddish song that attracted the students' attention: "*likht un zeyf un shvebelakh*" (candles and soap and matches). One day, the students' music teacher, Hanina Krachevsky, suggested that the students co-opt and recast the song. The students, he suggested, should translate the words into Hebrew ("It was totally forbidden to sing in Yiddish") and sing the song in four-part harmony. A few minutes later, an organized choir was going down Herzl Street, "marching in a mili-

tary procession and singing the song in Hebrew, '*ner, sabon, ve-gafrurim.*' "[57]
The lilting Yiddish song of the peddler was well known to the students, who
appear to have encountered it regularly and taken to singing it before being
instructed not to. In the story, the translation of the song into its Hebrew
equivalent appears to rectify the problem. But the appropriation of the song
by the pro-Hebrew teacher also transfigures it, re-forms it, and subverts its
utility as a peddler's mechanism for promoting his products and drawing
customers. Not only the words of the song but also its form is, in theory,
translated: from a lone man's chant employed in service of commercial ends
to a march performed by a regimented military procession for spectacle
alone. This intervention, however, made little difference. A portrait titled
"Voices of the Street" by Ziona Rabau-Katinsky mentions "the Jewish
carter, cap on his head, who whips his worn-out mule and announces his
wares in a pleasant cantorial tune and with a Galician accent: 'Oi, lekht un
zeyf un shvebelakh' " (Oy, candles and soap and matches).[58] A tourist from
Warsaw in 1937 commented that the corner of Ba'ale Melakhah and King
George Streets reminded him of Warsaw, Brisk (Brest), and Vilna (Vilnius),
where sellers would peddle cakes and call out, "Warm *kekim*, fresh *kekim*,
eight for a *grush*, buy, buy!"[59] But by the subversion of both linguistic and
commercial behavior and its reformulation in the language and tropes of
Zionist conquest, a quasi-military brigade had brought apparent, though
fleeting order to the streets.

This narrative might suggest that a group of ideologically inclined students was reforming a peddler who was indifferent to the demands of
Zionist national culture. But those immigrants who turned to peddling
often did so for lack of alternatives as much as for lack of conviction. A
1941 narrative poem by Emmanuel Ha-Rusi offered a literary reflection
on a fictional Hayim-Itzi, a shoemaker who, wounded as a soldier in the
Russian army, begins to sell *alte zakhen* (old things) in the streets of Russia.
Upon moving to Palestine, he is excited by the prospect of building the
land, but when he proudly displays his medals in the hope that he can
become a soldier, he is told by the clerk in the immigration division that
his services are not needed. He finds that he has no choice but to return
to the streets as a rag seller. His bleak fate is similar to that of the old can-
dle and soap seller remembered in the student's narrative cited above.
Hayim Itzi is a man mocked by children:

They know how to impersonate his singing voice
And when Hayim-Itzi comes by they meet him with song:
Alte shikh, alte zakhen! [old shoes, old things!; Yiddish]

One day, Hayim-Itzi sees a group of young men doing military exercises, and caught up in a fantasy, starts leading them in a march. But this illusion is soon broken:

Suddenly, the children started laughing
In a call of the wild, a howling of Tatars
"Guys—it's the rag seller!
Our rag seller! The rag seller!
Alte zakhen, alte shikh!"
Hayim-Itzi stood, he didn't continue on his way.
He slumped down and recoiled
And blushed, embarrassed, as the folly of his actions.
What stupidity! Stupidity!
The dream had passed by and reality had come.[60]

Emmanuel Ha-Rusi (born Emmanuel Novograbelsky in 1903) grew up in an avidly Hebrew-speaking home in Nikolaev (now in Ukraine) and led the Youths of Zion movement in Russia. After moving to Palestine in 1924, he worked draining swamps and at the port but moved to Tel Aviv after contracting malaria. There he became active in the Battalion of the Defenders of the Hebrew Language and founded the Matate theater, for which he penned the first Hebrew comedy revue, which included "An Anthem for *Totzeret ha-Aretz*," the somewhat satirical reflection on "Hebrew products" cited earlier.[61] His 1941 poem offered a picture of a different commercial sector in the figure of Hayim-Itzi, excluded from any meaningful production, speaking in Yiddish, hawking old things rather than new Hebrew products, and derided by all around him.

Whether or not it was their preference to do so, sellers roamed the streets because they had customers. They continued to speak in Yiddish because their customers understood this language; networks of informal sellers connected recent, impoverished Jewish immigrants (usually men) with a broader Jewish clientele, often of women. Yiddish-speaking sellers were not lone characters, transported, as it were, from another place and

time, but part of an active network of commercial activity. The high discourse of "only Hebrew" and "only Hebrew products"—itself a consciously counterfactual construction of Jewish self-sufficiency—ceded to a
different reality on the streets, a reality marked both by Jewish sellers
speaking Yiddish and by Palestinian Arabs speaking Arabic (and, as we
will see, Yiddish).

Yiddish-speaking Jewish immigrants shared the streets in many cases
with Palestinian Arab sellers. At least into the 1930s, these networks
brought Palestinian Arabs, particularly sellers of eggs and vegetables, in
contact with a consumer base of Jewish women.[62] Ziona Rabau-Katinsky
recalls in her memoir a mother "leaving her yard holding on to a
bucket and calling to the Arab shepherd: '*staneh ya walad—halib, halib*'
[Wait, boy—Milk! Milk! (Arabic)]."[63] Daniel Ofir recalls in an interview
that the Yishuv's economy relied on orange exports and so did not produce many fruits or vegetables for local consumption: "Arab women . . .
would come each morning with a basket on their heads, knock on the
door, and ask: 'Do you want to buy fresh produce?' "[64] Buying from
Palestinian Arabs, Tova Aharoni remembers in an interview, was common practice and proceeded despite appeals for *totzeret ha-aretz:*

A. They [the Arabs] would bring fruit on donkeys, with vegetables.
Mostly fruits, not vegetables.
Q. And people would buy from them?
A. They bought.
Q. Despite all the cries about *totzeret ha-aretz?*
A. No, they didn't yell so much about *totzeret ha-aretz.* Hebrew labor
yes. They came from Jaffa.

At this point, however, Aharoni insists in somewhat contradictory fashion
that her family was not among those who bought from Arab sellers:

A: We didn't have any contact with Arabs. We didn't see Arabs. My
grandmother would go to the market, she didn't buy from them. In
Jerusalem they bought from Arabs, on a donkey, oranges, I remember.
Q: Here people bought but not you? They would do it, they would
come with the wagons of goods like that?
A: Yes.[65]

Does her denial of the practice conjure an opposition to it that she held at the time but later discarded, or a newfound distaste for a practice that posed no problem at the time? Despite the limitations of oral histories, these stories clarify the persistence of such dealings and pinpoint their social context: a Yiddish-Arabic netherworld constituted of female Arab sellers and female Jewish customers communicating in a pidgin of forbidden tongues on the streets or on the doorsteps of private homes.

The interplay of Yiddish and Arabic within this "low" commercial sphere is expressed quite beautifully in an interview with Menahem Rogelski, whose memories from the late 1920s and early 1930s (he came to Palestine in 1925) include Yiddish-speaking Palestinian Arabs who would come around his neighborhood and offer to clean dishes before the Passover holiday. The image he painted included Arabs collecting dishes and scorching them in fire to make them kosher for Passover. In appealing to Jewish customers for business, they would call out in Yiddish, "*Vays in kesalakh, vays in feyle, vays in shinhas*" (Whiten your fabric! Whiten your tub! Whiten your copper!).[66] In this case, the provider of the service was an Arab and the consumer was a Jewish woman making sure her dishes were properly prepared for the Passover holiday. While the public market was, to a great degree, a Hebrew-speaking one, this liminal space between public and private, the sphere of women, new immigrants, and Palestinian Arabs, was surely not.

The cleaner of dishes might be classified as part of a group of Yiddish-speaking Palestinian Arab peddlers, generally subsumed in a category of sellers of *alte zakhen* who roamed the streets, often with horse-drawn wagons, hawking their wares.[67] Sellers of secondhand goods (whether Jewish or Arab) found ample business among immigrants, many of whom were poor. Popular discourse branded this market niche as aberrant. In a newspaper column of 1946, a seller of old things appears as an errant Kurdish Jew—likely a native speaker of Aramaic, not Yiddish—who wanders into the courtyard of the Jewish Agency and Jewish National Council buildings in Jerusalem, buying and selling "*alte zakhen, alte shikh*" (old things, old shoes).[68] The contrast between the symmetrical stone buildings on King George Street, housing the very nerve centers of the Zionist movement, and the haggard Kurdish Jew speaking in Yiddish, is striking. It appears that these figures were not only incongruous but also perceived as dangerous. An article in 1942 announced that "because of the increase of burglaries from apartments, residents [of Tel Aviv] are asked to make sure that entrances to homes are kept locked during day and nighttime hours and to be particularly wary of buyers of used goods who call out '*alte zakhen.*' "[69]

The Yiddish and Arabic-speaking sellers of *alte zakhen*, foods, and other goods were such dominant types in the Yishuv that their phrases, heard in the streets, became dominant metonyms for both the persistence of low language use and the unfortunate persistence of embarrassing, foreign, and diasporic forms of commerce, as the following text demonstrates. Before the founding of the Palestine Broadcasting Service in 1936, a fascinating (and difficult to translate) satirical piece in *Davar* imagined what the first Jewish radio broadcast would sound like:

> *Hello, Hello!* This is Tel Aviv speaking. Tel Aviv *spricht* [speaking (German)]. Tel Aviv is speaking. Tel Aviv *redt* [speaking (Yiddish)]. *Yalla fish, yalla fish* [Come on (Arabic); fish (Yiddish)]! *Yalla vayntroyb* [Come on, grapes (Arabic and Yiddish)]! Good grapes! *Farrekhten shikh* [Shoe repairs (Yiddish)]! *Alte zakhen* [Old things (Yiddish)]! *Alte benkele* [Old stools (Yiddish)]! *Hello, Hello!* Please don't pay attention to the interruptions . . . *Hello, hello!* Tel Aviv is speaking! The whole world, listen in! Please listen to the news of the day from Tel Aviv.[70]

The "broadcast" proceeds from this point as an all-Hebrew parody of politics and culture; this initial section, however, seems intended to call into question the very suggestion that Jews could produce a properly formal radio broadcast in standard language. The piece is relevant as a general reminder of linguistic mixing in the Yishuv; in this context, however, the particular languages used are significant. Arabic and Yiddish are presented in this caricature solely as languages of low commerce, the languages in which shoes, fish, grapes, and old things are sold; German and English, in contrast, are used solely in formal utterances. The mixture of Arabic and Yiddish ("*yalla fish*" and "*yalla vayntroyb*") indicates that the two languages had come to be seen as interchangeable symbols of an embarrassing and nonstandard form of commerce that, by extension, called into question the Yishuv's ability to be truly modern.

High Commerce: *Lo'azit* and Levantinism

The shadow realm of second-rate, second-class commerce conducted in Arabic and Yiddish was part and parcel of the commercial context in Tel Aviv and other cities as well as in agricultural settlements. In the case of Arab-made products, the perceived transgression involved the avoidance of Jewish products in favor of "foreign" goods; in the case of Yiddish-speaking Jews, the products were often Jewish-made, but the modes and methods of commerce were seen as imported and "foreign." The commercial sector, however, touched also on larger spheres of power relations between the Yishuv and the Western world, European imports, and international business. A society rhetorically focused on the labor movement, collectivism, and agricultural work also contained commercial agents, who, despite negative representations, were often quite strongly nationalist and courted by the labor movement. As time passed, labor, which had identified private capital with exploitative, antinational labor, became more amenable to cooperation with private business.[71]

Moreover, the political society of the Yishuv, for all its passion, was weak and ultimately influenced greatly by British economic policies and pressures, over which the Yishuv had little control. Already in late 1917, the writer Yosef Hayim Brenner warned of the power of the British Empire, which he feared would impose its capitalistic, imperialistic economic norms on Palestine. And indeed, clause 18 of the mandate ordinances opened Palestine to imports without tariffs. Imports were essential to the Yishuv—through the period 1922–39, imports exceeded exports by a ratio of approximately two to one, and at times more, an expenditure funded in large part by the capital brought in by new immigrants.[72]

Palestine's clear economic reliance on the West was a cause of discomfort for a society striving for a level of economic autonomy; the presence of foreign languages in certain economic spheres made this relationship of dependency visible and audible. On one level, imported products, particularly packaged consumer goods, were often labeled and marketed in languages other than Hebrew. Both the products and the language practices associated with their sale, then, appeared to be foreign intrusions. On a second level, the existence of import and export businesses in the Yishuv, as well as a robust banking industry, depended on contacts with buyers and sellers abroad.[73] These contacts—both those promoting highly encouraged exports and those bringing in more controversial imports—were fundamentally interlingual, and companies regularly exchanged correspondence in European languages, particularly English and French, to arrange deals. The presence of both import and export institutions, moreover, encouraged the training of young people in language skills and spawned a network of commercial schools and extracurricular training courses that focused on the acquisition of languages for commercial ends. The transformation of the Yishuv during the period of the mandate into an urban, industrial society was troubling to some, and their fears were expressed in part through discourses on the visible and audible linguistic effects of such commercial trends.

Economic activism directed toward consumers was bound up with linguistic activism precisely because foreign products tended to be marketed in, or with the help of, foreign languages. In April 1936 a group of young people smashed the windows of the Rivoli store, which sold luxury goods, and distributed propaganda fliers pointing out that the establishment was displaying foreign china and leather goods. At the same time, the group caused a stir about imported door handles installed at the Mizrahi bank on Lilienblum Street. The uproar came after the Battalion of the Defenders of the Hebrew Language had set off stink bombs in a hall screening a Yiddish film,[74] prompting Meir Dizengoff to write jointly to both pro-Hebrew-language and pro-Hebrew-labor extremist groups, saying, "If the path toward local goods and the protection of the language or the imposition of the language—if it is violence—then Tel Aviv will become a second Chicago and the results will be the opposite of what is desired."[75] Nonetheless, the uproar was limited to small groups. According to Alfred Kupferberg, describing Rivoli and other luxury stores in his book on German Jews in Palestine, "you would be hard put to it to find anything smarter or more elegant in Berlin's Tauentzienstrasse or the Jungfernstieg in Hamburg." This and other similar businesses, he continued, gave Tel Aviv "a cosmopolitan look; whether this is to be regretted or welcomed lies, so to speak, in the philosophical eye of the beholder."[76]

An analysis of advertisements from Tel Aviv, housed at the Eliasaf Robinson Collection at Stanford University, makes clear the extent of foreign-language use in advertisements and store signs. Many advertisements were written in two or three languages. Playbills in particular tended to be filled with advertisements for cosmetics, alcohol, and foods, many of the ads bilingual, and a good number of them with no Hebrew at all. To some extent, language patterns traced immigration patterns: from the 1930s, German was a mainstay on scores of fliers and advertisements. But language use was not entirely a response to speaking patterns: Yiddish was almost never used in written form on ads, and Polish is hardly found, despite the fact that these were common spoken languages.[77]

Multilingual ads appeared threatening to municipalities, pro-Hebrew organizations, groups of community activists, and labor and cultural leaders, all of whom stood on the lookout for Hebrew infractions. The Tel Aviv Municipality expressed shock about a 1937 advertisement for Weller's jam that reached its desks. The advertisement, alerting customers to a decrease in redemption fees for glass jam jars, was written in six languages—English, Hebrew, French, German, Russian, and Polish. Similar collections of languages can be found on other ads for foreign products.[78] The advertisement appears to have been submitted by a private citizen, Yehuda Finkelstein, who remarked in a note that "this form serves as a sad reminder of the lawlessness [*hefkerut*] that has taken root in our city" and affirmed that the municipality would find popular support for any activities it took against "this kind of transgressor [*poretz geder*]." The mayor, Israel Rokach, took this advertisement as an impetus to write to the Union of Industrial Owners (*hit'ahadut ba'ale ta'asiyah*) to stress "the insult to the public that is caused by the distribution of such bulletins" and to inquire into the steps being taken against Weller's. The head of the union, Arieh Shenker, expressed his sadness about the "anarchy of foreign languages that reigns even among manufacturers" and promised that the union would engage in "personal propaganda" to appeal to its members to change their advertising. While letters remarking on social transgressions often have a tone of pretentious shock and disbelief, the small word "even" in Shenker's letter points to an unspoken understanding among both sender and recipient that language transgressions, while perhaps expected elsewhere in the Yishuv, were particularly troubling in the commercial sphere.[79]

SYRUP
JAM
FACTORY

MONTEFIORE
near Tel-Aviv

בי"ח"ר
למיצים
ורבות

מונטפיורי
ע"י תל-אביב

הודעה

בית חרשת „וולר'ס" שמח להודיע לקונים שהחל
מהיום מקבל כל קונה בקנית צנצנת קונפיטורה
„וולר'ס" הנחה של 50% לקולנוע.
דרוש תוצרת„וולר'ס" בבל חנות מכלת!

Notice

Weller's Factory is pleased to inform her customers that
from today on purchasing a jar of Weller's Confiture you
will receive a 50% reduction to a Cinema.

Ask for Weller's Products at any Grocer !

Mitteilung

Weller's Marmeladen Fabrik beehrt sich mitzuteilen, dass
ihre Kunden beim Einkauf eines Glases Weller's Confiture
von heute ab eine 50% Ermäsigung in Kino erhalten.

Verlangt Weller's Producte
in jedem Delikatess Geschäft !

דפוס קאופ' „סגנון" בצ"מ, ת"א

Advertisement for Weller's Syrup Jam, date unknown. Courtesy of the
Department of Special Collections and University Archives, Stanford
University Libraries.

The CCEH report of January 1941 enumerated a variety of language
infractions. Several factories—Lieber, Elite, and Fishinger (confections),
Lodzia (textiles), Fromin (crackers and cookies), and Assis (juices)—sold
their products in the Palestine market with labels written completely in foreign languages, "with no mention of Hebrew."[80] Meanwhile the Culture

Department of the Jewish National Council mentioned in a report that the film companies Kodak and Salo were advertising in foreign languages. A mock "trial" of the denigration of the Hebrew language, published in *Ha-Mishmar*, listed as one of the accusations, "the wrappings and labels on products written in foreign languages [*lo'azit*]."[81] A 1944 newspaper article identified a contradiction between a commitment to Hebrew production and the tendency of merchants to advertise their wares in multiple languages, calling attention to "merchants who sell *totzeret ha-aretz* in foreign-language [*lo'azit*] packaging" and warning against the "Levantinism that is eating away all the good parts of us."[82] Another asked, "Is it conceivable that on the one hand it would be demanded of us to support Hebrew products and on the other hand get these products in foreign-language [*lo'azi*] wrappings?"[83]

For promoters of Hebrew, the demonstrative value of Hebrew obtained not only within the Yishuv but in foreign markets as well. For some, the use of Hebrew on labels of products for export would constitute an important step in demonstrating to Jews and non-Jews abroad the image of the new Hebrew man in place of the persecuted Jew. Through Hebrew, which was exportable and transmittable even to places without Jews, Jewish nationhood and Jewish transformation could be displayed through language, on the product itself. A letter from the CCEH to the Department of Commerce and Industry of the Jewish Agency stressed the importance of using Hebrew on packaging in such instances: "When something is sent to Singapore or Baltimore with Hebrew [packaging], [consumers] will see before their eyes not only the hounded, persecuted Jews but the Hebrew people's creativity in its own land." Therefore, the council continued, Hebrew has "political-national significance." A comparison was made to that paradigm of national normalcy, England: "Is it conceivable that the owner of a factory in England would sell his products to the residents of his own country and not put the language of his country at the top of every advertisement?!"[84]

The symbolism of the infraction is telling. A common Hebrew proverb is "Don't look at the jug but rather at its contents," the equivalent of the English "Don't judge a book by its cover." The implication here is the opposite, however: one who looks only at the Hebrew contents of a package without considering its foreign-language packaging endangers the product itself, and this was particularly dangerous when the package reflected values seen as foreign. Levantinism, it seems, was a malady that could take hold from the outside in, first tainting the external appearance of things by muddling cultures and languages, but soon contaminating the product itself, rendering even an appropriately manufactured product tainted.

Women, as we discussed above, were some of the primary consumers of food products and household goods marketed by speakers of Yiddish and Arabic, who were regarded as low or degenerate elements of the market. Female consumers were also, however, the assumed targets of many imported high-end goods. Bat-Sheva Margalit-Stern has investigated the tension women felt between their consumer needs and desires and the nationalist pressure to eschew luxury or individual comfort and adopt a more ascetic lifestyle.[85] A 1947 article in *Davar* mentioned a poster published as a joint enterprise of several women's organizations to encourage housewives and "daughters of Israel" to "stand on guard" for Hebrew and to defend it against "attack by the many business owners who were evading Hebrew in their advertisements."[86] Foreign-language wrappings on chocolate, wine, cosmetics, and cigarettes were cited as examples. The phrasing of the poster suggests that devoted women should serve as a bulwark against a group of business owners who were not sufficiently committed to the Hebrew project. If internationally focused businessmen were somehow external to the essence of the Yishuv, women, the masters of home and family, might still serve as its spiritual heart.

Nonetheless, the rhetoric of intrusion and foreign penetration disregarded the local network of producers, marketers, and consumers who created these foreign-language signs in the first place. The imperatives of international trade prompted many to employ their knowledge of European languages to cut deals. The linguistic practices inherent in the work of citriculturists, for example, are implied by the fact that Shimon Rokach, the manager of the Pardess citrus company, concluded a contract with a British shipping company in order to circumvent Arab traders and that he "sought new markets from Australia to the Far East."[87] Businesses seem frequently to have engaged in correspondence in languages other than Hebrew; we know this because of complaints about this practice and requests that importers and exporters shift to Hebrew.

The head of the Jewish Seamens' Agency in Haifa, Naftali Vidra, wrote to several local shipping agencies, including the "Yamit" company and the "Loire" Egypt-Palestine shipping company, asking them to write all of their letters in Hebrew. "We hope," he wrote, "that you will begin to arrange for translations and to write all of your letters in Hebrew."[88] The CCEH complained that factories and shops were publicizing their wares in the bulletin of the Palestine Philharmonic in foreign languages and that the newspaper of commerce and industry, *Plenius*, which formerly had come out in Hebrew and English, now came out only in English.[89] The prominence of foreign languages in the Yishuv was part and parcel of the success of private investors and the growth of the commercial sphere—and aside from interventions by purist organizations, was not normally viewed as problematic.

Advertisements too, in many cases, were not imported texts, produced outside Palestine, but rather the products of local Jewish advertising agencies. One such company was the Taf Decorative Advertising Company, with its office in Jerusalem. It advertised its signage services to Jewish businesses on the pages of *Davar*, promising to create advertisements that made an impression, were "unforgettable," and "accost people on the streets day and night." Its promotions made clear that the firm would design advertising copy to appeal not only to Jews but also to the British and Arab constituencies in Palestine. And so it needed employees who could handle multilingual work. It advertised once for employees who were "good-looking people who know the languages of the land [English, Arabic, and Hebrew] and are eager and industrious can earn well," adding, "The field of work promoted here is an important new branch of commercial propaganda and advertisement."[90]

"Good-looking people who know the languages of the land" (and perhaps some who were not so good-looking) also found employment in an auxiliary market providing language services that enabled businessmen to conduct overseas deals. The existence of translation firms, which advertised their services in newspapers and playbills, indicates that businessmen may not have been multilingual themselves, but rather relied on local polyglots to provide them with language services. A 1922 flier by the partners M. Z. Goddard and A. Pollack advertised their "Office for Translation and Correspondence," called Hamelitz, which would "serve the Public, in writing and arranging all kinds of private and commercial correspondence, applications, agreements, certificates, letters of recommendation, legal documents, etc.—in the following languages: Hebrew, English, Arabic, French, Russian, German, etc."[91] Another advertisement, for a woman named Minnie Manheim, implied that the proprietress could provide services in Hebrew, German, and English.[92] More esoteric services emerged as well. One Madame Gizell offered handwriting analysis services in a trilingual (Hebrew, English, and German) advertisement, and recommended that her famous services be used for "all questions of life and before concluding any commercial transactions."[93]

For Gedalyahu Zhokhovitzky (Zakif), who came to Palestine as a high school student in 1923 and subsequently engaged in pro-Zionist propaganda and fund-raising around the world, the eminence of European tongues in the business sector indicated that Hebrew had failed to achieve a basic precondition for national relevance: it was not necessary for economic life, and a person's lack of knowledge of that language did not pose an obstacle to economic success. Zhokhovitzky wrote in a newspaper

Advertisement for the Hakotew Correspondence and Translation Service, date unknown. Courtesy of the Department of Special Collections and University Archives, Stanford University Libraries.

We have the honour to draw hereby the attention of the Public, as well as of the various Institutions and Offices of our City, that we have opened

an Office for Translation and Correspondence,

under the title of "HAMELITZ",

which will serve the Public, in writing and arranging all kinds of private and commercial correspondence, applications, agreements, certificates, letters of recomendation, legal documents, etc. — in the following languages:

Hebrew, English, Arabic, French, Russian, German etc.

Our office experience in the past may stand as guarantee for the quality of our work wich will, surely, derive the satisfaction of the whole of our favouring clientele.

The work ordered for is being typed on the most modern typewriters.

Our office is to be looked for in the dwelling of Mr. Burstein, Tel-Aviv, (house of Sheikh Ali, at the corner of HERZL street), office hours as follows: 8-12 a. m. — 3-6 p. m.

With respect,

M. Z. GODARD,

A. POLLACK.

Tel-Aviv.

Flyer for the Hamelitz office of translation and correspondence, date unknown. Courtesy of the Department of Special Collections and University Archives, Stanford University Libraries.

article of the "unparalleled denigration of Hebrew" in business offices. Most of the hundreds of letters written in the large banks were not in Hebrew, he said, while insurance companies "don't recognize Hebrew as an accepted commercial language," carrying out all of their business in foreign languages. They demand that their clerks know many languages, but not Hebrew.[94]

There was no question to Zhokhovitzky that commerce and business were necessary, but he considered it critical that Hebrew become key to an individual's economic advancement, to become a language of symbolic power, in Pierre Bourdieu's sense. That had not yet occurred. "A man's level of intelligence," he noted, "is judged by his command of foreign languages [*leshonot lo'aziyot*]": "He boasts of his knowledge of English, German, or French, but he doesn't pride himself on having fluent Hebrew."[95]

Schools of Commerce

The spread of foreign goods advertised in foreign languages was enabled by a combination of enterprising sellers, eager buyers, and a secondary field of entrepreneurs, middlemen, clerks, managers, translation specialists, and others whose language expertise was essential in cutting deals and getting products to the store shelf. By necessity, companies that did business abroad and foreign companies with branches in Palestine conducted correspondence in European languages, particularly English, German, and French. As a result, a clerical staff trained in European languages was a necessity for a business in the Yishuv. From the early part of the British mandate period, a series of schools in Jerusalem, Tel Aviv, and Haifa promised a comprehensive education in commercial language skills along with the standard Hebrew education. An investigation of these schools of commerce, their students, programs, rhetoric, and, ultimately, reception lends insight into the ambivalence about European languages within an "all-Hebrew" economy.

The earliest school explicitly focused on commerce, it seems, was the Hebrew High School for Commerce (later the Gimnasya Re'alit) in Jerusalem. Founded in 1919 and headed by Shlomo Schurr, it received part of its operating budget from the Zionist Executive, the body responsible for carrying out the plans of the Zionist Organization.[96] Several other schools followed. The Safra School of Commerce, founded in Tel Aviv in 1926, was headed by Yosef Safra, the editor of the journal *Mis'har ve-ta'asiyah* (Commerce and industry).[97] According to an inspection at the

Safra School by Yosef Azaryahu, inspector for Zionist high schools, the purpose of the school was to train students for "low clerical jobs" in a two-year course to be taken after completing the regular eight-year primary-school sequence. The curriculum included the theory of commerce, commercial math, bookkeeping, and typewriting in addition to "general subjects," which included Zionism, English, general history, and a choice of Arabic or French.[98] Other similar institutions were the 'Atid School of Commerce in Haifa; the Tel Aviv School of Commerce; and the Pitman School of Commerce, also in Tel Aviv. All these institutions responded to a demand for specifically commercial education.

Languages were the cornerstones of these schools' programs. The Hebrew High School of Commerce taught Hebrew, English, Arabic, and French into the 1920s, as well as correspondence skills in English, Arabic, and French.[99] The seal of the 'Atid ("Future") School in Haifa included the words " 'Atid School of Commerce and Languages."[100] The inspector at Safra in 1942 noted that while students appeared to be deficient in Hebrew in some cases, "the progress of students in English is much better than in parallel classes in the academic high schools [*tikhonim*]."[101] And, indeed, a significant amount of time was devoted to English: six hours a week in the lower division, divided equally between language and commercial English, and between seven and eight hours a week in the upper division. "Our purpose," the school said, "was to impart to students the ability to express themselves orally and in writing (both commercial letters and summaries) and to develop their translation abilities both stylistically and technically by learning the structural principles of sentences and by emphasizing the oppositions between our spoken language (Hebrew) and the English language."[102]

These schools, though clearly committed to both Zionism and Hebrew, attracted the ire of pro-Hebrew organizations for their decision to conduct some classes in English. The Central Council for the Enforcement of Hebrew reported in August 1941 that it had written to the administration of the 'Atid School of Commerce, excoriating that school's use of English. The letter is worth quoting at length:

You surely know the looming danger of assimilation and Levantinism, which is undermining the education of this generation and the shaping of its character. How much more so, then, is it necessary to warn of any move that opens a door to imposing a non-Hebrew culture in the Hebrew schools? This sort of step amounts to the annulment of Hebrew as the exclusive language of instruction in your upper division. We are turning your attention to this matter because we have received many complaints about you and we assume you don't want this, as public opinion against your actions is being expressed openly. We therefore demand that you de-sist from this deviant method to Anglicize [*le'angel*] the young Hebrew in the Land of Israel rather than educate him in the spirit of our [Hebrew] civilization's foundations [*ruach mekor mahtzavtenu*].[103]

According to this fascinating statement, Hebrew culture faced two threats: Levantinism and assimilation. As we have discussed, Levantinism was usually defined as a diasporic form of low culture particularly char-acterized by the mixing of languages. This context, however, suggests an additional meaning of Levantinism: excessive obeisance to the West shown by a people possessing a deficient culture. The 'Atid School's per-ceived adulation of English, then, is an indication of the Levantine qual-ity of the Yishuv. The term "assimilation" is also noteworthy. A generic term of opprobrium within a community committed at root to opposing any ideology of assimilation, it evokes the inclination of some Jews, par-ticularly in western Europe from the late eighteenth century, to throw in their lot with European governments, languages, and cultures and to participate fully in civic life. Though early Maskilim, proponents of the Berlin Haskalah (Jewish enlightenment), proposed maintaining a robust commitment to Jewish life and culture, alongside full civic integration, the term "assimilationism" came to be associated in the Zionist context with a total rejection of Jewish linguistic and cultural identity.

This European fear of assimilation was adapted and rendered more symbolic in the Palestinian context. The nature of British colonial rule in Palestine was such that a decision to learn English could in no way be construed as a decision to assimilate into English culture. Assimilationism thus no longer meant assimilationism in the classical sense of full integra-tion: stripped of its original meaning, it had come to mean excessive adu-lation of foreign cultures and insufficient faith in the cultural strength or economic power of the national entity. When we understand the discur-sive overlap between these categories—all concerned with adulation of and overreliance on the West, combined with a deficient national spirit—we see that assimilationism was construed as a sort of Levantinism, and Levantinism as a form of exilic existence (*galutiyut*). Indeed, the same concerns that appeared to inflect discourses on low commerce pervade this attack on high commerce.

Proponents of commercial schools had to tread carefully to show that their commitment to commercial education would neither detract from the strength of the Hebrew economy nor encourage students to work abroad. In his commencement speech in 1928, Shlomo Schurr of the Hebrew High School of Commerce laid out in no uncertain terms that the study of commerce was intended not to direct students to live abroad, but to give them the necessary skills to stay in Palestine. The tension implied in harnessing global knowledge to support a local project was clear: ultimately, the success of the local was contingent on access to the global. As Schurr noted: "Young people who do want to stay in the country need to be armed with diverse and broad knowledge since our country is small and the field of its work is limited." In fact, he said, the very smallness of the enterprise required broader linguistic competence: just as the farmer in a small village needs to know how to provide for all his needs, and just as the proprietor of a small-town store needs to provide his customers all manner of products, likewise the average resident of Palestine needed to know more than the average resident of a larger country.[104] By this logic, a broad technical and commercial education using textbooks from abroad would train the provincials in Palestine to be truly self-sufficient in their isolated state—language education, counterintuitively, was the key to Hebrew progress that could remain within the bounds of Palestine and not seek fulfillment abroad.

Statistics indicate that graduates of commercial schools did indeed undertake a range of professions, some of which served the Hebrew economy directly, others of which assisted foreign firms. Of the 381 students who graduated from the Tel Aviv School of Commerce from its founding until 1936, 102 went on to private companies and law firms, 27 to British government offices in Palestine, 63 to study in universities in Palestine and abroad, 41 to public-sector jobs for entities such as the Tel Aviv Municipality and local and international banks, 33 to the stores their parents ran, 29 to agriculture, 16 to industrial factories, 5 to school teaching, and 8 to private teaching.[105] A similar survey of the class of 1937 showed that 9 of 16 graduates went into clerical work; we can assume they were employed by a mixture of the British government institutions, foreign corporations, and Jewish businesses that are explored in chapter 3.[106] While these categories are a bit difficult to parse, it becomes clear that only a small minority went into agriculture and became Schurr's "small town farmers" armed with the proper professional skills. Many built the overall economic strength of the Yishuv in private companies, some of which we can assume were Jewish run, some foreign run; others worked for international banks. In any case, their training was well rewarded. It appears that companies were satisfied with the students who came out of Safra, for example, and did recruiting among its graduates. A collection of school-related articles and documents contains admiring letters from bank and factory managers pleased with the quality of the graduates.[107]

In their promotional material, schools tended to emphasize both the range of professions available to students with knowledge of foreign languages and the higher salaries that they could command for their skills. The Safra School noted that a young clerk would typically begin at a salary of four to five pounds a month, while an experienced clerk with knowledge of foreign languages might begin at ten to twelve pounds a month, a 150 percent increase. The prospectus explained: "In Palestine there is generally a need to demand more of our students than is generally demanded of students of commerce abroad. Here it is necessary to know many languages (Hebrew, English, and Arabic) and an ability to get used to the modern technology associated with office work."[108]

The school's commitment to foreign-language instruction did not come at the expense of Hebrew study, and it felt the need to emphasize this point lest it be overlooked. The 1933 Safra School guidebook noted that regular primary schools were producing graduates who were not able to express themselves fully in Hebrew. By contrast, its goal was to give "students the practical and theoretical training necessary to take advantage of their linguistic knowledge through expanding their frame of understanding and improving it through scholarly explanation."[109]

Students themselves were adamant about the importance of foreign-language study in retrospective assessments of the school written for its promotional materials. In a letter written by a student named Yitzhak

Zamir after graduating, he remarked that the school "should be sure to teach an additional foreign language beyond English," in fact, French: "The French language also has made such inroads in the fields of banking and industry that an obligation rests upon the graduating student to learn it and to achieve competence in it by the time he leaves school."[110] Another student, Margalit Libman, reported that she had found a job in the "Institute for Foreign Commerce." Her duties engaged her language skills, since she was in charge of managing all the administrative matters of the office "and making contact both with producers in Palestine as well as buyers and visitors from abroad who were interested in industry." While she was thankful for her language knowledge, she admits that the study of German would have been helpful too.[111] The commercial society of the Yishuv was embedded in relationships both with foreign merchants and with foreign elements within Palestine itself, and schools understood that language was an essential element of improving these relationships for the Yishuv's own benefit.

The orthodox conception of a Hebrew labor sphere marked by exclusive use of the Hebrew language was challenged in practice from two major directions: from the apparently degenerate commerce lurking below, and the well-oiled machinery of foreign import and export, threatening from above with its economic power and leverage. Both pressures, the twin types of *totzeret zarah*—local and foreign products made by non-Jews—squeezed an emerging Hebrew economy that, in popular memory, fought heroically to maintain its market share and its language.

These slippages indicate that the association between Hebrew labor and Hebrew language was not absolute. With the sheer number of recent immigrants and the inherently social nature of a factory floor or assembly plant, it was only natural that workers would engage in conversations in their native languages. In effect, this meant that workers physically producing "Hebrew" goods—juice, soap, chocolate, or machine parts, to name a few—were doing so while conversing in languages other than Hebrew. The CCEH sent companies letters insisting that employees speak only Hebrew at work and to use foreign languages only with customers who don't understand Hebrew, but the tenor and repetitive nature of the letters indicate that they had little effect.[112]

Such opprobrium extended to meetings of businessmen and merchants. The owner of a chain of shoe stores, Y. B. Hoz, wrote a letter to Emil (Menahem) Shmurak at the Jewish Agency in Jerusalem, expressing sadness about a meeting of Haifa manufacturers convened in Shmurak's honor that was conducted in German. "There is no need to explain to you," Hoz wrote, "that industry [*ta'asiyah*] without Hebrew is neither Hebrew industry nor Zionist industry." Indeed, it was imperative that people of commerce in particular should know and speak Hebrew; this demand was so stringent that Hoz suggested that those who did not know the language should speak through a Hebrew interpreter or remain silent. The content of Shmurak's words did not justify delivering them in German, thought Hoz: "As important as your words might be, we will not exchange our language and let our country become a second Babel."[113] Hoz states the assumed association between the Hebrew language and Hebrew labor in a particularly clear fashion: a Hebrew product produced, marketed, or sold in a foreign-language context loses its status as a true Hebrew product.

The formulation is compelling. Its appeal to Babel, the mythological origin point of human—and Jewish—multilingualism, is made in a characteristically high rhetorical style. Such statements, moreover, are omnipresent in the activist literature around language practice in the commercial sphere. Nonetheless, the axiomatic association between Jewish labor and the Hebrew language, on the one hand, and a blanket rejection of language mixing, on the other, obscures a more variegated space of linguistic exchange in a variety of commercial settings, public and private, outdoor and indoor, stereotypically low and undeniably high. The persistence of what seemed like diasporic forms of commerce troubled some observers, but the depth and normality of these forms were more richly a part of the Yishuv than the doctrinaire reactions they sometimes received might indicate.

CHAPTER THREE

CLERKS, TRANSLATORS, AND THE
LANGUAGES OF BUREAUCRACY

Most of the members of the Yishuv came here with an exaggerated
romantic love in their hearts for England . . . that is, before they had the
opportunity to come into close, concrete daily contract with Englishmen,
flesh and blood just like them.
—*Isaac Abbady, Between Us and the English (1947)*

We chose English not because the English desired it, but because . . . we
needed its language to transact our business, including the business of
overthrowing colonialism itself.
—*Chinua Achebe, "New Songs of Ourselves" (1990)*

The importance of languages other than Hebrew, it might have
seemed, would wane with the assimilation of new immigrants to Hebrew
culture or the hypothetical creation of an all-Hebrew marketplace. But
the political reality of Palestine, so long as British rule persisted, ensured
interlingual contact and compelled a series of accommodations to
English in the bureaucratic realm.

Soon after conquering Palestine, the British took the monumental step
of making Hebrew an official language of Palestine, seemingly freeing
Jews to use only their national language even in official business. On

1 October 1920, a notice appeared in the *Official Gazette of the Government of Palestine*, titled "The Use of Official Languages." "English, Arabic, and Hebrew are recognized as the official languages of Palestine," it said. What is more:

> All Government ordinances, official notices and forms will be published in the above languages. Correspondence may be addressed to any Government Department in any of these languages. Correspondence will be issued from Government departments in whichever of the languages is practically convenient.[1]

This document, and clarifications published in 1922 and 1923 with the formalization of the mandate, came out not long after the Balfour Declaration had expressed the British commitment to the establishment of a Jewish national home in Palestine. The journalist Mordechai Ben-Hillel Ha-Cohen spoke of the near-messianic expectations that Jews attached to the proclamation by the British foreign secretary: "We heard the rumor about the Balfour Declaration, the great announcement, the first shofar blast of our freedom."[2] Enthusiasm for the newly official status of Hebrew was wrapped up in this broader promise that the British would give due attention both to the Jews' cultural claims and to their political aspirations.

A new era had begun. No longer, many believed, would Hebrew be a curiosity or the bailiwick of a small number of zealots. The implications of this ruling were wide-ranging and broadly symbolic. A formative period for Hebrew in the late Ottoman period had ended, and a period of maturity had commenced: Hebrew was now regarded by the British as an official language of Palestine, which meant it was to be used on all forms and official seals, and could theoretically be employed for any official governmental business or communication.

This new linguistic autonomy could be enjoyed by the many new Zionist institutions that had arisen around the end of the war. The advent of the British was followed by the founding of the Zionist Commission in March 1918, the Histadrut in December 1920, and the granting of municipal status to Tel Aviv in May 1921. These institutions, which were promised autonomy and conditional Jewish self-rule in antic-ipation of eventual independence, enthusiastically received the British promise of linguistic independence as well: if Jews could carry out their administrative business in their own language, gone would be the days when they would dwell as a minority under the rule of another nation, reminded of their subordinate status every time they went to fill out forms, pay taxes, or send mail. Such a promise was novel and heady; only a quarter century before, Theodor Herzl had scoffed at the idea that Hebrew could be a language of mundane transactions.[3]

"The [Tel Aviv Municipality] tried to impose Hebrew on the officials of the British mandate," says Zohar Shavit, insisting that the municipality, bolstered by the British ruling, had a far-reaching commitment to Hebrew.[4] But while the aspiration to use only Hebrew was far-reaching, the implementation of that principle was somewhat limited. The Labor leader Hayim Arlosoroff admitted in a 1928 essay that "the Jewish National Home must develop in the presence of the English," adding, "Many are the obstacles on this path."[5] Any attempts to use and promote Hebrew, even within circles committed to Hebrew, would occur in a broader multilingual space. From an activist standpoint, this meant language clashes and battles for language rights. But the nationalist emphasis on the promotion and protection of Hebrew also distorted the pervasiveness of selective English use by certain members of a community living and conducting its day-to-day activities—including manifestly Zionist activities—over three decades of British rule. Whereas certain imported goods and activities could be branded as foreign imports and stigmatized, the very structures of local governance and society, if denigrated, needed to be negotiated, oftentimes through language.

Reviews of archival records from both British and Zionist institutions reveal that mandatory functionaries felt both logistical and economic incentives to use English; that Zionist institutions felt, and often succumbed to, pressure to use English in correspondence with the British; and that a translation apparatus was pervasive. This bureaucratically created linguistic contact has been largely obscured by a narrative more concerned with instances of activism than instances of accommodation and negotiation. The emerging Hebrew bureaucracy often remained subordinate to the mandatory government; this subordination was repeatedly experienced in linguistic terms; and this state of affairs was often accepted out of recognition that English had a real, even if delimited place in the life in the Yishuv.

These negotiations were by no means novel for Jews. Palestine was not the first setting in which Jews found themselves under the rule of another government, found multilingual skills serviceable in bureaucratic contexts, or negotiated relationships with a government that was wary of granting new rights or recognizing existing rights. Broadly speaking, such situations were paradigmatic of the historical Jewish experience. Jews, writes Yuri Slezkine in his sweeping study of Jewish modernity, were the prime "professional internal strangers"; they had a level of literacy that usually exceeded that of the surrounding culture and naturally became "trained linguists, negotiators, translators, and mystifiers."[6] Jews did not take part in civil service work only as outsiders; in postrevolutionary France, for example, Jews' participation in civil service work was testament to their integration, not to their peripheral status, though their bureaucratic roles generated in turn a discussion about the degree of Jewish regeneration.[7] To Slezkine, such obligations to foreign bureaucracies were quintessentially diasporic. In the Zionist discourse, which he largely accepts, the Yishuv was to be the first context in which Jews would subvert the model of diasporic bilingualism or multilingualism through the imposition of Hebrew dominance. This characterization of rupture is not fully accurate, however. While the Yishuv was distinctive in that its members did not seek British citizenship or assimilation and in that emphasis on manual labor in the Yishuv often rendered holders of office jobs socially inferior, nonetheless, as in other historical settings, Jews hoped that the greater their representation in the bureaucratic apparatus, the greater the likelihood that those in power would accede to Jewish communal demands.[8] Pressures for multilingual competence in the Yishuv indicate a generally unacknowledged degree of continuity with such diasporic experiences.

Bureaucracy is an apparently emotionless, boring field, the opposite of the edgy, raucous space of the coffeehouse, cinema, or marketplace: "the only contact between the government and the public was the file and the file was a silent, mute object, without life or expression."[9] Within a history of language in the Yishuv, Jewish immigrant languages on the one hand and Arabic on the other might seem far more important to the long-term development of a society most openly concerned with its relationship to the Jewish Diaspora and the Arab world. But clerks' and translators' prevalence throughout the mandate period reflected more than just the occupational choices of a few or the technical needs of a society whose energies were otherwise devoted elsewhere; they signal the emergence of a society that would remain oriented toward English, both logistically and culturally, long after the British formally ended its Palestine mandate on 14 May 1948. Indeed, English was one of the more tenacious linguistic pressures Israel faced over the course of its subsequent history as the political and economic power of the United States grew. We can see the seeds of this orientation toward English in the mandate period, when the demand for English led to the founding of several private institutions devoted to training adults in language skills and when schools trained young people to be clerks. Already in this period, English use had become a mark of sophistication for bourgeois and professional elites, one belying opposition to foreign languages or a contravening sense that English should be purely instrumental. Significant sectors of the Zionist move- ment were caught between a rhetoric of rupture and distance from the social configurations of Europe and a desire for Western cultural attain- ments. English, increasingly, was a marker of such attainments.

The remainder of this chapter attempts to recover this foundational narrative of Jewish clerks, translators, English learners, and aspirants to the cultural cachet of English. Such actors were not nationalist leaders, but their experiences with English were nonetheless integral to the devel- opment of the Jewish national group in Palestine. In revisiting this class of Yishuv residents, we need to resist the urge to resurrect them only by attributing to them the role of unsung nationalist heroes. Rather, we should aim to understand both the texture and significance of their mul- tilingual lives, whether they were engaged in directly bolstering the Zionist position in Palestine or whether their work was purely technical, low-level office work away from the public view.

We learn about language-related activities and their significance obliquely, through mentions of language-learning bonuses in the British archival record, requests for work from young Jews who stressed their language capabilities in their applications, and recollections of those who remembered the behavior of their friends, relatives, and neighbors. Above all, the extent of English use becomes clear through correspon- dence protesting it. These sets of sources illuminate the tension between the ideal of bureaucratic independence on the one hand and, on the other, political subordination, differences in power, and the economic outcomes of foreign rule. Jewish culture under mandate rule evolved at the intersection of ideological demands for purity and practical needs for compromise. This nexus of conflict would come to define the Zionist and, later, the Israeli experience.

Distance and Protest

Emotionally distant and politically suspect, the British in Palestine had no great personal relationship with the majority of the Yishuv. Mordechai Ben-Hillel Ha-Cohen, whose multipart article on the early period of British rule in Palestine was cited above, spoke of a "conceptual difference" between Jews and Britons that led to "mutual miscomprehension."[10] British soldiers, usually in Palestine for short stints, rarely became integrated into their environments and lived in "ghettos" of their own.[11] Isaac Abbady, the head of the mandate government's Central Translation Bureau until 1944, concluded that the spiritual and mental distance between Jews and the British rendered any real closeness impossible.[12]

Scholars, moreover, have tended to emphasize the relative unimportance of English to the Yishuv before World War II, along with factors that "impeded the spread of the imperial language and . . . reduced the impact of this period of British rule," including the official status of Hebrew and the existence of a Hebrew school system. The British historian Edward Ullendorff stated: "Despite the existence of a British Administration for close on thirty years, the influence of English remained relatively minor until its massive burgeoning after the Second World War."[13] Ralph Poston, an aide to the high commissioner from 1931 to 1938, recalled that "there was virtually no mixing between the British and Palestinian Arabs and very little with the Jews at all." A. J. Sherman surmises that "one factor certainly was language: almost none of the British knew Hebrew . . . and knowledge of English was relatively rare among Jews."[14]

If, in this narrative, the British were largely absent and irrelevant, an alternate narrative implies an antagonistic British presence caused by the government's regular and egregious denials of Hebrew's official status and by breaches of its promises to provide the language full bureaucratic support. In truth, wrote Arlosoroff in his 1928 piece, British clerks had a huge amount of power over the budding Jewish national society: "In daily life the manager of the post office is the one who decides whether Hebrew will dominate in his office in practice or only in the official formulations of the mandate."[15] Zionist organizations responded in protest to continual breaches. The archives of Zionist institutions such as the Jewish Agency, the Jewish National Council, and the Palestine Office of the Zionist Organization preserve a narrative of engaged, fierce, and endless protest and activism against the lack of Hebrew and the dominance of English and Arabic in the bureaucratic sphere. Together, they tell a story of a small number of people passionately devoted to hunting out linguistic irregularities.

These protests addressed nearly every corner of the mandatory apparatus. In 1923, for example, the Zionist investor and land developer Bezalel Yaffe protested not having received receipts for his land taxes (werko) in Hebrew. Given that the main purchasers of land at the time were Jews, he thought, "the department exists on account of the Jews," and thus he had the right to demand Hebrew-speaking employees at the Werko Department and receipts in Hebrew for all taxes paid.[16] In the same year, Frederick Kisch, head of the Zionist Executive in Jerusalem, called attention to the language situation of Jewish settlements in the Bet She'an Valley region, which were not in one of the regions marked as an area of Jewish settlement, and which therefore did not qualify to receive Hebrew services. He claimed that although the 792 Jews in that area (out of 10,679 people total) were far below the 20 percent threshold for Hebrew to be deemed official, he asked—in English and with a level of intentional deception—that the government accede to the demands of "villages of Jews who can't use any other language but Hebrew."[17] We will return in a moment to such strategic claims of Jewish monolingualism.

Another locus of protest was the courtroom, where many cases were conducted in English or Arabic despite the presence (or predominance) of Jews in the case. "The status of the Hebrew language in the courts is not normal," said Mordechai Eliash to the Jewish Bar Association of Palestine in 1928. "When a Jewish judge is appointed, he is required to know all three [official] languages, something that is not true of Arab and English judges." Moreover, Eliash protested, protocols tended to be issued in Arabic even when the plaintiff, defendant, judge, and scribe were all Jews.[18] Hayim Nachman Bialik similarly griped that Jewish lawyers used English "because it is more convenient for them to appear before the judges in this language and their words are more effective."[19] Some of this rhetoric may have been overblown, and amid the enthusiasm for language policing, false claims and hysteria emerged. Nonetheless, the accretion of small and large cases of linguistic discrimination added to the perception that the British system was systematically discriminating against Hebrew.

Concerns about the *Official Gazette*, which was supposed to be published in all three official languages, reached the mandate government's desks from time to time. One letter complained that the envelope in which the Hebrew *Gazette* was sent had only Arabic and English on it. "I don't think there are ill intentions, just carelessness" said the writer, "but we suffer from a lot of carelessness."[20] The problems with the *Gazette* ran deeper: the Hebrew version of the paper was published with a delay, often of several months. Referring to the fact that the news was antiquated by the time it was received, one commentator wrote, "This newspaper has no purpose other than an archival-archaeological one." Moreover, the writer added, the Hebrew of the *Gazette* was hard to understand; it had a combination of archaic words and words coined "just yesterday" by the Hebrew Language Committee.[21] This problem didn't seem to abate. Shmuel Yeivin, the head of the Central Translation Bureau, indicated that when he took office on 3 July 1944, the Hebrew *Gazette* was still being published with a one-month delay.[22]

The list of objects for protest can be extended further; file after file in the Central Zionist Archive charts such activism from the earliest days of British rule. Other protests, for example, pertained to the lack of Hebrew in railway regulations, a eulogy for Lord Balfour given only in English, various types of forms printed in English and Arabic only, non-Hebrew-speaking clerks at the immigration department, and stamps on passports that did not have Hebrew on them.[23] Public texts—signs, stamps, and advertisements—also became major targets of group activism. As Yair Wallach points out, traditional religious relationships to text in both the Jewish and the Arab communities gave way in the mandate period to a secular understanding of text as a site of self-definition and political activism.[24]

One of the more colorful protest episodes, one that stretched on for nearly fifteen years, addressed the initial impossibility of submitting telegrams in Hebrew script at the post office. We will look first at the dogmatic nature of this fight and later return to it to explore the limits of drawing wide-ranging conclusions about linguistic zealotry. The issue derived from a point of inconsistency in the mandate's language ordinances. Despite general commitments to provide official services in Hebrew as well as Arabic and English, the laws of the mandate said that telegrams needed to be transcribed in Latin or Arabic characters. On 1 October 1920, an official government announcement said that although Hebrew was a recognized language for most official business, Hebrew script would not be recognized at the telegraph office: "Telegrams may be sent in any of the three languages, but if in Hebrew, they must be written in Latin characters, it not being practicable at present for the Post Office to transmit telegrams in Hebrew characters."[25]

Several activists got on the case quickly, including the Battalion of the Defenders of the Hebrew Language and the man who would become the protagonist of the story, an individual from Haifa named Israel Amikam. Amikam, who was born Masseoff and changed his surname to one that meant "my nation has risen," was an obsessive, solitary man who worked as a clerk at the electric company. In other words, he was a man quite familiar with the workings of the British bureaucracy. On 6 October 1922, Amikam wrote his first article in the newspaper *Haaretz*, "The Telegraph and the Hebrew Language," calling upon the British government to correct its oversight and allow telegrams to be transmitted in Hebrew script. A string of appeals to British and international organizations followed. On 18 December 1928, Amikam directed his appeal to the general manager of the post office and was refused. In May 1929, not long before a summer of political violence would leave the Yishuv further doubting Britons' goodwill toward the Zionist project, the Battalion of the Defenders of the Hebrew Language sued the general manager of the post office. But the court ruled against the battalion. Its reasoning was significant. Hebrew in Latin letters, it reasoned, was still Hebrew (it granted that if Hebrew had been entirely excluded, then that discrimination would have been overturned by Article 82 of the mandate laws). "A message in Hebrew does not cease to be in Hebrew because it is rendered in Latin characters," the ruling read, "any more than a message in English ceases to be in English when it is rendered in Morse Code."[26] Not so, thought the battalion. The ruling, they wrote in a letter to the Zionist Executive in Jerusalem, "is dangerous for the future of our language . . . and could negatively influence attitudes toward Hebrew in other branches of the mandate government."[27]

Amikam, undeterred, took his fight to higher levels of authority. In July 1929, he wrote to the high commissioner of Palestine, and on 12 September he wrote a memorandum to the secretary for the colonies in the Colonial Office, entitled "Violation by the Department of Posts and Telegraphs of the Government of Palestine of the Right of the Hebrew Language to Equality with the other Official Languages of Palestine." On 10 May 1931, he presented a memorandum to the League of Nations in Geneva. When Amikam contacted the high commissioner again, on 23 July 1933, he came bearing a petition with thousands of signatures. The Jewish National Council attached its own letter to this petition on 2 August, and Amikam visited the Eighteenth Zionist Congress later that month and got all the participants there to sign the letter, too. He then sent the petition in May 1934 to the Mandates Commission of the League of Nations, a body that regularly received petitions from many constituencies in the mandated states of the Middle East.[28]

Based on British records, it appears that the Colonial Office considered the issue carefully. While admitting that the government of Palestine was prepared "to consider admitting the thin end of the wedge," it acknowledged that "once that is inserted [that is, once Hebrew telegrams are permitted] the pressure for complete equality will probably increase—on the general Jewish principle that any concession must be regarded as an excuse for asking for more."[29] Nonetheless, the government considered the proposal and its limited application and ultimately accepted it.[30] On 7 December 1934, the Yishuv received an announcement that Hebrew would be accepted starting the following 1 January at twenty-one locations. The same day, Amikam received a letter from Arthur Wauchope, the British high commissioner, saying, "This should be seen as a sign of good will of the Government."[31] Amikam was jubilant. A video clip recorded by Nathan Axelrod's Carmel Newsreels in March 1935 shows Amikam, dressed in a three-piece suit, boutonniere, and gold rings, waving the first Hebrew telegram. His wife, hat askew, stands at his side holding flowers.[32] Victory had been won. By 1940, forty-four post offices were equipped to receive telegrams in Hebrew.

Taken together, these stories underscore the devoted nature of protesters aiming to rectify Hebrew's relative absence from Palestine's bureaucratic sphere. When we follow this line in the archival record, we perceive an activist population, largely unsympathetic to lapses or missteps and unremitting in its demands that Hebrew be an option for bureaucratic or administrative communication in all instances. Both individually and collectively, these records of protest suggest a deep and shared commitment to Hebrew and a lack of tolerance for foreign languages.

Israel Amikam holding the first Hebrew telegram, 1935. Nathan Axelrod, Carmel Newsreels, Israel Film Archive of the Jerusalem Cinematheque. Courtesy of the Israel State Archives.

Bargains and Concessions

Undoubtedly, the encounter with the British produced a space for Zionist activism and concretized the desire for political and cultural independence. In practice, however, outright rejection of British linguistic demands was less straightforward. The messiness that might be framed as a series of lapses from a monolingual norm constituted a set of implied norms in its own right, explicit and implicit recognitions of the multiple ways that a small nationalist group could interact with the government under which it was living.

While language barriers were a key issue early in the mandate period— few Jews in Palestine knew English—over time most conflicts arose not from absolute noncomprehension but from the politics of bilingualism. The issue, notwithstanding the protestations from Frederick Kisch that we encountered earlier, was not that Zionists were unable to speak the language of power but rather that a significant enough number *were* able to do so—thanks to language training of one kind or another—but felt pressure from nationalist elements not to do so. In such an environment, the politics of Hebrew-English bilingualism were marked by deliberate decisions, occasions for compromise, and tensions between maintaining hard-line positions and opting for procedurally easier courses of action.

This scenario of strategic monolingualism in the face of pressures for bilingualism was not unique to the Yishuv. Monica Heller recounts the following episode from Quebec that speaks to a similar strategic choice: An English-speaking man came into a French Language Promotion Office one day asking to take a French test. When he requested information about the test's whereabouts in English, the receptionist pretended not to understand and asked him to repeat himself in French. The man replied, "I have the right to be addressed in English by the government of Quebec according to Bill 101." The episode was finally resolved when the parties acquiesced to responding in their own languages to utterances in the other: the receptionist agreed to understand English and the man agreed to be spoken to in French. This exchange invites comparisons to the Zionist context where, similarly, linguistic choices and activism were often in the service of ideals rather than personal needs, and where rules protecting linguistic diversity (Bill 101 in the Quebec case, the laws of the mandate in our case) were widely disregarded but also selectively invoked to achieve particular ends. Bureaucratic exchanges, Heller shows, are spaces in which state policies (de jure and de facto) are contested and resisted, but also spaces for practical compromise and the loosening of ideologically conditioned norms. In instituting a French-language policy, the Quebec government had attempted to rid Francophone Quebecers of the English-French bilingualism that had previously been a marker of their subordination in Anglophone Canada.[33] In the Yishuv, insistence on Hebrew was intended to end a centuries-old situation in which Jews, a minority group, were required to be functionally bilingual. Hebrew dominance, like French dominance in Quebec, signaled an epic change of status, but it was functionally impossible or impractical in a range of settings, not all of them peripheral. Such tensions defined the experience of British rule in Palestine.

Who Were the Clerks?

The mythology of the monolingual rural physical laborer, itself problematic, ultimately excluded a large class of multilingual urban workers for whom a degree of multilingualism was implicitly or explicitly sanctioned. Some of these people, as we noted in previous chapters, worked for commercial outfits of one kind or another. An additional class of Jewish workers worked in the public sector as clerks or office workers for the ever-burgeoning bureaucratic apparatus, which included both British civil service and Zionist institutional jobs. The necessity of their work derived from the Yishuv's political context—under British rule, though with a good measure of communal autonomy—which entailed linguistic contacts and, thus, rewarded language skills. These concessions to circumstances, though not conditioned by a positive pro-British ideology, nonetheless shaped the contours of the emerging Hebrew society, revealing cleavages between relatively activist and relatively conciliatory or opportunistic segments of the Jewish population. In understanding the Yishuv within a broader, non-Jewish framework of power, we can recast Hebrew's own claims to hegemony over mother tongues (as presented in chapter 1) in light of its lack of political hegemony.

Some of the Jewish population worked directly in the British mandate offices, both in Jerusalem and in the regional districts. According to the 1922 census, Jews, though they were 13 percent of the population of Palestine, constituted 20 percent of the 181 clerks in the first division of the civil service and 27 percent of those in the second division. In 1945, the government employed 45,317 people, 20 percent of whom were Jews.[34] As Max Nurock, a British Jew who worked for the Zionist Commission, recalled, "Some Jews held very responsible positions in Custom and Excise, Post and Telegraphs, Surveys, and land settlement. They were not allowed to be very senior, but they were accepted because of their virtues, their qualities—technical and administrative." Clerical work offered a decent standard of living. According to a 1946 estimate, though Jews were 27 percent of those employed in clerical work, they received 36 percent of the total salary because they tended to be clustered in higher-status jobs than Arabs.[35]

Others worked for the Zionist movement itself. Clerks, even within high-profile national institutions, were generally not remarked upon and little remembered—in many cases they were viewed as bourgeois, non-Zionist, and generally irrelevant to the ideological progress of the movement. The word *pakid*, "clerk," was a term of derision. As Isaac Abbady recalled, "Since the essence of the Jewish clerk's job was unheard and unseen and not much read about and because he did his task humbly, one got the impression that he was somewhat unusual in Jewish public life."[36] Nonetheless, their numbers were significant. By 1946, 13.4 percent of the Jewish workforce, or 22,000 workers, were clerks.[37]

Reassessing the Activist Narrative

One revisionist approach insists that even those who seemed to collaborate with the British or were ensconced in anonymous clerical roles in the offices of Zionist institutions were actually upholding the mantle of Hebrew. Some people working as clerks for Zionist institutions, David De Vries shows, thought of themselves as engaging in *"Pekidut 'Ivrit le'umit"* (nationalist Hebrew clerical work), as opposed to the supposedly nonconstructive, noncreative diasporic model of clerical work; they also cultivated a sense of class consciousness by differentiating themselves from their bosses, whom they understood to be less nationalistic.[38] In De Vries's narrative, clerks were no less committed to Zionist tenets than their manually laboring counterparts, and indeed engaged in pro-Hebrew activism of their own. He cites a 1935 letter to the clerks' bulletin, *Pinkas,* in which a clerk wrote of indifferent managers who cared more about bookkeeping than the quality or universality of Hebrew in their offices or the use of Hebrew in their correspondence. Moreover, the clerk asked rhetorically, "Is it not common among some of our managers to respect the English speaker and scorn the clerk who knows 'only' Hebrew, be it the most perfect?"[39] This text offers a window into language practices in offices not devoted to Hebrew in practice. It also points to a perceived class divide between lower-level clerks engaged in Hebrew-language activism and their less Hebrew-oriented managers, whose notion of Zionist service did not necessarily imply an insistence on Hebrew.

Those who sought positions in the British bureaucracy, moreover, felt that they were promoting Jewish interests broadly, and the principle of Hebrew labor in particular, by occupying positions that might otherwise have gone to Arabs. Yaakov Reuveni, the writer of one of the few articles on the subject, notes that Jews often claimed that their greater tax payments (relative to the Arab community) should entitle them to proportionally better benefits, including proportionately greater representation within the mandatory bureaucracy. In the absence of a representative body in Palestine, employee hiring was one way for communities to exert influence. Because of this, "the Jewish aspiration to take part in Government work was interpreted as a pioneering mission and this based on the assumption that the authorities would take an active part in building the Jewish national home." In Isaac Abbady's assessment at the time, too, Jewish service in the British government in Palestine was one of the "most important achievements for national independence . . . along with the recognition of Hebrew as a governmental language."[40]

De Vries's argument is that clerks, far from being obscure nonnationalist figures, saw clerical work as a way to advocate for Jewish rights and the rights of Hebrew, both in British and Zionist settings. My claim is that, on the contrary, overt activism, even if visible and symbolically important, was relatively rare. The young clerk who stressed his pro-Hebrew activism in the face of his less than devoted boss serves De

Vries's argument about a nationally engaged body of clerks. But by alluding to colleagues less devoted to the cause of Hebrew, it also obliquely demonstrates that the segment of clerks devoted to Hebrew was small and that the demands of both the British government and the Jewish leadership made this devotion difficult to sustain. If, as De Vries argues, the strongly Zionist rank and file has been neglected by scholarship more interested in the upper echelons, even more neglected was that part of the rank and file that did not affiliate with the Histadrut or that participated in the organization but did not work as activists. As De Vries notes, the Union of Clerks of the Histadrut, the source of the most clearly Zionist rhetoric, succeeded in organizing "only a fraction" of clerks in the private sector and was "unable to gain control over the market and exert [its] influence over the unorganized clerical rank and file" more generally.[41]

If, on one level, this disconnection between ideal and reality provoked the sorts of protests we have begun to outline above, it also dictated a day-to-day set of linguistic relations that did not conform to stated ideals and—English document by English document—perennially reminded members of the Yishuv that the goal of making Hebrew reign in all sectors of the Yishuv would necessarily be limited by political expedience and practical needs. In considering the extent of English use in the bureaucratic sectors of the Yishuv, we quickly leave behind a rhetorical divide between pro-Hebrew, Zionist Jews and apathetic, foreign-language-using, non-Zionist Jews and enter into the workings of a society negotiating language diversity and linguistic accommodation in more complex—and not always surprising—ways.

The internal ambivalence about the importance of using Hebrew in bureaucratic settings—and about fighting any instances of foreign-language use—is visible even within episodes taken to underscore the pro-Hebrew fight. Let us return for a moment to the telegraph controversy mentioned above. The incident, on the surface, appears to be a classic example of a communal struggle against linguistic discrimination, a fight that in this case concluded when in 1934 the Post and Telegraph Office approved the submission of telegrams in Hebrew script. When we look more closely, however, we see a society divided about the merits of pursuing this fight.

We can see this ambivalence emerge from the moment when the activist parties begin soliciting ideological support and, especially, financial help from Zionist organizations. When the Battalion of the Defenders of the Hebrew Language wrote to the Zionist Organization for support, it received a tepid response. They were working on the issue, the Zionist Organization claimed, but they would not pay money to support the appeal of the 1929 trial.[42] Colonel Frederick Kisch of the Zionist Executive was more explicit about the reasons why the appeal might not be pursued. Aside from the cost of the appeal, he feared loss of political prestige in the event of failure, along with additional negative consequences for Hebrew in Palestine. Moreover, he questioned the value of pressing the issue: the Hebrew script would be used only for internal messages, since no other country recognized Hebrew telegraphic code. The stakes for Hebrew might have seemed large within Palestine, but considering the far broader network of communications in which the Yishuv took part, the inclusion of Hebrew would make only a small dent in what was already accepted to be a multilingual network of Zionist communications. Kisch made a final comment, too. The inclusion of Hebrew as a permissible telegraph language would not mean a further step toward the exclusive use of Hebrew by all Jews. Hebrew use, here as elsewhere, meant translation. New translators would have to be trained, and an increase in the cost of sending telegrams would follow.[43]

In arguing against the outcome of the 1929 trial, the Jewish National Council wrote to the chief secretary of the Palestine government, concerned that the Post and Telegraph Office was not accepting telegrams written in Hebrew. This, it said, "leads to confusion, because the transcription system differs depending on the European language known to the writer. . . . If he knows English, the transcription is English and if he knows German, French, or Russian, the transcription changes according to the language." Because of this, many Jews saw the need to avoid using Hebrew at all. In framing its argument in this way, the Jewish National Council made explicit something that was patently obvious but generally omitted in activist statements: Jews knew languages other than Hebrew, they thought according to the spelling conventions of these languages, and they were perfectly capable of using these languages instead of Hebrew when they believed that Hebrew would be too ambiguous. Far from recognizing or denying the language *needs* of the Jewish minority, the British government was in effect denying Jews the option to choose Hebrew over other languages in which they could have functioned equally well.[44] The chief secretary responded that "the possibility of using Hebrew characters in telegrams is a question which has engaged the sympathetic consideration of the Government at intervals since 1921," but claimed that "for now, financial and administrative difficulties are too formidable."[45]

When Israel Amikam began, after his victory, to solicit financial help to cover his outlays, he was again met with apathy on the part of the public. Amikam had successfully corralled public sentiment on behalf of the Hebrew language; when asked to symbolically support his petition, nearly all institutions had signed on. But when he asked these same individuals and institutions to support his quest financially (320 Palestine pounds [£P320] total), many refused. The Committee of the Jewish Community in Haifa, where Amikam lived, wrote, "Let us express respect for your work," but went on to suggest that the question at hand was a national one and should be addressed to the Jewish National Council.[46] The local council at Nahalal, concerned that the central Zionist institutions were not stepping up on the telegraph issue, volunteered to be "one of the public bodies that will remove this shame," though it hoped that "things would not get to that point."[47] By January 1944, Amikam had managed to raise £P50 from the Jewish Agency, £P50 from the Histadrut, £P5 from Mizrahi, £P10 from the electric company, £P5 from the teachers' center, and £P10 from private donors. None of the community councils had offered money, and Amikam was not close to covering his expenses.[48] Support for Hebrew telegrams, though vocally expressed, turned out to be more a collective posture taken for political reasons than a deeply held commitment. In any case, pro-Hebrew activities around education or culture likely took precedence over the telegram. Sir John Shuckburgh, at the Colonial Office, commenting on Amikam's petitions to the British government, was not entirely wrong to note of Amikam: "[He] is obsessed with this and it is really only this man . . . who rouses others to sign petitions on the subject."[49] Although the Hebrew telegram was celebrated on its tenth anniversary with great acclaim for Amikam, the concept of collective action was more important than the actual outcome, according to Amikam himself.[50] He was quite upset about this. He complained that he had "worked alone for twenty years without helpers."[51]

The telegram case was only one of many activist pushes spearheaded by a small group or an individual letter writer who claimed to be advocating for the general national rights of the whole group—a self-appointed language police force keeping law and order for the rest of the population. But in this case at least we find that the public, though willing to sign onto a pro-Hebrew campaign, was not willing to sacrifice its financial well-being or comfort for it. Living under British administrative rule meant that in practice English was omnipresent, though by no means dominant, in the bureaucratic, clerical, and administrative activities that occurred both in the cities and in administrative offices elsewhere in the country.

Incentives for English Knowledge

English was generally the language of work for civil servants, even in offices that dealt mainly with Jewish constituents, and for this reason a level of language proficiency was required. According to British policy, "Candidates whose customary tongue is other than English will be required to have passed the English Distinction Examination or another examination considered by the Director of Education to be the equivalent thereof before they are admitted to the Civil Service Examination."[52] According to a 1936 document, certain officers—for example, education officers, assistant secretaries, or land settlement officers—had to pass at least the lower-standard test within three years of their employment, and they received up to £P10 for language instruction.[53] Likewise, candidates for admission to law classes at the British Council of Legal Studies were required to sit for language exams, we learn from a letter to students (most with Jewish names) who failed to show up for such exams. Examinees, it seems from lists of those who sat for the "Law School English Test," were overwhelmingly Jewish.[54]

Even in positions for which English was not required for work, Jews (and Arabs) were offered incentives for passing standardized English exams. British civil servants had the option to sit for Hebrew and Arabic exams, and local Jews and Arabs could express proficiency in English and in the other local language. Two levels were offered, a lower standard and a higher standard. In 1926 the bonus amounts for police officers were five hundred mils a month for passing the lower colloquial standard and £1 a month (twice as much) for passing the higher standard (until 1927, Palestine used the Egyptian pound). In time, higher amounts were suggested, based on the assumption that "a lower reward will not secure a really good result."[55]

The incentives seem to have worked. Enough British civil service personnel were taking the exams—and passing them—that the amount allotted for bonuses proved insufficient. As British high commissioner Arthur Wauchope reported in 1934, "The large number of [police] constables who have now qualified for the receipt of such an allowance" has meant a supplementary allocation £P2,300 Palestine. One hundred thirty candidates had passed the language examinations in 1933, "a number considerably in excess of expectations." English was the language most often chosen by Jews and Arabs, since the language allowances, according to that report, were "not a sufficient inducement for Arab or Jewish constables to learn Hebrew or Arabic respectively."[56]

Translators for the Mandate Government

The great emphasis on English derived from the fact that the British mandate apparatus in Palestine, despite its official commitments to a trilingual policy, was never fully equipped to operate in languages other than English, and particularly not in Hebrew. Few British civil servants knew any Hebrew at all. According to the Palestine Royal Commission report of 1937, out of the 270 British officers in the first division of the civil service in Palestine in the mid-1930s, only six could speak Hebrew. Though the report recommended that appointments to the secretariat should be reserved for those British employees who have served in the districts "and know the people and their language," in practice Hebrew knowledge never became common.[57] If a Jew was to integrate to any extent whatsoever into the British bureaucratic system, it was incumbent on him to improve his knowledge of English.

Ronald Storrs, the military governor of Jerusalem between 1917 and 1920 and governor of Jerusalem and Judea from 1920 to 1926, mused in his memoirs that a more logical procedure would have been to make English the official language and simply provide Arabic translations and interpreters for other minorities, including Jews, as had been the case in Egypt.[58] Storrs's suggestion was not to be the policy of Palestine, though the assumption that English was the true official language of Palestine persisted in the minds of some who responded to early Jewish linguistic claims. In October 1918, for instance, Major General A. W. Money, who had been put in charge of the Palestine occupation immediately follow-ing World War I, wrote to Colonel Huggett, General Allenby's chief financial officer, seeking to dismiss Jewish complaints about having received their tax forms in Arabic: "We have no intention of giving every community in Palestine a receipt in their own language. English is the of-ficial language as I said above."[59] Arabic was a concession to the majority population of the country; no other linguistic demands were worthy of consideration.

Nonetheless, the OETA (Occupied Enemy Territory Administration, the military administration of Palestine) soon after expressed its commit-ment to multiple languages, a position that culminated in the declaration of three official languages in 1920, English, Arabic, and Hebrew, when the civil government took over. The inclusion of Hebrew derived in part from the British commitment to a Jewish national home as expressed in the 1917 Balfour Declaration; indeed, General Allenby, after entering the gates of Jerusalem in December 1917, read his first proclamation in Hebrew as well as Arabic, English, and several other languages.[60] However justified, the concrete result of this multilingual policy was great administrative strain. It entailed, writes Storrs, "an ever-increasing staff of Hebrew interpreters, translators, stenographers, typists, printers, and administrative officers, all supported by the tax-paying majority."[61]

The steep expenditures necessary to maintain a trilingual bureaucracy could be readily critiqued. George Antonius, best known for his survey of Arab nationalism, wrote a brief article in 1932 calling attention to the bloated bureaucracy of the mandate government. One source of this bloat was Britain's commitment to endorsing three official languages, which, he said, caused a "serious wastage," since every communication and all publi-cations needed to appear in the three languages, a fact that imposed an enormous burden on translators, who often ended up translating the same document twice. The result was not only a waste of precious time, he thought, but also "a crop of misunderstandings, of bewildering errors, and in certain cases, of miscarriages of justice."[62] The principle of language rights for multiple groups, as European Union members know well today, meant a series of bureaucratic nightmares on the ground and the frequent inability of the government to fulfill its stated language policies.

In practice, the official multilingualism of Palestine meant that translators were essential to the workings of nearly every part of the local bureaucracy, both British and Jewish. Whenever the Jewish community needed access to governmental services, many partook of translation services to transmit their documents and messages, services provided in practically all cases by members of their own community who had the requisite language skills. A vast enterprise of translators and translations sat not only at the heart of the British mandatory apparatus, but also, and more importantly for our purposes, behind the pretense of the Yishuv to operate in Hebrew only. Within the mandate government, this translation, by and large, occurred at the Central Translation Bureau in Jerusalem.

From 1920 to 1945, the bureau's Hebrew division was headed by Isaac Abraham Abbady, a Jew of Syrian descent who also translated the memoirs of Sir Ronald Storrs, whose pessimistic comments on the nature of British rule are cited above. The bureau appears to have gotten off to a rough start. In November 1924, the office of the assistant governor of the Jerusalem District wrote to Mayor Meir Dizengoff of Tel Aviv, admitting that the government translators were making mistakes. The translators themselves suggested appointing an advisory committee at that time, which would logically be constituted of representatives of the Hebrew Language Committee, but the committee refused. According to the letter, the only existing oversight was from Isaac Abbady himself, with additional help from a small number of others.[63]

The operations of the Central Translation Bureau appear to have gotten more stable at the end of the mandate. Between 1945 and 1948, the office was run by Shmuel Yeivin, more widely known for his work as an archaeologist, who appears to have begun issuing yearly reports about the bureau's activities, something not present for most of the period.[64] The scope of the office's work is possible to judge from records kept of translation requests during this period. In the year between July 1944 and June 1945, the secretariat had 664 documents translated from Hebrew to English and 221 documents translated from English to Hebrew. The figures were nearly the same the following year, while in 1947 the Hebrew-English translations went up to 1,039.[65] Expanding the corps of qualified translators became a pressing need during these years. Reports from 1945–46 recommend adding three new translators in both Hebrew and Arabic and promising the highest-paying vacancies in each bureau to those men who did best in their translation courses.[66] By 1947, on the eve of Israel's independence, the bureau had thirteen officers, including nine permanent employees. Lists of names suggest that temporary translators were not unusual: people went in and out of jobs such as "typist-translator," and "secretary proofreader."[67] These numbers—of documents and staff—presumably do not include translations in individual government branches (Education, Agriculture, etc.) or in the district offices, although the central office may have also served these other branches.[68] They also do not take into account translations done within Zionist institutions or in the private sector. When we imagine extrapolating outward, the number of English-speaking Jewish clerks in the Yishuv becomes much larger.

Reports indicate that the Hebrew section of the Central Translation Bureau was not only involved with translating to and from English. The great linguistic skills of its staff, Jews from various countries, meant that the Hebrew section was also entrusted with doing translations to and from other European languages. In 1944–45, the office translated eighteen German documents, fifteen French documents, and one Yiddish document to English.[69] The Hebrew translation office thus became the general European-language translation office for the British mandate: Jews, as usual in Jewish history, remained multilingual translators. The translators also occasionally played interpreter roles at interviews given by top British officials and administered the Hebrew exams taken by non-Jews who were applying to work as translators with the Palestine Railways and the Palestine Police.[70]

In general, translation services were not satisfactory, an indication that the bureaucratic apparatus would have been better served if more Jews had received a better education in English. The general manager of the railway wanted translators who knew English as well as Arabic or Hebrew, were experienced in translation, and had knowledge of railway terminology—and he expressed concern that too many unqualified candidates were being accepted: "Railways is not the only Department which is badly served in the matter of translations. In fact, the defect is universal throughout the Government of Palestine and there is no surplus of expert translators either for recruitment or for redistribution."[71]

Translators occupy an ambivalent place in a bureaucracy. On the one hand, they have little agency and must faithfully, mechanically transmit information without personal interference. On the other hand, they have historically exerted power in places where European power is weak or insufficient. As historians of Africa have noted, "The lack of direct communication created nodes of power used by interpreters," and "control over translation placed the African interpreter in the center of exchanges of information."[72] Translation was not neutral, neither in the English-Hebrew settings we have been discussing nor in settings where Arabic translation was demanded. In the context of the railway, it became a battleground as translators deliberately misconstrued the words of opponents. Arab members of the joint Jewish-Arab railway union believed that the union was becoming pro-Zionist and that they were being deceived by their Jewish counterparts. As the Arabic newspaper *Haifa* wrote, the language divide between the two parties "necessitated the employment of a translator in order to solve the problem; but this employee, who was not of the working class, curried favor for Zionism in the performance of his duties and abetted the spread of its influence and introduced it into the union's affairs."[73] The implications of this small affair are clear: a translator is a third-party intermediary in a relationship that is sufficiently complex even without intervention. He may hold views unacceptable to either side and may surreptitiously promote them.

The great and growing need for translators meant that many Jews who felt they had the linguistic skills for the job wrote to the Central Translation Bureau to apply for positions. They generally applied in English, presumably to show off their English writing abilities, though Hebrew inquiries were not uncommon. An applicant named H. Modlinger called himself a "simple Palestinian citizen" who had a "thorough knowledge of the three official languages and a Hebrew University education." He claimed to have worked as a clerk and translator at a British company and said he was submitting his application because the "office offers a splendid future and permanent position to young and energetic men."[74] Another writer, a Mr. Fuchs, thirty-two years old, had worked previously with the controller of light industries, as did Erich Goldstein, born in Glogau, Germany, who had worked also for the Palestine Manufacturers Association in Haifa.[75] Eliyahu Salamah seemed to have applied straight out of high school (at the Rehavia Gymnasium) and insisted that "aside from school, I learned the English language privately as well."[76] (A note appended to his application remarked, "He hasn't worked at all.")

The letters, including some recommendation letters written in behalf of candidates, indicate a pool of applicants who generally did not speak English as a native language but had built up their English knowledge through a combination of schoolwork, private lessons, study in England, and work in British offices and companies. This particular stock of letters, from 1946, is presumably typical of those from other years of the mandate, though, as we noted above, the volume was likely higher than in earlier years. This correspondence (only a fraction of the correspondence that surely existed on the topic) indicated that British government employment was increasingly perceived as a real option for Jews, but an option that could be achieved only through proficiency in English.

Candidates' language knowledge was subjected to testing. The texts in the application test ran the gamut from official documents, extracts from newspapers and business letters, and (in the Hebrew-to-English section) a technical publication, a newspaper article, and an extract from the Mishnah.[77] One text, in a translation exam offered at the Palestine Railways authority in 1946, was an excerpt from Nahum Sokolov's 1933 essay "Eliezer Ben-Yehuda," in which Sokolov lays out his thoughts about the act of translation: in some cases, he wrote, a writer should be judged not by his original work in Hebrew, but by his translation abilities.[78]

Most Jewish (and Arab) employees in British offices knew enough English that British officers increasingly found it pointless to invest time in learning Hebrew or Arabic; Jews, too, saw little need to learn Arabic to communicate with their Arab coworkers. This effect was marked enough that some Britons called into question the wisdom of requiring the

Hebrew and Arabic exams in the first place. A memorandum from 1937 by the British secretary of state, citing the need for assistants in some of Palestine's district offices, noted: "Knowledge of Arabic is far from necessary. Character and guts are more important as both such Arabs and Jews as they will have to deal with can speak English."[79]

The relative spread of English knowledge over the course of the mandate period concerned some Jews not only for ideological reasons but also because this trend meant fewer employment options for Jewish translators, who were most in demand if only a few Jews knew English. In 1942, a newspaper reported that the number of letters received in Hebrew by the inspector's office for heavy industry was declining, and the number received in English (and German) was increasing. This "causes the denial of employment for many Hebrew workers who had been invited as translators and for whom there is no longer any need." Ultimately, the writer thought, the government was getting a mistaken impression about the relationship of the Jewish community to the Hebrew language.[80] In a letter to the *Palestine Post*, a civil servant who signed his name as "Rigbi" said that he worked in a government office that dealt with Jews 75 percent of the time, but noted that only 10 percent of his correspondence was in Hebrew, "simply because most of the persons in contact with this office think it wiser to write and speak English to its officers." The outcome of this situation, which he affirmed was common in other government offices, was that clerks did not really have to know Hebrew. Rigbi was an advocate; he was writing to call "all those who had forgotten that Hebrew is also an official language to join in one common fight for one common language. . . . Every linguistic victory shall also be a political one."[81] Nonetheless, the very fact of his advocacy suggests that his desired outcome—universal commitment to Hebrew—had not been achieved.

The Law Courts

The law courts were a further setting for both linguistic activism and linguistic compromises in the British mandate context. Though oral arguments could be conducted in any of the three official languages of the country, Arabic was the most common language of the courts in Palestine, though summonses were issued to Jews in Hebrew. In reality, memoirs show, the linguistic situation was more complicated than this: some Jews did not know Hebrew and preferred to use languages like Polish or German. Moreover, "as time went by, the use of English became more dominant in the courts."[82] Nisan Rodeh, for example, recalled a case in which two Jewish lawyers pleaded before a Jewish judge for Jewish clients in English.[83]

A recurrent debate in the Jewish legal profession was the extent to which the concept of Hebrew law (*mishpat 'Ivri*) had a linguistic dimension, that is, whether the Hebrew language was essential to the development of a legal system that would be Hebrew (Jewish) in the cultural and historical sense. Just as some arbiters of culture insisted that culture in Hebrew (including translated culture) was more important than original Hebrew culture, some Jewish jurists and legal thinkers insisted that the development of a Hebrew legal tradition lay first and foremost in the insistence on the Hebrew language. Others, including Simha Assaf, who became an Israeli supreme court justice in 1948, felt that the Hebrew nature of the law lay in its link to the new Hebrews of Palestine, not to the Hebrew language per se.[84] Mordechai Eliash, a prominent lawyer and president of the Jewish Bar Association, was a member of the pro-Hebrew-language camp. In his leadership role, he implored Jewish lawyers to use only Hebrew in their correspondence with government courts, sought sanctions against lawyers who didn't use Hebrew, and inserted pro-Hebrew resolutions into JBA protocols: "It is an obligation upon every Jewish lawyer to use only Hebrew orally, in writing, and in all his correspondence and claims before all government institutions and in the courts in particular." The only exception he saw was in cases dealing with non-Jews or in private appearances before judges.[85]

Nonetheless, even a pro-Hebrew advocate such as Eliash did not use Hebrew in all instances, claiming that because the British judges knew that he was fluent in English, they would not tolerate him speaking to them in Hebrew. Gad Frumkin, a high court judge during the mandate period, recalled that even the heads of the Histadrut, normally known for their zealous commitment to Hebrew, did not follow the decree to use Hebrew only in court. A barrister such as Eliash feared, logically, that his testimony might be heard by a young translator who knew even less English than he did. As a result, his words might be translated into a "stammering English."[86] The class dimensions here are again worth noting: a lawyer such as Eliash was of a far higher social standing than a translator, who stood at the level of a court clerk. In this case, a higher-status, more highly educated lawyer was more competent in his multilingualism than a younger, lower-class man assigned to translate for him. Under these circumstances, lawyers naturally sought to deploy their own multilingual skills.

"Things have gotten to such a point," wrote the pro-Hebrew Organization for the Enforcement of Hebrew, that Jewish lawyers considered English knowledge a "necessary condition" for work in the courts, leading to the curious situation that "English judges have requested that the Jewish lawyers speak in Hebrew rather than broken English."[87] The stakes of Hebrew use were foremost symbolic; the organization's letter spoke of the language as "one of the most important foundations of building a healthy nation in its land," but offered a far more technical justification, not unlike that used to justify the exclusion of Yiddish films in Jewish-run theaters: by demonstrating what could be interpreted as apathy toward Hebrew, users of English suggested to authorities that Hebrew "has no importance even for Jews" and that Hebrew translators are not really necessary.[88] The chair of the organization expressed the related concern that lawyers were tending to read the English version of the *Official Gazette*, perhaps because the Hebrew version often came out with a significant delay. This "insulting, scathing attitude toward Hebrew," they wrote, "is likely to cause the stoppage of the Hebrew edition by the government. The authorities will conclude that the Hebrew language holds no importance even for the Jews themselves."[89]

English in Zionist Institutions

Jews in the mandate apparatus or those working in the British court system were commonly users of English, but this did not mean that they were the only Jews to confront situations of official language contact. Faced with a government both unwilling and logistically unable to deal fully with Hebrew correspondence from Zionist institutions, Jewish municipalities, parties, and organizations corresponded with British offices in English—sometimes but not always by way of English translations.

Some of the links between the Yishuv and the British were accomplished by British Jews or by Jews who had spent time in Britain. Max Nurock, a British Jew who worked with the Zionist Commission (the forerunner of the Jewish Agency), sat somewhere between the Zionist movement and the British. He claimed to have learned Hebrew from Mordechai Eliash, Bialik, Ahad Ha-'Am, and Saul Tchernichowsky as well as Eliezer Ben-Yehuda. But Hebrew fluency was not the main skill he needed: "Because English was my mother tongue," he wrote, "I was naturally used as a liaison with the British occupying military authorities." In fact, he said, "The Mandatory Government looked upon me as . . . a channel of communication with the Yishuv and its leaders. That was quite clear and openly recognized."[90]

A similar situation comes up in a Hebrew University oral history interview with a man named Daniel Ofir, whose uncle Yahalom had left Jaffa in 1907 for England, where he grew up. When the British took over Palestine, Yahalom worked as a translator for the Hebrew newspaper *Haaretz*. "It was good that they had a Jewish officer who had been educated in England," Ofir remarked with pride, "who knew both Hebrew and English, whose job would be to translate from English to Hebrew." This family became part of the English-speaking elite. Yahalom's daughter Sarah studied at the Evelina de Rothschild private school, which taught English, and married a British Jew who was a district officer in Tel Aviv.[91]

These outsider personalities, Jews who either were not part of the Yishuv in the first place or had left it to live in England, were not the only ones to make connections between the Yishuv and the English—English-language contact was simply too important and widespread to be restricted to the small number of native Jewish English speakers in Palestine. Overwhelmed by translation demands, the mandate apparatus regularly asked Jewish institutions to provide their own English translations along with the Hebrew original. In 1925 the Principal Medical Office, Jaffa District, asked the Tel Aviv Municipality for English translations, suggesting that writing in English would be in the municipality's best interest: "The fact that Saturday is a Jewish holiday and Sunday a Christian holiday means that any letter written in Hebrew which arrives here after Friday morning is not dealt with until Monday morning."[92]

While this request was framed as a gesture of goodwill to the municipality, other communications simply demanded English use. In 1927 the Southern District commissioner complained to the Tel Aviv Municipality that despite his request for English translations, "a number of letters, some urgent, others not, have been sent without any English translation." This failure imposed a financial hardship: "I must regretfully inform you that I am unable to bear the cost of translating letters both from the Council into English and to the Council into Hebrew." He offered the municipality the option either to write in Hebrew but receive replies only in English or to attach English translations and receive English and Hebrew replies.[93] In other words, he was willing to translate once but not twice over the course of any given exchange. In a further communication, the Southern District commissioner wrote that while "fully sympathising with the Township's [municipality's] desire to conduct all its correspondence in Hebrew," he "would suggest that a somewhat more liberal and tactful attitude should be adopted in the future." Local conditions required it: "Tel Aviv is situated within a trilingual area and it is hardly possible to maintain that in that area English is a foreign language."[94] In 1927, the Businesses Ordinance (*Pekudat ha-hevrot*) decreed that all businesses needed to send all memorandums and ordinances to the registrar of businesses in English or with an approved English translation.[95] In 1928 the district police commissioner from Jaffa explained his use of English for correspondence by saying that "the licensing clerk who is a British constable was busy at the time and stated that he could not read Hebrew and requested that the application be translated into English in order to save time."[96]

The Tel Aviv Municipality and the Jewish National Council got angry at the British bureaucratic apparatus for its lack of sufficient resources to process Hebrew—they repeatedly chalked it up to deliberate discrimination against or suppression of Hebrew. Occasional orders to send Arabic correspondence to district offices—for example, the police office in Jaffa—further heightened the feeling of unequal treatment and denigration (*zilzul*).[97] The Jewish National Council angrily wrote the chief secretary of the Palestine Government in 1929, incensed that the Tax Department had refused to engage in Hebrew correspondence. The Yishuv, it said, would not give up on the importance of Hebrew, "because of a lack of needed clerks." If a Hebrew-speaking clerk is required, he should be found, especially given the important contribution of the Jewish community to overall governmental tax revenues.[98]

But the rhetoric around British intransigence and the oppression of Hebrew didn't change the basic linguistic situation: there were three official languages in Palestine, and Hebrew was not chief among them except in a limited set of circles. Therefore, translators remained in demand within Jewish institutions just as in British institutions. As early as 1919, before the language ordinance recognizing Hebrew became official, the Haifa Municipality made arrangements for translation services: it hired a Mr. Suleiman Bey Nassir, formerly of the Khedival Mail Steamship Company, to translate Arabic, and a Mr. Silverman, an economic agent in the OETA, for Hebrew.[99] Another man who was recommended as a potential hire, Baruch Bina, had been in the British army as the censor for the OETA, was "well versed in local affairs and relations," and had "a perfect knowledge of English, French and Hebrew."[100]

Over the ensuing decades, employment inquiries flowed into the Tel Aviv Municipality from those possessing language skills who hoped to gain employment in the bureaucracy of the First Hebrew City. A man by the name of Ezra David wrote to the Tel Aviv Municipality in April 1935 (in English), offering his services as a clerk: "I am a Jew and aged about 21 years. I am well conversant in the three official languages: Hebrew, English, and Arabic, and hold excellent certificates and testimonials. In case I may kindly be granted [a] post you may be confident that I shall always endeavor to discharge my duties to your entire satisfaction."[101] David received a standard curt reply from the municipality, letting him know that letters requesting work at the municipality should be written in Hebrew, the language of Tel Aviv—this was a standard response to non-Hebrew correspondence. But passionate assertions of the municipality's monolingual policy did not result in a monolingual staff. Similar inquiries came in at other points during the mandate period from people showing off their language skills. Shlomo Aharoni, who described himself as a twenty-one-year-old Jew from Aden, wrote, "I know how to read, write and speak in the three official languages."[102] Shimon Taberski, who described himself as a new immigrant from Russia, wrote in a request for work: "I know Hebrew and a little English (it will be just a few more months before I gain proficiency in the language)." Taberski, it seems, was aware that his lack of English was an impediment to employment, and he stressed his willingness to improve further in that language.[103] Some mentioned prior experience: L. Rotstein had previously worked as a correspondent in Hebrew, French, and English.[104] Others mentioned a whole range of language skills besides the official languages: Y. S. Sharafi, from Tehran, stated that he had "good knowledge of English, Persian, Hebrew, Arabic, and French," and Avraham Naiman claimed to have fluency in English, Arabic, German, and Polish.[105] The noted Sephardi journalist Nissim Malul, who wrote on behalf of a man named Sh. Shapira, noted, "In addition to Hebrew, the aforementioned Mr. Shapira also knows Arabic to a degree that not all Ashkenazim achieve."[106]

Translators, it becomes clear, were necessary employees at the municipality of the First Hebrew City, both despite the official languages policy of the British mandatory government and because of it. The importance of English knowledge was so great that even those who did not speak Hebrew felt they could apply for jobs because of their English skills. Leah Donberg wrote a letter to the mayor in which she touted her English and French skills but explicitly noted, "Unfortunately I don't know Hebrew well."[107] These translators are largely invisible to the historian except whenever someone called attention to a problem with translation or when indignant employees protested the need for translation services in the first place.

The translation office, we might expect, was a kind of hidden space where foreign languages could be translated and, thus, neutralized. But it would be incorrect to assume that Hebrew was in fact the original language of all Zionist correspondence. Largely through the wording of protests, we learn that many Jews in Yishuv institutions used English to the extent that they could, finding it either desirable or simply easier; the aforementioned applicants, if hired, would likely have prepared correspondence in English in addition to translation work. We know this in part through complaints raised by Zionists who felt that the Zionist organizations were not upholding their linguistic duties. The major Zionist institutions, the Zionist Organization and the Jewish Agency, were regularly cited for using English in their offices and in correspondence with the British or with overseas Zionist groups. They did so even when English was not specifically demanded; many felt that it was simply advisable to use that language to avoid misunderstandings.

"We considered it a national duty to address the authorities always and only in our language, in Hebrew," wrote Mordechai Ben-Hillel Ha-Cohen. "There was something demonstrative about this, and there is no doubt that it prepared the ground for Hebrew being declared one of the legal languages of Palestine." But problems remained: "There was always a feeling of a lack of understanding. We brought in translators, but it still felt as if there was a lack of communication. But in Jerusalem, where there were some activists who knew the British language, there were better relations."[108]

The use of English by Zionist organizations continued for this basic reason. Attempts to promote Hebrew occasionally came up against protestations that, in other contexts, English was being used without a problem. The Aliyah Division of the Jewish Agency in Jerusalem, for instance, attempted to get its offices abroad to use Hebrew in their correspondence: "Lack of Hebrew use is not appropriate in correspondence between the highest institution of the Zionist movement and its branches abroad." While the Paris and Trieste offices agreed to the demands, the Johannesburg office did not, claiming that it "conduct[ed] a continuous correspondence" with Zionist headquarters in Jerusalem and London, regularly received correspondence from Zionist offices in English, and "knowing as they do that the state has not been reached when correspondence can be readily and easily conducted by us in Hebrew, they not only do not make the stipulation that you do, but they actually write to us themselves, with few exceptions, in English."[109] In this case, the recipient of English correspondence was not the British government, but branches of the Zionist movement in the English-speaking world. This particular use of English, which we have not discussed in detail here, became increasingly important over time as English-speaking countries became the place of residence for a significant percentage of world Jewry and as Zionist institutions were perennially engaged in communication and fund-raising efforts with their Jewish communities.

The Language of Correspondence

Using the language of "officialness" and citing the unique status of Hebrew, Yishuv institutions regularly discriminated against languages other than Hebrew in correspondence—but selectively used English under certain circumstances. The Tel Aviv Municipality Archives has folders full of non-Hebrew letters returned to their senders. While the typical response was brief—"Please write to us in our official language, Hebrew"—other responses were more impatient. A response to a letter in French rhetorically asked one Efraim Freudmann, a Belgian citizen, whether "one of us could likewise write to the Brussels municipality in Hebrew," indignantly implying that the Hebrew municipality was not being treated respectfully as a national institution.[110] A letter to a Mr. Fritz Epstein in March 1940 likewise stated: "It seems to me that we are allowed to demand of you that you behave with the same courtesy that you would show in any place where you lived outside your homeland."[111] If the Hebrew-speaking community of Palestine had been granted autonomy to operate in its national language, it followed that one should not even think of addressing the Tel Aviv Municipality, or other institutions, in another language. In 1940, the CCEH devised another means to convince Jewish institutions and individuals to write only in Hebrew; noting that many were not insisting on receiving correspondence in Hebrew, they distributed pro-Hebrew stamps to attach to pieces of correspondence, with the words: "We respond only in Hebrew and only to letters written in Hebrew."[112]

But the principle of Hebrew exclusivity was not evenly applied, and evidence of exceptions lends insight into the impossibility, or at least the difficulty, of enforcing a fully Hebrew bureaucratic policy. The strictest enforcement of the Hebrew-only policy was for letters in Jewish immigrant languages: Yiddish in the early years of the mandate, and German increasingly later. English, too, was rejected when the writer seemed not to have sufficient standing. A letter in English from a Mr. Munzer reported that the water supply on Bezalel Yaffe Street had been turned off, and as a result, "the whole house is full of disgusting odours."[113] Munzer received a request to write back in Hebrew; given the postal delay, residents of his building presumably suffered from the stench for several more days.

The policy on English-language correspondence was more complicated, however, in cases of English and American businesses or individuals who simply had no knowledge of Hebrew. The official position was straightforward, as in a letter to a Jewish engineering company in

Palestine. The Tel Aviv Municipality expressed shock that the company would "continue to address us, the highest institution in the Hebrew city of Tel Aviv, in a foreign language," adding, "It might interest you in connection with this to know that even non-Jewish companies . . . see it as their duty to address us in our language."[114] In reality, non-Jewish companies were not so meticulous in their Hebrew use, and the Tel Aviv Municipality nearly bent over backward to accommodate their linguistic infractions. In response to inquiries from two foreign companies, the Shell Petroleum Company (British) and the Prudential Insurance Company (American), the municipality sounded a different tone from the one projected to Munzer, the man suffering from unfortunate odors in his home. Mayor Israel Rokach, who employed a less than polite style in responding to non-Hebrew letters from other senders, sounded a different tone here.

> Now that the Shell interests in this country are increasing on a large scale and business connections between yourselves and the Jewish community of this country are on the increase, we consider it our duty both to you and to ourselves to point out that it is time that you adopt the system of addressing the members of the Jewish community or their representatives in their own language, Hebrew. The expense which this would entail would surely be warranted and I am sure that you will appreciate that this courtesy if shown by you to the Jewish community of Palestine in general and to ourselves in particular will be worthwhile.

The letter to Prudential, meanwhile, acknowledged that the request for Hebrew might seem petty: "We would like to draw your attention to one little matter which, trivial though it may appear, is of great importance. It is the question of language."[115] The tone here is overwhelmingly deferential and respectful. Though Rokach is clear about the community's desires, he by no means speaks in the language of demand and, moreover, allows himself to write in English in reply, something that would have been anathema in general. The municipality knew that it had to be careful about seeming too doctrinaire about languages; the economic fortunes of the Yishuv and the city of Tel Aviv depended on the maintenance of positive relations with suppliers, commercial entities, and certain governmental offices.

Economic power was not the only leverage that an entity could use to defend the use of English. The laws of the mandate themselves provided a defense for those who chose to write in English when they did not know Hebrew—just as the laws of Quebec, as we saw earlier, provided a defense for a man who addressed a French-speaking clerk in English. A British Jew who was rebuked for writing to the Tel Aviv Municipality in English had his attorney complain to British government offices in Jaffa about the municipality's claim that English was a "foreign language": "My client is Mr. J. B. Amzalak who is a British citizen," wrote the lawyer, "and has every right to use the British Language in this country."[116] After receiving a standard letter from the Tel Aviv Municipality chastising him for writing a letter in English, a Th. D. Schatz responded politely, in English: "May I remind you that there are three official languages in Palestine, which I assume are all known by you. Two of these languages are used on each of your letter heads and therefore I had to take the choice of one in which I can make myself understood."[117]

English, moreover, sometimes became a default lingua franca between Jewish institutions and Jewish immigrants, particularly German immigrants, who did not know Hebrew. Bruno Cohn, a German speaker whose letterhead marked him as a specialist in internal and nervous diseases, replied to a request for Hebrew correspondence by saying that his knowledge of Hebrew was not yet sufficient for letter writing and thus, "as the english language is as well an official language in Palestine as the hebrew language, I repeat my letter in english language [all errors *sic*]."[118] Likewise, the Haifa resident Max Tuchner, after having his German-language request for a marriage license returned with an admonition to write in Hebrew, appealed in English to the Haifa Municipality: "I am very sorry to tell you that cannot enough hebrew to write a letter in this language. Jbeg pardon for this case and sent me please my certificate of married on my new address" [all errors *sic*].[119] The recourse to English, it seems, was not simply the product of individual initiative; the practice was explicitly sanctioned by the newspaper of the Union of German and Austrian Immigrants: "We repeat our appeal and demand: one who knows Hebrew to a greater or lesser extent must speak *only Hebrew* in public; otherwise, he may use the English language."[120] English, because of its official status and growing international prestige, became available as a lingua franca perceived as less offensive than German, the language of the Nazi enemy. But in this role, English had the capacity to supplant the linking function of Hebrew, that is, to become the actual shared language of Jews. Mordechai Ben-Hillel Ha-Cohen realized this threat early when he wrote, speaking of English and Arabic, "threats are bursting forth [against our language] from two sides, fighting with all their might."[121] We will return to this dual threat in chapter 5. And indeed, if we look forward several decades, we find that English indeed has become the lingua franca of world Jewry, just as it became the lingua franca of the world at large.

At the outset of the mandate period, few Jews knew English. Zionists had come mainly from eastern Europe, sometimes by way of central Europe, and were far more likely to be proficient writers, readers, and speakers of German, Russian, or French than of English. The lack of English was nearly immediately felt. Mordechai Ben-Hillel Ha-Cohen wrote that the multiplicity of languages and the lack of English knowledge on the part of Jews "did not work to [their] benefit." Though the "demonstrative" insistence on addressing the authorities in Hebrew was considered a "national obligation" and certainly prepared the ground for Hebrew becoming an official language, "in practice our interests suffered from strange relations that are created unwillingly when people don't understand one another."[122] The ideal of language unity and exclusivity, Ben-Hillel Ha-Cohen is suggesting, was not technically feasible at this point—Jews could be as demonstrative as they wanted, but they soon realized the frustration of speaking in a language that could not be understood. Activists could be indignant about English, but the demand for it was undeniable, and this became more and more the case over the course of the mandate period. Those who wished to progress in this direction went one of two ways: to a school of commerce or to one of a range of other private programs offered to adults.

Some of the clerical staff of Palestine studied at one of the commercial schools in the country, which were mentioned in chapter 2 as spaces where languages were taught for commercial ends. Data on enrollees indicates that students at these schools were notably middle-class (not wealthy) and mostly average (not high-achieving) young people looking for training to get a decent job.[123] A good number of the Safra School's students in 1933 were new immigrants who were simultaneously enrolled in remedial Hebrew courses. Three of the new arrivals that year were from Salonika; others came from Poland, France, and America. The students included one "truly foreign boy," an Arab from Jaffa "who entered the school and aspired to become like his Hebrew friends." A list of enrollees from the 1932–33 year, though primarily composed of Tel Aviv residents, also included students from other surrounding towns.[124] In 1942, the inspector noted that there were many more girls than boys in the Safra School. "It appears," he said, "that the girls tend to be the ones who aspire to clerical work, and it is they who have the greater chance of realizing their aspirations."[125] The predominance of women presumably arose from the fact that offices liked hiring female secretaries and typists.

In his 1937 report about the Tel Aviv School of Commerce, Eliezer Rieger noted: "There aren't many students of the spoiled types who find a place in the larger institutions in the country. Because of this there is less chutzpah and more diligence among the students and perhaps less imagination."[126] In a note, a former student named Dina Pugatzki had a similar experience. She had intended to learn medicine or become a pre-school teacher, but "for various reasons" was not able to pursue those goals and decided on a clerical career.[127] Shulamit Yerushavski entered the school so that she "wouldn't be groundless [*netulat karka'*] in [her] life" and with the perception that clerical work was a way to "do something practical."[128] It appears, then, that schools of commerce attracted middle-income or lower-income students, not children of the wealthy or well connected. In this sense, the Yishuv differed from other countries in the British Empire where knowledge of English and the acquisition of white-collar skills were directly correlated not only with social class, as was the case here, but also with proximity to the nationalist project in later colonial and postcolonial years.

While schooling was the most common way for some number of middle-class Jews to enter jobs in the Jewish or British bureaucracy, adults too old for the school system also availed themselves of English-study courses. In 1939, J. S. Bentwich, chief inspector for English in the Hebrew schools, received an inquiry from Allan Drinkwater, the director of the London publisher and bookseller Longmans, Green. Drinkwater, noting an increased number of orders for books oriented toward English learning for adults, asked whether there were language programs in Palestine that taught English to adult immigrants.[129] In fact, Bentwich replied, there had indeed been several efforts to teach English to adults— some within the Yishuv itself. The Jewish Agency's English Committee, in addition to its work in developing an English-language curriculum for the Zionist schools (which are discussed in chapter 5), had set up a committee to teach the language to adults and had worked with the British Council to build a central English library. But official British-Zionist partnerships represented only a small portion of adult education in English, as Bentwich acknowledged: "The bulk of adult teaching is still done by private teachers, in small groups, and is practically unorganized."[130]

This unorganized adult English teaching, because it was done by private institutions with no link to the Zionist enterprise, is undocumented in the official Zionist archives, and records of these activities are therefore difficult to come by. Nonetheless, what documents do survive indicate the existence of English courses at institutions called the Golden School of English in Tel Aviv, the Tel Aviv School of English, and Berlitz schools in Jerusalem, Haifa, and Tel Aviv.[131] English courses were also offered at Hebrew University and the Workers' Seminary in Jerusalem, the School of Law and Economics, Tel Aviv, and the Hebrew Technical Institute, Haifa.[132] An extract from a letter from C. A. F. Dundas to Lord Lloyd (secretary of state for the colonies and leader of the House of Lords) in 1941 noted: "The Jaffa Institute [referring to the British Institute in Jaffa] and the Tel Aviv School of English are both making progress. The latter is, I think, rapidly becoming a real force in the life of the town."[133]

Adults seem to have signed up for these courses out of a vague, usually unrealized desire to improve their economic situation or gain the more intangible benefit of acquiring a connection to the then-ruling power. The director of the Tel Aviv School of English, writing to a woman who had previously expressed interest in the school, wrote encouragingly: "I am aware of the difficulties at the present time, but may I suggest that study can be all-absorbing and refreshing. In a time like the present a knowledge of English is essential and may even be the factor that will decide your future."[134] Whether or not this statement was true in this woman's case, the demand for English courses exceeded supply. With the opening of a British Institute location in Tel Aviv, English seekers had a highly developed option for English courses and cultural activities. It appears from British Institute statistics from May 1943 that the largest number of students in the courses was of Polish origin (206 of the 749) and the second-largest constituency was of German origin (145). These are small numbers relative to the total population, but it should be noted that there were waiting lists at the British Institute, an indication that demand for English courses exceeded supply.[135] Correspondence between one Religious Zionist community, Kevutzat Rodges (later Yavneh) and the *Palestine Post*, the English-language newspaper in Palestine, requested that copies of newspapers be sent to be used in kibbutz English classes for adults.[136] Some number of adults, the vast majority of whom, we can assume, had little exposure to English before they came to Palestine, were finding that they wanted a bit of English knowledge regardless of their general commitment to the Hebrew project.

The British came to power before most Jews commanded Hebrew, let alone spoke it as their mother tongue, but their decision to declare Hebrew an official language of Palestine gave legitimacy to the claim, emergent during the prewar years, that Hebrew was and should be the dominant language of the Jewish community in Palestine. Organizations and individuals could press the British to uphold its language rules, citing linguistic discrimination; these sorts of campaigns are part of the heroic narrative of Hebrew revival. The real front of mandate-era language wars, however, was internal. Jews attempted to convince other Jews that they needed to make Hebrew dominant in their professional lives; if they did not, the British might subtly or overtly deny national rights to the Jews as a whole.

The outside impression of Jewish linguistic solidarity could be fairly effective. Because the British maintained a level of distance from Jews, most were aware mainly of activist Jews. British writings thus tend to support the impression of ideological fervor—including linguistic fervor—in the Zionist camp. In October 1918, soon after the British took military control of Palestine, a young officer wrote to Colonel Huggett in the Foreign Office about the Jews' tenacity about Hebrew: "If there is one point on which Jews here are fanatical, it is the language. Quiet, law-abiding, elderly citizens are able to go to prison rather than submit to a set-back of the Hebrew language."[137] Horace Samuel, a British military judge early in the period, wrote, picking up on not only the intensity but also the secularity of the pro-Hebrew movement, "The Hebrew language has not merely become a fetish, but has actually superseded Jehovah himself as an object of worship in the more advanced circles."[138] Jewish activists would by no means have wished to correct this perception; maintaining an impression of Jewish devotion to Hebrew was an important part of the Zionist demand for rights, both linguistic and more broadly national. The overall impression of the Jewish community, in both British and Jewish sources, is of a group bent on achieving ethnic autonomy and eventually sovereignty, and concerned with the British only to the extent that they could manipulate them to achieve national objectives.

Meanwhile, however, a different sort of story was unfolding. Over the course of the mandate, a growing bureaucracy granted employment to many who had the requisite language skills. In tandem, more and more organizations were founded to promote English learning. Attraction to English could be portrayed as the result of a stealth plot by the British— one writer suspected that "the rulers of the country, based on the principle of 'divide and conquer,' aspire to exploit the [linguistic] anarchy in order to impose English on the Yishuv," and accused Hebrew officers of not standing up to the British. But that same writer suggests later in his article that the fault might lie internally: "A nation like ours needs to learn the healthy and independent secret of survival [*sod ha-kiyum*] from other nations. Look at England, whose language circles the whole world."[139]

The appeal of English, though it was conditioned by a particular bureaucratic configuration, transcended the walls of translation offices or clerical bureaus. Though some lawyers used English only occasionally, others used the language with impunity and even went so far as to impersonate the British: "They travelled to England, joined the English bar and returned as barristers with a wig on their head, since this was the outward mark of difference between . . . 'native' and [British] lawyers."[140] "As in many other fields," Gabriel Strassman writes, "specific professional demands were stronger than general national demands." But a functional need for English coexisted with a far more complex relationship with the British overlords, a relationship that could include respect, admiration, and jealousy as much as simple professional duty. There were, "without a doubt, psychological impetuses to use English in the mandatory courts," Strassman writes, describing a situation of mimicry and deference typical of colonial settings: "It is not impossible that there was also habit or acceptance of the customs of the foreign ruler."[141]

A 1944 article by P. Azai (Pinhas Elad) in the newspaper *Haaretz* captures the complex dynamics of jealousy, mimicry, and interest increasingly wrapped up in the English language. Toward the end of World War II, English books had, according to the article, "made a lightning conquest of the display windows of the fancy stores." This perceived conquest was helped by the great allotment of paper given by the government for the printing of books: the 20 bookstores selling foreign books before the war had mushroomed into 180 stores by 1944, 50 in Tel Aviv alone. Whereas before the war, consumers of English books were mainly "clerks and intellectuals," those filling the roles discussed earlier in this chapter, during and after the war "the chief purchaser [was] the public and, as is clear, the Jewish public."[142] Further English penetration came through the British army, in which approximately ten thousand Palestinian Jewish soldiers served. Whereas the English soldiers' newspaper came on time every day, the Hebrew newspaper came out later on, and so those who knew English (and especially those who had only an intermediate knowledge of Hebrew) came to prefer the English news.[143]

It was ironic, thought Azai, that the market was overrun by English books and newspapers "at an hour when every voice is talking about revival, about an independent Hebrew state." Azai explained the incongruity of excessive English use, paradoxically, as a product of insufficient Westernization. The Western nation would hold fiercely to its national language, in this case, Hebrew. The Yishuv, by contrast, had been overtaken by "a Levantine desire for cheap spiritual absorption into the ruling nation," that is, a typically Eastern tendency to mix East and West in an inauthentic, culturally inferior way. This absorption, though, was by no means a passive process, the swallowing of a weak-willed people by the great maw of British cultural imperialism; it was an active process built by the individual choices of Palestine Jews, some of whom were attracted to the symbolism of English language and culture. The books purchased in the numerous bookstores of Tel Aviv, Azai pointed out, were not read only in the privacy of the home but also in public. Azai explained: "The yearning for the English book held in the hand, with the large title facing outwards so that people will see it, is not different from the yearning for a *pipe* or flinging back the collar of the shirt."[144] (In the original, the word "pipe" is transliterated in Hebrew letters.) The power of the English book was not only in its contents, banal or subversive as they were, but also in the semiotic power of the English language as a symbol.

Though the language of power was in other respects tucked away in offices, out of sight and out of mind for the majority of the Yishuv, the language was by no means neutral. Over the course of thirty years of British rule, English had emerged as not only the language of administration, but also an arbiter of social power more broadly, the linguistic gateway toward individual and collective success, even within a society deeply committed to the principle of Hebrew exclusivity. This tension persisted through 1948 and beyond.

CHAPTER FOUR

ZION IN BABEL

The Yishuv in Its Arabic-Speaking Context

Unless there is very careful steering it is upon the Arab rock that the
Zionist ship may be wrecked.
—*Herbert Samuel, British high commissioner for Palestine, to
Chaim Weizmann, 1921*

While negotiating both the proximate power of the British Empire and
the growing global power of English, Jews in Palestine found themselves
early on reflecting on another linguistic force, one that was native and
thus inextricable from the landscape: Palestine's majority Arabic-speaking
population. Recounting his 1914 visit to the new Zionist agricultural colonies of Palestine, the Yiddish writer Yehoash (Solomon Blumgarten)
called the lack of Arabic knowledge he had found among immigrant Jews
"one of the weakest points of the settlement." Arabic was a language
that Jews used to address employees, he had found, not a language of
widespread daily usage: "Colonists who have been living in Palestine for
decades know only sufficient Arabic to converse with their Arab 'Arabaji'
[wagon-driver] or their Arab help. As to writing and reading Arabic, that
is out of the question."[1] During the year of the poet's visit, the citricultur-
alist and writer Moshe Smilansky had also spoken critically of immigrant
Jews: "Over the course of thirty years we did not learn the language of

the land. In the entire Hebrew Yishuv there are not even ten people who can read and write Arabic. This fact might seem absurd to the reader; but to our disgrace, this is the reality."[2]

These statements about the lack of Arabic proficiency among Ashkenazi immigrant Zionists, expressed in the second decade of the twentieth century, reflected a concern that persisted in the mandate period as well: a concern about being linguistic outsiders in their homeland. As noted in earlier chapters, Jews in the Yishuv were concerned about the weakness of Hebrew and were sensitive about the perceived invasion of a Hebrew space by outside languages. In this case, however, the source of language difference was internal to the land and the region; in this view, the Zionist immigrants themselves were the foreign linguistic presence. Zion, the antidote to a diasporic Babel, was a Babel of its own, a place of multiple languages and speakers who did not understand one another. While those who wrote about Arabic did not fear it becoming overly dominant within the Jewish community (this fear briefly surfaced in the very earliest years of Zionist settlement but quickly subsided), they saw great peril in allowing the majority language to remain alien to them.[3]

Arabic was the linguistic substrate of Palestine, the bedrock upon which the Yishuv was built and into which it penetrated as Jews built the foundations for a Hebrew society on an Arab landscape, a process they often depicted in maps showing points of Jewish settlement on an otherwise unmapped Arab landscape. Meron Benvenisti has appropriately criticized the Zionist supersessionary move, writing that settlers' lives were conducted "inside a Jewish 'bubble' and their only contacts with the outside world were with neighboring Jewish communities, with Jews living in the city, and with the English."[4] But the divide from Arabic—as from Yiddish, German, or English—was not so clean-cut. The rhetoric of separation was real and had important and fateful implications for the development of Palestine, but separation did not entail uninterest in or ignorance of Arabic. The story of Ashkenazi Jewish encounters with Arabic, whether inadvertent or closely planned, is also the story of a deeply ambivalent process of Jews simultaneously distancing themselves from, being curious about, appropriating, and controlling a Middle Eastern space. The story of Arabic is also the story of an Arabic-speaking Jewish population, a group committed to a more conciliatory Zionism in the late Ottoman period and to using language to bridge populations, but a group mostly absent from histories of the mandate period.

This chapter maps four discrete but interlinked ways and settings in which some Jews encountered, sought out, or deployed Arabic: Jewish contact with Arabic in the region of Tel Aviv, a Jewish city that had separated itself from the mixed city of Jaffa but remained enmeshed in quotidian encounters with that region's populations; community Arabic courses offered to—and requested by—kibbutz dwellers and other agricultural communities in rural regions of the country; Zionist Arabic-language newspapers intended to shape Arab public opinion; and intelligence and military operations that gathered information about communal goings-on through the use of Jews—often Middle Eastern Jews—who knew Arabic. These activities were diverse with respect to their contexts and aims, and took place in often-unrelated social spheres. What they share, however, is a collective sense of Palestine as an Arabic-speaking space, the recognition that Hebrew would not be dominant in all of Palestine, and an awareness that, despite desires to the contrary, Zionist Jews were not the majority population in the land they were settling.

Increasing physical and institutional separation under the British mandate did not make Arabic disappear from Jewish consciousness. Rather, it shifted what Smilansky had called "the language of the land" into particular social spheres that became objects of continual Jewish reflection. As Gil Eyal has pointed out, intercommunal distance—and the violence that accompanied and further compelled it—resulted in the cultivation of cadres of orientalists and Arabists whose cachet lay in their stores of expertise. These experts served as the kernel of the Israeli intelligence and Arab affairs services after the establishment of the State of Israel in 1948.[5] Nonetheless, emphasis only on those who mastered Arabic or deployed it professionally excludes the story of a larger subset of Jewish society that, even as opportunities for Jewish-Arab contact waned, continued to seek a modicum of proficiency in Arabic, found meaning in token or symbolic contacts, or supported Arabic-language activities for others even without knowledge of Arabic themselves.

This book has contended, first, that the Yishuv's diverse language encounters required a complex set of accommodations and negotiations and, second, that these encounters could be symbolically important even for those without knowledge of the languages in question. The significance of Arabic, too, lay not only in the research activities taken up by experts and scholars; partial competence or theoretical desires for competence were meaningful in a society deeply aware of the stakes of multilingualism and concerned with an inability to cope with the original inhabitants of the land. In this case, any such contacts, even unilateral, could give Jews who were idealistic about convincing Arabs of the legitimacy of Zionism a basis for believing that the Jewish-Arabic conflict could be resolved, whether through personal contact, propaganda, or espionage.

Knowledge of Arabic, as conceived by those who reflected on the subject, encompassed two sets of skills: colloquial competency, and reading and writing skills. Depending on context, both could be sources of consternation or points for comment. As the Zionist program of market separation and "Hebrew labor" proceeded apace (a trend discussed in chapter 2) and as increasing European immigration shifted the demographic and political balance of the Yishuv toward its Ashkenazi elements, both forms of Arabic knowledge became increasingly rare. Many Zionists found themselves facing consternation over a linguistic situation that they themselves had engineered. With time, "the Sabra was cut off from Arab culture not only spiritually and intellectually but also physically."[6] The lack of a common language was this reality's most accessible symbol.

Memories of Contact

The trajectory of development in Palestine was not in the direction of shared lives between Jews and Arabs, whether in the urban core of Tel Aviv–Jaffa or in the agricultural communities, but some contacts persisted. Mark LeVine and Zachary Lockman have discussed institutional attempts at establishing contact between these populations, particularly their laborers.[7] These contrived contacts were organized alongside more spontaneous, day-to-day encounters that were not systematically documented. Frequent conflicts and outbreaks of violence from the 1920s onward meant that neither community was inclined to emphasize instances of cooperation or good relations, in part out of the knowledge that there could be retaliation against Arab collaborators.[8] In official protocols, moreover, mentions of language contact are strikingly absent: Arabs, even when mentioned, are relevant as working bodies, instigators of violence, or figures who might displace Jewish labor, but are rarely presented as named individuals.[9] Jewish-Arab relations—and the role of Arabic in these contacts—have thus been obscured by the historical record.

Jewish communities in Jaffa during the late Ottoman period "mixed with the local residents and spoke their language" and solved intercommunal tensions by using traditional methods of arbitration (*sulh*), religious courts, and Ottoman state courts.[10] But urban distancing brought a linguistic split. When the Ahuzat Bayit society was founded in 1906 to investigate the possibility of creating a Jewish suburb of the ancient port city of Jaffa, it envisaged settling Jewish immigrants in a new nationalist society where a Hebrew culture could be cultivated away from Arabs. Separation, not integration, was the recommended path toward a safe, hygienic, modern, prosperous, and fundamentally Hebrew community, in both linguistic and nonlinguistic senses.[11]

Nonetheless, the principle of physical separation, significant as a conduit to labor separation, did not occlude all contact, though it is important to note that many of these contacts, like conversations between Jewish settlers and their "Arabaji," or wagon driver, were strongly hierarchical, unequal encounters. Starting from the choice of Ahuzat Bayit members to hire Arab laborers to build their homes, Tel Aviv saw a persistent flow of Arab laborers: "Palestinian Arabs could not be kept out of Tel Aviv, but at best only regulated."[12] Much of the texture of these encounters is recoverable only in retrospect, through oral histories that are likely to be deeply tinged by nostalgia and conjecture. Nonetheless, if we forgo a concern with the legitimacy of claims to Arabic "fluency" and presume that memories of Arabic knowledge reflect at least a minimal familiarity with the language, we can learn quite a bit about the dynamics of encounters involving Arabic between children, men, and women and the simultaneous curiosity, revulsion, and distancing that overshadowed the more organized engagement with Arabic in formal or institutional settings.[13]

Some of these language contacts, residents recalled in oral interviews, occurred between children, whose tendency toward play and whose less developed sense of social barriers enabled them to converse with less stigma than adults did. Rivka Rabinovitz, who grew up in Tel Aviv in a Viennese Jewish family, recalls having Arab friends, the children of household helpers or laundresses, who came by their home on Herzl Street. Economic contacts, of the sort discussed in chapter 2, led to subsidiary language contacts: "I spoke fluent Arabic," she said. When asked by her interviewer whether the knowledge might have come from school, she confirmed that she learned French rather than Arabic in school and therefore learned Arabic entirely from these acquaintances.[14] Zvi Elpeleg, born in Poland in 1926, lived in an area of Tel Aviv where Bedouins also lived (now the Florentine neighborhood) and recalled: "There simply wasn't anyone to talk with other than children whose language was Arabic. And I began to speak Arabic then."[15] Though Tel Aviv over time expanded into and overtook the villages of Salama, Shaykh Muwnnis, Jammasin al-Gharbi, and Summayl, located at the edges of the original settlement, these boundaries were not hermetic. Through much of the prestate period, quotidian contacts, though never encouraged, persisted.

What sort of judgments did Jewish children form as a result of these happenstance encounters? A repeated trope in the memoirs and oral histories, as in the rhetoric of the Labor Zionist camp, is a divide between friendly and unfriendly Arabs, coupled with a sense that personal relations could persist despite the corrosive presence of anti-Jewish violence, apparently perpetrated by unseen, malicious Arabs.[16] Tzipora Brenner, born in 1917 and around six years old when her family immigrated from Kovno (Kaunas, Lithuania), made such a distinction: "[Arabs] would bring fresh eggs and excellent vegetables . . . On the other hand, they also stole things from us. During the day they were friendly. Apparently. Maybe not the same Arabs."[17] Perceptions of congeniality could coexist not only with bad feelings but also with perceptions of murderous violence occurring in the community. Asher Asher (same first and last name), who emigrated from Bulgaria at age two in 1921, recalled: "We played in the orchard with everyone. There were excellent relations. I tell you, we didn't even lock the door."[18] But these good relations were local, not general. His father had sold his property in Jaffa and moved to Tel Aviv, Asher said, because of fear of what he called "*itbah al-Yahud*" (a Hebrew corruption of the Arabic phrase meaning "slaughter the Jews!")—in other words, murderous Arab threats.[19]

In this dynamic, individual friendly Arabs were seen as instrumental in protecting Jews from their murderous Arab counterparts, often through forms of personal communication and the helpful, almost subservient issuing of warnings to Jews. Shoshana Kirstein, from Rovno (Rivne, Ukraine), recalls that one time in 1929, the year of a wave of anti-Zionist violence particularly focused in Jerusalem and Hebron, her father went to Jaffa to buy vegetables and was approached by an Arab acquaintance named Ibrahim. "Musa, Musa," Ibrahim said, speaking to him using the Arabic version of his Hebrew name, Moshe—a deferential practice to which Yehoash also attested in the colony of Rehovot—"They are going to do something over there. Run home to your wife and kids and don't come anymore."[20] Ibrahim also once offered to walk Shoshana home: "I wanted to walk," she recalled, "and he offered to walk with me, behind, [he said,] so they won't think you are walking with an Arab." "We had good relations with the Arabs," she concluded after recalling this exchange. In both cases, a claim of Arabic knowledge was an important part of the story, the final evidence that these relations were legitimate and fruitful. After recalling that Ibrahim called her father "Musa," Kirstein noted of her father, "He already understood a little Arabic." In recounting the story of being escorted home, she says about herself as well, "I already spoke a little Arabic."[21] The veracity of these claims is not at issue; they may well have been false. What is telling here is the constructed impression that language enabled and reflected a type of positive Jewish-Arab encounter that left the Jew in a position of safety and control, but that was both atypical and fleeting.

Zimra Livneh's story about Arabic and language contacts between women, also conveyed in an interview, demonstrates the complex multilingual setting where language contacts occurred. The story involves Livneh's mother's attempts to learn Arabic in an act of solidarity with an Arab woman. Her mother, who came from an assimilated Russian-Jewish family, developed a friendship with this woman, who came by to deliver fruit. The friendship developed when, one day, the mother walked in to find the Arab woman being beaten by her husband. She took the stick away from the husband and yelled, in Russian, "*Nyet, nyet, nyet, nyet.*"

> This is how the friendship developed. My mother would come every day and would teach this Safa—her name was Safa and the children were runny-nosed with pus, trachoma, what have you. She would teach them

how to wash, how to dress. She sewed them undershirts and underwear from white cloth and would write in Russian every word in Arabic. For example, if they said to her *"tafadal"*—please—then she would write *"tafadal"* in Russian and after that would write please in Russian so she would know what it was. She learned enough this way that she could, more or less, manage to get along with them.[22]

This is a rich story of language learning. Zimra's mother was explicitly engaged in a civilizing mission toward the local fruit seller: she declared that her mission was to save the woman from her violent husband, himself a symbol of Arab tyranny, and save the entire family from their sickness and squalor through simple changes in clothing and hygiene.[23] Safa—a common Arabic name meaning "purity," but also, coincidentally, the word for "language" in Hebrew—became the purveyor of language; the Arab woman provided the Jewish woman the verbal tools necessary for the Jewish woman to "save" or "heal" the Arab and to secure her own status as the beneficent provider. Without language, the story implies, these civilizing activities would not have been possible.

Hebrew, interestingly enough, does not figure in this story. The exchange was thus not an encounter between Hebrew and Arabic, the prototypical Jewish-Arab linguistic encounter in a land where nationalism was marked in language by both communal preference and British linguistic policy. Rather, it was an encounter between Arabic and Russian. In this case, Russian was the language of health and civilization, and Arabic was correlated with sickness. But Russian did not represent the dominant language. When Livneh's father moved into an empty Arab house on the edge of the Nordiya neighborhood—now the site of the Dizengoff Center mall—these civilized Russians found themselves in a geographic and linguistic wilderness: "There was wasteland around us. You have to understand, no one could describe this wasteland. Wasteland with sand and the howling of jackals and everything connected to that. We were thrown in there. We didn't know Hebrew. We didn't know Arabic. Yiddish we knew only a little of because we were a quite assimilated family in Russia, that is, my parents."[24] The moment of intimacy between Arab and Russian women was not a simple microcosm of Zionist-Palestinian relations, the meeting of Hebrew and Arabic, or the

encounter of Zionism with the Arab. The Jew in question was an alien-
ated woman who felt herself detached as much from the Jewish linguistic
community as from Arabic. Her civilizing instinct was classically
European, but it was not in this case tied to the Hebrew cultural program
of Zionism; if anything, the island of civilization she attempted to create
in the Arab fruit seller's house was an island of European order in a sea
of Jewish disorder as much as a Jewish island in an Arab sea. Arabic was
both a means to a classic civilizing end and a path toward belonging for a
family whose excess of civilization—as they understood it—rendered
them alien in the local landscape, Jewish and Arab.

These encounters were haphazard, and the language gains supposedly
made were not lasting—those who claimed to know Arabic in the 1920s
and 1930s inevitably no longer knew the language when they were interviewed six or seven decades later. Two other caveats are necessary as well.
First, boundaries between communities were strictly maintained. Rivka
Rabinovitz recalled a family across the street from hers "that thought of
itself as aristocratic" but grossly transgressed social norms: "One daughter married an Englishman, another married an Arab." This was not
widely accepted behavior: "In practice everyone excommunicated
them."[25] Second, these are demonstrably not stories of equals. Every one
of them has a hierarchical element: the Jew condescends to use Arabic as
part of a civilizing mission, or the Jew is clearly the "more civilized" of
the pair, as in the case of the Arab man walking behind the young Jewish
girl. But in noting these limitations, we begin to see, through these personal accounts, the perceived (though limited) importance of Arabic
despite and alongside a more official discourse of communal separation.

Community Arabic Courses

Narratives of happenstance urban encounters with Arabic were part
and parcel of a Jewish discourse of distance between Jaffa and Tel Aviv.
As presented in interviews and memoirs, they seem to be historical curi-
osities whose tellers are not sure how they fit into a history more concerned with intra-Jewish cultural developments, on the one hand, and
direct conflict with Palestinian Arabs on the other. However, they coexist
with and provide the backdrop for more concerted efforts on the part of

the Zionist establishment to bring Arabic knowledge to Jewish communities and then to redeploy this knowledge to persuade Arabs of the legitimacy of Zionism and improve relations between Jewish settlements and neighboring Arab villages.

Yosef Eliyahu Chelouche, a leader of the Sephardi Jewish community who was born in Jaffa to Algerian parents, wrote in his memoirs, "The bitter truth must be told: many of those who came from abroad to build our enterprise did not understand the vital importance of good neighborly relations." Lack of contact served to reinforce existing Jewish stereotypes of Arabs as backward, uncivilized, and cunning. Chelouche was correct to note that Zionist immigration and settlement activity were directly or indirectly conducted at the expense of the Palestinian Arab community: "Every act that was part of the process of nation building, especially the purchase of land, the founding of settlements, and the very act of immigrations, was not only a political act, but one directed against the Arab Palestinian community, which is how the Arab side perceived them. This concern was common among the Sephardi Jewish community at the turn of century."[26] But Chelouche was wrong to suppose that European Jewish elements of the Yishuv, so often tone-deaf to Palestinian Arab concerns about Zionism, ceased to be aware of the importance of intercommunal relations. Indeed, even as relations became increasingly strained and violent, segments of the Jewish community persisted in their often naïve reflections upon precisely such relations (or their absence). Increasing numbers of Zionists, according to a 1946 article from the newspaper *Ha-Boker*, were recognizing "that knowledge of the language of our neighbors is a fundamental obligation and that shared lives will not be possible in this land and in the vicinity without a common language."[27] Arabic seemed to be a bridging device over a chasm that perhaps could not be bridged.

Yehoash observed in his visits to the Ashkenazi colonies that "more than any other thing, [the colonists] discussed the problem of neutralizing the anti-Jewish agitation being carried on by the Arab newspapers and, especially, informing Jewish colonists as to what their Arab neighbors were thinking and saying about them."[28] This two-pronged approach—which could be framed in reverse as learning to read Arabic and using the language in propaganda newspapers—became the overall strategy of the Jewish Yishuv. Such activities were significant, it should be noted, not because either part of this equation was successful, but because the act of language learning and deployment served as a proxy for understanding and managing what could neither be satisfactorily understood nor wholly managed.

In a climate of overall opposition to foreign-language study—explored in chapter 5—Arabic courses were somewhat welcome. As Nirit Reichel points out, those elements of the Jewish population most opposed to (European) language study in general were some of the staunchest supporters of Arabic study, though not of the establishment of true Hebrew-Arabic bilingualism.[29] The British report to the Permanent Mandates Commission in 1926 noted that in addition to Arabic courses in Jewish high schools, some cities had arranged evening courses in Arabic—though it noted that Arabs were not making parallel efforts with Hebrew.[30] Particular local interest in Arabic emerged, according to a 1938 letter to the Jewish Agency, in response to the 1929 Arab riots in Hebron and Jerusalem and grew further in the wake of the Arab Revolt of 1936–39.[31]

One key player in this organized push for Arabic literacy was the Jewish Agency, formed to engage in negotiations with the mandatory government and intended as a vehicle for seeking international support, particularly financial, for the settlement project.[32] It took a more organized role beginning in the late 1930s, when it began to field a large number of local requests for Arabic courses. Though many of the Jewish Agency's activities were regional or international in scope—in the late 1940s, its Political Department became engaged in diplomacy with Egypt and Trans-Jordan—in a number of instances the department became involved in local affairs.[33] The major proponents of Arabic instruction within the Jewish Agency were Moshe Shertok (later, Sharett), the director of the Political Department between 1933 and 1948, and Eliyahu Sasson, the specialist for Arab affairs in the department (and a native of Syria). Sasson and Shertok became known by educators for their commitment to resolving Jewish-Arab conflict through Arabic-language knowledge.[34] "It is known from experience," wrote Sasson, "that lack of knowledge of Arabic among the new settlers is not only not conducive to forming honest neighborly relations to the minimum degree necessary, but it is certainly likely to cause needless clashes between the Hebrew settlements and the Arab villages alongside them."[35] Cognizant of the perils of mis- and noncommunication, the Arab Division of the Political Department elected to send ten Arabic teachers to offer courses for Jewish community leaders (referred to by the Arabic term *mukhtar*) at twenty-five locations. Over the course of the 1940s, they added more teachers and programs.

Members of the department stressed the importance of rigor in these courses. Michael Assaf (Osofsky), an editor of the Arabic-language propaganda paper *Haqiqat al-Amr* (discussed later in this chapter), lamented the trend of adults "beginning but not continuing" Arabic study and stressed that the motto of "quality not quantity" should motivate the efforts of the Jewish Agency.[36] Sasson commented that though all Jews might come into contact with Arabs, many were "unable to learn foreign languages and Arabic in particular." Courses, therefore, should be intensive and limited to a small group of students.[37] These objectives were reflected in the composition of Jewish Agency–sponsored courses in the 1940s. In a report back to the Political Department, a teacher described a program consisting of ten hours of study daily, with additional opportunities for informal speaking in the evenings.[38]

A focus merely on this top-down implementation, however, obscures the dialogic development of Arabic programs in rural locales. The Political Department promoted Arabic not only because some of its leaders deemed this activity important but also because communities had been requesting assistance from this central body for some time. The teacher Menachem Na'or, for example, wrote a beseeching letter in 1935 recounting how he had been trying for over a year to publish an Arabic textbook, without success. Perhaps Shertok could expedite this process: "Who knows the importance of understanding with Arabs more than you, the director of political work?"[39]

Community leaders also called upon the Jewish Agency to lend financial and logistical support for Arabic courses. The archives of the agency contain hundreds of letters directed to Miriam Glickson at the Arab Department, requesting Arabic teachers in cities, towns, and kibbutzim.[40] These records contain correspondence mainly from 1937 to 1948.[41] Letters most often requested financial support or Arabic teachers. A 1944 letter from Kibbutz Gan Shlomo, for example, reads: "We are turning to

you to please help us organize courses in our kibbutz in Arabic. Our location is surrounded by Arab villages and in the field of Arabic knowledge
we are very behind."[42] A similar letter from Giv'at Brenner concludes,
"The demand for knowing this language is great and the need is felt. We
will await your positive reply."[43]

The Jewish Agency received two main types of correspondence regarding Arabic study: reports of ventures toward personal contact and evidence of attempts to impart to Jews systematic knowledge of Arabs, often
with no personal contact implied. Reports of personal visits between
Jewish settlements and Arab villages, categorized in the archives as
"Activities for Cultivating Neighborly Relations," tell the stories of encounters that tended to be represented as strikingly idyllic. A report from
a Jewish trip to the northern Arab village of al-Dawwara (in the Safed
district) commented that a kibbutz group shared its newest produce—
tomatoes, peanuts, and sunflowers—with its hosts and received sacks of
grapefruit in return. In this romanticized scene, reminiscent (perhaps
ominously) of the first American Thanksgiving, all discussed their hope
that the coming year would "bring peace that would relieve all of hu-
manity" and that all would merit "good neighborly relations."[44] Trading
produce and engaging in pleasantries with Arabs certainly did not
require comprehensive historical and political knowledge of the Arab
world. The desire for personal knowledge seems to have emerged from
and contributed to the sense that people could transcend political conflict
precisely by leaving the academic sphere and engaging in dialogue.

Organizations affiliated with the Labor Zionist movement, Mapai (the
consolidated labor party), and the Histadrut were particularly active in
cultivating personal relationships with Arabs by planning and supporting
colloquial Arabic courses. Proposals for conversational Arabic courses as
late as the 1940s reflect a faith that personal contact could solve political
problems. In 1944, Y. Y. Kurstein began a series of mail-order courses for
members of Mapai. According to an introductory letter, one lesson
would be sent each week, to be completed and returned by mail to the
party's headquarters. There it would be corrected for mistakes and returned together with the next week's lesson. The lessons in colloquial
Arabic were printed in Hebrew transliteration. The first installment
taught the phrase *Kif halak* ("How are you?") and asked students to trans-

late a fictional exchange between the Jewish Drori, "a kibbutz member," and the Arab Abu Diyab, "a grocer."[45] These lessons were intended to teach the student, it seems, how to have regular, quotidian contact with Arabs, including shared commerce and communal visits.

A series of Mapai documents from early 1948 indicate that this romanticized vision of contact persisted until the establishment of the state, even as a civil war was under way in Palestine. Zvi Rosenstein (Even-Shoshan), a member of Mapai's Education Committee, stated early that year that Arabic would be important not only because Jews had been forced into contact with Arabs, but also because "we strive for mutual understanding" and "we want perhaps to educate our coming generations, by means of the language, not in hate, but rather in a relationship of respect so that they won't view the Arab child contemptuously."[46] Another member of the committee, Aryeh Yaffe, called himself a "big Arabophile," claiming that his knowledge of Arabs "from daily life" made him optimistic about the possibility of coexistence. He exhorted the group: "Let's not create a ghetto. And let's not erect barriers, because if we do, it will be the greatest crime and political suicide."[47]

Personal contact, according to this approach, could be a potent political tool even when its promoters doubted the potential for positive relations. At an assembly of Mapai members in 1943, a member named Y. Burstein noted that there was no single body, either in the Yishuv or among Arabs, authorized to conduct negotiations. In consequence, he said, "our policy towards the Arabs cannot be done like in other countries." Rather, "our politics in the Arab field is *personal politics* . . . Relations with Arabs determine the solution to the problem." Such a stance required unity among members of the party: "Every member is required to take interest in this problem as in the rest of the party's questions."[48] Both Yaffe and Burstein articulated the premise shared by other advocates of a personal approach to Arabic study: long-term coexistence was possible and could be accomplished by building goodwill through language study.

The binationalist Ha-Shomer Ha-Tza'ir movement had a particularly strong commitment to the study of colloquial Arabic and local Arab society; it discussed the value of Arabic education more than any other Labor Zionist group.[49] A writer in the newspaper of Kibbutz Kfar Masaryk, affiliated with the movement, lamented in 1936, "We have not even begun to learn the ABCs of approaching Arabs."[50] One year later, a columnist from Kibbutz Mishmar Ha-'Emek rebuked his fellows for their unwillingness to learn more than the minimum amount of Arabic necessary to address Arab workers in the fields.[51] Newspapers associated with Ha-Shomer Ha-Tza'ir were known to publish "Arabic corners," with phrases and dialogues in Arabic, often written in both Arabic script and Hebrew transliteration. One such feature from 27 January 1933 was oriented toward facilitating social gatherings between Jews and Arabs: it instructed readers in how to invite guests to their homes for a party. Perhaps in the spirit of respect, or with the intent that these words would be used in a print invitation, the expressions are in formal Arabic rather than the Palestinian dialect. Alongside this feature, a dialogue in colloquial Arabic and transliterated into Hebrew letters modeled a general exchange of pleasantries (*Ta'al, khallina nat'haddath qalil. Tayeb, shu fi jadid?*—Let's talk a bit. Good. What's new?).[52] The cultural committee of Kibbutz Kfar Masaryk reported in May 1936 on the inception of an Arabic-language course and anticipated that the demand would be so great that the class would be split into two sections.[53] These grand expectations were not to be fulfilled, however, because of limited funding and students' apparent lack of perseverance. In September the committee reported that the number of students in the course had dwindled to between ten and twelve and that funding for the class would run out unless the kibbutz waged significant fund-raising efforts.[54]

Ongoing efforts to teach Arabic within Ha-Shomer Ha-Tza'ir got a more formal, institutional structure in the last decade of the mandate period. When the first murmurs of partition were heard in the Labor establishment following the Arab revolt and, in particular, with the 1942 Biltmore Program, Ha-Shomer Ha-Tza'ir was put on the defensive; it felt itself hard-pressed to affirm the viability of its binationalist scheme in the face of a clear trend in favor of partition. In light of these challenges, a group of Arabists within Ha-Shomer Ha-Tza'ir gathered in 1940 to found the Department of Arab Activities. The leaders of the department were the Germans Eliezer Be'eri (formerly Ernst Bauer) and Josef Waschitz, the Romanian-born Aharon Cohen, and the Warsaw-born Mordechai Bentov (formerly Gutgeld).[55] Together, they strove to create a base of language knowledge necessary if Jews were to seek out Arab partners and organize the Arab community. As its first act, a group of six kibbutz members were chosen to receive instruction in elementary Arabic and learn about "the problems that are involved in Arab activity in the Land of Israel." A total of nine hundred work days were allotted for this purpose.[56]

As part of his work establishing the Department of Arab Activities, Be'eri advocated for basic courses in spoken Arabic, just as other kibbutz members had. In a request to Sasson at the Jewish Agency, Be'eri wrote that he had visited two Ha-Shomer Ha-Tza'ir kibbutzim and had learned that there was an "urgent need" for an Arabic teacher. Kibbutz Gat's situation was particularly critical, since it was "surrounded by many Arab villages and it is far from places of Jewish settlement." In this situation of geographic and linguistic isolation, Arabic was essential in particular to the head of the kibbutz, who had so devoted himself to learning the language that he had "even succeeded in creating an atmosphere of sympathy among its neighbors," though he needed a teacher in order to progress further. Awareness of the need for Arabic was widespread among kibbutz members there, Be'eri wrote, since they "frequently come into contact with Arabs—on the roads, in the fields, on guard duty, etc., and they need to know a little Arabic."[57] The wording of Be'eri's request on behalf of the kibbutzim indicates different reasons for knowing Arabic among different people: greater proficiency on the part of those who served as more formal liaisons; more limited, instrumental skills for those whose contact with Arabs, though frequent, was more basic.

The call for Arabic knowledge was a protective response to a feeling of being both isolated, as they saw it, and surrounded by Arab neighbors, the letter implies. The Jewish settlements of Gat and Negba, in the southern plain between the Judean Hills and the coastal city of Ashkelon, were flanked by Arab villages, but since the centers of Jewish population were some distance away, their situation was perceived as one of abandonment. Be'eri's letter implies positive relations and quotidian contacts "on the roads, in the fields," but language is presented here not only as a means to integrate with these neighbors and passersby but rather as a way of neutralizing their threat and turning self-imposed Jewish isolation from a dangerous state to a safe one.

The Department of Arab Activities of Ha-Shomer Ha-Tza'ir sought to improve these contacts by conducting a six-month seminar in the Druze village of Ussefiya (Isfiya in colloquial Arabic), in the Haifa district.[58] In a letter to the participants, Be'eri announced the details of the seminar, which began on 17 June 1941 and was taught by a Christian Arab from Haifa. The announcement gives the impression that the course was a curious cross between a camping trip and a research expedition. Each participant was required to bring bedding, clothing, a plate and utensils, paper, and writing instruments as well as Arabic textbooks and dictionaries. An electric pocket flashlight was also recommended.[59]

The letter creates a striking portrait of a haphazard group of idealistic men, armed with notebooks, descending on a Druze village. A series of photographs chronicle the experience of the group: ascending to Ussefiya by foot in their button-down shirts and rucksacks, meeting with Arabs over coffee and food, engaging in the study of Arabic texts, and mingling in outdoor spaces with men in Arab headdresses. Such undertakings constructed the imagery of Jewish-Arab contact and interpersonal exchange. Photographs taken at the Ussefiya seminar reflect a clear sense of idealism on the part of the department and its belief that personal contact, enabled by systematic knowledge of the Arabic language and Arab society, would ultimately avert conflict. For the participants—young, idealistic, and still believing that labor cooperation between the two populations would bring about peaceful relations—this camping trip–cum–Arabic lesson was an adventure of discovery and mastery.

While related communications to the Jewish Agency implied that natural contact had waned and that the ability to converse freely needed to be revived through programs such as the one described above, requests for more systematic, text-based courses presumed, as both Yehoash and Smilansky had, that the absence of reading and writing skills was the main issue for Jews. The goals of these sorts of courses went beyond language acquisition for practical ends and also focused on understanding Arab society, culture, and history. Beginning in 1940, the Reuven Mass publishing house in Jerusalem released a booklet of excerpts from Arab newspapers, compiled by Shlomo Dov Goitein, Israel Ben-Ze'ev, and Moshe Brill, all of whom had been active in Arabic promotion in other contexts. The publisher suggested that the resource might be of interest to schools and communities. The introduction to the first issue of the series, a sample of which was sent to the Jewish Agency, stated its intention to teach the form of

Photos from the Ha-Shomer Ha-Tza'ir Arabic seminar in Ussefiya 1941.
Courtesy of Ruti Herman, Kibbutz Hazorea.

Arabic used in newspapers so as to provide access to the social, economic,
and cultural life of the Near East. The contents reflected an expansive
and ambitious curriculum, including articles on Arab folkways, local and
regional news, and religious practice.[60] The justification for these textually

oriented courses came from the recognition of increasing distance between the Jewish and Arab populations of Palestine. Miriam Glickson summarized this tension between organic contact and systematic knowledge in a memorandum to Moshe Shertok about a conference of Arabic teachers convened by the Arab Department of the Jewish Agency in August 1942:

> Today there is a lack of direct contact between Jews and Arabs such as existed in the first settlements. Then there were Arabs in every house and community and every resident knew how to conduct a conversation with them. But today the settlements are separate, most of their residents don't know Arabic at all and the work of spreading the language is only beginning. On the other hand, thanks to systematic study, an important thing that was lacking in the early settlements, we imparted to some of the residents an elementary knowledge of the literary language, of the Arab question, and of Arab folkways.[61]

The exigencies of settlement, her thinking went, had drawn Jews away from the natural interchange with Arabs that had existed in a mythologized earlier period, but the introduction of methodical study could build a different kind of knowledge about Palestinian Arabs based on a knowledge of facts rather than of people.

Such methods had a central place in left-leaning circles as well, the same circles so explicit about the importance of human contact. While Be'eri was promoting practical language courses, he was also concerned to build a more regimented program of historical and cultural studies, based on the methods he had learned while a student at the University of Berlin between 1932 and 1935.[62] He wrote in 1940 that each teacher of the Arab Department's language courses "needs to have a comprehensive knowledge and scientific education [haskalah] and also didactic experience and ability," a formulation that implied that only a European-trained orientalist would be suited for the job.[63] At different points throughout the 1940s, Be'eri laid out intensive curricula for the study of the Arab world. A twenty-part curriculum of May 1946, for example, covered classical Arab history and geography, anthropology, and politics; the final sessions discussed the development of Zionist thought on the Arab question and considered "how to achieve a bi-national solution."[64] This broad-ranging study needed to be grounded in scholarship, Be'eri thought. In his 1944

Bibliographic Anthology, he laid out European sources for the study of the Orient.[65]

Be'eri claimed to be uncomfortable with adopting European methods wholesale. "It is necessary to root out the Romantic attitude," he wrote, which sees the Arabs as "the heroes of *One Thousand and One Nights* and tends to idealize all the phenomena of their life."[66] In the preface to his *Anthology*, he emphasized that the purpose of the compilation is "useful and not scientific," a seeming rejection of the wholesale focus on "scientific" learning characteristic of the School of Oriental Studies in Jerusalem, a bastion of classical orientalist philology. Yet Be'eri was clearly enamored of European models of systematic study. While offering an apology for including so many non-Hebrew books, he wrote, "Nevertheless there is a large portion of foreign-language books, English in particular. And this, necessarily, because the British not only have command of the Middle East, they have also written the best books about it, in particular about its history and problems in the modern period."[67]

Arabic study was a means of responding to a feeling of Jewish isolation within an Arabic linguistic space, a sentiment expressed clearly in Be'eri's letter about Gat and Negba. Less clear was whether the accompanying courses should require engagement with Arabic speakers. This tension was visible in a February 1940 meeting of Yishuv representatives who gathered to discuss Arabic courses in the communities. In a memorandum following the meeting, Eliyahu Sasson reported that certain delegates had called upon the others to go beyond language courses and "meet with the Arab shepherd and farmer in all walks of life." But this suggestion touched an ideological sore spot. If this more personalized approach to Arabic were approved, Sasson thought, the information headquarters (*lishkat ha-hasbara*), which was responsible for propaganda materials, should be asked to make this known to the public in a sensitive way so as not to create the impression that this suggestion was made by Ha-Shomer Ha-Tza'ir or the League for Rapprochement and Cooperation (a socialist organization founded by members of Ha-Shomer Ha-Tza'ir and headed by Hayim Kalvarisky).[68] In other words, the Zionist consensus as it stood in the late 1930s and early 1940s definitively excluded those approaches to Arabic that would entail too close an interaction between the populations. Language, perhaps paradoxically, did not need to be about human contact. It could be oriented as much toward persuasion and management at arm's length.

Arabic for Propaganda

Learning Arabic was, on the one hand, an inwardly focused project to help Jews—many of them not especially engaged with Arabs— understand a population that appeared foreign and threatening. These efforts, however, were closely interwoven with more deliberate attempts to exploit Arabic knowledge in order to communicate Zionist positions to Arabs. Newspapers in the modern era, as Benedict Anderson points out, were tools for disseminating national ideas and cultivating national con- sciousness in populations of like-tongued, even if not like-minded, indi- viduals. Many were deployed within groups sharing a language by governments concerned that their citizens were not properly ideologically oriented. But as the European powers came to realize, media and communications not only were available for internal communications but were powerful means of reaching foreign populations as well. Propaganda efforts (alternatively known as information warfare, "win- ning the hearts and minds," or, in the British context, "publicity") were typically imperial projects, employed by empires sensing that their power might be in decline.[69] These projects nearly always involved translation and information gathering within populations they did not understand.[70] The Zionist propaganda effort, on a much smaller scale and without a state apparatus, occurred in a similar context.

Those publications produced for colonial subjects or ethnic minorities sought to shape beliefs and behavior through content intended to be attractive to the target public.[71] In 1943, the British produced a newspaper called *Heshima* (Respect) for the thirty-five thousand East African soldiers (*askari*) they had deployed in Ceylon. Published in Swahili, the lingua franca of East Africa, and Chinyanja, spoken in Zambia, Malawi, and Mozambique, *Heshima* "was part of a major propaganda concept" that aimed to shape relations between soldiers and their officers and to main- tain discipline while providing information on the movements of Allied forces. Through articles structured to be of interest to the soldiers, "minds were disciplined for times of war and peace."[72] Information delivery, as understood by the British and believed by Zionists, was not a one-time transfer of key information but a step toward the cultivation of a new kind of mind with radically transformed political attitudes.

Propaganda efforts were a mainstay of the Zionist movement from its early years. In the late Ottoman period, such efforts were dominated by Sephardi intellectuals, who, because of their proficiency in Arabic, could be involved in crafting persuasive texts without the aid of non-Jewish Arab middlemen.[73] In claiming a lack of Arabic knowledge among Jews, both Yehoash and Smilansky were focused on new Ashkenazi settlements and overlooked those North African, Yemeni, and native Palestinian Jews who spoke Arabic as a primary language, as well as those members of the pre-Zionist Ashkenazi community who often knew some Arabic and incorporated its words into their spoken Yiddish.[74] These populations, prominent in the late Ottoman period, had become increasingly over-shadowed by linguistic foreigners in the overall narrative of Zionism, but nonetheless played a key role in the Yishuv's deployment of Arabic.[75] As Abigail Jacobson argues, during a period when Ashkenazi Zionists were debating the merits of separating the Arab labor market from the Jewish labor market, key Sephardi leaders focused on cultivating positive relationships with Palestinian Arabs in order to convince them of the merits of Zionism.[76] According to testimony by Abraham Elmaliah (rendered as El-Maleh in Arabic), editor of the Sephardi Jewish newspaper *Ha-Herut*, these efforts emerged out of desire to counter the defamation of Jews in Arabic newspapers. Overall, he and his collaborators felt, the Arab press was portraying the Zionist movement as "a kind of monster that had come to banish all the Arabs from the country, to take their land, etc." The goal of the propaganda effort was to demonstrate that this was not the case, that the movement would "bring a lot of good to the land."[77]

So emerged Hevrat Magen (Society for Protection), founded in Jaffa by Elmaliah and David and Esther Moyal, which tasked itself with explaining the interests of the Jews of Palestine to the Arab world on the pages of the Arab press, and emphasizing that the Zionist program was not opposed to the interests of the Arabs and, moreover, would benefit them.[78] Yosef Chelouche, who was married at the age of seventeen to a daughter of the Moyal family, expressed his participation in Hevrat

Magen as follows: "We, some of the natives of the country who knew Arabic, who were reading these provocations in the Arabic press on a daily basis," decided to get together and do something about it.[79] Elmaliah, the editor of *Ha-Herut*, noted in an interview later the unique abilities of Sephardim in this regard: "I have to tell the truth that [the Ashkenazim] didn't read Arabic in those days and couldn't know what was going on. There were a lot of Arabic readers among the Sephardim and because of that we felt an obligation to answer the Arabs and stand in the breach against them."[80] A similar editorial objective motivated the founding of *Sawt al-'uthmaniyya*, a newspaper that the Moyals had founded along with Jerusalem-based journalist Nissim Malul.

An initial strategy on the part of Hevrat Magen was to financially support existing Arabic newspapers that expressed sympathetic views. For example, every time an anti-Semitic article was published in *al-Karmil*, known to be hostile to Jews, Hevrat Magen would pay *As-Safir*, which had a more moderate view of Zionism, to run a response. This sort of financial support involved a process of bribery and incentivizing that continued into the 1930s.[81] Rashid Khalidi, in his study of Palestinian newspapers, cautions that assessments of newspapers' attitudes toward Zionism can be skewed by the pro-Zionist pieces that were simply reprints of material written by Zionists themselves.[82] Hevrat Magen also contributed articles to Arab newspapers in other Arab countries such as Syria and Egypt in order to offer "answers to the provocation," in Elmaliah's words.[83]

Elmaliah's activities also lay in the realm of translating non-Hebrew texts for readers of Hebrew, another activity reserved (as we saw in chapter 3 regarding English) for segments of the Jewish society that had the requisite multilingual skills. From 1913, Elmaliah worked for the newspaper of the socialist Zionist organization Ha-Po'el Ha-Tza'ir, initially covering both the Arab and Sephardi worlds. His responsibilities extended beyond Arabic: he also translated Ladino articles from Istanbul, Salonika, and Izmir, thinking that this would give Ashkenazi readers a sense of the Sephardi world. In 1919, after becoming disillusioned with the worker's movement, he went to work for the newspaper *Do'ar Ha-Yom*, which had been founded by Palestine-born Jews that year. He also became involved with the Zionist Commission, the forerunner of the Jewish Agency, where he also worked as an interpreter and a translator. He told the commission each day what was being written in the daily Arab press, including in French. In turn, he attempted to write responses in the Arab press, writing letters to those papers that would allow it. Elmaliah was one part of a larger translation apparatus oriented toward newspapers in multiple languages: "There was a large staff," he remembered, "that dealt with Yiddish newspapers and also English newspapers. But I was the head of the entire newspaper division."[84] Language abilities could thus serve the dual function of conveying Zionist perspectives to Arabs and conveying Arab perspectives to Jews, which Sephardim were able to accomplish through their role as translators. According to Elmaliah: "We wanted to bring to the Hebrew reader what was being written about him in the Arabic press and also bring to the Arab reader our responses and reactions to what the Jewish Yishuv was doing."[85] After World War I, Elmaliah became involved with the Sephardi Federation and later became the official Sephardi representative on the Jewish National Council. In building relations with Arabs, language proficiency remained the key element: "I was a good friend of theirs . . . because I knew their language and had a hand in Arabic literature. And maybe because of my Sephardi-ness [*sefardiyut*] I could understand their mentality. We were really good friends."[86]

As important as the actual effect of the newspapers on public opinion was the rhetoric of cultural synthesis cultivated by this small group of Sephardi Arabic-speaking intellectuals who presented themselves as uniquely capable of cultivating better relations through language, and carried on by Ashkenazi Arabic promoters in the mandate period.[87] For Nissim Malul, linguistic assimilation (to Arabic) was the ultimate goal, and he essentially downplayed the importance of Hebrew as a cultural marker.[88] Most Palestine Sephardim, however, like most Ashkenazim, saw fluency in Hebrew as a primary goal, but believed that Arabic knowledge was also essential. While the late-Ottoman founders of Hevrat Magen regarded themselves as unique in their ability and willingness to use Arabic for such purposes, the principle of Arabic for propaganda persisted into the mandate period among Ashkenazim also committed, though now usually from a Labor Zionist standpoint, to the idea that if only Zionists could use Arabic to explain themselves, conflict could be averted.

The Evolution of Propaganda during the Mandate Period

With the beginning of the mandate period, this relatively limited effort on the part of a group of Sephardi intellectuals also became the concern of the central organizational bodies of the Yishuv: the Histadrut, the Jewish Agency, and the Jewish National Council, which flailed around for decades while insisting on the importance of propaganda efforts in Arabic but remaining uncertain of how to put this project into action. Nissim Malul, already seasoned in journalistic efforts in Arabic, put out a pro-Zionist Arabic newspaper, *al-Salam*, in Jaffa in 1920, but the central Zionist institutions tended to feel that it was of low quality. In the 1920s and 1930s, nary a month went by without discussions about how to influence existing Arab papers. The three major Hebrew newspapers at the time, the centrist *Haaretz*, the rightist *Do'ar Ha-Yom*, and the leftist *Davar*, published frequently on the Arab question, repeatedly expressing a fear that not enough *hasbara*, or propaganda work, was being done. All the while, efforts were under way to do just that: Hayim Kalvarisky was building up contacts with Arab journalists and paying them to write articles supportive of Zionism. In 1929, the Zionist Organization founded the United Bureau for Addressing the Arab Question in an attempt to improve Zionist-Arab relations. Michael Assaf (Osofsky), an Ashkenazi orientalist of Polish origin who was then writing on Arab issues for *Davar*, wrote that the time had come "to start to talk to the Arabs" and suggested that while "there aren't Ashkenazi Jews who write in Arabic and journalists like this among the Sephardim are also rare," nonetheless "it is possible to overcome this."[89] Debates continued in the Zionist Organization over the ensuing years, with persistently unresolved questions about finances and leadership, and disagreements about which organizational auspices were appropriate for such a project.[90] Kalvarisky continued to seek contacts in the Arab world, including the editor of *Al-'ahd al-jadid*, in Beirut, but members of the United Bureau were doubtful that paying money would achieve the proper aims. Yosef Meyuhas wrote, "I have had bad experience in this area. I remember negotiations with an Arab paper that had gotten a lot of money from us that then wrote specifically against the Jews." Nonetheless, around 1930 about 14 percent of the bureau's total expenditures, or £P826, were going toward promoting pro-Zionist coverage in Arab newspapers.[91]

Into the 1930s, the Jewish National Council and the Zionist Organization, along with the labor organizations Mapai and the Histadrut, continued to bring up the matter of printing a Zionist newspaper in Arabic. In April 1936, the general Arab labor strike and countrywide riots caused leaders across the labor spectrum to feel increasingly dubious about turning Arab workers toward Zionism.[92] As tensions flared at home and abroad, a more concerted push for a local foreign-language propaganda newspaper arose in the Yishuv. That year, a group of some of the most prominent Zionist leaders met again to discuss the feasibility of putting out a newspaper in Arabic.[93] After years of debates and discussions, a multipartisan group of labor leaders and General Zionists, relative peaceniks, and relative hawks gathered to affirm a consensus: Arabic-language propaganda was, one way or another, the way forward, though it must be stressed that the agreement came as much from the need to assure Jewish constituencies that the leaders were doing something as from the hope that such steps would be effective in changing Arab opinion.[94] Just as language spotted on packaging or overheard in a coffeehouse could be meaningful for its semiotic value as much as for its semantic content, language printed in a newspaper could be meaningful even if it was only rarely read. The medium, indeed, was the message.

When a committee did finally convene with the goal of getting a newspaper off the ground, disagreements focused mainly on the frequency of the paper (weekly or daily) and on which organization in the Yishuv would be responsible for publishing it: the Jewish Agency or the Jewish National Council, both formally nonpartisan organizations that represented the entire Jewish community of the Yishuv, or the Histadrut, an organization with an explicitly labor-oriented socialist platform. In part, the eventual decision to choose the more partisan arrangement came from a desire to remove the Arabic-newspaper project from the hands of Sephardim. As Eliyahu Golumb pointed out, the general organizations had "many competing blocs and groups," and moreover, "some in the Sephardi community think that Arab relations is their bailiwick." More important to this final decision, though, seems to have been the sense that a clear political line would result in a more effective paper. Reuven Zaslani (Shiloah) commented, "The paper is directed to Arabs, and the Arabs we [the Histadrut] can deal with are workers and intelligentsia, who can be attracted to socialist ideas."[95]

By December 1936, it was decided that the Histadrut, which had briefly tried publishing another Arabic newspaper, *Ittihad al-'Ummal* (Union of workers), between 15 April 1925 and 7 January 1928, would host the newspaper.[96] The Arab Committee of the Histadrut continued making plans for the newspaper into 1937. Just before the first issue came out, on 24 March, Assaf stated that it would not deal with the internal politics of the Histadrut but rather with "significant economic, cultural, and social matters." One section would deal with the Arab press, but it would be a real newspaper with original content rather than a collection of other papers' articles. Distribution would be largely through Jews, particularly Jewish coffee shops and doctors with Arab clients, but it would also be sold in kiosks, sent in the mail by subscription, and sent to Arab teachers in the villages. The initial budget was £P1,500.[97]

Assaf, a member of Ha-Shomer Ha-Tza'ir whose concern with Jewish-Arab coexistence led him to study Arabic at Hebrew University, was chosen as editor, along with Eliyahu Agassi, of Iraq origin and the head of the Arab Department of the Histadrut: the paper would thus in practice be an Ashkenazi-Sephardi coproduction.[98] Other Jews of Arab origin also worked in the office, including Nissim Malul and the translator Yitzhak Shamosh, whose family was originally from Aleppo.[99] Records also indicate that a large number of non-Jewish Arabs were also recruited to participate in the compilation, editing, and distribution of the newspaper—a 1949 list contains nearly one hundred names.[100]

The first issue of the newspaper was published with the following note to the reader (in Arabic):

> Any unbiased person must acknowledge the great creative enterprise of the Hebrew people in its sole and eternal homeland. The enterprise has brought blessing to all the residents, disproved all speculations about the country's absorptive capacity, broadened and continues to broaden opportunities for the good of the whole country: the number of Arabs has increased and their situation has improved.
>
> The Jewish workers' movement organized in the Histadrut, the backbone of the Zionist movement, has and continues to call for building and peace and the development of the land for the Jewish people and the Arabs who live in it.

Despite this glowing report of achievements, the introduction continues, Arab propaganda had gotten the upper hand, calling the Zionist movement "imperialism" and employing anti-Jewish stereotypes to claim that the Histadrut was acting contrary to the interests of the Arab peasant. The Histadrut, which was committed to disproving these claims, said that it would extend its hand to any Arab, believing that knowledge, the plow, and the tools of building would help raise the status of all peoples. The newspaper, whose name meant "the truth of the matter," would begin to clear the way.[101]

In this first issue, the paper exhibited a heavy editorial hand, stating explicitly how events should be interpreted and questioning interpretations offered by others. "The intellectual wing of the Zionist movement," a front-page article read, "has been and will be pushing for construction and for peace and for improving the country for the good of the Jewish people and the good of the Arabs who dwell in it." Another paragraph of the same article argued that "adding population to the Arab world [that is, by Jewish settlement] is a good way to improve the Arabs' situation."[102] Another front-page article listed the names of Jews killed in the ongoing riots, asking, "Will Islamic and pan-Arab glory be revived this way?"[103] Other articles dealt with the new Tel Aviv port, the number of marriages in the past year (showing that Muslim marriages went down during the Arab revolt and thus obliquely demonstrating the liabilities of violence), prodemocratic activities in England and France, and the dire economic situation in the Arab world (suggesting that conditions could improve if Arabs abandoned violence). When it cited articles from Arab papers (*al-Liwa, al-Difa', Filastin*), it questioned their veracity. The issue concluded with prolabor slogans such as "True nationalism cares about workers and peasants" and "The builder will rise and the destroyer will fall."[104]

The principle of propaganda, however, was in the main a principle of selection rather than proclamation. Intended to be openly pro-Zionist, the paper's articles were selected to create a particular political impression. Wartime articles were strongly pro-Allied (and anti-Vichy). Book reviews highlighted anti-Nazi tracts in Arabic, such as Abbas Aqad's *Hitler fi al-mizan* (Hitler in the balance), about the struggle of democracy against Nazism.[105] These stories identified anti-Nazi trends in Palestine and the Arab world and presented them as evidence of common cause between Arabs and Jews.[106] Stories of Jewish-Arab collaboration were frequent: joint Jewish-Arab rallies in support of Charles de Gaulle received attention, as did a party in Ra'anana that had both Jewish and Arab guests.[107] Finally, the paper interpreted events in order to claim their benefit for Palestinian and other Arabs. For example, in the issue of 1 July 1941, an article about a fashion exhibition in Tel Aviv emphasized two points: the exhibitors, new Jewish immigrants, were bringing improved techniques for sheep and goat cultivation to Palestine; and the exhibition was improving commercial connections between Palestine and neighboring Arab countries.[108]

How did the editors of the paper conceive of their goals? Assaf said in early 1937 that the goal was "to fight the journalistic monopoly of the Arab inciters" through "objective and Zionist" reporting.[109] This framing of propaganda as objectivity placed the paper within an evolving Zionist (and later Israeli) tradition of *hasbara*, "explaining."[110] While the rhetoric of personal contact anticipated and sought human relations, the voices behind the newspaper—or smaller publications such as the daily bulletin of "Jewish news" in Arabic that the Jewish Agency put out between 1938 and 1939—stressed that Arabic could enable Jews to undertake a one-way public relations project of explaining Zionism to Arabs.[111] In a statement from 1941, Assaf further explained the paper's purposes, being careful to distinguish between mere propaganda and true or empirical evidence: "Explaining [*hasbara*] our undertaking in the country not simply by propaganda [*ta'amulah*], but by demonstrating our activities and deeds to the Arabs by way of emphasizing the positive value of these activities for the whole country, both its Jews and its Arab residents." Assaf hoped that the paper, which would not intercede in internal Arab or Palestinian politics and would take a positive view of the Arab world as a whole, would have literary value for its Arab readers, who would see it as a source of economic news and solutions to problems they were facing, as well as humor. In the process, these readers would be exposed to a "progressive, democratic, active liberal worldview." Finally, the paper would help Arab intellectuals get to know Jewish literature "and even gain some knowledge of our language." To this end, the paper had begun including Hebrew lessons and Hebrew expressions and proverbs with Arabic translations.[112]

The Histadrut did its best to gather evidence that this Arabic propaganda work was effective. The editorial staff collected letters from Arab readers in 1937 testifying to the importance of the paper. Mahmud Ya'qub from Tul Karem wrote in March, "I read the first issue of your paper and found that *Haqiqat al-Amr* is a free newspaper that has important articles, particularly on the oppressed workers' movement. I was very pleased with this phenomenon." Yusef 'Azar praised the paper's "constant defense of the worker without distinction of religion," saying in May that Jewish-Arab rapprochement is essential for the good of Arabs in Palestine. Others wrote from Bethlehem, Qalqilya, and Nablus, expressing support for the fact that this newspaper spoke for workers across religious lines.[113]

The paper also collected testimony from Jews involved in distributing the paper to Arab communities. One from Rehovot said that the papers were being received "with great support and interest."[114] Another, from Gedera, noted that the landowners were trying to keep the newspaper from peasants and workers, who were increasingly reading the paper, an indication that there was great interest among the proletariat. Yet another, from Kfar Giladi near the Lebanon border, spoke of Lebanese Arabs receiving the newspaper in secret. Jews based in Alexandria, Beirut, Damascus, and Aleppo also affirmed that they were finding interest in the newspaper in their countries. Shamosh, who was functioning as the administrator of the paper at the time, wrote a report about visiting with three young men, ages eighteen to twenty, from the Al-Najah school in Nablus. One of them testified that he had been reading his father's subscription to the paper with great interest since it first came out in 1937. Another had just started receiving the paper a few months before, and the third asked for a copy. All three affirmed that the paper was being read with great interest in Nablus, thanks to its appealing content, nice language, and nice pictures. As young intellectuals, they were particularly pleased with the translated stories. They also claimed to enjoy the Hebrew lessons and were sorry that these were not available in a book. One suggested sending copies to all the students in Al-Najah. After Shamosh read the boys the list of subscribers in the city—apparently, 108 copies were being circulated, and the Histadrut was receiving more subscription requests—the informants confirmed that the list included doctors, pharmacists, teachers, the principal of Al-Najah, small and large businessmen, students, and craftsmen. They also offered to contribute articles.[115] As far as the editors of *Haqiqat al-Amr* were concerned, Arabic propaganda seemed to be working.

The desire to show that the propaganda was changing minds in the Arab community persisted even as relations plummeted and as Assaf's "ongoing dealings with the problems of Jewish-Arab relations brought about, in dialectical fashion, the hardening of his Zionist stance," in the words of Assaf's colleague Yehuda Gotthelf, the editor in chief of *Davar*.[116] Even while working on this project, Assaf was toying with a more cynical approach. Indeed, in a 1938 pamphlet on Zionism, social- ism, and the Arab question, Assaf went as far as to question the possibil- ity of joint organization and to recommend the transfer of Arabs to other parts of the Arab world, speaking of this as a good solution to the tragic Jewish situation in Europe.[117] Nonetheless, Assaf wrote in May 1947 of ongoing Arab approval of the newspaper. *Haaretz* noted in a March 1947 article that the commander of al-Najada, a Palestinian Arab paramilitary organization founded in 1945, had spoken of the bad relations between the two peoples, but cited both *Haqiqat al-Amr* and *'Al Ha-Mishmar*, the Hebrew paper of Ha-Shomer Ha-Tza'ir, as exceptions to this rule. Shimon Landeman, a worker in the Jerusalem Municipality who also wrote textbooks for spoken Arabic, wrote a letter to the editor of *Haaretz* speculating that Arabs were looking to the paper for a way to understand Jews.[118]

These supportive comments about the Histadrut and *Haqiqat al-Amr* from Arabs might appear suspicious, perhaps even fabricated, and indeed we learn more from them about the hopes and dreams of the Histadrut than about the real experience of the Palestinian community. Nonethe- less, we know from the work of Hillel Cohen that the networks of Arab- Jewish collaboration were wide and extensive, that the Palestinian allegiance to the strongly anti-Zionist Husayni family was only partial, and that internal Palestinian divides made receptiveness to and coopera- tion with Zionist groups contextually appropriate or feasible in certain instances.[119] Moreover, Zachary Lockman reminds us that some Arab workers sought out labor-organizing support from the Histadrut despite their uneasiness with or opposition to Zionism.[120] Thus, the people profi- cient in Arabic who were working for Zionists did not need to be Jews;

they could be Arabs hired for the cause. Just as Jews in Tel Aviv could be convinced of the possibility of coexistence by individual Arabs who appeared well disposed to them, propagandists as well found what they considered sufficient evidence of support and collaboration to make their vision of potential coexistence not seem entirely fanciful.

Fund-Raising for Haqiqat al-Amr in the United States

The nexus of Jewish-Arab relations (and Hebrew-Arabic translation) might appear to have existed purely in the realm of local interethnic relations, detached from the other planes of interlinguistic and intercultural contact that defined the Yishuv. It turns out, however, that the *Haqiqat al-Amr* operation was international in scope. In addition to Hebrew translations of the Arabic text distributed around the Yishuv, similar to the work undertaken by Hevrat Magen, English translations of some issues were distributed in the United States. Indeed, even at this stage, *hasbara* projects directed at Arabs aimed, in tandem and indirectly, to convince foreign Jews of the rightness of the Zionist cause. In promoting the Arabic propaganda newspaper, the Histadrut made financial appeals in English to wealthy Americans by way of the New York office of the National Labor Committee for Palestine, a special fund-raising department that engaged in a range of projects to help the Histadrut and its labor activities in Palestine.[121] Israel Mereminsky, a representative of the Histadrut in the United States between 1939 and 1945, wrote to A. K. Epstein, an American Zionist, noting that the budget of *Haqiqat al-Amr* had nearly tripled in the years since the newspaper's inception, but that financial support from American Jews was unfortunately waning. Only two large individual donors, Epstein and a Mr. Harris, were supplementing the broader fund-raising campaigns by the Histadrut in Palestine and America.[122] Other potential donors, records show, had received appeals and turned them down. One reply, from Elias Brown, of Brown's Smart Apparel for Men and Women, in Los Angeles, noted that Brown had read the appeal letter "with very much interest" and assured the writer that "the paper [*Haqiqat al-Amr*] is doing a great piece of work for Palestine." But he was skeptical about its message: "When you speak of encouragement for the project, I suspect somehow that that means money. . . . You know life today is one campaign after another and we are already embarked on the United Jewish

Welfare Fund, to which we owe a distinct obligation."[123] Brown, committed to this general pro-Zionist Jewish welfare organization, the precursor of the United Jewish Appeal, chose to disregard this narrower project.

Though the appeals were not always successful, the aspirations of the fund-raisers indicated that they saw *hasbara* not merely as the production of Arabic propaganda material to use with Arabs but also as an international project to win the support of foreign donors. Hoping to move in that direction, Mereminsky included five to ten copies of the paper, translated, so that the Histadrut would "be able to conquer and acquire special and major donors."[124] But neither foreign donors nor local minds were "conquered," it seems, by these propaganda activities. Mereminsky wrote to the Executive Committee of the Histadrut in 1944, complaining that it had not done enough to arm him with more propaganda material—in this case, propaganda material that would appeal to American funders. Back in Palestine, the projects faltered because of lack of funds or political will. Elmaliah's impression of similar Arabic-language propaganda efforts before World War I appeared to be the consensus after, too: "I can't know the effect because the atmosphere was so poisonous, but it certainly didn't have a large influence."[125] The overall preference for a society in which language contact would be unnecessary was pitted against a demographic and political context that seemed to compel a form of linguistic engagement but provided few clear answers about how this engagement was to proceed and whether it would succeed

Arabic in Military Intelligence

Ultimately (in retrospect), the trajectory of Jewish engagement with Arabic led not toward reconciliation but toward military intelligence. In his 1923 essay "The Iron Wall," Vladimir Jabotinsky claimed that because "there are no more uninhabited islands," the creation of a Jewish state in Palestine would necessarily entail protests from the native population. The urgent moral need for a Jewish state, in his estimation, justified and necessitated a military confrontation as well as a geographic "revision" of mandate borders. In the mid-1930s, the Revisionists withdrew from the organized Yishuv but remained a powerful oppositional force.[126] Militaristic responses to the perception of Jewish-Arab conflict were not limited

to the Revisionists, however. Though personal contact and faith in ultimate reconciliation were among the tenets of the socialist Labor movement in its early years, this belief, as Anita Shapira explains, shifted as
Arab opposition mounted in the 1930s, eventually crystallizing into what
she calls the "offensive ethos," a turn to arms based on the perception
that Zionists had "no choice" but to fight back.[127] In 1920 the Histadrut
set up a militia, the Haganah, which was highly organized by the end of
the mandate and employed many of the same intelligence strategies as
the Revisionists. By the end of the mandate period, such activities were
occurring under the auspices of the Shai, the intelligence division of the
Palmach (itself the fighting force of the Haganah paramilitary group);
Shahar, the Shai's unit of *mista'arvim*, or Jews from Arab countries who
dressed and acted as Arabs; as well as Delek, the Revisionist movement's
intelligence division. Each of these organizations built elaborate systems
of intelligence information about Arabs using both high-level research
about political trends in the Arab world and a network of personal agents
who used personal contacts and their knowledge of colloquial Arabic to
amass bodies of information.

The Shai, founded in 1939–40 and headed by Ezra Danin, was formed
to organize Jews involved in "getting to know Arabs [*hakarat 'Arvim*]" and
"creating contacts and cultivating relations," according to an account by
Yehoshua Palmon, a member of the organization.[128] Language was at the
center of these individuals' activities. Yaakov Eini, a Jerusalemite of
Syrian-Jewish descent, remembered going to an Arab intellectual in
Jerusalem who agreed to help him with his Arabic "because he was interested in just making money." Such individuals—native speakers of Arabic
located outside the target Palestinian-Arab community—took on small-
scale undercover tasks, for example, dressing in Arab clothing and trying
to pass in the Hebron area, Eini reported. In these cases, clothing, not language, was the protective device. As Eini said, when members of the
group were suspected by the British, they would say that they were Jews
who were traveling and were wearing Arab clothes for their safety.[129]

Real reconnaissance, however, required authentic-sounding language
abilities, and in 1943 the Palmach established the Shahar unit of
mista'arvim, undercover agents, to mingle in Arab populations and collect
information. The term is derived from the Arabic word *musta'rib*, which

means "to act as or pretend to be an Arab." The term arose with the beginning of Muslim rule in Spain in the eighth century. Though many Jews and Christians converted to Islam, it was common even among those who did not to speak Arabic to adopt Arab customs. The term was transformed in the Christian north of Spain to the Spanish *mozárabe*. With the use of this technique in Palestine, a hierarchy of knowledge was reflected in a social hierarchy. Military organizations used native Arabic-speaking Jews for lower-level information gathering and employed European Jews in higher-level analysis. As Gil Eyal argues, this separation of personal contact and systematic analysis, and stratification of European and Mizrahi Jews, persisted in the Israeli military following the creation of the state.[130]

Mista'arvim, writes the former *mista'arev* Gamliel Cohen, were "Hebrew, Zionist, Palestinian-born fighters who were able to mix in and even act, for short or long periods of time, within the Arab population, within Palestine or throughout the Middle East, in the framework of intelligence missions or even clandestine guerilla operations." "The conditions for being accepted," he continued, "were knowledge of Arabic and an 'Oriental' appearance." The *mista'arvim* used their Arabic skills not merely to observe and record but also to gain intimacy with what they understood to be the Arab mindset. According to Palmon, such goals were achieved. "Over the course of some time," he said in an interview, "we gained experience with the Arabs; I came to understand their mentality, their characteristics and ways of fighting." These activities expanded well beyond Palestine; the Palmach established an undercover intelligence network stretching from Turkey to East Asia.[131]

A related system of intelligence gathering operated among the Revisionists, whose political philosophy was premised on the impossibility of reconciliation and who from the outset predicted that military engagement, not diplomacy or propaganda, would determine the solution to Jewish-Arab conflict. In his 1931 article "Round Table with the Arabs," Jabotinsky criticized the Left for seeking reconciliation with Arabs. Committed to the idea of complete separation, he rejected any need for knowledge of Arabic and spoke of purging its influences from the Hebrew language in his extensive writings on the importance of Hebrew promotion. In a 1919 letter he wrote: "In official capacities there is no need for knowledge of Arabic. This is fair; for we don't require Arabs to command

Hebrew." Yet over time, the Revisionists found themselves in need of information that could be gathered only through language proficiency. In response to these needs, Delek, the intelligence division of the Revisionist military organization, the Irgun, constructed an elaborate system of informers, mainly native Arabic-speaking Jews, to collect information. In a February 1948 letter, G. Binyamin of the central office wrote, "It is necessary to seek ties with Arabs. It is necessary to look for Jews who are tied in all manner of friendships and knowledge [*heiker*] with the Arabs. It is necessary to pressure these Jews to connect in some way with the Arabs and obtain information."[132]

Intelligence activities required a forced and spurious intimacy that employed the terms of friendship ("understand," "recognize") for the purposes of classifying a foe. Both the Haganah and the Irgun privileged systematic knowledge (*yedi'ot*) over personal contacts (*hakarah*) but depended on the latter, and indeed in the process of learning and teaching Arabic for military-intelligence purposes found common cause with those on left-wing kibbutzim or in the Histadrut who claimed to be using Arabic for peaceable or propagandistic aims. Shimon Somekh, "the spiritual father of the *mista'arvim*," according to Gamliel Cohen, was also engaged in other kinds of Arabic-language activities, including community language education for the Histadrut and Ha-Shomer Ha-Tza'ir. Somekh, who was born in Baghdad in 1916, came to Palestine as a Zionist—"by taxi, through the dessert, holding a travel visa, textbooks, a notebook, and a tennis racquet," as he described it. Bolstered by his fluency in Iraqi Arabic, he continued to study Palestinian Arabic in the Culture Division of the Histadrut, the heavily Ashkenazi organization where his uncle Eliyahu Agassi, the future editor of *Haqiqat al-Amr*, worked. With his Arabic knowledge, acquired both natively and through the educational structures of the Ashkenazi Labor Zionist movement, Somekh went on to teach Arabic in surrounding villages, especially the kibbutzim of Ha-Shomer Ha-Tza'ir.[133]

The nexus of casual encounters, local learning, propaganda, and intelligence became part of the classic narrative of Zionist engagement. Retrospective descriptions of Shahar and the *mista'arvim* are highly laudatory. In hindsight, it was their facility with Arabic that seemed to set these members of the population apart from and above their peers, who, for the most part, did not know Arabic. A *Haaretz* article from 15 January

2004, on the occasion of the death of the noted *mista'arev* Shimon Horesh, said that Horesh "educated generation upon generation of *mista'arvim*, those who spoke and understood Arabic, [as well as] generations of activists and researchers in Arabic." Horesh, a sixth-generation Palestinian Jew, grew up in the Shabazi neighborhood of Jaffa in the 1930s and studied at both Christian and Jewish schools before enrolling in the Herzliya Gymnasium. He was so "authentic," reported the article, that he was dismissed from his job teaching English in Damascus because his Arabic accent was too strong. Horesh's friend Yaakov (Jack) Zviya, also a commander in the Palmach in 1948, summed up Horesh's patriotic language teaching well: "You, a field worker and a man of action, chose to impart your knowledge of Arabic, Arab culture and ways of life to tens of thousands of security forces and to the intelligence community, men of the Mossad and the General Intelligence Service and special commando units."[134] In this case, the purpose of Arabic knowledge was entirely to serve the Zionist cause through presumed, colonial-like mastery over the Arab, and language acquisition could be presented as a patriotic act embedded in what it meant to be an elite Zionist in the intelligence community.

Perceptions of a Golden Age

Despite the increasing militarization of Arabic learning by Jews, the language continued to symbolize, counterfactually, the amelioration of distance. Arabic could point either to a golden past from which contemporary relations had declined or to a utopian future, usually in which Palestinian Arabs would give up their opposition to Zionism. For scholars of classical Islamic history at the School of Oriental Studies at Hebrew University, this ideal past period was located in medieval Baghdad and Córdoba, where Jewish exegetes wrote in Arabic, and Hebrew poets drew from the Arabic poetic tradition. As the faculty member Levi Billig wrote in a memorandum about the school: "It is felt that understanding of common cultures leads to mutual sympathy, such as existed between Jews and Moslems in the Middle Ages."[135] Writing for the Sephardi-edited monthly journal *Mizrah u-ma'arav* (East and West), edited by Abraham Elmaliah, the historian and noted Revisionist Joseph Klausner wrote of connecting "what is worthy in the East with what is excellent in the West," adding, "This ambition for a synthesis between East and West is our legacy from the period of Sepharad," referring to the period of the Spanish Golden Age. Martin Buber, who moved to Palestine in 1937, called the Jewish people a "between people" (*'am benayim*), and Jerusalem "the gate between East and West."[136] Sephardi intellectuals shared a related ethos, arguing that they, with their hybrid identities and knowledge of Arabic, might shepherd in a coexistence of Occident and Orient such as had occurred in medieval Spain.

Advocates of a more personal, colloquial relationship to the Arabs also alluded to the past, but in their case to the more recent past: the late Ottoman period, when the tiny Jewish community interacted more often with Muslim and Christian Arabs than it did later, and when new Ashkenazi immigrants were likely to mimic Arab dress and seek proficiency in Arabic as part of an orientalist appropriation of the East.[137] There are differing assessments of the degree of Jewish-Arab interaction in the late Ottoman period, the period that Yehoash and Smilansky referred to as a period without Jewish proficiency in Arabic. What is clear, however, is that this earliest period of Zionist settlement was later portrayed as a golden age of Jewish-Arab contact and coexistence that, even if deliberately overturned by Zionist policy decisions, represented a halcyon moment. Thus, while Hebrew University orientalists alluded to Jewish-Muslim coexistence in the medieval period, a 1946 article in the Hebrew daily *Ha-Boker* (associated with the non-Labor-oriented General Zionists), reflected on bad relations in the present and urged a renewed commitment to the study of Arabic, implying that this commitment would help revive a state of coexistence that had been present in the relatively recent past but had been lost: "We must not forget that the first immigrants [to Palestine] from the West to stake a claim in the land of our forefathers wandered about along its length and breadth and were welcomed in brotherhood and friendship by the Arab residents of the land and with the help of our Sephardi brothers who commanded both Arabic and Hebrew."[138]

This rosy image of Arab-Jewish relations, deployed in 1946 regarding the late Ottoman period, has been redeployed more recently to refer to the mandate years themselves. Muhammad Amara claims: "During the British Mandatory period . . . in spite of the fact that the communities,

Arab and Jews, had separate school systems, there was language contact, generally with the Jews learning Arabic."[139] This historical assessment is largely spurious, since language contact was haphazard and Jews often did not learn Arabic well in school (as the next chapter explores). Nonetheless, this nostalgia reflects a striking ideological current: the discursive longing for organic relationships in light of and in spite of policies that imposed distance and stressed difference. Arabic use oriented toward Jewish-Arab contact, whether in academic circles, among lay learners, or among native-speaker intelligence or propaganda experts, occurred with the assumption that greater linguistic contact in the past had been correlated with better political relations and, conversely, that declining language abilities reflected—even precipitated—political strife.

Arabic knowledge and use seemed—to denizens of Tel Aviv, to kibbutz language learners, and to promoters (both Arabic-speaking and not) of Arabic propaganda—to be an antidote to both the loss of a past coexistence and the apparent impossibility of future harmony. But Hebrew-Arabic symbiosis, idyllic and symbolic though it may seem in retrospect, was never an operative goal of any but the most peripheral of these language operations. In the cases we have surveyed, Arabic stood for and negotiated the occasional (and often unwelcome) appearance of the Palestinian Arab within an environment depicted as all-Jewish, the effort to make this local other familiar, and the desperate and ultimately fruitless attempt—through language—to stave off its attacks, both literal violence and political pressure. The norm of Hebrew monolingualism not only protested the importation of a European Babel but also resisted full integration with the Middle Eastern linguistic context, a context that in any case did not welcome Hebrew's linguistic intrusion any more than it welcomed Zionist settlement—few Arabs took it upon themselves to learn Hebrew.[140] But like European languages, which could not entirely be kept out, Arabic, persistently present, engendered real accommodations. Zionists were reminded that the construct of Zion was itself a foreign presence in Arabic-speaking Palestine, a homeland that could penetrate but could not erase the multilingual space that it had entered.

CHAPTER FIVE

HEBREW EDUCATION BETWEEN
EAST AND WEST

Foreign-Language Instruction in Zionist Schools

Regarding a foreign language, I don't think we need it at all. We should
learn just one language: Hebrew and specifically Hebrew. The
multiplicity of languages is unnatural.
—*Menahem Ussishkin (1903)*

The Yishuv was awash in linguistic contacts, some unwelcome, some
sought out. But one space seemed to sit apart from this mixing and to
provide a laboratory for the growth and cultivation of Hebrew: the
school. Zionist schools in British mandate Palestine were, in reality as
much as in the popular imagination, places where Hebrew reigned even
when it did not permeate other settings. Attention to the ways in which
reflections on multilingualism occurred in this space, however, suggests
that no setting in the Yishuv was fully removed from outside pressures.

The Hebrew pedagogical sanctum had been built with great collective
effort, much of it oriented toward the exclusion of other languages.
Early-twentieth-century battles to remove European tongues as languages
of Jewish instruction, together with the institution-building efforts of
highly committed teachers and students, led to the creation of a full
Hebrew-language school system by the end of World War I.[1] Reflecting

on the history of Hebrew schools in 1953, fifty years after the foundation of the Hebrew Teachers' Federation, Aharon Ne'eman called the revival of Hebrew the organization's first achievement. The teachers, he said, had zealously promoted Hebrew against "parents who demanded the study of French, [then] the language of clerical work; Arabic, the language of the country; and Yiddish, the language of the home," as well as against "intellectuals . . . who recommended teaching the sciences in European languages." Against all these forces, Ne'eman wrote, the teachers persevered in their commitment to Hebrew "through deep faith, great passion, and a fundamental revolution."[2]

But despite teachers' bombast about the creation of a Hebrew school system, indeed a monumental achievement, Zionist schools in the mandate period did not exclude all other tongues. Nearly all of them taught English, and many taught Arabic—the two languages that, as we have seen, exerted pressure on the Yishuv as the languages of the land. High schools also offered French, a nearly universally taught language in the Jewish colonies of the late Ottoman period, but one that was less actively remarked upon during the mandate period, even when it was taught.[3] School administrators would not have denied the existence of foreign-language instruction or deemed it entirely antithetical to their mission: their goal was to exclude instruction *in* foreign languages, not instruction *of* foreign languages. Nonetheless, their enthusiasm for Hebrew's victory—shared by scholars of Zionist education in later generations— has meant that the existence of foreign-language instruction in the prestate period has been largely overlooked and often minimized.[4] Bernard Spolsky and Elana Shohamy, for example, offer a brief, summary judgment of prestate Arabic study before more extensively treating the state period: it "did not gain real strength during the mandate."[5]

Nonetheless, for a marginal enterprise, foreign-language study attracted a disproportionate amount of attention from educators and political leaders. The words and ideas of educators and others who spoke about, in favor of, or against the inclusion of foreign languages in the Zionist curriculum lend insight into the symbolism attributed to such study in general and to the study of Arabic and English in particular. Although the entrenchment of the Zionist movement in Palestine meant an escape from European Jewish institutional pressures for multilingual education, this reorientation of Jewish life did not mean an escape from language contact more generally. Indeed, the schools, the space most explicitly tasked with shaping the future of Hebrew and its culture, became key sites for considering Hebrew's limits. English and Arabic remained prominent in the Zionist and (later) Israeli psyche even as Jewish immigrant languages were largely (though not totally) swept aside in each generation by the forces of assimilation. The history of language in Palestine must thus address not only the languages and language skills that the Zionist movement intended to eliminate but also those that its students were asked to acquire.

Zionist foreign-language instruction addressed, most fundamentally, the fact of Jewish interaction in its immediate context: British-controlled, Arab-majority Palestine. English was the language of the British mandatory government, which, though it recognized Arabic and Hebrew as official languages, clearly privileged (and, more practically, was more adept at processing) correspondence in its native tongue, as chapter 3 demonstrated. English, moreover, had become the international language of commerce, academia, and politics. Meanwhile, Arabic was the language of Palestine's majority population as well as the chief regional language, a language whose diverse meanings for the Jewish population were enumerated in chapter 4. Any practical engagement with the Arab world thus required knowledge of Arabic. For all its promise of monolingualism, the reorientation of Jewish life toward Palestine could not mean a total escape from language contact and foreign-language needs.

Yet justifications for language study were not concerned only with functional needs (which themselves could be multiple and contested); they were also inward looking, cognizant of the functions and limits of Hebrew. Both English and Arabic, as we will see, could serve as symbolic markers for essentialized values esteemed by the Yishuv and deemed critical for the incipient Hebrew nation: in the case of Arabic, a renewed connection to the Semitic East and to the Semitic roots of Hebrew; in the case of English, a strengthened commitment to democratic values, civic pride, and European modernity. Set against a notion of Diaspora marked by Jewish rootlessness, alienation, and economic and civic underdevelopment, Arabic and English represented two opposite antidotes, one the escape from Europe toward a more authentic East, and the other the removal of tendencies deemed "Oriental" and the fulfillment of cultural and democratic ideals characteristic of the ideal European nation. The chief linguistic antidote to exile, Zionists felt, was Hebrew, but foreign-language study itself—paradoxically—could also be a concrete way to imbibe antidiasporic values and establish an authentic, vibrant Hebrew society. The symbolic force of Arabic and English study becomes clear in the presentation of several educators' reflections in the second half of this chapter, with an emphasis on two educators in particular: Shlomo Dov Goitein, who taught Arabic at the Re'ali School in Haifa before moving to the School of Oriental Studies at Hebrew University, and Hayim Yehuda (Leon) Roth, a professor of philosophy at Hebrew University who came to Palestine from England in 1928 and wrote extensively on the subject of education. Conversations about foreign-language study, taken together, help illuminate the self-fashioning of a society that understood itself as potentially an ideal blend of East and West, but nonideally as inauthentic aspirants to both in practice.

Who Was Studying What?

A survey of curricula makes clear the consistent place of foreign languages in Zionist schools. Though English and Arabic were conventionally listed last in lists of subjects, the hours devoted to them were in some cases greater than the hours apportioned for the Bible, mathematics, or other core subjects.[6] Until World War I, Arabic was taught alongside French, and often Turkish and German in academic high schools. In 1910–11, the Hebrew Gymnasium in Jaffa, for example, taught six hours of French a week starting in the equivalent of the fifth grade, as well as between two and three hours of Arabic.[7] The Re'ali School in Haifa in 1913–14 taught four hours of German, three hours of French, and three hours of Arabic, Turkish in the upper grades, and English in a special commercial track.[8] During this early period, graduates of these Hebrew schools, as well as those who studied at the Alliance israélite universelle schools, often expected to find jobs overseas and wished to gain the language skills to pursue them. As Abraham Elmaliah, the noted Sephardi Jewish educator and journalist, said in a 1963 interview, a typical Sephardi student in Palestine "would finish the Alliance school and then he would have to go far away to find work." Many were successful: "All the banks in Egypt and Paris were full of students from the Alliance schools [in Palestine]."[9]

The curriculum changed dramatically after World War I. German, Turkish, and Latin were eliminated, and English became de rigueur at schools of all three Zionist educational streams: General, Labor, and Religious. This was a positive development, wrote Yosef Luria, director of the Zionist Department of Education, for Turkish was "difficult for students and lacking any cultural value," whereas English "easily introduces students to a wide and rich culture."[10] In the earliest years of the mandate, it seems, only some urban schools taught English, but this changed quickly, perhaps under pressure from Jewish students themselves.[11] A letter from six religious students to the administration of the Doresh Zion School in Jerusalem in 1919 demonstrated their desire for English to be added to the curriculum: "Seeing as every person comes to a point in the course of his life when he requires a European language, we, young people at the present time, find it appropriate to study the language of the nation that has redeemed us from the terrible troubles, that is, the English language, which is the ruling language in the whole world."[12] Such a view, suffused with a great degree of hope and promise, was shared by other writers in the immediate years after World War I. For example, the journalist Mordechai Ben-Hillel Ha-Cohen wrote that the British and the Jews were "brothers" and recalled that as the troops advanced into Palestine, Zionist activists "welcomed the new rulers with blessings."[13] Even as good feelings faded with the British response to the 1921 riots and the 1930 Passfield White Paper—which attempted to restrict Jewish immigration and land purchases—English instruction continued. In General and Labor primary schools, intended for those not going on to higher education and encompassing grades one through eight, students began English study in the fifth grade, studied five hours a week until the sixth grade, and then four hours in both the seventh and eighth grades.[14] The Religious Zionist schools offered a similar schedule, for both boys and girls.[15] Gymnasia offered this level of English instruction through the high school years; the Re'ali School, for example, taught six hours a week of English in the last two years of instruction.[16] Schools of commerce, discussed in previous chapters, offered correspondence courses in English in addition to the usual hours of language instruction:

in the late 1940s, the school of commerce in Tel Aviv taught two hours of English correspondence, as compared with just one hour of Hebrew correspondence.[17]

This instruction, often by Anglophone Jewish immigrants, was not particularly successful in conferring proficiency; accounts make it clear that students learned little in their English studies. The Alliance israélite universelle, which operated outside the Zionist school system, taught French in a serious way alongside Hebrew to between three thousand and four thousand students, but the Zionist schools didn't do a credible job teaching English.[18] At the Gan Meir school, where a woman named Tamar Nahshon (born 1926) studied, "kids learned English but didn't know English." The distaste for English among the students was palpable to her: "We hated the British so we didn't want to learn English."[19] In retrospect, some of those who received education in European languages outside the Zionist system came to realize how unusual it was. Another interviewee, Menahem Rogelski (born 1919), was transferred to the Alliance school between the second and third grades because the Zionist school system had gone on strike. "I am thankful to the teachers to this day," he said in an interview many years later, "because I learned almost four languages there rather than just one language. We learned until four in the afternoon and we really learned well—I've been happy about that ever since."[20]

Arabic was regularly taught in Zionist elementary schools before World War I. After the war, though, the promotion of Hebrew spelled the end of regular Arabic teaching in the elementary schools, and in most cases Arabic was confined to the gymnasia, which accounted for 15–20 percent of the student population.[21] The curriculum at the Hebrew Gymnasium of Jerusalem in 1924–25 was typical: students studied only Hebrew in the fifth and sixth grades, English beginning in the seventh, French and Arabic in the eighth and ninth grades.[22] It would be wrong, however, to see Arabic as only an elite pursuit, as French clearly was; Labor schools, particularly on kibbutzim, included Arabic either in their formal curricula or in extracurricular activities.[23] Moreover, some educators who specifically opposed instruction in European languages promoted Arabic study.[24] Thus, articles advocating for more widespread Arabic study were published at intervals, and educators generally felt that Arabic should be taught more widely and at earlier stages.[25] Particularly early on, Arabic educators contended with a dire lack of instructional materials. "The study of this language is difficult for students who lack appropriate textbooks," wrote Luria in his 1921 report.[26] A further problem was some teachers' apparent lack of skills. Often, English teachers knew English fluently but not enough Hebrew, whereas Arabic teachers—generally not native speakers—were more likely to know Hebrew quite well but to make many errors in Arabic.

English and Arabic curricula were developed through the interaction, not always smooth, of several institutional bodies. Until late 1932, Jewish education was officially coordinated by the education department of the Zionist Executive, which, under the leadership of Yosef Luria, offered recommendations for both English and Arabic study that were adopted at least in general outline. At the end of 1932, supervision of education was transferred to the Department of Education of the Jewish National Council (Ha-va'ad ha-le'umi shel keneset Yisra'el), based in Jerusalem.[27] Education was conducted within three separate "streams" (*zeramim*), each of which had its own school committee and inspector and remained semiautonomous within the department.[28] Religious schools were run by the Mizrahi, the Religious Zionist organization influenced by the thought of Rabbi Abraham Isaac Kook. Schools of the Labor stream were overseen by the Histadrut. The General stream, which constituted 53 percent of the total school enrollment in the 1940s, served nearly everyone else except the small number of students educated privately or in ultra-Orthodox schools.[29] Within these streams, students were generally divided into two types of schools: the majority (85 percent) into primary (*'amami*) schools for grades one through eight, and the remainder into gymnasia, which covered grades five through twelve and prepared students for higher education.[30]

Bodies were formed within the Jewish National Council's Education Department to address specific curriculum areas, including committees devoted to both English (first convened in September 1935) and Arabic (1937). These were the only two Jewish National Council committees devoted to the study of languages other than Hebrew. Both committees were made up mainly of schoolteachers; they discussed issues of teacher recruitment, hiring, and professional development; textbooks; and curriculum. The two committees faced similar apathy on the part of schools, students, and parents, and the protocols of their meetings are filled with complaints about lack of respect and lack of resources.

These committees themselves were substantially influenced by outside bodies. The Arabic committee members included representatives from departments of Arab affairs, including those from the Histadrut, the Jewish Agency, the British mandatory government, and the Department of Education itself. Moreover, faculty members from Hebrew University's School of Oriental Studies (founded 1927) sat in on meetings, proposed textbooks, and influenced the discussions.[31] English education, for its part, was influenced by several British-run or British-funded bodies. English was taught at Hebrew University from 1937; with funding from the Jewish community in England, the university hired a lecturer in English: Adam A. Mendilow, a Jewish PhD from the University of London, who had recently taught English in India.[32] Mendilow became involved in the promotion of English at the public and school levels and sat on the English advisory committee. The British mandatory government's Department of Education produced recommendations on the teaching of English in Hebrew schools that were, from the early 1930s, largely adopted. Moreover, the Jewish Agency founded its own English-language committee in July 1936, which included representatives from the Jewish National Council committee and Hebrew University but also the mandatory Department of Education, thus cementing a link between the Zionist and the British bodies. The Jewish Agency committee, which received half of its funding from Jewish donors in London, held courses for teachers on the teaching of English, planned English libraries, offered English classes for adults, and offered lectures for broadcast by the Palestine Broadcasting Service.[33]

Further pressure for English teaching came from the British Council, which had begun worldwide efforts to promote English studies. Its involvement was initially financial—it offered a £75 grant to the Jewish Agency's English committee in 1937, though it was not consistent in its funding, owing to the unwillingness of the schools themselves to offer additional hours of instruction. Despite its fickle funding policies, the British Council continued to cooperate with the Jewish Agency's English committee in other ways to recommend books for purchase, arrange teacher-training courses, and offer advice.[34] On 23 September 1940, the council set up a Palestine location in Jaffa to offer English courses for those who did not know the language, and English lectures for the more proficient.[35] "Today English is well-nigh a universal tongue spreading to the four corners of the globe," reported the *Palestine Post*. "It has been learned rapidly in Palestine, yet there are still many deprived of a convenient opportunity to acquire a knowledge of the language of Shakespeare." The war, suggested the article, made it imperative that British ideals of freedom and love of liberty be known in the colonies.[36] The ultimate effect of this outside involvement is not certain. The Zionist leadership ignored or denounced this intervention, but it does appear from British reports that Tel Avivians made use of the British Institute. More importantly, as we will see, the sentiments on behalf of English offered by the British Council were not wholly rejected by Zionist educators.

Voices against Foreign-Language Study

What little has been written on foreign-language study in the Yishuv has emphasized the overall apathy and opposition toward foreign languages. Indeed, many teachers were committed to removing foreign influences in the schools and sought to minimize foreign-language study, particularly European language study. At times this sentiment was directed at lower-level or rural students and was based on an assumption that the "nationalist farmer"—the paradigmatic Zionist figure—ought to be monolingual. In 1892, when the first groups of Zionist teachers attempted to organize, the teacher and pioneer of Hebrew education Israel Belkind stated that foreign-language study had no place in the schooling of children in agricultural settlements, though it might be appropriate for urban children: "While children in the cities need to learn other languages, too, like for example Arabic and French . . . because who knows where they will go when they finish their schooling, teachers in the agricultural settlements need to . . . teach children the love of labor at home and the love of the soil in the field and in the garden. Thus it is unnecessary to learn foreign languages in the agricultural colonies."[37] The perceived division between multilingual students and monolingual ones could also fall along gender lines. Ahad Ha-ʿAm had once commented that women had no need for foreign-language skills: "French, why do they need it?"[38]

Perhaps students who intended to go abroad or engage in international trade might need foreign-language skills, but, these men thought, those at the heart of the Zionist mission, who would stay put in Palestine, could be monolingual. Such dictates, patronizing as they sound, appear to have been shared by some workers themselves, who privileged practical education and real-world experience over book learning. Tzvi Elpeleg, the son of a carpenter and a homemaker who had immigrated in 1934 from Poland, recalls that he went to school only until the age of fourteen because "in the eyes of my parents and other parents—not everyone, but the majority of the neighborhood—[up to age fourteen] was the maximum level of education that a person needed to have."[39]

A division of Zionist labor between elites who might be multilingual and workers who would remain (in this case become) monolingual might be contrasted with a division recommended by colonial administrators in the British Empire, who thought it best to educate the vast majority in the national vernacular while reserving English for a group of elites. "The immediate result of affording an English education to any large number of Malays," wrote E. C. Hill in his 1884 "Report on Education in Malaysia," "would be the creation of a discontented class who might become a source of anxiety to the community." English was for the few: "A certain number of Malays educated in English are of course required to fill clerical appointments and situations of the kind which do not include manual labor."[40] Similar dynamics were at play in Africa.[41] Though the context in the Yishuv was distinct from that in Malaysia or the other colonial locales where English was recommended for elites—most importantly because a robust Hebrew-language educational system was being constituted and because recommendations on English were being made by Jews, not by the English—a similar consensus existed there that the masses simply had no use for English and that it would be pointless, even dangerous, to compel them to take up foreign-language study.

But while it was self-evident that some elites in India or Malaysia would need English, this was not so clear in mandate Palestine. Unlike a colony, the Yishuv was largely autonomous, both because of the mandate system and because, as largely European immigrants, Zionists were not seen as a typical native population in the eyes of the British. Looking forward, as the mandate itself stated, to a day of eventual Jewish sovereignty, it seemed that even elites could manage in Hebrew. The education of advanced students in other languages, therefore, was not a straightforward proposition or an obvious project even for the elites. Thus, although the Yishuv was a small economy under the rule of a European colonial power, few explicitly acknowledged that the language of that power would have any central role in the operations of the society. As Oz Almog has noted, the Labor movement had a deeply suspicious view of higher education in general and foreign-language study in particular, since such study appeared to have no connection to the quotidian needs of farm labor. Kibbutz schools did not prepare students for university entrance exams.[42] But the sentiment extended beyond the Labor movement. The proposition that any segment of the Jewish population would be educated in multiple languages appeared unnatural and unpleasantly evocative of the diasporic Jewish experience.

One response to these concerns was to sideline other languages as much as possible, thus emphasizing the national and spiritual benefits of Hebrew. Izhac Epstein, whose writings on the teaching of "Hebrew in Hebrew" became a standard for generations of teachers, wrote extensively on the danger of multilingual education. "One of the widespread errors among the public regarding education," he wrote, "is the belief that increasing the number of languages increases knowledge." Noting that many parents were demanding foreign-language study for their children, he proceeded to outline the main psychological danger of combining languages. Cultivating expressive abilities in multiple languages meant, in practice, teaching multiple words for the same concepts, words that ultimately would become confused with one another in the mind: "The languages that we learn weaken one another."[43]

For Epstein, foreign-language instruction in the schools would exacerbate the typical Jewish condition of multilingualism, against which the schools were enjoined to fight. "Members of oppressed peoples have to divide their language abilities into two languages from early childhood," he wrote. While people from other nations are often isolated in their own language, Jews regularly heard two or more different languages at home and in the street—it was impossible, he thought, for powers of expression to develop normally under these circumstances.[44] Worse yet, these characteristically diasporic conditions did not appear to be dissipating in Palestine, where he observed that individuals regularly switched between languages in their conversations. Not only would this mixing and switching impair students' powers of thought in Hebrew, it would lead to another phenomenon, which he called "*hal'azat ha-'Ivrit*," (the "foreignizing" of Hebrew). A person who knew—or learned—languages besides Hebrew would be influenced in his or her Hebrew speech and would come to make errors.

Epstein was aware that foreign languages could not be eliminated completely—"we are enslaved to our environment and its demands"— but he was insistent that languages should be studied no more than necessary. A student learning a language for commercial purposes should focus on commercial language. A language course focused on reading, likewise, should not include speaking exercises or essay assignments.[45] Language should, in his view, be absolutely functional and never allowed to become natural or effortless, for if it does, the language and its words will begin to harm the students' expressive abilities in Hebrew. Epstein's words, written just before the British came to power in Palestine, were held up as a model by the Hebrew Teachers' Federation, which called his research "broad, full, and comprehensive" and repeated his arguments in their assessments of the important work done by early Hebrew educators.[46]

The supposed psychological harm of language multiplicity, which so concerned Epstein in the years before World War I, was a central plank in later educators' opposition to foreign-language study. There was much on which to base this fear, given the climate of bilingualism research at the time, and teachers actively reflected on the phenomenon. Fishel Schneerson, a psychologist and pedagogue, conducted a study for a seminar on bilingualism convened in 1939 by the Tel Aviv branch of the Hebrew Teachers' Federation. Influenced in his work by the large variety of European studies of bilingualism over the preceding several decades (including a 1928 conference in Geneva on the problem of bilingualism), Schneerson began with the premise that "bilingualism is a problem even when it comes during childhood, during the period of the development of language."[47] Schneerson was concerned with the bilingualism of students who spoke one language in the home and Hebrew at school; he did not consider that schools would expose students to any language other than Hebrew. And yet his concern for the deep psychological harm caused by bilingualism was indicative of a generation of educators who could not allow foreign-language study ever to become serious, out of fear that it might begin to impede Hebrew fluency.

This fear that Hebrew would be overwhelmed by foreign languages persisted despite the relatively limited place of foreign languages in schools. In 1924, the journalist Mordechai Ben-Hillel Ha-Cohen reflected on the linguistic situation of the Yishuv under British rule, noting the parallel threats posed by English and Arabic.

> Threats are bursting forth [against our language] from two sides, fighting with all their might. English has come to our country, the language of the authorities, which has not only political value but also—and this is perhaps even more important—a very rich literature, literature in all fields, inestimably rich and more imaginative than our poor Hebrew literature. . . . And from the other side our Arab neighbors are attacking our language with great exertion. Their literature isn't vast and from this perspective our literature might be able to compete with it and it doesn't have the power to subdue our language. But Arabic is supported by a great mass of people who speak it, by the daily life lived in that language, and by the Arab reality.[48]

Ha-Cohen was highly aware that the Yishuv would come into contact with both English and Arabic and, moreover that these languages offered models for Hebrew, the one for its great literature and the other for its rootedness in the landscape. Whereas concerns about Arabic tended to fall in the general realm of educational overload and lack of practicality, concerns about English tended to evoke both the power of the British government and the historical tendency of Jews to slavishly mimic the cultures of the West. The principal of the Hebrew Gymnasium in Jerusalem warned of a "flood of Anglicization" if the British were to have too much influence on the Jewish schools. Joseph Klausner, alluding to English, warned that Hebrew culture could not "stand up to stronger elements."[49]

These anxieties engendered a fundamental uncertainty about the place of foreign languages in the Yishuv's schools, a debate that became more earnest over the course of the mandate period. Some of the most vocal concern came in schools that were teaching more than just English and Arabic. The Balfour Gymnasium in Tel Aviv, for example, began to teach Italian in the school as a response to an Italian government initiative to spread its culture in the Near East, a proposal that was apparently accepted in a few other gymnasia for a period in the 1930s (until the Italian invasion of Ethiopia rendered the entire pursuit problematic). The Herzliya Gymnasium also taught Italian in the 1930s, in addition to English, Arabic, and French.[50] But the educational director of the school expressed his opposition to foreign-language study more generally: "If a student needs to know a language, he can learn it in a short period of time."[51] In other words, there should be no need to devote precious school hours to foreign-language instruction. This wholly incorrect assessment—languages cannot be learned in a short period of time—reflects a dismissive desire to simply kick languages out of the schools.

But even the normal dose of English and Arabic could be a matter of concern to those uncertain whether Hebrew was on a solid foundation. A letter to parents from Kibbutz Ein Harod, whose school taught English from the fifth grade and Arabic from the sixth grade, made clear its ambivalence about the entire project: "Learning three languages at once (Hebrew, too, is a language) is not an easy or simple thing. The question of *bilingualism* in the primary school . . . is being discussed and discussed again by the best pedagogues and researchers—there are those who approve of it and those who oppose it. How much the more so [should the study of] three languages [be discussed]."[52] In the Conference on Language and Culture of 1942, sponsored by the Jewish National Council, "strong sentiments arose" against the fact that the Jewish Agency was funding English and Arabic courses in Zionist schools while "casting off Hebrew education." The sentiments came at a time of increasing insecurity about the state of Hebrew after a massive immigration of German speakers and a perception that gains achieved over the 1920s and early 1930s were giving way to a society built not of ideologically committed citizens but of those who simply had nowhere else to go and who were waiting for any opportunity to leave: "A large portion of the Yishuv is sitting on their suitcases waiting to go back into exile."[53] The inclusion in the curriculum of English and Arabic, though not the languages of those immigrants' Diaspora, evoked the Jewish Agency's perceived tendency to privilege the Yishuv's foreign contacts over its core Hebrew mission. The anxiety was palpable—how could a school that professed to care first and foremost about Hebrew reasonably and fruitfully include not one but two additional languages on its already cramped schedule?

These alarmist, dismissive, and concerned views fit easily into a historical narrative of Hebrew's tireless fight against linguistic rivals. Indeed, they mimic coexisting fears about Yiddish or German: the languages were seen as stronger, more natural, and more vibrant, and thus as threats to Hebrew. But if such sentiments were real, they were not universal and, more to the point, did not prevent foreign languages from being taught nearly universally. As Nirit Reichel notes, the overt Zionist rejection of any educational undertaking not directly tied to Jewish national aims coexisted with a "covert model" of a student who would receive a wide general education.[54] A widespread discomfort with multilingualism coexisted with a real sense, at least among some Zionist educators, that Hebrew could not fully evade its linguistic and cultural others and, moreover, that it should not, for its own sake.

Language for Practical Purposes

The fact was that the study of Arabic and English had clear practical justifications and could not be neglected, even in the rural agricultural settlements that Belkind had earlier sought to exclude from any such studies. In a 1936 lecture on "general studies" given to the left-wing Ha-Shomer Ha-Tza'ir labor organization, the educator Zvi Zohar discussed foreign-language study as part of a labor-oriented curriculum that, among other goals, familiarized students with general human culture and provided a basis for professional life. English courses, he thought, should prepare students to read scientific texts and newspapers and carry on negotiations with English speakers. Instruction in Arabic, which he called "the language of the neighbors," should aim at teaching both "understanding and free conversation" and recognition of the lives of the Arabs. Language skills, in this formulation, were heavily practical and, more to the point, oriented toward local, Palestinian needs.[55]

On one level, the purpose of language study was practicality: if the languages were necessary, they should be taught, and they should be taught with an eye to the contexts in which they might actually be used. English courses in particular were most often justified this way: "Our political situation has made it necessary for us to learn a foreign language, something that isn't necessary in other countries," wrote Yosef Luria in 1921.[56] The most commonly used English texts in the Yishuv advanced these quotidian goals. Isaac and Rachel Morris's 1932 textbook *Second Year English for Palestine Schools* (like his first-year book), was "designed to meet the needs of Palestine schoolchildren" by considering "colloquial, narrative, and descriptive" language forms.[57] Meir Diengott and Samuel M. Bender's *First Steps in English* (1937, 1947), published by the Re'ali School in Haifa, was clearly oriented toward local practical purposes as well. A collection of children's rhymes is interspersed with thematic lessons titled "Time," "Breakfast," "Go to school," "Train Journey," "Ride in a Bus," and others. "These themes are simple," the writers emphasize, "taken first of all from the room in which the pupils are found, passing into the home and later going out into the street."[58] Grammar books, too, were careful to note that they did not want to teach more grammar than that necessary for spoken and written proficiency—grammar was "primarily a means and not an end in itself."[59] A 1941 report titled "The Teaching of English in Hebrew Secondary Schools" by J. S. Bentwich, English teacher at the Re'ali School and later an inspector for Hebrew schools at the mandatory Department of Education, emphasized that a student who completed the secondary-school course "should be able to understand spoken Standard English and to express himself more or less freely on ordinary topics."[60]

The British were the most obvious target for spoken English use, but a more unusual suggestion about the benefits of competence in spoken English is worth noting. W. J. Farrell, head of the mandate's education department in Palestine and a regular attendee at the Jewish Agency's English Committee meetings, suggested that perhaps the agency could require incoming Jewish settlers to acquire a knowledge of English while still abroad, "as a means of communication with the Arabs, since only a few [Jews] can acquire knowledge of Arabic."[61] Moshe Shertok, head of the Political Department of the Jewish Agency, opposed this proposal, however: "As a means of communication with Arabs he did not think English to be of great importance."[62] Though the idea was pooh-poohed in this instance, English indeed has become a chief language of communication between Israeli Jews and Palestinian Arabs in high-level negotiations as well as in citizen-led peace initiatives.

Practical goals could be oriented toward written as well as verbal competence. English had particular relevance for clerical workers, and from the beginning of the mandate period, educators even outside commercial schools considered adding stenography and correspondence courses for those interested in this profession. English could also be the language in which farmers read agricultural manuals or industrial workers learned new techniques.[63] A reading knowledge of English could thus be defended even in the absence of personal contact with Britons. Sections of Bentwich's curriculum focused on reading to allow students to understand the context of modern plays, novels, newspapers, or science and history textbooks. Though proficiency is key, Bentwich did not support the direct method, concluding that "the best method . . . is something of a compromise" between English speaking on the part of the teacher and explanations in Hebrew, as well as Hebrew-to-English translations in the intermediate stages, when students are learning grammar.[64]

In seeking to achieve these practical goals, Yishuv educators had direct recourse to a series of textbooks prepared for a different colonial setting: British India, where educators had for decades been debating the best ways of teaching English to Indians. The majority of Hebrew schools in the Yishuv—both primary and secondary—turned to one series in particular: Michael West's *New Method Readers*, texts oriented toward reading proficiency. West, who had been posted to Bengal in 1912 as part of the Indian Education Service, was critical of the "English-only," direct-method approach that had motivated British English teaching in India since Thomas Babington Macaulay's *Minute on Indian Education* in 1835. Convinced that some level of English would be profitable for all students, he designed a reading-based curriculum that would give practical skills to all students regardless of their future educational goals. As the principal of the Teachers' Training College in Dhaka, West experimented with reading curricula based on a limited vocabulary. Incrementally, West added speaking components to his reading courses.[65] In 1935, he published his *New Method English Dictionary*, which became a common reference in the Yishuv. In addition to New Method books directly imported to the Yishuv through the series' publisher, Longmans, Green, the New Method model was more deliberately adapted to the Yishuv. Realizing that many students wanted to work on their speaking skills as well as on reading literary texts, West asked Bentwich to write a textbook in 1938 as part of the New Method Series, consisting "mainly of conversation-lessons centring on topics of daily life and leading up to short stories with questions and answers as in the New Method Readers." This text, like West's other courses, did not focus on grammar.[66]

Arabic, too, could be justified by reference to its practical importance—both spoken and written—for a society in the middle of an Arabic-speaking region. Some educators rejected grammatical study outright and promoted colloquial Arabic study alone (sometimes using Hebrew transliteration rather than Arabic script), focusing on the customs and traditions of contemporary communities, and supporting Jewish visits to Arab villages, similar to those being organized for nonschool outings. One advocate of a communicative approach was Israel Ben-Zeev, the inspector for Arabic at the Department of Education of the Jewish National Council beginning in 1938. Ben-Zeev was born Israel Wolfenson in the Me'ah She'arim neighborhood of Jerusalem in the summer of 1899.[67] He received a traditional religious education but later studied Hebrew language and literature, European languages, history, and the sciences at the German-run Läemel School in Jerusalem and eventually left his traditional religious practice. After the British conquest of Jerusalem in December 1917, he began to worry about the future of Jewish-Arab relations in Palestine, and in 1919 made the decision to study Arabic at the Arab Teachers' College in Jerusalem. "I was the first and last Jew in this Arab institution," he later wrote.[68] Later, Ben-Zeev traveled to Egypt, where he taught Judaic studies at the University of Cairo for part of the year while pursuing a PhD at the University of Frankfurt de Main under the guidance of Josef Horovitz and Gotthold Weil, the future directors of the School of Oriental Studies at Hebrew University.[69]

Though he had been educated in Frankfurt in the German orientalist tradition—which focused on grammar and classical texts—when he assumed the role of inspector for Arabic for the Jewish National Council just before World War II (a position he held until 1965), Ben-Zeev decried classical methodology as artificial and divisive. He believed that drawing Jews and Arabs together through spoken-language proficiency should be the first priority of the secondary schools. In 1938 he argued, "It is necessary to adapt the sounds, expressions and accents of Arabic to the student's ear before the eye adjusts itself to the dead letters." After all: "Students do not learn Arabic as a dead language for scientific purposes. They learn it for use in reading, writing, and conversation. Personal contact with Arabs is a vital need in all respects."[70] He later emphasized these opinions in his textbooks for colloquial Arabic, which were published in several editions over the course of the 1940s.[71] Other educators echoed these calls. Jochanan Kapliwatzky, an independent iconoclast continually at odds with the university establishment, called "understanding the masses" the "most important purpose" of Arabic study and proposed a curriculum in spoken Arabic that required no knowledge of the literary language.[72] A 1942 memorandum by Yitzhak Shamosh, sent to the Jewish Agency and the Jewish National Council, also pushed for a communicative approach at all levels of schooling. In the primary schools, said Shamosh, a native of Syria who taught Arabic language at Hebrew University, the focus should be on spoken Arabic to be used "at times of need" and "for day-to-day uses"; in the gymnasia, students "would be able to use their knowledge [of Arabic] for their own good in life"; and at the university, highly skilled students would complete their studies with the ability "to write, converse, and speak easily" and, moreover, become representatives of Zionism to the Arab world.[73]

Sephardi and Mizrahi educators were particularly likely to promote spoken Arabic, the legacy of a longer trend in the Sephardi Zionist community of desire for communication with Arabs, particularly during the late Ottoman period.[74] In his 1928 Arabic textbook, the Sephardi leader Abraham Elmaliah argued that existing textbooks were simply not adequate for Jewish children in Palestine: "All the methods that have been compiled in Europe, Egypt, and Syria, both by European scholars and by religious Arabs—though excellent from the scientific-research-linguistic-grammatical perspective—are nonetheless not at all appropriate for the Hebrew student who wants to derive useful and not scholarly benefit from textbooks in Arabic."[75] In a meeting of the Jewish National Council's Arabic Committee in March 1931, educators disagreed over the merits of Avinoam Yellin and Levi Billig's *Reading Selections*.[76] While the university scholars in the group spoke highly of the book, likely in support of their colleague Billig, two Mizrahi educators, Yosef Mani and Eliyahu Habubah (the second of whom composed his own textbook for colloquial Arabic), were concerned that the material was "too historic and Islamic" and not sufficiently focused on practical contact.[77]

These pro-communication educators stressed the practical benefits of real contact with Arabs, always with the assumption that such contact was conducive to peaceful relations. Few textbook introductions explicitly mention the practical benefit of Arabic study for managing or monitoring an enemy or hostile population, a motivation more visible in community-education-type settings, including on kibbutzim. Nonetheless, the actual curriculum used in most schools was focused far less on knowing Arabs personally than on "Knowing the Arab," a methodology explicitly or implicitly tied to surveillance, control, and mastery. In a 1934 speech, Yellin sketched a model of educating in the "living language," by which students would focus on literary Arabic and contemporary texts as a way to understand Arab society.[78] In the 1931 introduction to *Reading Selections*, he emphasized, "We took care to choose chapters that have cultural value in the lives of the nations whose language is Arabic, as well as general cultural value."[79]

This focus on comprehending rather than personally knowing Arabs was common and represents an important third path between classical and colloquial studies. This lack of focus on formal grammatical instruction, in other words, the refutation of the traditional classical method, did not mean a turn to colloquial Arabic but rather the choice of a program focused on understanding the modern Arab world through written texts.[80] Indeed, to the extent that Arabic came to be seen as "practical," it was because it was the language of surveillance and propaganda. As the intelligence divisions of the Irgun and the Haganah became more developed, and particularly after the state was established in 1948, the clear benefit of studying Arabic in school was the prospect of a job in the intelligence services, a point that Gil Eyal has made persuasively.[81] Once the state came into being, English and Arabic thus increasingly became pre-professional skills for students who intended to go into certain careers.

Beyond the Practical: Finding Models for Zionism in Foreign Languages and Cultures

To the extent that English was viewed as simply "technically helpful" or Arabic was seen as a practical tool, study could be utilitarian.[82] But language study is rarely justified on the basis of practical needs alone; educators around the world have attempted to attach loftier, more broadly humanistic goals to their teaching and to rebuff those who care only about the practical (notwithstanding a trend in interwar American education away from nonpractical studies).[83] Yishuv educators retained a great respect for the exalted, the symbolic, and the intellectual even as they discussed how to impart practical skills. Any assessment of practical language study alone thus overlooks what was for Jews the historical importance and symbolism of Arabic on the one hand and western European languages on the other. Arabic, for its part, was conceived of as a natural undertaking for Ashkenazi Jews, who had long recognized the great production of Jewish philosophy and literature in Arabic, had identified Arabic as a sister Semitic tongue, and from the mid-nineteenth century had been engaged in its study within the academic institutions of Europe.[84] The Jewish interest in Arabic was not simply a product of the encounter with Arabic-speaking populations in Palestine, and the practical benefits of using that language to understand or influence Arabs was not the only reason it seemed important.

English, in contrast, did not have a broad role in the intellectual development of modern Jewish thought and (outside Anglophone countries of course) was not considered central to Jews, Judaism, or Jewish history in the way that Arabic was. Though the Zionist Organization was originally headquartered in London, Zionists by and large encountered English only in Palestine after the British took control. But English, unlike Turkish during the Ottoman period, had more than simply instrumental associations. As a European language, it evoked a broader set of cultural discourses about culture, modern education, assimilation, economic opportunity, prestige, access to power, and integration with the West—concerns that had occupied Jewish thinkers since the early Haskalah period in the late eighteenth century and that were by no means neutralized by the radical Zionist move to leave Europe physically behind. While the set of discourses about Arabic were exclusive to Arabic, those pertaining to English might well have been applied to French if the colonial politics of the age had proceeded differently, but the discursive link between modern values and European language would have likely followed a similar path.

Long-standing Jewish associations between language and associated values—Arabic with Semitic authenticity, European languages with modernity—led to a situation in which language study itself could appear conducive to the transmission of values. In the case of Arabic, classical methods were held up as a path toward proper Hebrew authenticity. In the case of English, modern reading courses with texts that focused on contemporary British culture seemed best to advance the Yishuv's quest for modernity. These values-based motivations, as much as practical ones, directed choices about language studies and help explain why aspects of the language curriculum, whether extensive translations of Qur'anic passages or essays on British municipal services in England, do not immediately appear relevant to the Palestinian context.

The Symbolism of Arabic

Arabic appeared to have the potential to draw students toward a richer and more rooted Hebrew identity in two ways. First, grammatical similarities between Arabic and Hebrew might lead students to a deeper understanding of the linguistic structure of their new mother tongue, and, second, Arabic study could be part of a more symbolic, amorphous project to draw nearer to the East. Eliezer Ben-Yehuda had emphasized early on the importance of Semitic—and thus, Arabic-like—traits in Hebrew and stressed the importance of drawing on words from other Semitic languages. Thus, he recommended including instruction in Arabic pronunciation in the study of Hebrew. "One of the living veins of our language is pronunciation," he wrote in a letter to the editor of the educational journal *Ha-Hinukh* in 1910. He expressed concern that Hebrew speakers were eliminating the unique sounds of the letters tet, ayin, and, kof, which give the Semitic languages "their Oriental tone and sound," and by omitting doubled consonants (still a feature of Arabic), were negating "the power and strength of [their] language." Noting the difficulty of Semitic pronunciation for Westerners, Ben-Yehuda's Hebrew-language committee had turned to heads of schools to institute pronunciation classes led by native Arabic speakers, who "can produce the true tone of each letter naturally and in a way that is neither affected nor artificial."[85]

Whereas communication-based textbooks downplayed grammar, other texts explicitly focused on this component of the language, seeing it as a conduit to a better understanding of Hebrew. Martin Plessner, in his *The Theory of Arabic Grammar: A Guidebook for Hebrew Schools (1935)*, clarifies his understanding of Arabic as a linguistic tool to draw students closer to

Hebrew. The book, one-quarter of which is composed of verb tables, is intended to encourage students to compare Arabic and Hebrew "in order to come to a greater understanding of their mother tongue." Arabic is a particularly powerful tool for this purpose, said Plessner, a teacher of Arabic at the Re'ali School in Haifa, so long as it is taught according to European orientalist principles rather than native Arabic ones:

> The great precision with which Arabs construct their sentences makes the Arab language a one-of-a-kind tool to accustom the Hebrew child to logical thought. From this recognition we explain the syntactic phenomena—in opposition to the accepted method among the Arabs—from a logical point of view on the basis of the scholarly work that has been done in Europe in the last century. The teacher who knows how to use this tool properly will educate his students to be more precise in linguistic matters generally and in matters of our own language in particular.[86]

Systematic study, not colloquial proficiency, was the goal. In response to an article by a man advocating for "practical" Arabic study in the gymnasia, Plessner asserted that this approach would be a mistake: "Arabic is the only Semitic language that children learn at school, the language closest to his mother tongue. Other than it he learns only European languages, which won't enlighten him about his mother tongue in the way that European languages support one another abroad."[87] While European students, Plessner implies, could learn about their own tongues through Greek, Latin, and modern tongues, classical Arabic was the proper way for Jews to come to an understanding of their own language.

Some textbooks reflected the related notion that just as Arabic was the "root" of Hebrew, contemporary Arabic culture could be understood as a reflection of the ancient Hebrew past. Jochanan Kapliwatzky, who had so vociferously promoted spoken Arabic, suggested elsewhere that a benefit of studying the Arab present could be insight into the Jewish past. His textbook *The Arabic Language and Its Grammar*, for example, includes passages describing the life of Bedouins, "whose content," he writes, "offers a comparison between the lives of the ancients in the land of the Fathers and the lives of the Bedouins."[88] In either case, Arabic was a conduit to Hebrew linguistic authenticity and to Jewish cultural roots. While practical studies were oriented toward mastery of a local context, classical studies claimed the East for Zionism in a far deeper way, by integrating it and its language into Zionism itself.

Zionist educators agreed that textbooks from Iraq, Syria, and Egypt, which some Jewish students of Arabic used through the 1930s, were not ideal. Most Jews in the Yishuv, after all, learned Arabic as a second language and benefited from books tailored to Hebrew-speaking students. Plessner's critique of the Arab textbooks, however, runs deeper. There was a fundamental methodological difference, he thought, between European and Arab pedagogy. While Arabs taught holistically, on the level of meaning and sound, European methodology attuned students to deeper structural elements of the language.[89] Only the rigor of methodical classical Arabic, Plessner believed, would give Jewish students the deep understanding of Hebrew they required. This reasoning was also instrumental in the founding of the School of Oriental Studies at Hebrew University in 1927. "The Hebrew language demands knowledge of the Semitic languages, the development of the Oriental spirit," said the noted Hebrew teacher David Yellin at a meeting to plan the establishment of the school, "and therefore one of the first things [in the establishment of a university] needs to be the opening of a department of Oriental studies."[90]

Arabic study appeared to some to have a second benefit beyond its linguistic value: it would ease Zionists' integration in the East and allow them fully to divest themselves of Europe. Accordingly, one of the most commonly heard arguments in favor of Arabic study in Hebrew schools was that in order to truly return to an authentic Hebrew identity, Jews had to get in touch with their Semitic roots, roots that some felt had been severed during the long sojourn in the European Diaspora. An article in the newspaper *Ha-Boker* made this explicit: "In order to free ourselves from the influence of foreign [European] languages whose family and race are different from ours, there is a need to draw nearer to our Semitic sister [Arabic]."[91] Levi Billig at the School of Oriental Studies likewise spoke of disseminating "an understanding of Arabic culture, which is so foreign to Jews brought up in the West or among Slavs."[92]

An appeal for local literacy involved vaguely stated calls to connect with Arabs and get rid of an excessive concern with the West. Shlomo

Dov Goitein, in a meeting of the Jewish National Council's Arabic Committee, denied any chance that Jews would lose their identities by "assimilating" into the East: "There is no danger of assimilation; on the contrary, there is a positive need to get closer to the East."[93] In a 1927 article in *Hed ha-Hinukh*, a writer identified as "Y. M." argued that schools were not sufficiently committed to promoting knowledge of Arab populations. The Arab school, which he called "terra incognita," was unknown though at hand: "We have not even tried to get to know it. Our sights are directed overseas, to the West: we've gotten used to denigrating that which is going on around us with one nullifying word—Levantine—and to treat it as though it is worthless." Perhaps, he suggested, Zionists could "at last come to a point of mutual understanding, which is the only way to draw near those who are distant and estranged."[94] The denigration of the East as "Levantine," the writer believed, was ultimately hindering Jews' integration into it. Indeed, he thought, some amount of the Levant needed to be incorporated into the Zionist self.

Connecting with the East seemed to be the best way to resolve a host of Zionist limitations, both linguistic and spiritual. "The only way by which we can effectively fix the [Hebrew] language" wrote Yosef Y. Berlin in the educational journal *Hed Ha-Hinukh* in 1927, "is by delving into Orientalness [*mizrahiut*]."

> Delving into Orientalness, or better yet Semitic-ness [*shemiyut*], is necessary for us for several reasons. A Western people won't be established in an Oriental land . . . The nation among whom we are settling and which will always surround us on all sides won't understand us, and we won't understand them, if we don't become that which we need to become: a Semitic people. It is a mistake to think that we will succeed by diplomacy. Only in a place where there are direct relations, where there are good Jews in whom the Semitic vein has returned and has been aroused by the smell of the earth and the sight of the skies is there the possibility of a relationship, of talks, or negotiations . . . We need to educate ourselves to be a Semitic people, and the desired day will come of its own accord. We need to cultivate the Orientalness inside of ourselves.[95]

Toward this end, Berlin recommended a solution suggested by Rabbi Eliezer Meir Lipschuetz the Hebrew gymnasium should teach Arabic and Aramaic in the way that European schools teach Latin and Greek—both to introduce students to the roots of their own language and to help them understand the classical, civilized culture from which their own culture derived.[96] Of course, Arabic was a cognate language, not an ancestor of Hebrew. Moreover, Ancient Hebrew, not Arabic, would be the primary source of classical models. Nonetheless the orientalist conception that Palestinian Arabs, and particularly Bedouins, preserved the cultures of biblical times buttressed the claim that the Arabic language, too, might reflect Hebrew's linguistic origins.

We can see several of these strains of thought come together in the words of Shlomo Dov Goitein, the Hebrew University scholar of classical Islam and medieval Jewish communities, a chief interpreter of the Cairo Genizah materials, and one of the most impassioned advocates of the symbolic value of Arabic. His 1946 article in the educational journal *Shevile ha-hinukh*, "The Question of Arabic Study: Toward a Decision," articulated justifications for Arabic study in the schools. "It is not difficult," he wrote, "to define the general purpose of Arabic-language instruction in our schools."

> Arabic study is a *part of Zionism*, a part of the return to the Hebrew language and the Semitic Orient, which today is wholly Arabic-speaking. We wish that our children, when they go out into the world, *be able to feel themselves to be at home in the East and to be able to act within it*, just as we desire that they do not lose the precious inheritance of European spirituality that we brought. And in order for our young people to be able to feel at home in the Arab Orient and to act within it, it seems that they need to know Arabic to a certain degree and to know something about the life, institutions and spiritual world of the contemporary Middle East.

Goitein's ultimate proposal emphasizes practical studies of contemporary Middle Eastern "life and institutions," as the last sentence indicates, but his justification is essentially internal: he stresses that Arabic knowledge will facilitate Jews' return to two aspects of their authentic identity: the language and the land. Because Arabic is a "close sister of our language," he argues, its study can be part of "preserving the original character of the Hebrew language and enriching it." Arabic knowledge can be a path to Jewish authenticity in another sense as well; after the recent destruction of European Jewry, there remained a "stable bloc" of "original Judaism" in Yemen and North Africa with which relations needed to be cultivated.[97] Arabic and Islam were thus both the analogue of Hebrew and Jewishness and, in the form of contemporary states, the incubators for the most authentic forms of Judaism.

Further, Goitein stresses that teaching Arabic can be one step in making Jews feel that they are "at home" (*bene bayit*) in the Orient. He argues, articulating a central tension in the Zionist movement, that Jews should not blend into the East at the expense of their European identities, but should be a kind of hybrid, manifesting the best of Europe and Asia. Jews should, he implies, fulfill the assessment of several European orientalists including Theodor Nöldeke, who wrote that Jews "have maintained many features of their primitive type with remarkable tenacity, but they have become Europeans all the same; and, moreover, many peculiarities by which they are marked are not so much of old Semitic origin as the result of the special history of the Jews."[98] More, even, than a program to give students practical skills, Arabic study appears here to be a deeply symbolic gesture, a commitment to return to the East, reassert identity, and declare a commitment to Hebrew culture.

The curriculum for Arabic in most schools was based heavily on reading, but combined an orientation to the practical with the recognition of the deep symbolic value of Arabic. At a meeting of the Committee for Arabic Study in the High Schools, on 10 October 1934, Avinoam Yellin, inspector for Arabic in the Hebrew schools, gave a presentation on the challenges facing Arabic-language educators in the Zionist secondary schools. The 1939 publication of this piece in the journal *Ha-Hinukh* sparked, according to Shlomo Dov Goitein, an intense debate about the merits of Arabic study.[99] The purposes of Arabic study, the document said, fell into two categories: "practical" and "general educational." The "general educational" functions mirror the aims of the School of Oriental Studies and the guidelines set out by Plessner. From this standpoint, Arabic could help students "recognize one of the important world literatures and cultures," "develop the ability to discern and to use grammatical structures which require precision in thought and expression," by "cultivating comparisons between the mother tongue [Hebrew] and a second Semitic tongue for the sake of a more foundational understanding of the mother tongue," and, finally, "value reciprocal relationships between the intellectual elites of the Jewish people and the Islamic peoples." The "practical" goals, in contrast, emerged from the lived experience of Zionists in Palestine. They encompassed "day-to-day needs," administrative roles, reading Arabic newspapers, and "cultivating social relationships with the Arabs in this land and neighboring lands."[100] Learning Arabic had the potential, Yellin believed, to promote multiple aspects of a young student's development. The deep grammatical structure of the language could be a means to cultural awareness and self-understanding, as Plessner argued, but the spoken language could also be a tool for contact among ordinary people.

Noting the limitations placed on students by limited hours, Yellin sketches a model of education by which students focus on literary Arabic and contemporary texts for understanding Arab society. In contrast to Plessner, he believed that the study of grammar was simply instrumental to understanding and should not be considered a subject in its own right.[101] Other educators adopted this composite of classical and contemporary sources in their textbooks. Josef Joel Rivlin included four categories of readings in his 1936 textbook: excerpts from the Qur'an and other classical sources; Arabic texts written by Jews; excerpts from contemporary newspapers; and selected Arab legends.[102] Ultimately, practical and symbolic justifications could not entirely be separated. Indeed, given the great symbolism of returning to the East, the establishment of harmony within Palestine through personal communication had a symbolism of its own.

These visions aside, the movement to teach Arabic often stalled at the recognition of present discord with real Arabic speakers. While English seemed threatening as a foreign language, Arabic most often simply seemed unwise, or untimely. A teacher identified as "Y. S." disagreed with Yosef Y. Berlin, who had recommended drawing closer to the Orient. The truth, Y. S. wrote, is that the Arabs should turn to the Jews "and learn something from Westerners." "As long as they don't take the first steps, we'll continue teaching our curriculum in our own ways. For the time has not yet come for one language and pure, unified words [*safah ahat u-devarim ahadim tehorim*]."[103] Such concerns about the Arabs' lack of readiness to learn Hebrew—or, more specifically, their lack of interest in doing so—were common in articles questioning the value of the operation. While the appeal of the authentic past was theoretically attractive, the encounter with modern Arabs pushed Y. S. to accentuate not the Zionists' Semitic nature but their Western sensibilities, not the Jewish desire to shed Europe but a coexisting urge to flaunt their Europeanness and bring it as an offering to the underdeveloped East.

The Symbolism of English

The pro-Western resistance visible in Y. S.'s response to Berlin evoked a civilizing mission never far below the surface of Zionist rhetoric.[104] For all the emphasis on the authentic Semitic character of the Jews, members of the Zionist movement by and large wished to act and appear European. But the appeal for Zionists to act as Western moderns—in their relations with Arabs or otherwise—was no more straightforward than the appeal for them to be Semites. Zionists' anxiety over their lack of Semitic authenticity and lack of claim to Palestine was matched only by their concern about insufficient modernity and development, a concern bred by years of exclusion from and within the societies of modern Europe. This second insecurity, too, was reflected in discourses on acquired language. If Arabic was presumed to be an entry ticket into the East and its conventions, English could be seen as a way out, an antidote to the corrosive influences of the East and a means of ensuring the European quality of the Yishuv.

Shoshana Sitton, who has written on English in the Yishuv, emphasizes the conflict between the British government, which wished to impose its own educational principles on Palestine, and the Yishuv, which balked at any foreign involvement in the Hebrew Zionist schools. Speaking of the early years of the mandate, when the extent of British control was still undetermined, she writes, "It was feared that British financial support would undermine the justification for adopting the Hebrew language in Jewish schools and encourage the introduction of English as the governing language." Aware of the "superiority" of British culture, Sitton argues, educators worked to create a Hebrew culture that could stand up to it. A focus on Zionist ideas and a rejection of foreign ones would be central to this endeavor. The Zionist scout movement thus was shaped as a counterpoint to the British system, as was the curriculum itself. Overall, she writes, "the creators of the young, secular, Hebrew culture tried to isolate schools from the influence of other cultures and to emphasize its exclusivity by over-emphasizing its unique qualities."[105] Sitton is not wrong in emphasizing the strength of Hebrew Zionist culture and its fierce independence from British oversight, but in overlooking those aspects of British culture included in the curriculum, she elides a coexisting tendency to see English—though not British—oversight as a means of inculcating desirable values.

For some refugees in Palestine before and during World War II, English promised a ticket to Europe, almost literally. An article in *Ha-Mashkif* from 1944 noted, certainly hyperbolically, that 90 percent of Polish Jewish immigrants that year were sending their children to Christian Polish schools. Even if we discount its premise, the anecdote makes clear why some might have made that choice: the missionary schools taught English. And English was a way back to Europe: "A young girl in the [school] dormitories was learning English. She was asked by our writer whether she was also being educated in Hebrew. The answer was 'And why do I need that?' and she added, 'At the end of the war, in the event that I can't return to Poland, I'll try to have the government send me to London. And if I am forced to stay here it will be a tragedy for me.' "[106] English was indeed occasionally a conduit for physically leaving Palestine and getting employment in Europe. More common, however, was a perception that English, which Ben-Zion Dinaburg (head of the Hebrew Teachers' Training College in Jerusalem) called "the chief conduit of European influence" in the Yishuv, would help Jews escape the degenerative effects of the East and establish a functioning European society in Palestine.[107] This impulse, we should note, was similar to the feelings of colonial and postcolonial African elites. As Moredawun Adejunmobi writes: "To the extent that Western society itself was constructed as a model of modernity, African access to this ideal would be mediated at least in part through selective appropriations of the modalities offered by the Western world. . . . There was little doubt that European languages played a vital role in the formation of the novel political and economic structures associated with modernity."[108]

Two impulses were characteristic of Zionist educators, who, though they did not find the structures of modernity "novel," were similarly concerned that such values were incompletely or only tenuously held by the Yishuv. First, from the beginning of the British presence in Palestine, some expressed the hope that the study of English literature might serve as a model for the still incomplete Hebrew literary tradition. Second, many felt that an introduction to the modern culture, nature, and political system of the English (seen as a beacon of democracy, particularly in the Nazi era) might serve as a model for the emerging Hebrew society.

A great strength of English was its rich literature. Just as knowledge of Arabic's Semitic grammar could strengthen the linguistic core of the Hebrew language, familiarity with English literature could serve as a model for the still-lacking Hebrew literary tradition. English, Mordechai Ben-Hillel Ha-Cohen noted in 1923, has "a very rich literature, literature in all fields, inestimably rich and more imaginative than our poor Hebrew literature."[109] A report on English in Hebrew secondary schools, published by the Education Department of the Jewish National Council in 1941, asserted that the gymnasia in particular needed to move beyond language itself to broader cultural concerns. The report cited a 1918 British document that recommended "Modern Studies," including the study of modern European languages as "an instrument of culture" that could help "develop the higher faculties, the imagination, the sense of beauty, and the intellectual comprehension." Applying that document's conclusions to the Palestine context, the report noted that "a similar cultural aim should pervade the study of English in our schools." Exposure to English in Palestine was even more important than the study of other European languages in England, for "Hebrew literature is poorer than English both in content and form."[110]

Literature was not the only exemplary creation of the English; their culture, society, and civic structures, too, could serve as models for an emerging Zionist polity. At its heart, the recommendation to study foreign languages was premised on the idea that, like Hebrew literature, Zionist civic culture was stunted in its development and needed an infusion of Western sensibilities. The Safra School of Commerce in Tel Aviv, which taught English largely for professional reasons, noted in its promotional material that through foreign-language study "every educated person can probe the international world of cultures and recognize their achievements."[111] English was at the core of this proposition. The Jewish National

Council report on English insisted that the curriculum focus not only on English literature, but also on English life: "Pupils who have been fed only belles letters remain often with only a poor understanding of the English people." Moreover, a connection with modern people would transmit a set of modern values to the Yishuv, for "the study of modern English thought and institutions can provoke useful discussion and help to correct provincial tendencies."[112] The use of language here is revealing. The word "provincial" evokes the parallel term Levantine/*levantini*, a word used to describe failed or incomplete Europeanization, ill-formed institutions, and illogical cultural mixtures. As we have seen from other statements about *levantiniyut*, the main feature of cultural provincialism was multilingualism, and its main antidote was adherence to Hebrew only. But in this case, ironically, one path away from *levantiniyut* was the study of a foreign language understood to embody an opposite tendency.

No doubt, it was England that first promoted itself as a model society with model values, in Palestine as well as in the rest of the empire. British publishers offered accessible English texts about the greatness of the empire for distribution in numerous countries overseas. In a small book called *Here and There in the British Empire*, published in 1902 and transported to the Yishuv, students read that "Greater Britain" had become "a power to which Rome in the height of her glory was not to be compared," and the text goes on to suggest that this stunning success can be attributed, "in no small measure, to the fact that the British are a hardy, determined, persevering, maritime race" who love adventure, order and justice, and the spirit of law.[113] Tendentious as they may seem to today's reader, these texts by and large confirmed beliefs that Zionists held already. The West's embodiment of modern values was broadly assumed; its epistemic privilege was unquestioned and unquestionable.[114] The particular texts available to Jewish students, whether written abroad or in Palestine, reflected educators' own search both to justify the Zionist project in Western eyes and to find Western blueprints for Jewish self-government and civil society.

Three books "recommended for English" by the English Committee of the Jewish National Council in 1935–36 lend insight into the process by which, implicitly, British values were understood to be models for the Yishuv.[115] These texts were not used by every school—indeed, textbooks, not nonfiction, were the basis for elementary study—but appear to have been used in the upper grades in some institutions. In this case, the implicit principles behind their selection make them relevant for this analysis. The first is Robert Baden-Powell's 1908 *Scouting for Boys: A Handbook for Instruction in Good Citizenship*, recommended for reading in the tenth grade. Baden-Powell's book, directed to British audiences (though ultimately distributed throughout the world) was written during a period of flagging self-confidence in Britain following the Anglo-Boer War. As Elleke Boehmer writes in a 2004 introduction to the text, "Where the failing strength of the nation was mirrored in the alleged deterioration of the male physique at the time, a practical handbook that proposed physical training as well as lessons in strategy derived from the writer's own military experiences, could not but be a winner."[116] As Sitton has noted, the Zionist scout movement worked to inculcate explicitly Zionist rather than British values, but a closer look indicates that the deeper self-understanding of the two movements was not so different.[117] The parallels between the British concern with diminished masculinity and the Zionist commitment to building a new sort of man can hardly be ignored. Baden-Powell saw the colonial space as a realm characterized by strong, selfless, nationalist men working for peace. The frontiersmen of all parts of the British Empire were "peace scouts": "They understand living out in the jungles and they can find their way anywhere . . . They are accustomed to take their lives in their hands and to fling them down without hesitation if they can help their country by doing so."[118] Baden-Powell's vision is a colonialist fantasy of manhood and self-reliance in a harsh natural environment far away from the coddling and enervating city. The protagonists become epitomes of the modern British nation by mastering the survival techniques of primitive peoples who have an intuitive understanding of nature. Likewise, a Jewish reader of Baden-Powell might believe that his description reflected Zionist mastery of the Palestine environment.

A second book recommendation was Charles Higham's 1931 text, *The Good Citizen: An Introduction to Civics.*[119] This highly idealized portrait of British civic life was directed at the urban British schoolchild. It asks students to pay attention to the efficient postal service, roads, schools, and electric lights in their own neighborhoods and to understand that these services work well because of the civic commitments of British citizens.

The book also reviews governmental structures and the makeup of the British Empire. Whereas for a British student the book evokes respect for the homeland and a sense of civic pride, for a Palestinian Jewish student the text functions partly as a guide for the perplexed to English society and partly as a manual and instruction book for the creation of a working society elsewhere. The act of reading this text as part of a language class abroad would indelibly link the English language with a set of idealized social portraits and, ultimately, to Jewish communal aspirations. A further indication that such primers were taken seriously by the Yishuv is the fact that Adam A. Mendilow, English lecturer at the Hebrew University, co-authored a similar book called *How the English Are Governed*, tailored to the Palestinian audience and repeatedly acquired by school libraries and academic programs.[120] The exemplary nature and political leadership of British society was highlighted in some courses: the English final exam authored in 1935 by the Jewish National Council committee required an essay titled "The British Nation as the Defender of the League of Nations."[121]

A third selection, Paul Cohen-Portheim's *England: The Unknown Isle* (translated from German), is notable for having been written outside England by a Jew, in this case an Austrian. Cohen-Portheim, a regular traveler to England, was detained there between 1914 and 1918 as an enemy combatant because of his citizenship. Undeterred, he moved to Paris and went on to write, in the words of a *Time* magazine review, "one of the most tolerant, friendly, sympathetic retaliations imaginable."[122] Although "never brilliant or startlingly original," according to the review, the book seems to have offered several characterizations of England intriguing or appealing to the English Committee of the Jewish National Council. First, Cohen-Portheim insisted on England's uniqueness, using words that could have been used by Jews to describe themselves: "England is a phenomenon that needs a special terminology to describe it. . . . The British nation is the least understood and the most extensively misrepresented in the world." Second, Cohen-Portman points out England's remarkably tolerant treatment of Jews and attributes this respect, in part, to Britons' "deep reverence for everything ancient with a long tradition behind it."[123] Not only did this text remind Jews of Britain's supposed respect for them, but Zionists could also infer that if the British devotion to tradition and the ancient made them tolerant of Jews, then Zionists, with similar traits, would certainly become a nation tolerant of others. Cohen-Portheim's estrangement from England is always palpable; indeed, it may have been a particularly attractive feature of the book. The author felt—as many Zionists did—that British society was bizarre and inscrutable, yet he ultimately came down on its side, praising British society as stable, respectful, and worthy of emulation. Though Zionists' feelings toward their British overlords were surely ambivalent and at times sharply negative, the proposals themselves suggest that in the eyes of some educators, Britain was a society to be emulated—particularly after the Nazi rise to power. English courses—imposed initially for more practical reasons—were the logical forum in which to communicate that country's civic values. The attractive qualities of this book may also have led Jews outside the school system to read this volume in the original German.

Where, in the case of Arabic, we considered the position of Shlomo Dov Goitein, professor of Islamic Studies at the Hebrew University, let us turn in the case of English to Hayim Yehuda (Leon) Roth, an Anglo-Jewish professor of philosophy at Hebrew University who received his training at Balliol College, Oxford. In his 1943 article "The Desired Direction in the Teaching of English" (*"Ha-kivun ha-ratzui shel limude ha-Anglit"*), Roth justifies the instruction of English in a way that showcases the multiple, often conflicting sentiments bound up in the decision to teach English in the Zionist schools.

Roth's first question, one that follows him through the essay, is the following: to what extent do we (Jews, Zionists, or the Yishuv) want to be English or be like the English? He begins by stressing unequivocally that "we are not engaging in these studies in order to be English." Immediately, however, he allows himself a bit of wistful musing—"it is true that if we did want to change our skin, we would prefer them over any other nation"—and then cuts himself off abruptly: "This isn't a choice we can make, because we have already chosen—or been chosen by—another choice. We are Jewish and we have returned to the land of our fathers in order to rebuild Jewish life. And a principal part of this life is Hebrew language and culture." At the end of these serpentine musings, he attempts to distance himself from the English language entirely: "English for us is a secondary language, a foreign language." Roth, a native English speaker, makes this point as one who chose to leave England behind and cast his lot with the Hebrew project in Palestine. His uncertainty, however, appears to run deeper than a personal crisis of identity: speaking in the name of the Jewish collectivity in Palestine, he admits that the Yishuv experiences the conflicting desires to be a society much like England and to be a society whose uniqueness is marked by and bound up in its commitment to Hebrew.[124]

Why should a society principally committed to Hebrew devote time to English as a foreign language? He proceeds first to discount the older generation's attraction to "great world literature," calling this attraction a characteristic of the "transitional generation" (*dor ha-ma'avar*) that the younger generation might be able to overcome. Echoing voices cited earlier, he holds that the need for English derives from a set of practical demands: "commercial needs, recreational needs, and social needs." English is necessary, he writes, first for understanding the words present on road signs, packaging, and advertisements; second, for reading textbooks and manuals in fields from agriculture to commerce; and third for comprehending the many English words that have made their way into Hebrew newspapers and radio broadcasts.[125]

But English for Roth is not merely a means of satisfying day-to-day needs that derive from unavoidable contacts between the Yishuv and the British. The study of English, as with Arabic, could also be an important means of strengthening the otherwise deficient Hebrew culture: "Hebrew is important and it will remain important, but it needs completion. This completion must come from outside, from a secondary language, an assisting language [*lashon-'ezer*], a foreign language." While some may ask why this additional language has to be English and cannot be French, Russian, or German, history, he says, has shown that English must be the language. "Who are we connected to through family, literary, commercial, political, and diplomatic ties?" he asked, and answered, "With English-speaking countries." Indeed, English was to be "the center of gravity of our future."[126]

How are we to formulate the Yishuv's relationship to these two languages, one the quintessential language of the Islamic East, the other quickly becoming the arbiter of the West? Several competing paradigms can be used to place these discussions. The first is the contemporary European debate on classical languages versus modern languages, which pitted Latin and Greek against French, English, and German and can be used to think about tensions between culture and practicality, classical knowledge and modern applicability. The second is the context of colonial Arabic study and the increasing tendency within Europe to study Arabic not for philological reasons but as a means of managing colonial encounters in the Middle East. The third is the long history of non-Western people's colonial and postcolonial encounters with English (as well as French), a history of small nation-states attempting to balance the desire to promote a national language with economically and politically generated needs to learn a European language.

The late nineteenth and early twentieth century saw a major shift from classical studies to modern languages in Europe. Until the 1880s, Latin and Greek were the hallmarks of a proper education, and as the pioneer of English teaching H. E. Palmer stated in 1942, "The teaching of French, German, Italian and English (to foreigners) was modeled on the classical tradition."[127] When English was first adopted as a school subject in other parts of Europe, commented the Danish professor of English K. V. Olsen in 1947, "the methods employed were those inherited from the teaching of Latin."[128]

But as modern language education began to spread across Europe, a new emphasis on communication and practical skills emerged. Germany's educational system had been restructured after the Napoleonic Wars into a two-tier system in which the higher level, the *Gymnasien*, maintained the grammar-translation method used with Greek and Latin, and the second-tier *Realschulen* focused on modern languages.[129] In 1882, Wilhelm Viëtor, who had taught German in England (1872–73), sounded his call for a renewed methodology in the study of modern languages: "*Der Sprachunterricht muss umkehren!*" (Language teaching must be radically modified).[130] At about this same time, Maximilian Berlitz began to systematize in France what would become the direct method, a method of language learning that focused on spoken competence and real-world knowledge and eschewed formulaic grammatical studies or the translation method.[131] The transition from classical to modern (or "realist") language studies was not effortless, nor was it complete; the classics maintained their value. The question, however, became who should learn which languages and at what stage in school.

The tension between classical and modern language education persisted in the Yishuv as well. But whereas the choice in Europe was between classical and modern European languages, the discourse in the Yishuv found its own linguistic objects: English and Arabic. Latin and Greek were not cognate to Hebrew and thus did not appeal as clues to the structure of the national language.[132] But the prospect of using language to access both universal and nationally particularistic values remained, taking over in large part from the discussion about Latin as a universal language, which had persisted through the early years of the twentieth century.[133] In a world decisively shifting from the classics to modern languages, English was the more logical choice as the global tongue.

But to the extent that classical studies were intended to encourage linguistic and grammatical precision, the Yishuv opted for a Semitic alternative: Arabic. Classical Arabic, as a foreign language that could be taught to familiarize students with Hebrew grammar, could, along with Biblical Hebrew, occupy the place that Latin had in the European schools. At the same time, however, Arabic had a self-evident modern role to play: it was the major regional language, the language that could be studied in order to understand the Yishuv's neighbors. Thus, one facet of a larger debate over humanist and realist education was negotiated over Arabic. A 1940 report by the Re'ali School in Haifa, which had long excelled in foreign-language teaching, made this parallel explicit. Referring to a past suggestion that Arabic be studied the way Latin had been studied elsewhere, the report concluded, "We certainly exaggerated when, in previous years, we said that the function of Arabic in our studies is like the function of Latin in European countries." In fact, it continued, the more modern applications of the language were equally important, or even more so; it needed to be studied "as a living language."[134] In discussing whether the purpose of Arabic study was fundamentally intellectual or fundamentally functional, Arabic-language educators reenacted aspects of the humanist-realist debate that had been applied in Europe to Greek and Latin on the one hand and modern languages on the other.

This analogy, though illuminating, is not wholly satisfying. Arabic could, as we have seen, be construed as a parent language or as a regional language that could help promote peace (in the way that Latin and German could be seen by the French, for example); it could also, however, be seen as the language of a primitive people that needed to be civilized. This colonial relationship to Arabic cannot be overlooked. Many of the discourses of Arabic study—to understand the political leanings of natives, to study their folkways, and to create propaganda—traced trends that have come to be understood as typically colonial.[135] These needs shaped the way that Arabic was taught in European settings. At the same time that European states were reconsidering their approaches to modern (European) languages, the colonial powers (Britain and France in particular) were promoting a new emphasis on modern Arabic. With the expansion of British and French colonial holdings in the Middle East after World War I, a practical focus began to emerge. The foundation of the School of Oriental Studies at the University of London in 1916 (later, the School of Oriental and African Studies) exemplified this shift in Arabic study in England. "My own belief has always been," said a Cambridge professor of Arabic on a 1909 panel to consider the organization of Oriental studies in London, "that really understanding the literature of a people is impossible unless you understand their mind by being brought into direct contact with them."[136] The Department of the Languages and Cultures of the Near East thus was structured to include "the modern literary and colloquial languages of the Near East" in its curriculum, a choice that made it different "in many important respects from ... the corresponding departments in other British Universities."[137] A Cambridge University report on Oriental languages in 1947 affirmed the importance of understanding modern cultures: "If we are to preserve close and intimate relations with the nations of Asia we must develop in our own country an interest in the cultures of the East."[138]

Thus, while tracking the modern-languages debate in one sense, the discourse on Arabic in the Yishuv also tracked another: an emergent shift in European Oriental studies from a curriculum concerned with classical texts, grammar, and literature to one concerned with functional Arabic studies and oriented toward modern (and particularly colonial) uses. This shift was propelled by the public as well as by figures within the Yishuv's

Arabic-teaching establishment. An article in *Davar* put it succinctly: "The fundamental defect of every Oriental school made in the European mold is the lack of knowledge of living Arabic."[139] Leo Ari Mayer, professor of Arabic at Hebrew University's School of Oriental Studies, argued back, saying that his school's graduates "have to be absolutely completely at home in ancient Arabic literature and the more they forget the common parlance of our own days, the better their style will be."[140] Nonetheless, the trend was clear and the pressure was palpable: an Arabic curriculum that didn't somehow respond to the modern region was undesirable.

Reading language discussions in light of European trends in both modern-language and Oriental-language learning is useful for understanding approaches to Arabic. Considering the Yishuv fundamentally colonial doesn't get us far in understanding its attitudes toward English, however. The argument about Zionist representation of and appropriation of the East may be familiar. What remains less discussed, however, is whether this move of appropriation, so often inherent to the act of language learning, may extend to studies of English as well. The Zionist movement enjoyed fashioning its homeland as a proto-nation-state, on track to become a nation like its European models. But although the Yishuv's language-related discussions mimicked European ones in important ways, its status as a small national society under (indirect) European rule and at a significant geographic remove from Europe set it apart. English was not simply another modern language to be learned as an analogue to Hebrew, but rather the language of the sovereign. In its discussions about English, the Yishuv was more typologically similar to a colonized or postcolonial population. Like postcolonial states in Africa and Asia, it created an educational system that cultivated knowledge of the national language. Nonetheless, like those communities, it was forced to acknowledge the benefits of English-language knowledge for administration, commerce, and politics—even if, unlike elites in the majority of African states, its elites were not primarily English speaking. As in these other emerging national societies, educators in the Yishuv expressed anxieties that their emerging national language could be swept away by the language of the occupier. At the same time, they felt that British society could offer models for development—indeed, that there existed no models for modernity outside those offered by the West. If mastery of

Arabic meant the mastery of the East for a movement that was, quite evidently, not Eastern, mastery of English meant the appropriation of the West by a society that, though its majority was European in origin, was not sure it was reliably, deeply Western.

All three comparative models illuminate aspects of the Zionist discourse on Arabic and English—none is a perfect analogy. Taken together, however, they present a discordant image that includes internal European trends, European colonial trends, and non-European postcolonial trends. This dissonance must be central to our understanding of the Yishuv's history and culture. Derek Penslar has noted that the Zionist movement sat in the uneasy gray area between the two halves of a world increasingly split between colonizers and colonized.[141] In this case, the recognition of being ruled, if indirectly, by one nation (the British) and potentially ruling over another (Palestinian Arabs) provoked an inconsistent set of reflections about the Yishuv's relationship to what lay outside of it. The discussion about how and why to teach foreign languages was particularly sensitive because it asked educators to confront not only their position in Palestine between Arabs and British but also their status as outsiders in relation to both the East and the West. Jews' familiarity with (and ambivalence toward) European tongues long preceded the Zionist encounter with the British colonial power. Likewise, the encounter of Jews with Arabic study far preceded the encounter with Palestine. The Jewish fascination with the Orient grew and developed alongside the Jewish fascination with the Occident. Beyond the evidently important practical considerations involved in creating educational programs, the prospect of foreign-language teaching could not but invite deeper reflections about Jewish desires, fears, and uncertainties about becoming both European and Semitic. In the end, the sanctum of Hebrew education—like the more evidently multilingual spaces of the home, the coffee shop, the cinema, the marketplace, the street, the government office, and the propaganda operation—became a setting for a self-consciously Hebrew society to reflect on the nature of its relationship to its linguistic and cultural others and to understand the limits of a monolingual ideology in an interconnected world.

CONCLUSION

THE PERSISTENCE OF BABEL

"The threat of a Babel of languages . . . is menacing the young state of Israel as it takes its first steps," warned Aharon Shekhtman in *Davar* in March 1949, less than a year after Israel declared its independence.[1] A report prepared by the Israel National Commission for UNESCO in 1953 spoke of the fear that, with continuing immigration, "immigrants would divide themselves into their own communities according to the language they spoke, that a Babel of languages and idioms would destroy originality and creativeness in the country."[2] The Tower of Babel metaphor, used in the mandate period, continued to surface after statehood as a response to language diversity. Where it did, concerns about the persistence of the Jewish Diaspora inside the homeland were never far away. In February 1949, expressing a similar set of concerns about language mixing, the journalist and writer Avraham Sharon had penned an article warning of a phenomenon he called *filogalutismus* (philo-*galut*-ism, or philo-exile-ism). Jews, he explained, have "wanted to dance at two weddings: the Israeli one and the exilic one. They had the homeland on their tongues and exile in their hearts and minds."[3] His metaphor bespoke both a misplaced target for enthusiasm and a deep sense of confusion about the object of communal and individual loyalties—it was a tension that had existed since the early days of Hebrew cultural production.

There was reason to revisit the concept of Babel in these first days of the state. Along with the increase in the number of languages heard in the streets after a lull caused by British restrictions on Jewish immigration around World War II, a sort of Yiddish revival seemed to be in the air. New Yiddish books were being published in the newborn Israeli state: an edition of Melekh Nayshtat's *Destruction and Uprising of the Jews in Warsaw* had come out in Yiddish, as had a book of poems by Abraham Sutzkever. Moreover, and to the great chagrin of some veteran observers, the first issue of *Di Goldene Keyt*, a significant Yiddish literary journal, was published under the editorial oversight of Sutzkever and Abraham Levinson and was held up by worried observers as evidence that Yiddishists now wanted to turn Israel into the center for their activities.[4] Moreover, questions surfaced about the acceptability of the German language in the public sphere; about the integration of new immigrants from North Africa, the Levant, and Iraq; and about the structure of education, including language education, in the new Israeli school system.[5]

With language mixing and language questions abounding, the satirical Matate Theater in Tel Aviv ran Yigal Mossinsohn's comic play *The Tower of Babel* in June 1951. A reviewer wrote that, with its comic renditions of immigrants' bad Hebrew and odd cultural tics, the performance had captured "something of the comic linguistic void around us—this mixed multitude of intonations, speech with foreign dialects aplenty."[6] The symbolic weight of this new wave of language diversity added to the practical considerations of immigrant absorption.

It would not be proper to think that the state could absorb so many new immigrants without "language pangs and suffering," wrote Shekhtman in his tract on the return of Babel.[7] Looking at a linguistically diverse reality and what felt like an uncertain future, he deemed it appropriate to tell a retrospective narrative of pro-Hebrew courage that might be reapplied in the present. His story returned to the years before World War I. Starting with the Second Aliyah period (1904–14), he wrote that the community had "accepted a prohibition on Yiddish and other foreign language performances"; it protested visits by Yiddish writers; and it "was shocked" at the suggestion of allowing German-language teaching at a new Haifa technical school, later the Technion. A Hebrew school system, he continued, took major steps to assimilate new immigrants from various backgrounds, and the Battalion of the Defenders of the Hebrew Language policed offenders. But those efforts, he lamented, had not achieved Hebrew dominance: "Foreignness still lurks with every step." Bezalel Elitzedek, writing for *Haaretz*, praised Shekhtman's narrative, claiming that this "excellent" article, along with Sharon's statement on philogalutism, showed a recognition of the threat of Yiddish in particular among the labor mainstream.[8] This was not a new narrative, however: it was the narrative of language diversity from as early as the 1920s, when the Battalion of the Defenders of the Hebrew Language was active. The sense that an ideologically committed period had ended is not the legacy of the post-1948 period, but rather of the British mandate period.

Nostalgia, protest, and anxiety were not new. What was new was the availability of state legislation to assist in language policing—in this case, firmly directed at manifestations of Yiddish and German and oriented also toward the rapid linguistic assimilation of Arabic-speaking Jewish immigrants, whose language, the language of the enemy, made their assimilation into Israeli Jewishness (figured as Ashkenazic) seem particularly urgent. Nahum Levin of the Culture Department of the Jewish National Council called for a law defending Hebrew by banning foreign-language newspapers, schools, and theaters; he cited the appearance of ten new foreign-language newspapers and plans to create a Yiddish theater.[9] The Tel Aviv Municipality met to discuss a new signage law requiring that signs should be in Hebrew only (this was a more stringent requirement than those promulgated during the mandate, which stated that Hebrew should be the most prominent language). One participant in that meeting, Mr. Shoshani, expressed concern that many new immigrants were congregating in areas such as Jaffa, where they were speaking only Yiddish.[10] Writers on language policy in Israel have argued, incorrectly, that "the prewar bitterness of the struggle against Yiddish was not renewed."[11] Indeed, the revival of this fight in the 1950s reflected a deeper and more existential anxiety about the return of exiles to a country tentatively carving out a distinct culture.

Language restrictions were also directed at German. On 15 December 1950, the Cinematographic Censorship Board passed a ban on the use of German in public artistic performances after there were public protestations directed at a language that to many evoked the Nazi era.[12] "The

Danger of Foreign Languages [*la'az*] Is Growing," warned a headline from the *Herut* in February 1949. The concern was not only the symbolism of foreign voices; the abundance of other languages might negatively affect the development of Hebrew. Other headlines at the time expressed concerns that Hebrew itself was becoming incorrect and improper. It had become *lashon 'ilgim*, an inarticulate language, warned one of the scores of articles written in these years.[13]

Nonetheless, not all felt the threat of foreign tongues so acutely. Conciliatory attitudes surfaced in a population half full of new immigrants, both out of the belief that Hebrew was sufficiently well rooted to withstand challenges and out of the perception that it would be unwise or improper to bar other languages. Speaking at a December 1949 banquet of the Histadrut 'Ivrit 'Olamit (International Federation of Hebrew), which had undertaken the promotion of Hebrew overseas, Moshe Sharett (Shertok) proclaimed, "Yiddish has ceased to be the language of children and young people and as the number of young grows, Yiddish becomes more and more an old-person's language. This fate is expected for Ladino as well."[14] Perhaps in these circumstances, a minority language would not pose such a danger to Hebrew. An article in *Ha-Mashkif* in December 1948 speculated that the Jewish population of Palestine had turned over a new leaf: "There is no doubt that the young State of Israel, although it was established by the Zionist movement, is now going beyond the framework of this movement." Now the state belongs to the Jewish people, it proclaimed, and Yiddish perhaps could have a place.[15] The ban on German, which bears comparison to short-lived bans on German imposed in the United States following World War I, was not accepted universally either. A letter to *Haaretz* thought the ban would make Israel the laughingstock of the world and pointed out that the new ordinance would technically outlaw a public reading of Herzl's writings in the original. Emotions and politics were getting in the way of culture, the writer thought.[16] An article in *Herut* thought that a ban on the language was an inappropriate response to the horrors of the Nazi regime, pointing out as well that Herzl's *Altneuland* was written in this language. The stakes of Babel for this writer were not quite so dire. "It is natural," he continued, "that in an era of immigration we are reminded of Babel on the streets of Tel Aviv," and Israelis should not be overly concerned about it.[17]

The dance between exclusivity, measured in commitment to Hebrew, and openness to the world, the region, and the Jewish past, measured in tolerance of other tongues, has over the years not only been directed toward immigrant languages, as we showed was also the case in the mandate period. Over the course of the late twentieth century, Israeli academic programs increasingly supported writing and publication in English as a way to make Israeli scholarship accessible to the broader world, but met resistance from Hebrew purists. A particularly telling conflict arose in 2008 when the Technion, the same university that had excluded German from its instruction in 1914, chose to teach its business administration courses exclusively in English. According to Boaz Golani, the dean of the Faculty of Industrial Engineering and Management, "We came to the conclusion that if we continue to prepare our graduates by teaching in Hebrew, we are putting them at a disadvantage in the conditions of global competition." An analysis by *Haaretz* saw this move as a symptom of a broader globalization of education and a desire to recruit foreign students, a trend that has increased over the decades of Israel's statehood. Voices of protest came, among others, from the Academy of the Hebrew Language, whose president called it a "serious development." Golani admitted he was aware of the history of Hebrew promotion in general and at the Technion in particular, but claimed a need to "look squarely at reality and adapt to changing circumstances."[18] Commenters on the article by and large lauded the decision, with one pointing out, "Instruction in Hebrew was appropriate for the period of nationalism in Europe, but the period of globalization requires changes."[19] A look back in history, however, suggests that the circumstances to which the Technion was adjusting in 2008, perhaps new in degree, would have been familiar in kind to educators in the interwar period as well, educators who seriously considered the place of English, other European languages, and Arabic throughout the mandate period.

These post-1948 negotiations over the place of Babel in Zion had been percolating for decades. Sharon's comments about the desire to dance at "two weddings," the Israeli one and the exilic one, implied a psychological disorder that had to be overcome. In practice, however, this contradiction was not always felt so sharply. Residents of the Yishuv during the mandate period and onward celebrated the national and communal values reflected in their valuation of Hebrew, but found their linguistic ambitions tempered by recognition of the foreign, the international, and the outside. The embrace of the national did not seem inconsistent with a limited multilingual policy, one that tolerated or condoned language diversity in certain social spheres—commerce and leisure—and effectively recommended it in others—bureaucratic settings, foreign-language classes, and organizations committed to engaging with Palestinian Arabs. This equilibrium, though delicate and constantly in need of negotiation, persisted into the state period and beyond.

Indeed, the progression of world and regional events meant that three linguistic pressures of the pre-1948 period—English, Arabic, and German—were increasingly powerful as symbols of specific cultural developments. English remained and grew as the language of global power and the sine qua non for Israel's global relevance; Arabic has continued to mark the seemingly intractable Israeli-Palestinian and Israeli-Arab conflicts as well as the waves of Mizrahi Jewish integration in the 1950s and 1960s; German remains associated with the Holocaust. These three languages became more, not less, symbolically charged in the years after the state's creation, though for new and evolving reasons. The particular constellation of Jewish mother tongues in Israel has remained fluid as the dominant ones have shifted from Yiddish and Polish to Arabic and later to Russian and Amharic. But the public campaign of shaming that was endemic in the Yishuv period has not persisted. Political loyalty and national service rather than cultural and linguistic conformity have become the primary markers of national belonging, while broader Western trends toward multiculturalism have led to greater (though certainly not unqualified) tolerance of linguistic diversity. A 2008 report prepared by the Ministry of Immigrant Absorption noted: "It seems that there is reason to increase the legitimacy of multilingualism among the younger generation of immigrations in the context of a multicultural society."[20]

Those complaining about immigrants' linguistic recalcitrance, on the one hand, and about Western media and economic penetration, on the other, often imagine a purer time in the past when the Zionist collective was united in its commitment to Hebrew and its rejection of other tongues.[21] This harmonious vision of the past, though, is no more accurate than the decidedly opposite description of linguistic chaos and libidinal urges going awry. In the most intimate realms of the Yishuv as well as in more public ones, other languages were present. In discussing their relevance, roles, and acceptability, the Jewish community of Palestine negotiated the limits and cultural boundaries of a Hebrew society aware of the local and global networks in which it operated. Organizations such as the Jewish National Council, the Jewish Agency, political parties, teachers' organizations, and newspapers openly and consistently confronted and commented on the resulting language practices. The responses of those organizations were not universally negative. In various ways they protested, accepted, interpreted, and concurrently shaped the behavior going on around them.

This diversity of responses to linguistic phenomena surfaces in surprising ways in the existing archival record. My search led me to offbeat sources, such as the stunning photograph of Paula Gottlieb Sutker with which I began my introduction. She is pictured in a dress covered over with language names and national flags, a garment that could be interpreted as either a doctrinaire statement or an ironic response to the language battles around her. Her photo, saved and ultimately made accessible to the public through a family archive and then a municipal collection, clearly struck a chord. Such photographs, along with advertisements, fliers, memoirs, and oral histories, invite further reflections on the nature of archives as repositories for the hegemonic narrative of the past.

But the sources that most suggest clarity often hide a history of uncertainty. Mementos of what might be called language activism—pressing against what seemed the inappropriate presence of Yiddish, German, Ladino, English, Arabic, Polish, and others in a Hebrew-dominant space—often hide within them stories of complex interpersonal relations, mixed motivations, and uncertainty about outcomes. The Yishuv was deeply aware of linguistic choices and their symbolic significance and demonstrated a complex attitude toward them. When we recover those linguistic phenomena sidelined or ignored, we access a vibrant and diverse story of Zionist dealings with the Jewish community, the Middle East region, and the Western world.

The history of culture, we learn through these inquiries, is the story of a meeting between engagement and apathy, ideology and expedience, insistence and compromise. We must move away, therefore, from the study of the Yishuv as only the site of nationalist victory and pro-Hebrew cultural construction. Choices and attitudes about language in Palestine were tinged by economic as well as ideological pressures, personal as well as collective preferences. Languages could be symbols to be lauded, defended, or excoriated, but also tools for accomplishing real communication objectives. In considering the extent of a range of mother tongues in leisure and commercial settings, English in the bureaucratic sectors of the Yishuv, and Arabic in the realm of political activism as well as the everyday, we quickly dispense with a clear divide between invented categories of pro-Hebrew, Zionist Jews and foreign-language-using, apathetic, non-Zionist Jews—precisely the dichotomous categories insisted upon in much of the archival record—and confront a society aware that it was negotiating language diversity and linguistic accommodation in more complex ways. In practice, a people historically marked by their multilingual skills continued to seek and deploy language proficiencies in Palestine for both personal and collective ends. This space of contradiction, ambivalence, and inconsistency is the place of Babel in Zion. We must reckon with it as we rewrite our narratives about the history of the Zionist project.

NOTES

Abbreviations

AHH	Haganah Archive, Tel Aviv
AYA	Aviezer Yellin Archives of Jewish Education in Israel and the Diaspora, Tel Aviv
BB	Beit Berl, Moshe Sharett Israel Labor Party Archives, Kfar Saba
TNA, BW	British National Archives, London, British Council Records
TNA, CO	British National Archives, London, Colonial Office Records
CAHU	Central Archives of the Hebrew University, Jerusalem
CCEH	Central Council for the Enforcement of Hebrew
CZA	Central Zionist Archives, Jerusalem
ER	Eliasaf Robinson Tel Aviv Collection, M1522, Department of Special Collections, Stanford University Libraries
HMA	Haifa Municipality Archive
IFA	Israel Film Archives, Jerusalem Cinematheque
ISA	Israel State Archives, Jerusalem
JA	Archives of the Jabotinsky Institute in Israel, Tel Aviv
JMA	Jerusalem Municipality Archive, Jerusalem
KZA	Kibbutz Ha-Zore'a Archives
LA	Pinhas Lavon Institute for Labour Movement Research, Tel Aviv
OETA	(Occupied Enemy Territory Administration)
OHD	Oral History Division, Institute for Contemporary Jewry, Hebrew University of Jerusalem
TAMA	Tel Aviv Municipality Archive
YTA	Yad Tabenkin Archives of the United Kibbutz Movement, Ramat Ef'al
YYA	Yad Ya'ari Archives, Ha-Shomer Ha-Tza'ir Archives, Givat Haviva

Introduction

Epigraph: Flier for Hebrew courses administered by the Jewish National Council Culture Department, CZA DD1/1915; original in four languages: Yiddish, Hebrew, Ladino, and German.

1. Azaryahu, *Tel Aviv: Mythography of a City*, 85; Shavit, "Tel Aviv Language Police"; Shur, *Gedud megine ha-safah be-Eretz Yisra'el 1923–1936*.

2. One example of this reading of this photo is in Kalif and Rinat-Benbenishti, "Rega'im gedolim be-'ir ketanah," 16.

3. Purim is also a traditional context for the discussion of Jewish languages and the feasibility of translation. The Talmudic Tractate Megilah, commenting on the Book of Esther's comment that King Ahasuerus sent his correspondences to "to each province in its own script and to each people in its own language" (1:22; 3:12), considers whether it is appropriate to translate scriptures into Jewish vernaculars. I thank Naomi Seidman for this insight.

4. Aaron, "The Doctrine of Hebrew Language Usage."

5. Eliezer Ben-Yehuda, "Mah na'aseh li-leshonenu she-yedubar bah?" [What should we do to our language so that it is spoken?], *Ha-Or*, 23 January 1912, 1. Naomi Seidman has remarked on the fact that in creating a symbolic, collective, or metaphorical "mother tongue," the "fathers" of Hebrew had to silence many actual mothers who would have otherwise spoken Yiddish to their children: "As a collective myth of the Hebrew revival, it seems clear that the mother's silence, self-sacrifice, and absence (or, alternatively, her transgression) are built into the mythical structure" (Seidman, *A Marriage Made in Heaven*, 109); Arendt quoted in Berend, *Decades of Crisis*, 74.

6. Hroch, "From National Movement to the Fully Formed Nation." For analyses of language and nationalism in central and eastern Europe, see Carmichael, " 'A People Exists and That People Has Its Language' "; Tornquist-Plewa, "Contrasting Ethnic Nationalisms."

7. Eliezer Ben Yehuda, *Ha-halom ve-shivro*, 95; translation from *A Dream Come True*, 63.

8. Bartal, introduction to *Ha-'agalah ha-mele'ah*, xv; Saposnik, *Becoming Hebrew*, 69; Chaver, *What Must Be Forgotten*, 17; Zohar Shavit, "Tel Aviv Language Police," 208–9.

9. These fights for Hebrew dominance were aimed at establishing a pro-Hebrew official policy; it is generally agreed that they benefited from the diverse linguistic origins of Jewish immigrants, the strongly negative ideological stance taken toward Yiddish, and the concomitant construction of Jewish institutions whose language would be Hebrew. See Efrati, *Mi-leshon yehidim le-leshon umah*; Ben-Hayyim, *Be-milhamtah shel lashon*; Morag, "Ha-'Ivrit ha-hadashah be-hitgabshutah," and Karmi, *'Am ehad ve-safah ahat*. Shlomo Haramati has offered several hagiographies, including *Sheloshah she-kadmu le-Ben-Yehuda* and *Leviyim be-mikdash ha-'Ivrit*. A body of scholarship also considers the battles to establish Hebrew as the language of instruction at the Technikum in Haifa, an event seen as a seminal victory for Hebrew; see Shilo, "Milhemet ha-safot ki-tenu'ah 'amamit" and Ben-Yosef, *Milhemet ha-safot*.

10. Shavit, "Tel Aviv Language Police," 209.

11. The linguists Bachman and Palmer (1996) distinguished between organizational competence, which reflects knowledge of grammatical rules and the production of coherent speech or text, and pragmatic competence, which refers to subtler understandings of what language or register is appropriate in which setting, as well as sensitivity to cultural difference and dialect, that is, learning to speak like a native; see Baker, *Foundations of Bilingual Education and Bilingualism*, 14. But competence is measured not only by the ability to integrate, for example, into a host society. As Jan Blommaert writes, language in the context of globalization (that is, cultural contact and movement) should be understood as a "collection of semiotic resources" that may belong to several languages and not reflect what would be classically deemed "fluency." Partial competence in such settings is as significant as full native competence; see Blommaert, *Sociolinguistics of Globalization*, 102–3.

12. See, for example, Efrati, *Mi-lashon yehidim le-leshon umah*; Blau, *Ha-lashon ha-ʿIvrit be-hitpathutah uve-hithadeshutah*.

13. For an overview of scholarship on Hebrew's rise to dominance, see Nahir, "Micro Language Planning and the Revival of Hebrew," and Nir, "Maʿamadah shel ha-lashon ha-ʿIvrit be-tahalikh ha-tehiyah ha-leʾumit." A second debate, particularly during the 1950s, centered on whether Hebrew was a complete language distinct from the language-in-the-making of the prestate period or an incomplete language still in need of promotion and development; see Kuzar, "Linguistic and Political Attitudes towards Israeli Hebrew."

14. Saposnik, *Becoming Hebrew*, 254; Fishman, "Interwar Eastern European Jewish Parties and the Language Issue," 182.

15. Harshav, *Language in Time of Revolution*, 174. Harshav drew from Itamar Even-Zohar's work on the emergence of Hebrew amidst other cultural-linguistic forces from which the Hebrew center adopted elements. Even-Zohar and others at Tel Aviv University were known for developing terminology on culture as a polysystem; see Even-Zohar, "Ha-tzemihah veha-hitgabeshut shel tarbut ʿIvrit mekomit vi-yelidit be-Eretz Yisraʾel, 1882–1948"; Chaver, *What Must Be Forgotten*, 16. On the Hebrew University incident, see Myers, *Re-Inventing the Jewish Past*, 77–80; Pilowsky, "Yiddish Alongside the Revival of Hebrew." On other battles over language use, see Helman, *Or ve-yam hikifuha*, 223–30.

16. Carr, *A Land Divided*, 85; Shavit, "Tel Aviv Language Police," 203.

17. David Gurevich, ed., *Statistical Abstract of Palestine, 1929*, 35.

18. Bachi, *A Statistical Analysis of the Revival of Hebrew in Israel*, 182, 190.

19. Ibid., 194. Bachi's statistics may be inexact, however, since the 1916 survey excludes Jerusalem and the matter of survey taking is always suspect (what does it mean to be a person "speaking a language other than Hebrew"?).

20. The languages that the teachers named were Arabic, Bulgarian, Danish, English, French, German, Greek, Hebrew, Hungarian, Italian, Ladino, Latin, Polish, Romanian, Russian, Ruthenian, Spanish, Turkish, and Yiddish; see AYA 9.42, Surveys; Arnon, "Ha-moreh be-misparim," 309.

21. Anderson, *Imagined Communities*, 77.

22. Shapiro has argued that Hebrew, a limited language, acted as an "internal censor, which prevented them from seeing certain aspects of the reality around them" to the point that when they reached adolescence, "these native born children educated in the Hebrew schools did not have a language with which they could analyze public life in modern society" (*'Ilit le-lo mamshikhim*, 77).

23. Moss, "Unchosen Peoplehood."

24. Alex Bein, a biographer of Herzl and the erstwhile head of the Central Zionist Archives, spoke of a Jewish landlord in Germany who had criticized him for his Zionist commitments and warned him against becoming involved with her daughter, lest the daughter go to Palestine; this same daughter found herself living near him in Palestine a few years later; see Bein, *Kan en mevarekhim le-shalom*, 146.

25. Frankel, *Prophecy and Politics*; Harshav, *Language in Time of Revolution*; Moss, "Arnold in Aysheshok, Schiller in Shnipishok"; Seidman, *Marriage Made in Heaven*; Parush, "Another Look at the Life of 'Dead' Hebrew"; Pilowsky, "Yiddish alongside the Revival of Hebrew"; Rojanski, "The Status of Yiddish in Israel, 1948–1951"; Rojanski, "Ha-umnam 'safah zarah ve-tzoremet'?"

26. Divine, *Exiled in the Homeland*, 110.

27. On the romanticization of the Bedouin, see Almog, *The Sabra*, 198–201. On Arabic at the Hebrew University, see Milson, "The Beginnings of Arabic and Islamic Studies at the Hebrew University of Jerusalem"; Lazarus-Yafeh, "The Transplantation of Islamic Studies from Europe to the Yishuv and Israel"; Kramer, introduction to *The Jewish Discovery of Islam*. On Arabic study as a means of contact, see Beinin, "Knowing Your Enemy, Knowing Your Ally"; Eyal, *The Disenchantment of the Orient*. On the post-1948 period, see Suleiman, *The Arabic Language and National Identity*; R. Talmon, "Arabic as a Minority Language in Israel"; Abu-Rabia, "The Learning of Arabic by Israeli Jewish Children"; Joseph, *When Languages Collide*.

28. This configuration recalls Albert Hourani's discussion of the "politics of notables"; see Hourani, *The Emergence of the Modern Middle East*, 35–66.

29. Bailey, *Images of English*; Pennycook, *English and the Discourses of Colonialism*.

30. On the national everyday, see Kotkin, *Magnetic Mountain*; Edensor, *National Identity, Popular Culture, and Everyday Life*; Zahra, *Kidnapped Souls*, 5; Heller, *Paths to Post-Nationalism*, 4.

31. The nexus of language and globalization has been most extensively studied around English, which, as it inserted itself in large and small societies around the world, led to accommodations as well as resistance and reentrenchment. These studies tend to pertain to the postwar and post–Cold War periods, and with their presentist focus tend not to look for precedents of these trends further in the past; see Saraceni, *The Relocation of English*; Crystal, *English as a Global Language*; Pennycook, *Global Englishes and Transcultural Flows*; Fairclough, *Language and Globalization*; Calvet, *Towards an Ecology of World Languages*.

32. Burke, *What Is Cultural History?*, 128. On language ideology, see, for example, Bambi B. Shieffelin, et al., *Language Ideologies: Practice and Theory*; Schaefer, "Linguistics, Ideology, and the Discourse of Linguistic Nationalism," 7. A good example of the "ideology in lan-

guage" approach by a social historian is Sewell, *Work and Revolution in France*, 1–15; Burke, *Languages and Communities in Early Modern Europe*, 2–7. For recent examples of this trend in other fields, see Burke, *Towards a Social History of Early Modern Dutch*; Mir, *The Social Space of Language*; Mitchell, *Language, Emotion, and Politics in South India*.

33. Both Anat Helman and Maoz Azaryahu consider discourses and realities around language use in Tel Aviv, which was compelling both because it was a meeting point for immigrants—and thus palpably multilingual—and because, as a planned Jewish city, it wrestled with the meaning and contradictions of being the "First Hebrew City"; see Helman, *Young Tel Aviv*, 30–33; Azaryahu, *Tel Aviv*, 33–71. For linguistic and sociolinguistic assessments of Modern Hebrew, see Shohamy and Spolsky, *The Languages of Israel*; Ornan, "Le-toledot tehiyat ha-lashon"; Ornan, " 'Ivrit ke-safah zarah ve-'Ivrit le-dovere safot zarot"; Morag, "Ha-'Ivrit ha-hadashah be-hitgabeshutah." On the revival of Hebrew as a literary language, see Alter, *Hebrew and Modernity*; Alter, *The Invention of Hebrew Prose*; Gluzman, *The Politics of Canonicity*; Hochberg, *In Spite of Partition*. Yael Chaver's implication is that literature offered a space apart from the crushing hegemony of Hebrew culture in which to explore ambivalence both about Hebrew and about the Zionist project; see Chaver, *What Must Be Forgotten*. Lital Levy also offers an insightful study about reflections on (and in) Arabic within Hebrew and some Arabic-language fiction in Israel; see Levy, *Poetic Trespass*. Na'ama Rokem and Na'ama Sheffi consider the politics of German-language literature and its translation into Hebrew: see Rokem, *Prosaic Conditions*, and Sheffi, Germanit be-'Ivrit.

34. Gallagher and Greenblatt, *Practicing New Historicism*, 51, 69.

35. Goffman, *The Presentation of Self in Everyday Life*.

36. Piterberg, *The Returns of Zionism*, 101.

37. Clifford, *Routes*, 250.

Chapter 1. Languages of Leisure in the Home, the Coffeehouse, and the Cinema

Epigraph: Cited in Carmiel, *Bet-kafeh*, 30.

1. Neumann, *Land and Desire in Early Zionism*, 4–7; Zakim, *To Build and Be Built*.

2. Yehi'eli, *Li-she'elat ha-safah*, 5.

3. Yehudah Gotthelf, "Ba-hazit ha-tarbut ha-'Ivrit" [On the Hebrew culture front], *Ha-Shomer Ha-Tza'ir*, 1 November 1936, 7.

4. Revusky, *Jews in Palestine*, 103; Wirth, "Urbanism as a Way of Life," 5.

5. Online versions of Levinson's two speeches are available at http://www.benyehuda.org/bialik/dvarimo6.html and http://benyehuda.org/levinson/hatarbut_bagola.html; on Hebrew culture in the Yishuv, see Jacob Shavit, *Ha-historyah shel Tel-Aviv*, 322–32; Sovran, "Ha-'Ivrit ki-sefat tarbut," 52; Bialik cited in Sovran, "Ha-'Ivrit ki-sefat tarbut"; Nathan Alterman, *'Ir ha-yonah: shirim* (Tel Aviv: Mahbarot le-safrut, 1957), 265, cited in Sovran, "Ha-'Ivrit ki-sefat tarbut," 52.

6. Exodus 20:8–11; compare Deuteronomy 5:12–15, which also refers to the Exodus as a rationale for the observance of the Sabbath. Rabbis who recommended the practice of Hebrew speech on the Sabbath included Shene Luhot ha-Berit (Yeshayah Ha-Levi Horovitz, 1558–1630), R. Yitzhak Lampronti (1679–1756), and Rabbi Nahman of Bratslav (1770–1881); see Federbusch, *Ha-lashon ha-'Ivrit be-Yisra'el uva-'amim*, 325–27. Shim'on Berman, in his 1870 travel journal to Palestine, recalled a woman named Sheine Rivka Sheikovitz who, though she spoke Yiddish regularly, spoke Hebrew on the Sabbath; see Shilo, *Princess or Prisoner?*, 144.

7. "Ha-profesor gelui lev," *Ha-'Erev*, n.d., in *Be'ayot lashon ve-tarbut: leket devarim she-ne'emru ve-nikhtevu be-hodshe Adar B[et]-Nisan 5706 [1946]* [Issues of lanugage and culture: A selection of things written and said between Adar Bet and Nisan 5706 (1946)], Jewish National Council, Culture Department / Institute for Hebrew Language and Culture, 1946, CZA DD1/3250. I was unable to locate a publication called *Ha-'Erev* and thus do not know the source of the original publication.

8. Hinitz, *Gedole Yisra'el bi-vedihah*, 20. Another version of the anecdote reads: "One Sabbath, friends came to visit Bialik at his home and found him speaking Yiddish. 'You, Bialik, speaking Yiddish!?' they asked him, 'Yiddish speaks itself,' he responded to them, 'and speaking Hebrew is difficult labor, which is forbidden on the Sabbath' "; see Adir Cohen, *Sefer ha-humor ha-Yehudi ha-gadol*, 256.

9. "Of all informing details," writes Joseph Boskin "few more readily offer insight into societal affairs than people's laughter" (*Rebellious Laughter*, 202). Robert Darnton suggests that jokes or proverbs meaningful to "natives" can be among the "best points of entry" into the historical past, the points at which one can "grasp a foreign system of meaning in order to unravel it" (*The Great Cat Massacre*, 78).

10. Segal focuses on the irony that Bialik was crowned national poet despite the fact that he continued to write poetry in the earlier Ashkenazic accent (which produced a particular poetic meter) rather than a version of the Sephardi accent, usually with ultimate stress; see *A New Sound in Hebrew Poetry*, 139–48.

11. Gotthelf, "Ba-hazit ha-tarbut ha-'Ivrit," 7; Bialik, "Ha-zilzul ba-lashon ha-'Ivrit u-va'ad ha-lashon" [The denigration of Hebrew and the language committee], in *Devarim she-be'al peh*, 2:132.

12. On "mobilized culture," most often discussed with regard to literature, see Gluzman, *Politics of Canonicity*, 6. The tension between "recruited culture" and "free culture" is nicely summarized in Jacob Shavit, *Ha-Historyah shel Tel-Aviv*, 312–16; Zakim, *To Build and Be Built*, 91; Leheny, *The Rules of Play*, 20, 31. This imperative to shape citizens through leisure is visible in the 1941 report prepared for the American Youth Commission, which, while promoting the expression of "individuality," insists that youth "need guidance" to cultivate the right kind of individuality, lest they yield to deleterious influences, delinquency, crime, and debauchery; see Wrenn and Harley, *Time on Their Hands*, xix, 25. E. P. Thompson discusses a similar exercise of leisure controls in early industrial Britain; see, for example, his discussion of leisure and the English working class in *The Making of the English Working Class*, 57–59.

13. The body of research on leisure and leisure-time activities grew up in the 1950s and 1960s as historians focused on material culture and the practice of the everyday; see the exchange in *Past and Present*, 146 (1995) and 156 (1997). On the Hebrew quality of the Yishuv, see Azaryahu, *Tel Aviv*, 79.

14. Part of the Haifa Sabbath-related activism is found in Protocols of the Va'adah le-havtahat ha-tzivyon ha-'Ivri shel ha-shekhunah (Committee for Ensuring the Hebrew Character of the Neighborhood), 1942–49, HMA 6075–00312/19.

15. Kolatt, "Religion, Society, and State during the Period of the National Home," 277.

16. Ibid., 291.

17. Shapira, "Religious Motifs of the Labor Movement," in *Zionism and Religion*, 254.

18. On school Sabbath rituals, see Naor and Shavit, *Staging and Stagers in Modern Jewish Palestine*, 65.

19. Brown, *The Israeli-American Connection*, 96; Patai, *Journeyman in Jerusalem*, 213–16.

20. Leheny, *Rules of Play*, 27; White, *De-Stalinization and the House of Culture*, 21–23. White cites the Soviet politician Konstantin Chernenko's comment at a June 1983 plenum on ideology that socialization work "achieves lasting results ... when it encompasses all aspects of a person's life and world including their daily lives, their leisure and their family relations" (22).

21. Kotkin, *Magnetic Mountain*, 220.

22. Rozin, *Hovat ha-ahavah ha-kashah*, 10.

23. "The informal state" has been defined as a collection of organizations "either pressing for a change to the status quo or seeking to sustain a status quo that is in danger of being eroded." Breaches of morality are common targets for these efforts; see Borsay, *A History of Leisure*, 54–58.

24. The discussion about children's speech pertained to the quality, tone, accent, and vocabulary of spoken Hebrew. For one such exploration, based on a study of children in the Yishuv, see Israel Rubin Rivkai, " 'Al ha-spetzifiyut ha-leshonit be-fi yaldenu be-Eretz Yisra'el" [On linguistic specificity among our children in Palestine], pts. 3–4, *Leshonenu* 5, no. 1 (1933): 73–77; *Leshonenu* 5, nos. 3–4 (1933): 231–42; also published in Rivkai, *'Al sefat yeladenu ba-aretz*, 15–91.

25. Goffman, *Presentation of Self*, 9.

26. Yehoash, *Fun New York biz Rehovos un tsurik*, 1:158.

27. Helman, "Even the Dogs in the Street Bark in Hebrew," 367.

28. Goffman, *Presentation of Self*, 112, 128. Other writers have applied Goffman's terminology to multilingual situations in which "backstage" language use serves as a source of solidarity between minority actors; see Codo, *Immigration and Bureaucratic Control*.

29. Kotkin, *Magnetic Mountain*, 220.

30. Rivka Avrahmson interview, 24 August 1999, 12, OHD 30(240).

31. For the politics of the census in another Jewish setting, see Lichtenstein, "Making Jews at Home."

32. Roberto Bachi calculates that Hebrew accounted for 71.1 percent "of total use of languages," on the assumption that those who used it as a "primary language" were using it, on average, 75 percent of the time and those who used it as an additional language were using it, on average, 25 percent of the time. This kind of statistical aggregation tells us little about the context of language use, but does offer a baseline number; see Bachi, *Revival of Hebrew in Israel*, 186–89.

33. P. B., "Lashon 'Ivrit u-sevivah 'Ivrit" [Hebrew language and Hebrew environment], *Ha-Boker*, 22 November 1939.

34. "Shetah hefker" [No-man's-land], *Haaretz*, 9 October 1940.

35. Rachel Katznelson, *Devar ha-po'elet* [Writings of the Female Worker] (1943), 179, cited in Bernstein, "Human Being or Housewife?," 251.

36. Bernstein, "Human Being or Housewife?," 251.

37. Like most sociolinguistic studies, this area of research has focused on the United States and western Europe and has dealt with the recent past by using the methods of sociology, methods that require living subjects. One good example of such work is Menard-Warwick, *Gendered Identities and Immigrant Language Learning*.

38. Yitzhak Bitansky interview, 1 November 1998, 16, OHD 1(240).

39. Zion Falah interview, 24 January 1999, 9, OHD 41(240). In light of the massive suppression of Jewish speakers of Arabic that occurred in the 1950s and 1960s, the comparison of Tripolitanian Arabic to Yiddish suggests a degree of foreboding. "For us," Yehouda Shenhav writes in an autobiographic introduction to his book on Arab Jews, "the story is . . . about how 'Arabness' was underscored, erased, and otherwise managed in order to fit us into the Jewish collectivity" (*The Arab Jews*, 2). See also Shohat, *Taboo Memories, Diasporic Voices*, 205.

40. Seidman, *Marriage Made in Heaven*, 109.

41. The language problems of the eastern European immigrant household derived, Rivkai thought, not only from the mother's "bastardized language" but also from the father's tendency to speak a very high, formal, and unnatural Hebrew. The result: the child ends up "between a rock and a hard place"; see Rivkai, *'Al sefat yeladenu ba-aretz*, 20–25; quotation on 23.

42. Ibid., 31.

43. Peiss, "Gender Relations and Working Class Leisure," 99. Women, instead, tend to adopt certain forms of leisure that can be "fitted into a fragmented time schedule," such as reading, writing letters, needlework, or knitting; see Deem, *All Work and No Play*, 80–81. See also Henderson, *Both Gains and Gaps*; Green, *Women's Leisure, What Leisure?*; Henderson, *A Leisure of One's Own*. Whereas those books tend on the whole to focus on the experience of women as a group, later books focus on the multiplicity of women's experiences and complicated binary notions of gender; see Aitchison, *Gender and Leisure*.

44. Groups of women formed to promote Hebrew on behalf of the Hebrew Language Committee; see "Tel Aviv: Mo'etzet nashim lema'an Va'ad ha-Lashon ha-'Ivrit" [Tel Aviv: Council of women in support of the Hebrew language committee], *Davar*, 18 July 1939, 7.

45. Peiss, "Gender Relations and Working-Class Leisure," 101.

46. Aitchison, *Gender and Leisure*, 45–46.

47. Guy Miron, "From Bourgeois Germany to Palestine," 119, 125.

48. Bernstein and Lipman, "Fragments of Life," 146.

49. Sarah Rafaelovich interview, 8 July 1998, 17–18, OHD 22(240); Yitzhak Bitansky interview, 1 November, 1998, 16, OHD 1(240); Tzvi Elpeleg interview, 23 July 1998, 11, OHD 31 (240).

50. Zohar Shavit, "Lemale et ha-aretz sefarim."

51. Heinrich Loewe, "Ha-sifriyah ha-'ironit Sha'ar Tziyon," [The Sha'ar Zion City Library], *Yedi'ot 'Iriyat Tel Aviv: sefer ha-yovel, 25 shanah le-hivasedah shel Tel Aviv* [Tel Aviv Municipality news: Anniversary volume, 25 years since the founding of Tel Aviv] 5, nos. 6–7 (1933–34), 286.

52. The debate over "Hebrew culture" and "culture in Hebrew" dominated the Hebrew literary scene for decades. Though translation appeared inevitable, some doubted whether Hebrew, lacking much vocabulary, was a sufficiently rich target language. Y. H. Brenner asked whether one could empty the beauty of Japeth [Europe] into the little canisters of Jacob. On debates around translation into Hebrew, see Cutter, "Translation and the Project of Culture"; Miron and Wirth-Nesher, "Modern Hebrew Literature."

53. A slightly disproportionate percentage of the books borrowed from the collection were in Hebrew (76 percent), with the next most popular reading languages being Russian (12.5 percent) and Yiddish (6.7 percent); see "Sifriyot tziburiyot," *Yedi'ot 'Iriyat Tel Aviv: sefer ha-shanah 5699 [1938–39]*, 140.

54. Loewe, "Ha-sifriyah ha-'ironit Sha'ar Tziyon," 288. The writer Hayim Nachman Bialik wrote of Bet Ahad Ha-'Am that it would be a sanctuary of Hebrew, housing cultural foundations that no person would denigrate, "even those who have no part in the God of Israel" (Bialik, " 'Al 'Bet Ahad Ha-'Am," 6 February 1928, in *Devarim she-be'al peh*).

55. Y. Edelshteyn, " 'Al ha-sifriyah ve-kore'ehah" [On the library and its readers], *Mi-bifnim* 7 (1924): 122.

56. Ibid.

57. " 'Al sifriyat ha-gimnasyah," *Be-Finatenu* (Balfour School), 6 July 1926, AYA 4.145/12.

58. The original materials are organized as collection 9.42 in the AYA, with a variety of apparently arbitrary secondary designations. The original surveys are sorted alphabetically, one folder for each letter of the alphabet. Not all surveys are complete. The volume, published in 1929 after some delay, contained a range of articles on the state of teaching in the Yishuv, in addition to the aforementioned survey; see Mikhtav hozer #15/11, Merkaz histadrut ha-morim, 2 March 1928, AYA 9.174/498, and Dov Kimche, *Sefer ha-yovel shel histadrut ha-morim*.

59. The questions were as follows: #8: Mother tongue; #9: List of places studied, including language of instruction; #11: Literatures in which you were educated and which influenced you the most; #12: Knowledge of foreign languages and Jewish dialects

(speaking, reading, writing); #13: In which languages do you regularly read books and newspapers?

60. Arnon, "Ha-moreh be-misparim," 305.

61. Many teachers listed multiple languages, so the table includes separate entries for "Hebrew-Yiddish-Russian," "Hebrew-Russian-Polish," "Hebrew-German-French," and all manner of other combinations. The published statistics go on to disaggregate the statistics.

62. Arnon, "Ha-moreh be-misparim," 308.

63. German was the most common, with nearly 50 percent of respondents saying they regularly read in that language. Russian was not far behind at 40.9 percent, followed by English (27.9 percent), French (15.8 percent), Yiddish (6.7 percent), and Arabic (4.7 percent). Small numbers cited other languages as well; see Arnon, "Ha-moreh be-misparim," 309–10.

64. In many cases, respondents qualified their answers about knowledge of languages by pointing out which languages they knew only a little. The most common languages to know "a little of" were French, Arabic, and English, presumably languages they had begun to acquire in Palestine. The rate of reading in German is striking, a decade before the influx of native German speakers, who certainly accessed German literature in even greater numbers.

65. AYA Surveys 9.40/163; 9.42/28b.

66. Ullendorff, "Hebrew in Mandatary [*sic*] Palestine," 302.

67. Shachar Pinsker, "Mah zeh ha-'Franconi' ha-zeh she-atem yoshevim bo yomam va-lailah? zeh hu o hi?" [What is this "Franconi" that you sit in day and night?], *Haaretz*, 24 April 2008. References to coffee shops include Gal, *Berakhah Fuld*, 163, 190; Carmiel, *Bate ha-kafeh shel Tel-Aviv, 1920–1980*, 61–63.

68. "Bishvil ha-meltzarim" [For the waiters], originally in "Mi-pinkas ha-hulin," *Davar*, 5 September 1939, 4; reprinted in *Be'ayot lashon ve-tarbut*, 1946, 39, CZA DD1/3250.

69. Gotthelf, "Ba-hazit ha-tarbut ha-'Ivrit," 7.

70. Sylvia Gelber, *No Balm in Gilead*, 79.

71. Groman, *Ha-mis'har ha-kim'oni be-Eretz Yisra'el*, 28.

72. Carmiel, *Bate ha-kafeh shel Tel-Aviv*, 61.

73. Lockman, *Comrades and Enemies*, 164.

74. Benjamin Tammuz, cited in Carmiel, *Bate ha-kafeh shel Tel-Aviv*, 10.

75. Hayim Feierberg, "Mizrah pogesh ma'arav: bate ha-kafe be-shule Tel Aviv 1936–1960" [East meets West: Cafes on the margins of Tel Aviv, 1936–1960], in Carmiel, *Bate ha-kafeh shel Tel Aviv*, 296.

76. Zohar Shavit, "Boire un café en hébreu."

77. Pinsker, *Literary Passports*, 68–69, 90–91; Pinsker "The Urban Literary Café and the Geography of Hebrew and Yiddish Modernism in Europe."

78. Chaver, *What Must Be Forgotten*, 120–21, 173.

79. Y. Nitzani, "Be-'edot ha-mizrah be-tokh 'ami" [In the eastern communities within my people], *Davar*, 17 May 1936, 4.

80. Lapid, *Kol Noa*, 14 July 1933, 6, in Carmiel, *Bate ha-kafeh shel Tel-Aviv*, 104.

81. "Kabaret Germani ba-'ir ha-'atid" [A German caberet in the city of the future], *'Iton Meyuhad*, 30 May 1937; cited in Carmiel, *Bate ha-kafeh shel Tel-Aviv*, 104.

82. Letter to Haifa Business, 3 October 1938, HMA 6075.

83. Y. Gur-Arieh and M. Rozen, Jewish National Council, Culture Department / Institute for Hebrew Language and Culture to multiple recipients, 26 March 1946, CZA DD1/3250.

84. May 1923, cited in Carmiel, *Bate ha-kafeh shel Tel-Aviv*, 25.

85. Carmiel, *Bate ha-kafeh shel Tel-Aviv*, 31–32.

86. D. N. Brinker, "Ha-murshe ha-artzi le-hashlatat ha-'Ivrit be-tzibur ha-dati" [The National Council for Enforcing Hebrew in the Religious Community], "Sekirah: le-hashlatat ha-'Ivrit ba-hayim ha-datiyim" [Survey: On the enforcement of Hebrew in religious life], 17 February 1941, CZA S8/744.

87. Yahef, "Yamim ve-lelot be-Tel Aviv" [Days and nights in Tel Aviv], *Tesha' Ba-'Erev* 6, 15 April 1937, 15; in Carmiel, *Bate ha-kafeh shel Tel-Aviv*, 138.

88. On film reception in non-Western countries, see Arvind Rajagopal, "Mediating Modernity"; Katz and Wedell, *Broadcasting in the Third World*; Akyeampong and Ambler, "Leisure in African History."

89. Curran and Park, "Beyond Globalization Theory," 7.

90. See *Ha-Ahdut*, 3 Heshvan 1914, cited in Zimerman, *Simane kolno'a*, 14–15; Helman, "Tzerikhat kolno'a ba-Yishuv uvi-medinat Yisra'el bi-shenotehah ha-rishonot," 78.

91. Tartakover et al., *Hatzagah rishonah*, 103.

92. Shalit, *Makrinim koah*, 20–24.

93. Ibid., 74.

94. Yuval, *'Ilan natu'a be-admato*, 52–53.

95. This feature has been observed in the study of film-watching behavior in colonial Africa: "In place of the regimented and reverential silence imposed on filmgoers in North America and Europe, African film shows were characterized by the noise, commentary, and engagement typical of spectacles" (Ambler, "Popular Films and Colonial Audiences," 96).

96. Ayelet Cohen, "Reshit ha-kolno'a ha-Eretzyisre'elit," 149–50; "Yitzhak Molkho," in Tidhar, *Entziklopedyah la-halutze ha-Yishuv u-vonav*, 4:1984–85; Yerushalayim Segal, *Zikhronot Yerushalayim be-Tel Aviv*, 203–4. I was not able to identify Krichevsky's first name—it was also not known by a contact at the Jerusalem Cinematheque. On the history of Israeli and Zionist film, see Tryster, *Israel before Israel*; Ayelet Cohen, "Reshit ha-kolno'a ha-Eretzyisre'eli"; Feldestein, *Halutz, 'avodah, matzlemah*; Shohat, *Israeli Cinema*.

97. Yerushalayim Segal, *Zikhronot Yerushalayim be-Tel Aviv*, 210–11.

98. He first worked for free, but after eighteen months was hired by the Eden Cinema for £1.5 per evening film and £1 for daytime films. In 1927, Segal joined up with a new immigrant to Palestine, Nathan Axelrod, and they opened the Moledet Studio, which became famous for its documentary film reels; see Yerushalayim Segal, *Zikhronot Yerushalayim be-Tel Aviv*, 211, 227–29.

99. Ibid., 240.

100. Tartakover et al., *Hatzagah rishonah*, 102.

101. Rieger, "Ha-'itonut, ha-kolno'a veha-radio," 178.

102. Shalit, *Makrinim koah*, 26.

103. Jacob Shavit, *Ha-historyah shel Tel-Aviv*, 333.

104. An Eden Cinema program from 1934 presented Frank R. Strayer's Spanish film *El Rey de Los Gitanos* (King of the gypsies). A program from Migdalor accompanied a screening of William Thiele's 1933 Viennese film *Großfürstin Alexandra* (Grand Duchess Alexandra), starring the famous opera singer Maria Jeritza as Alexandra. A list of future showings included *Ball im Savoy* (Ball in Savoy, 1935, Czechoslovakia); *Polenblut / Polska Krew* (Polish blood, 1934, Germany); *Tarzan and His Mate* (1934, US); *Wonder Bar* (1934, US); *Eine Frau, die weiß, was sie will* (A woman who knows what she wants, 1934, Germany); *The Prince of Arcadia* (1933, UK); *L'opera de quat'sous* (*The Threepenny Opera*, 1931, France); *Abdul the Damned* (1935, US); *Amok* (1934, France); and *As You Desire Me* (1932, US). A photograph from 1937 reveals an advertisement for a showing at the Migdalor of Sacha Guitry's 1936 *Le Roman d'un Tricheur* (*The Story of a Cheat*) in which the title of the film was rendered also in German for German-speaking audiences: "Roman eines Schwindlers"; see Eden Cinema program for 17–22 November 1934, ER, box 6, folder 2; Migdalor Program, ER, box 6, folder 2; photograph [undated, probably 1937], ER, box 12, folder 5.

105. Ambler, "Popular Films and Colonial Audiences."

106. Land of Promise flier, ER, box 6, folder 2; Carmel Newsreels 1-036, part C, Nathan Axelrod Collection, IFA.

107. Feldestein, *Halutz, 'avodah, matzlemah*, 168.

108. Shoshana Persitz was a stunningly multilingual woman. Originally from Kiev, she attended the University of Moscow, the University of Paris, and the Sorbonne. She was active in the Tarbut schools and spent time in Germany before coming to Palestine in 1925. In Palestine she served on the Tel Aviv city council, the education department of the Zionist Organization, and later the education department of the Jewish National Council.

109. Shoshana Persitz, Eden Hotel Jerusalem, to Colonel Frederick Kisch, Jerusalem, date unclear, 1930, CZA S30/2038.

110. J. Luria to the managers of Talking Cinemas in Jerusalem, 15 September 1930, CZA S25/6733.

111. Werner Senator to Members of the Jewish Agency Executive, 30 September 1930, CZA S25/6733.

112. *Mayne Yidishe Mame* was directed by Sidney L. Goldin and produced by the Judea Film Company in New York. There are no extant copies. For coverage of the release in the United States, see "First Yiddish 'Talkie' Films Produced by Judea Film Co.," *New York Jewish Daily Bulletin*, 28 April 1930. See also "Jewish Films in Own Tongue," *Variety*, 22 January 1930; "Yiddish Short Film Booked in Fox Houses," *Motion Pictures Today*, 7 April 1930; "A Yiddish Talkie," *Jewish Outlet*, 17 April 1930; A. Mandelbaum, "Khazeray De-Luks: Felyeton," *Morgn Frayhayt* (New York), 3 July 1930; "Yiddish Film Starts Rioting in

Palestine," *World*, 27 September 1930 (cited in Helman, "Tzerikhat kolno'a ba-Yishuv uvi-medinat Yisra'el bi-shenotehah ha-rishonot").

113. Helman, *Or ve-yam hikifuha*, 50; Gedud Megine Ha-Safah to Israel Rokach, mayor of Tel Aviv, 8 September 1930, TAMA, 4-140A.

114. Aviezer Yellin and Asher Ehrlich, Histadrut ha-morim, to the Eden Cinema Administration, 7 September 1930, CZA S30/2038.

115. Dr. Yosef Rivlin and Aviezer Yellin, Histadrut ha-morim, to the Jewish Agency Administration, Jerusalem, 17 September 1930, CZA S30/2038. This Yosef Rivlin is Yosef Yoel Rivlin, an educator of Arabic, who is not the same as the Josef Rivlin who worked for the film agency.

116. Helman, *Or ve-yam hikifuha*, 50.

117. Yerushalayim Segal, *Zikhronot Yerushalayim be-Tel Aviv*, 246.

118. "Compromise Settles Fight over Showing of Initial Yiddish Talkie in Tel Aviv," *Jewish Daily Bulletin*, 30 September 1930.

119. Helman, *Or ve-yam hikifuha*, 50.

120. Yerushalayim Segal, *Zikhronot Yerushalayim Be-Tel Aviv*, 246.

121. Helman, *Or ve-yam hikifuha*, 48.

122. Josef Rivlin, Yehudah [Judea] Film Company, to the Jewish Agency Administration, Jerusalem, 16 September 1930, CZA S30/2038.

123. Ibid.

124. Ibid.

125. Abravanel Weimar (Vimar) to the Battalion of the Defenders of the Language, 7 September 1930, TAMA 4/140A.

126. Va'adat ha-herem le-totzeret Germanyah [Committee to Boycott German Goods] to Department of Culture, Tel Aviv Municipality, 28 April 1939, TAMA 4/141A.

127. District Commissioner (British), Jerusalem District, to mayor of Jerusalem, 31 December 1940, JMA, box 837, 1-61/11/6.

128. Y. Ben-Zvi and M. Gelerter to the administration of the Edison, Orion, Eden, and Zion cinemas in Jerusalem, 16 April 1941, CZA S23/757.

129. Yerushalayim Segal, *Zikhronot Yerushalayim Be-Tel Aviv*, 248.

130. Ben-Zvi and Gelerter to the administration of the Edison, Orion, Eden, and Zion cinemas.

131. Y. S., "Tel Aviv ha-'arbit," *Ha-Tzofeh*, 23 December 1937, 2, cited in Helman, "Tzerikhat kolno'a ba-Yishuv uvi-medinat Yisra'el bi-shenotehah ha-rishonot."

132. Tartakover et al., *Hatzagah rishonah*, 103; emphasis added.

Chapter 2. Peddlers, Traders, and the Languages of Commerce

1. A. Ludvipol, "Ha-mis'har veha-hinukh ha-mis'hari" [Commerce and commercial education], *Haaretz*, 3 October 1919, 1.

2. Bialik, "Ha-zilzul ba-lashon ha-'Ivrit u-va'ad ha-lashon," *Devarim she-be'al peh*, 131.

3. Helman, *Young Tel Aviv*, 91–92.

4. The Babel story as we have it was constructed of two strata, an earlier, antiurban tale involving the construction of a city-tower and its destruction by God, and a later addition that identified the place as Babylon and added the text about language; see Abusch, "Notes on Two Passages in the Biblical Account of Prehistory," 1–7.

5. Ian Buruma and Avishai Margalit situate distaste for the West within a longer history of distaste for capitalism, urbanism, and modernity, originally among Europe's own internal critics; see See Buruma and Margalit, *Occidentalism*, 17.

6. Tel Aviv was the first planned Hebrew city, but it was also, for many decades, the only one. With the rise of what has been called the pioneering ethos, which was oriented toward agriculture, national institutions ceased to invest in city planning, and no other cities were planned during the mandate period. The urban centers that did arise were products of urbanization of older *moshavot* (Rishon Le-Zion, Petah Tikva, and Rehovot), and the transformation of urban satellites into towns (Holon, Bat Yam, Ramat Gan, and the Kerayot around Haifa); see Bein, *Toledot ha-hityashvut ha-Tziyonit*, 429; Erik Cohen, *The City in the Zionist Ideology*, 3–20, 62.

7. Helman, *Or ve-yam hikifuha*, 104–5.

8. Groman, *Ha-mis'har ha-kim'oni be-Eretz Yisra'el*, 9.

9. Anat Helman nicely summarizes the tension between national and consumerist tendencies and the discourse around "luksos" (*Or ve-yam hikifuha*, 117–37).

10. As a Christian middle class rose, Jews became objects of resentment; their role as financiers to kings and princes only aggravated relations. At moments when protecting Jews seemed too costly to relations with the Christian middle class, rulers sometimes turned to expulsion. In the medieval period, indeed, the verb "to judaize" came to mean "to lend money at interest"; see Jeremy Cohen, *The Friars and the Jews*, 15; Little, *Religious Poverty and the Profit Economy in Medieval Europe*, 56.

11. Dohm, "Concerning the Amelioration of the Civil Status of the Jews," 33.

12. Joseph II, "Edict of Toleration," 39.

13. According to Marx: "As soon as society succeeds in abolishing the *empirical* essence of Judaism—huckstering and its conditions—the Jew becomes *impossible*, because his consciousness no longer has an object" ("On the Jewish Question," 52).

14. Sombart, *The Jews and Modern Capitalism*, xx–xxviii; see also Penslar, *Shylock's Children*, 164–65.

15. Karp, *The Politics of Jewish Commerce*, 2; see also Penslar, *Shylock's Children*, 45–46; Liberles, "On the Threshold of Modernity," 58; Endelman, *The Jews of Britain*, 82, 93.

16. Segev, *One Palestine, Complete*, 288.

17. Keren Ha-Yesod booklet, 1936, cited in Schlor, *Tel Aviv*, 105.

18. Slater, *Consumer Culture and Modernity*, 31.

19. The Fourth Aliyah was not only a time of increased industrialization in Palestine, but also a period when Jewish industrial firms, most notably Nesher (cement) and Shemen (oils), extracted concessions from the British government to introduce protective tariffs.

Thus, the public campaign for local goods occurred not in the context of hostile government policy but of British policies that further strengthened the Jewish industrial sector; see Barbara Smith, *The Roots of Separatism in Palestine*, chapter 8, "Protecting Jewish Industry."

20. Rieger, "Shene piske-din," 79.

21. "Le-ahar ha-ta'arukhah," 1.

22. Shimriyah Levin, composition notebook, Läemel School, Jerusalem, 1931–32 academic year, CZA A580/22.

23. Patai, *Journeyman in Jerusalem*, 103.

24. The song continues: "Solely from the produce of our land / Solely from the fruit of our might and our energy / You want satiation / and immigration, brother / from your hat to your shoelace / you are obligated to buy" (Emmanuel Ha-Rusi, "Zemer le-totzeret ha-aretz," available [in Hebrew] at *Zemereshet: A Project to Save Early Hebrew Music*, www.zemer.co.il/song.asp?id=1766).

25. In his 1946 summary of retail commerce in the Yishuv, Yaakov Groman points out the dual threats of the Middle Eastern goods and the goods coming in through Ha'avarah, the goods-for-immigration transfer agreements with the Third Reich (Groman, *Ha-Mis'har ha-kim'oni be-Eretz Yisra'el*, 8); see also Livni, *Ha-ma'avak she-nishkah*.

26. British products were not technically imports: the Yishuv was part of the British Empire, the local currency was a version of the British pound (the Palestine pound), and the British government had adopted tariff policies to promote the sale of British goods in Palestine to the point that they were often the cheapest alternatives. These "imported" goods therefore appeared particularly widespread and threatening to a community that defined "local" and "foreign" in ethnic rather than geographic terms. A fair amount of work has been done on British economic policy, including tariff policy in the Yishuv; see, for example, Nahum Gross, who stresses the massive role of the British in structuring and developing the economy of the Yishuv, in "Ha-mediniyut ha-kalkalit shel ha-mimshal ha-Briti ha-mandatori be-Eretz Yisra'el."

27. See references to these imports in Michaely, *Sehar ha-hutz vi-yevu ha-hon be-Yisra'el*, 11, and a fuller discussion of the Ha'avarah agreements—and the controversy between labor leaders and Revisionists about their merits—in Yehuda Bauer, *Jews for Sale?*, chapter 1. These agreements provided for a number of German Jews to come to Palestine and transfer their assets in exchange for a commitment from the Yishuv to buy German imports.

28. Liberles, "Threshold of Modernity," 63; Lowenstein, "The Beginning of Integration, 1780–1880," 132–33.

29. Ibid., 131.

30. Gilman, *Jewish Self-Hatred*, 133–34.

31. The Hebrew root *r.kh.l* means "to go about from place to place" and is likely related to the word *regel*, meaning "foot" or "leg." In its biblical context in the Song of Songs, it seems to refer to a spice merchant, an itinerant trader who traveled long distances to bring exotic goods (Song of Songs 3:6). The most famous explications of Jewish prohibitions on

gossip are found in the Hafetz Hayim, the book of moral prescriptions first published in 1873 by Rabbi Yisra'el Me'ir Kagan (who came to be known as the Hafetz Hayim). Many editions followed, with practical guides to avoiding *lashon ha-ra'* and *rekhilut*, some directed specifically at women; see also Ben-Zeev and Ben-Zeev, *Rekhilut*.

32. Tebbutt, *Women's Talk?*, 5.

33. Ibid., 6.

34. " 'Iske ha-toshavim be-Tel Aviv," *Yedi'ot 'Iriyat Tel Aviv*, 7 November 1926, 10.

35. "Survey of Business in Tel Aviv," *Palestine Post*, 20 May 1936, 9.

36. "Ha-ashamot ve-suge ha-ne'eshamim be-vet mishpat 'Iriyat Tel Aviv" [The charges and types of the accused in the Tel Aviv Municipal Court], *Yedi'ot 'Iriyat Tel Aviv*, 15 June 1926, 12.

37. Sh. Zaltzman, "Mah la'asot le-shikhlulah shel Tel Aviv?" [What should be done to improve Tel Aviv?], *Yedi'ot 'Iriyat Tel Aviv*, January 1933.

38. Brawer, *Perek ge'ografyah*, 316, cited in Helman, *Or ve-yam hikifuha*, 106–7.

39. The divide between *galutiyut* and *levantiniyut*, and between the anti-Yiddish politics of the first half of the twentieth century and the anti-Arabic politics of the second half is absolute in the historiography. On the notion of *galutiyut* (rejection of exile), see Zerubavel, *Recovered Roots*, chapter 2; Berg, *Exile from Exile*, chapter 1; Hochberg, *In Spite of Partition*, introduction and chapter 2; Hochberg, "Permanent Immigration"; Shohat, *Israeli Cinema*.

40. Penslar, *Shylock's Children*, 39–42.

41. Steven Aschheim traces the evolution of German-Jewish perceptions of their eastern European brethren who made their way to the German-speaking states in waves of immigration between the seventeenth and nineteenth centuries, most in response to anti-Jewish violence in eastern lands. Initially, these Jews were received positively, but antagonism developed with German modernization as eastern Jews appeared to be the very epitome of those traditional, primitive, or backward traits that German Jews wished to slough off. The *Ostjude*, he claims, were both the target of westernizing reforms and a symbol of all Jews' inability to cast off markers of difference; see Aschheim, *Brothers and Strangers*, introduction.

42. Selzer, *The Aryanization of the Jewish State*, 43–46.

43. Cohen-Hatav, "Yazmut, tikhnun u-fituah merhavi."

44. Boneh, *Eretz Yisra'el*, 165; Jacob Katz et al., *'Al Prof. Alfred Boneh*, 3, 11.

45. Groman, *Ha-Mis'har ha-kim'oni be-Eretz Yisra'el*, 7; emphasis in the original.

46. Marcia Gitlin, "A South African's Impressions of Palestine," in TAMA 2674/4, cited in Helman, *Or ve-yam hikifuha*, 107.

47. Aviva Askrov interview, 8 May 2000, 5–6, OHD 36(240). I refer to several interviews from this collection. They were recorded in most cases between 1998 and 2000 in the homes of the interviewees, all of whom were being asked to recall the Tel Aviv neighborhoods in which they grew up. These oral histories have inherent limitations as historical documents; nonetheless, they offer portraits of the past that can be read against texts from the period in question.

48. Tzipi Dagan interview, 10 October 2000, 7, OHD 35(240).

49. Cited in Shohat, *Israeli Cinema*, 116; Ben-Gurion's statement came in an interview with *Le Monde*, 9 March 1966. Gil Hochberg, who traces the origin of the word "Levantine" to the French colonial denigration of the East, shows how several later Arab Jewish writers, among them Ronit Matalon and Jacqueline Kahanoff, reclaimed Levantinism in a literary project of resistance against Zionist norms; see Hochberg, "Permanent Immigration," 220–21.

50. *Yedi'ot 'Iriyat Tel Aviv* 5:203 (1934).

51. Karni'eli, *Hoterim tahat kiyum sefatenu*, 6; also in Karni'eli, *'Al kipuah zekhuyot sefatenu*, 2.

52. Letter to Tel Aviv Municipality, Tevet 5687 [1927], TAMA 334/4A; cited in Helman, *Or ve-yam hikifuha*, 107.

53. *'Iton Meyuhad*, 1 Elul 5698 [1938], 7, cited in Helman, *Or ve-yam hikifuha*, 111.

54. Irgun le-hashlatat ha-'Ivrit [Organization for the Enforcement of Hebrew] to Mayor Israel Rokach, 1 Aug 1939, TAMA 4/141A.

55. Azaryahu, *Tel Aviv ha-'ir ha-amitit*, 114–15.

56. Nedivi Mazkir to administrator of the Organization for the Enforcement of Hebrew, Herzl 14, 7 August 1939, TAMA 4/141A.

57. Barukh Ben-Yehuda, *Sipurah shel ha-Gimnasyah "Herzliyah,"* 136–37. Hanina Krachevsky, known as the "Father of Hebrew Song," came to Palestine in 1908 but committed suicide in December 1925, at the age of forty-eight.

58. Rabau-Katinsky, *Be-Tel-Aviv 'al ha-holot*, 45.

59. Azaryahu, *Tel-Aviv ha-'ir ha-amitit*, 113.

60. Emmanuel Ha-Rusi [Emmanuel Yinon Novograbelsky], "Ma'aseh be-Hayim Itzi ha-hayal" [A story about Hayim Itzi the soldier], *Davar*, 27 June 1941, 4.

61. Ha-Rusi, "Zemer le-totzeret ha-'aretz."

62. The sale of Arab goods to Jews was relatively small—Szereszewski estimates that 10 percent of Jewish purchases were from the Arab sector; see Smith, *Roots of Separatism in Palestine*, 168.

63. Rabau-Katinsky, *Be-Tel-Aviv 'al ha-holot*, 45.

64. Daniel Ofir interview, 22 April 1998, 15, OHD (8)240.

65. Tova Aharoni interview, 4 December 1998, 14, OHD, (19)240.

66. Menahem Rogelski interview, 10 September 1998, 21, OHD (2)240.

67. This phenomenon has had echoes in recent years. On 2 November 2009, Tel Aviv acted to ban the entry of horses into the city in an effort to prevent the entry of junk traders, who tend to use horses as their means of transport. An article describing the decision was titled "Tel Aviv: 'ir beli alte zakhen" [Tel Aviv: A city without *Alte Zakhen*]; see Mako (Channel 2 News), 3 November 2009, http://www.mako.co.il/news-israel/local/Article-9646o4a7907b421004.htm.

68. A. Belin, "Mahalat ha-peh veha-tzahevet," *Davar*, 10 May 1946, 3.

69. "Tel Aviv," *Davar*, 2 July 1942, 4.

70. "Ha-radio shelanu," *Davar*, 9 August 1935, 18. All words not in italics are in Hebrew in the original; italicized words are non-Hebrew words that were transliterated into

Hebrew. On the history of Israeli radio, see Penslar, "Radio and the Shaping of Modern Israel," 81–82.

71. Hagit Lavsky argues that the commercial sector of the Yishuv was characterized by what Yossi Katz calls "nationalist capitalism"; see Lavsky, "Ha-umnam kayam kesher 'mahuti' ben Yehudim ve-kapitalizm?" On the relation between labor and capitalism, see also Ben-Porat, *Between Class and Nation*; Karlinsky, *California Dreaming*, 41.

72. Jacob Shavit, "Ben 'hevrah yishuvit' le-'hevrah politit' "; Brenner, 19 November 1917, cited in Shavit, "Ben 'hevrah yishuvit' le-'hevrah politit,' " 11–12; Michaely, *Sehar ha-hutz vi-yevu ha-hon be-Yisra'el*, 8–18.

73. The Yishuv had a large number of banks relative to the population, particularly in the 1930s. Some were subsidiaries of foreign banks; others were local (Michaely, *Sehar ha-hutz vi-yevu ha-hon be-Yisra'el*).

74. Shohat, *Israeli Cinema*, 54–55.

75. Quoted in Livni, *Ha-ma'avak she-nishkah*, 8.

76. Rivoli was founded by a German immigrant from Berlin; it sold luxury goods; Kupferberg cited in Schlör, *Tel Aviv*, 90, 93.

77. See, for example, the playbill for the Palestine Folk-Opera in its production of *Madame Butterfly*, 1941, ER, box 6, folder 7. Ads are found in ER, boxes 1, 6, 10–13.

78. An advertisement for Kruschen Salts, produced by the E. Griffith Hughes pharmacists in Manchester English, is printed in Hebrew, French, English, and Arabic, with much briefer text in German, Spanish, Italian, and Greek for good measure. Clearly, this company did not want to leave out any potential body of customers; see ER, box 1, folder 5.

79. Exchange of letters, November 1937, TAMA 4/140B.

80. Moshe Rat to CCEH, memorandum titled "Kipuah ha-'Ivrit ba-shetah ha-ta'asiyah veha-mis'har" [Discrimination against Hebrew in the field of commerce and industry], 3 January 1941, CZA S8/744.

81. "Be'ayot lashon ve-tarbut: leket devarim she-ne'emru ve-nikhtevu ba-hodshe Adar B[et]-Nisan 1946" [Issues of lanugage and culture: A selection of things written and said between Adar Bet and Nisan 5706 (1946)], Culture Department of the Jewish National Council, Institute for Hebrew Language and Culture, CZA DD1/3250.

82. "Ketzad yishamer ha-tzivyon ha-'Ivri shel yishuvenu ba-'ir ha-me'orevet" [How will the Hebrew character of our community be preserved in a mixed city?], *Davar*, 25 December 1944, CZA S71/2154.

83. Efraim T., "Madu'a Lo'azit?" [Why foreign languages?], *Davar*, 16 February 1947, CZA S71/365.

84. Letter from Yitzhak Ben-Zvi, CCEH, to Nahum Levin, Department of Commerce and Industry, 23 January 1941, CZA S8/744.

85. Margalit-Stern, "Imahot ba-hazit."

86. Cited in Efraim T., "Madu'a Lo'azit?"

87. Karlinsky, *California Dreaming*, 57.

88. Sea Department, Jewish Agency, Haifa, to local business owners, November 1936 [various dates], CZA S9/1612.

89. Rat to CCEH.

90. "Hadash ba-aretz!," advertisement in *Davar*, 30 August 1931, 4.

91. Flier for Hamelitz, ER, box 1, folder 3.

92. Advertisement for "Hakotew," ER, box 1, folder 9.

93. Flier for Madam Gizell, ER, box 1, folder 2.

94. Gedalyahu Zhokhovitzky, "Ha-Yehudi ha-melumad," *Ha-Boker*, 25 October 1940, CZA S71.

95. Ibid.

96. "Tidhar, *Entziklopedyah la-halutze ha-Yishuv u-vonav*, s.v. "Schurr, Shlomo," 15:4700–4701.

97. *Bet Sefer le-mis'har Safra, Mosad tikhoni le-haskalah kelalit realit u-mis'harit* [The Safra School of Commerce, a high school for general and commercial education], Tel Aviv Eretz Yisra'el [n.d., likely 1940 based on one photo dated 1940], CZA DD1/3085.

98. Y. Azaryahu, *Dokh mi-bikuri be-vet ha-sefer la-mis'har "Safra" be-Tel Aviv* [A report from my visit to the Safra School of Commerce], based on a visit on 2 January 1942, CZA J17/6576.

99. Blank form for report card, showing list of subjects, n.d. [1924–29], CZA A531/17.

100. Taikher, *Hanhalat pinkasim*, title page.

101. Y. Azaryahu, *Dokh mi-bikuri be-vet ha-sefer la-mis'har "Safra" be-Tel Aviv*.

102. *Bet sefer Safra: likrat shenat ha-limudim 5694 [1933–34]*, 27–28, 31.

103. CCEH, report, 27 August 1941, CZA J1/2228/7.

104. Schurr, photocopy of speech given at the end of the 1927–28 academic year of the Bet Sefer Tikhoni la-Mis'har, CZA A531/17.

105. Principal Sh. Auerbach, High School of Commerce, Tel Aviv, to Education Department of Knesset Yisra'el, 22 October 1936, CZA J17/429.

106. B. Ya'akovson, Secretary of High School of Commerce, to Keren Ha-Yesod Education Department, 20 April 1938, CZA J17/429.

107. *Tzeror mikhtavim*, 25, 27, 29.

108. *Bet sefer Safra*, 8–9.

109. Ibid., 22.

110. Yitzhak Zamir to the Safra School administration, in *Tzeror mikhtavim*, 14.

111. Margalit Libman to the Safra School administration, in *Tzeror mikhtavim*, 16.

112. CCEH report, 27 August 1941.

113. Y. B. Hoz, Rishon le-Zion, to Emil Shmurak, Jewish Agency, 22 January 1939, CZA S8/744.

Chapter 3. Clerks, Translators, and the Languages of Bureaucracy

Epigraph 1: Abbady, *Benenu le-ven ha-Anglim*, 38–39.

Epigraph 2: Chinua Achebe, "New Songs of Ourselves," *New Statesman and Society*, 9 February 1990, cited in Adejunmobi, *Vernacular Palaver*, 21.

1. *Official Gazette of the Government of Palestine*, no. 28, 1 October 1920, 5. The transition took a bit more time to be formalized. On 10 August 1922, the League of Nations passed a Palestine Order-in-Council affirming Arabic, English, and Hebrew as the official languages of Palestine (it was enacted in September). Article 82 read: "All ordinances, official notices and official forms of the Government and all official notices of local authorities and municipalities in areas to be prescribed by order of the High Commissioner shall be published in English, Arabic, and Hebrew. The three languages may be used in debates and discussions in the Legislative Council, and, subject to any regulations to be made from time to time, in the Government offices and Law Courts" (Palestine Order in Council, Article 82, 10 August 1922, UNISPAL database). Finally, Article 22 of the official League of Nations Mandate for Palestine in 1923 stated: "English, Arabic, and Hebrew shall be the official languages of Palestine. Any statement or inscription in Arabic on stamps or money in Palestine shall be repeated in Hebrew and any statement or inscription in Hebrew shall be repeated in Arabic." Article 15 prescribed "the right of each community to maintain its own schools for the education of its own members in its own language."

2. Ha-Cohen, "Eretz Yisra'el tahat shilton ha-tzava ha-Briti," 46.

3. "Who among us," Herzl famously wrote in his 1896 treatise *The Jewish State*, "has a sufficient acquaintance with Hebrew to ask for a railway ticket in that language? Such a thing cannot be done" (89).

4. Zohar Shavit, "Tel Aviv Language Police," 203.

5. Arlosoroff, "Ha-pekidut ha-Britit veha-bayit ha-le'umi [1928]" [British clerks and the national home], in *Kitve Hayim Arlozorov*, 1:80.

6. Slezkine, *The Jewish Century*, 20.

7. Birnbaum, *Jewish Destinies*, 4–5.

8. Studies of Jewish claims to integration through government service come mainly in studies of Jews in European militaries; see Rozenblit, *Reconstructing a National Identity*; Presner, "Muscle Jews and Airplanes."

9. Abbady, *Benenu le-ven ha-Anglim*, 34.

10. Ha-Cohen, "Eretz Yisra'el tahat shilton ha-tzava ha-Briti," 49.

11. Sherman, *Mandate Days*.

12. Abbady, *Benenu le-ven ha-Anglim*, chapter 1, "The Spiritual Distance." This chapter considers negative portrayals of Jews in English literature, the lack of a real reckoning with the Jewish question, and the lack of British understanding of the Jews' desire for revival in their homeland.

13. Ullendorff, "Hebrew in Palestine," 302; Shohamy and Spolsky, *Languages of Israel*, 158–59.

14. Poston, cited in Sherman, *Mandate Days*, 60.

15. Arlosoroff, "Ha-pekidut ha-Britit veha-bayit ha-le'umi [1928]," 1:74.

16. Bezalel Yaffe to Jaffa District Governor [English and Hebrew], 22 Sivan 5683 [June 1923], CZA S25/6311.

17. Kisch to chief secretary, Government House, Jerusalem, 18 December 1923, CZA S25/6311.

18. M[ordekhai], Histadrut orekhe ha-din ha-Yehudiyim be-Eretz Yisra'el, *Protokol, Ha-ve'idah ha-rishonah*, 8–9 April 1928, Session A, 8 April, 10.

19. Hayim Nachman Bialik, "Ha-zilzul ba-lashon ha-'Ivrit u-Va'ad ha-lashon," Adar B[et], 1929, *Devarim she-be'al peh*, 132.

20. Ariav to Max Nurock, 8 October 1929, CZA S30/2040.

21. Y. Ha-Timhoni, "Ha-'Ivrit ha-rishmit shel ha-'iton ha-rishmi" [Culture Department of the Jewish National Council, Institute for Hebrew Language and Culture], *Be'ayot lashon ve-tarbut: leket devarim she-ne'emru ve-nikhtevu ba-hodshe Adar B[et]-Nisan 1946* [Issues of lanuage and culture: A selection of things written and said between Adar Bet and Nisan 1946], CZA DD1/3250.

22. Shmuel Yeivin, "Report on the Hebrew Section of the Central Translation Bureau for the year July 1944–June 1945," ISA, M 5078/120-9-4-9.

23. CZA S30/2039, S25/6733, S30/2041, S6/4491, S30/2042.

24. Wallach, "Readings in Conflict," 59–61, 177–211.

25. *Official Gazette of the Government of Palestine*, no. 28, 1 October 1920, 5.

26. Court Ruling, High Court no. 88.29, Application for an order to issue to the Postmaster General Directing him to accept telegrams in the Hebrew language, 9 May 1929; petitioner: Mr. Lehrer; respondent: Postmaster General; CZA S20/2039.

27. Y. Strod, Battalion of the Defenders of the Hebrew Language, to the Zionist Executive, Jerusalem, 9 May 1929, CZA S30/2037.

28. Several scholars have focused on the culture of petition writing that emerged in the Middle East Mandates; see Provence, "Protest, Counterinsurgency, and the League of Nations in Syria," and Bailony "Transnationalism and the Syrian Migrant Community."

29. O. G. R. Williams, comment on Mr. Amikam's petition to the League of Nations 97246/32, 28 August 1934, "Palestine Original Correspondence," TNA, CO 733/262/13.

30. Cunliffe-Lister, 13 September 1934, in ibid.

31. " 'Esrim shanah le-hakhnasat ha-ot ha-'Ivrit ba-telegraf" [Twenty years since Hebrew script was brought into the telegraph], *Ha-Tzofeh*, 2 January 1941, CZA S71/1828.

32. IFA, Carmel Newsreels 1–002, March 1935.

33. Heller, "Language Choice, Social Institutions, and Symbolic Domination," 378; see also Conrick, "Legislating for Language"; Conrick and Regan, *French in Canada*, 59–78.

34. Reuveni, "Ha-markiv ha-yehudi be-manganon memshelet ha-mandat," 52; see also Reuveni's chart that discusses the specific numbers of Jews in the police force (Reuveni, *Mimshal Ha-Mandat Be-E. Y., 1920–1948*, 145).

35. Reuveni assesses the proportion at 33 percent. For Nurock, see Max Nurock, second conversation with Yehuda Oppenheim, 8, OHD 1(82). In fact, Jews and Arabs were generally excluded from all but the bottom three or four levels of the seven-level civil service, though Jews of British origin were eligible for higher positions; see Reuveni, "Ha-markiv ha-yehudi be-manganon memshelet ha-mandat," 48.

36. Abbady, *Benenu le-ven ha-Anglim*, 89.

37. These numbers appear to include clerks in both Jewish and British settings; we can assume, though, that the numbers were much higher in Jewish institutions; see Reuveni, "Ha-markiv ha-Yehudi be-manganon memshelet ha-mandat," 43.

38. De Vries, "National Construction of Occupational Identity," 381, 387.

39. A. Argov, "Al hilufe pekidim" [On the replacement of clerks], *Pinkas* 3 (October 1935): 24; cited in De Vries, "National Construction of Occupational Identity," 387.

40. Reuveni, "Ha-markiv ha-yehudi be-manganon memshelet ha-mandat," 44, 48; Abbady, *Benenu le-ven ha-Anglim*, 82–91, 89.

41. De Vries, "National Construction of Occupational Identity," 383.

42. H. Ariav, general secretary of the Zionist Organizations, to Battalion of the Defenders of the Hebrew Language, 20 May, 3 June, 7 June 1929, CZA S30/2037.

43. F. H. Kisch to the Zionist Executive Political Department, London, 14 May 1929, CZA S30/2039.

44. Jewish National Council to chief secretary, Palestine government, 16 January 1929, CZA J1/70/2.

45. Chief secretary to the Jewish National Council [English and Hebrew], 31 January 1929, CZA J1/70/2.

46. The Haifa Committee sent a letter to the Jewish National Council suggesting this; see chairman of the Va'ad Ha-Kehilah ha-'Ivrit, Haifa, to the Jewish National Council Jerusalem, 31 December 1943, CZA J1/3532.

47. Kefar Nahalal Committee to the Jewish Agency, Jewish National Council, and the Executive Committee of the Federation of Workers, 17 December 1943, CZA J1/3532.

48. Israel Amikam to the Jewish National Council administration, 9 January 1944, CZA J1/3532.

49. Sir John Shuckburgh, comment on Amikam's petitition 97246/32, 30 August 1934, TNA, CO 733/262/13.

50. "Hodot lo mekablim ha-yom telegramot be-otiyot 'Ivriyot" [Thanks to him, it is possible today to receive telegrams in Hebrew script], *Ha-Mashkif*, 1 January 1945, CZA S71/2154; Israel Amikam to Committee of the Hebrew Community, Haifa, 12 December 1943, HMA 4469.

51. Israel Amikam to the Administration of the Anglo Palestine Bank, 12 December 1943, CZA J1/3532.

52. "Extracts from Cyprus General Orders," ISA, P 657/1.

53. Language Examinations, 1936, TNA, CO 733/320/13.

54. Secretary, Council of Legal Studies, to Gobernik, Bronzaft, Gordon, Shriebman, Maklev, Schebalg, and Abramov, 3 December 1936, ISA, M 1288/5; "Law School English Test," [1936?], ISA, M 1288/5.

55. "Regulations for the Payment of Language Allowances, 1926," ISA, M 334/4; C. F. Strickland to chief secretary, 7 March 1933, ISA M 125/12.

56. Sir Arthur Wauchope to Sir Philip Cunliffe-Lister, 10 February 1934, TNA, CO 733/254/2.

57. Extract from Report of Royal Commission, n.d. [1937], TNA, CO 733/320/13. This is not to say that there weren't attempts to teach Hebrew to British officers, for example, in the Palestine police. The Jewish National Council appears to have offered courses for British officers in Haifa. A report at the end of 1937 claimed that ten officers had passed the tests and spoke Hebrew fluently; see Ben Zion Klein, "Hora'at ha-safah ha-'Ivrit be-huge ha-shoterim ha-Britiyim be-Haifa" [The teaching of Hebrew in British officers' clubs in Haifa], 26 December 1937, CZA J1/3552.

58. Storrs, *The Memoirs of Sir Ronald Storrs*, 317.

59. A. W. Money to Colonel Huggett, 13 October 1918, CZA L4/25.

60. The proclamation was in English, French, and Russian, the languages of the Allies, as well as Hebrew, Arabic, and Greek, considered local languages (Greek was the language of the Greek patriarchate, which wielded significant power in Jerusalem); see Grainger, *The Battle for Palestine, 1917*, 215.

61. Storrs, *Memoirs*, 374.

62. Antonius, "The Machinery of Government in Palestine," 60–61.

63. Epstein, in the name of the assistant governor, Jerusalem/Jaffa District, to Meir Dizengoff, Tel Aviv, 17 November 1924, TAMA 3/1B. The advisers mentioned were the Jerusalem judge Mordechai Eliash; Rabbi Samuel Aaron Veber (Shazuri), who had recently been the secretary of the Chief Rabbinate's office; and Josef Klausner, who at that time was editing the literary journal *Ha-Shiloah*.

64. It is unclear whether the numbers present in the late 1940s are similar to those for the 1920s and 1930s. We can speculate that the later numbers grew somewhat as the British bureaucracy expanded its ranks, but discussions about the need for translators, such as Antonius's, suggest that the office engaged in similar activities from its inception.

65. "Annex II, Correspondence, Circulars, etc. Translated for the Secretariat July 1944–June 1945"; "Annex II Correspondence, Circulars, etc. Translated for the Secretariat July 1945–June 1946, ISA, M 5078/120-9-4-9.

66. Minute to the director of education, draft, 13 March 1945, ISA, M 5081/10.

67. "Third Annual Report on the Hebrew Section of the Central Translation Bureau, July 1946–June 1947," 14 September 1947, ISA, M 5078/120-9-4-9.

68. Ibid., annex III (paragraph 39), "Translations Made for Various Government Departments (other than Secretariat)," ISA, M 5078/120-9-4-9. These included twenty-one Hebrew-to-English translations, twenty-five English-to-Hebrew translations, and two English-to-Russian translations. The departments in question were Accounting, Antiquities, District Administration, Health, Income Tax, Police, War, and Post and Telegraph.

69. "Annex II, Correspondence, Circulars, July 1944–June 1945."

70. Shmuel Yeivin, "Report on the Hebrew Section of the Central Translation Bureau for the year July 1944–June 1945," ISA, M 5078/120-9-4-9; "Second Annual Report on the Hebrew Section of the Central Translation Bureau, July 1945–June 1946," 7 August 1946.

71. W. J. Farrell, "Memorandum on Translators," Department of Education, 16 October 1945, ISA, M 5081/10.

72. Lawrance et al., "Introduction: African Intermediaries and the 'Bargain' of Collaboration," 14–15.

73. Lockman, *Comrades and Enemies*, 144.

74. H. Modlinger to chief interpreter, 26 November 1946, ISA, M 4892/10.

75. Mr. Fuchs to chief interpreter 1 November 1946; Erich Goldstein to Central Translation Bureau, 4 September 1946; both in ISA, M 4892/10.

76. Eliyahu Salamah to S. Yeivin, 29 September 1946, ISA, M 4892/10.

77. "Third Annual Report on the Hebrew Section of the Central Translation Bureau, July 1946–June 1947," 14 September 1947, ISA, M 5078/120-9-4-9.

78. Palestine Government, Palestine Railways, Behinah be-tirgum, April 1946. Students were given half an hour to translate the 200-word text into English; see ISA, M 4892/13.

79. "Extract from Minute by the Secretary of State," 5 July 1937, TNA, CO 733/320/13.

80. Yehudah Even-Shemu'el (Kaufmann), director of the Culture Department, Jewish National Council, to the Central Committee of the Union of Industrial Owners / Hit'ahadut ba'ale ha-ta'asiyah, 2 November 1942, CZA S25/6741.

81. Rigbi, letter to the editor, *Palestine Post*, 29 November 1945, 4, CZA S25/6741.

82. Likhovski, *Law and Identity in Mandate Palestine*, 29–30.

83. Gabriel Strassman, *'Ote ha-gelimah*, 54.

84. Likhovski, *Law and Identity*, 103.

85. Federation of Jewish Attorneys in the Land of Israel, Protocol, Second Conference, 2–3 May 1928, Tel Aviv, CZA, J108/2.

86. Cited in Strassman, *'Ote ha-gelimah*, 53.

87. Organization for the Enforcement of Hebrew to Jewish Lawyers, Tammuz 5697 [June/July 1937], TAMA 4/140C.

88. Ibid.

89. Chair, Organization for the Enforcement of Hebrew, to chair, Histadrut orkhe ha-din, 21 December 1939, TAMA 4/141A.

90. Max Nurock interview (by Bernard Wasserstein), 6 July 1970, 1–2, 5, OHD 1(82).

91. Daniel Ofir interview, 22 April 1998, 13–14, OHD 8(240).

92. Principal Medical Office, Jaffa District, to Dizengoff [English], 20 January 1925, TAMA 3/1B.

93. District Commissioner, Negev District, to president, Township of Tel Aviv [English], 19 May 1927, TAMA 4/140A.

94. Crosbie, Southern District commissioner, Jaffa, 10 July 1927, TAMA 4/140A.

95. "Shuv hitnakeshut rishmit bi-zekhut ha-'Ivrit" [Another official assassination of the rights of Hebrew], *Davar*, 16 August 1927, 1.

96. District police headquarters, Jaffa, to Tel Aviv Municipality [English], 20 April 1928, TAMA 4/140A.

97. Leadership of the hanhagat mahleket ha-mosedot to the Jewish National Council, 26 January 1927, TAMA 4/140A.

98. Jewish National Council [sender unclear] to chief secretary, Palestine Government, Jerusalem [Hebrew], 16 January 1929, CZA J1/70/2.

99. "Report on the Haifa Chamber of Commerce," 21 November 1919, CZA L3/20/1.

100. Acting chairman, Zionist Commission, to chief administrator, OETA Headquarters, 23 December 1919, CZA L3/20/1. Bina was not hired on the spot; the Chief Administrative Office of the British government considered the role unnecessary but said that it might hire him in the future. It appears that Bina by January 1920 had become the representative of the Zionist Commission in Haifa.

101. Ezra David to Tel Aviv Municipality, 14 April 1935.

102. Shlomo Aharoni to Meir Dizengoff, 18 January 1929, TAMA 3702A.

103. Shimon Taberski to Tel Aviv Municipality, 19 March 1930, TAMA 3702A.

104. L. Rotstein to vice mayor, Tel Aviv Municipality, 30 December 1930, TAMA 3702A.

105. Y. S. Sharafi to mayor, Tel Aviv Municipality, 26 January 1930; Avraham Naiman to mayor, Tel Aviv Municipality, 11 February 1930; both in TAMA 3702A.

106. Nissim Malul to M. Block, Tel Aviv Municipality, 12 September 1928, TAMA 3702A.

107. Leah Donberg to Meir Dizengoff, 2 December 1929, TAMA 3702A.

108. Ha-Cohen, "Eretz Yisra'el tahat shilton ha-tzava ha-Briti," 50.

109. E. Dobkin, Aliyah Department, Jewish Agency, to Palestine Offices in Konstanza, Trieste, Paris, Saloniki, Vienna, Johannesburg, Harbin, and London, 4 April 1937; to Trieste office, 16 April 1937; to Paris office, 7 May 1937; secretary of the South African Zionist Federation to E. Dobkin, Aliyah Department, Jewish Agency, Jerusalem, 3 June 1937, CZA S6/4487.

110. Nedivi to Efraim Freudmann, 29 April 1937, TAMA 4/3642B.

111. Nedivi to Fritz Epstein, 14 March 1940, TAMA 4/141B.

112. "Shipur ha-lashon veha-ketav" [Improving the language and the writing], AYA 9.8/4, folder 010; the stamps are found in the archives of the Tel Aviv Municipality at the CZA, too, which indicates that they were distributed widely.

113. Munzer to the Tel Aviv Municipality, 14 June 1934, TAMA 4/140A.

114. Tel Aviv Municipality to Hevrah Eretz Yisre'elit le-handasah, October 1935, TAMA 4/140B

115. Israel Rokach to the Shell Petroleum Company and the Prudential Insurance Company, 9 November 1934 [English], TAMA 4/140A.

116. S. O. Richardson, solicitor, to the district commissioner, Southern District, Government Offices, Jaffa, 22 June 1927, TAMA 4/140A.

117. Th. D. Schatz to Mr. Nedivi, 9 June 1940, TAMA 4/141B.

118. Dr. Bruno Cohn to Tel Aviv Municipality, 30 January 1934, TAMA 4/140A.

119. Max Tuchner to the Va'ad Ha-Kehilah, Haifa, 5 January 1943, HMA, folder 5453.

120. "Wir wiederholen unsere Mahnung und Forderung: er hebräisch mehr order weniger beherrscht, möge in der Öffentlichkeit NUR HEBRÄISCH sprechen; andere können sich der englischen Sprache bedienen," *Mitteilungsblatt der Hitachduth Olej Germania we olej Austria* 4, no. 25 (21 June 1940), 3, TAMA 4/141B.

121. Ha-Cohen, "Eretz Yisra'el tahat shilton ha-tzava ha-Briti," 231.

122. Ibid., 50.

123. Eliezer Rieger, "Dokh 'al bikuri be-vet ha-sefer ha-tikhoni le-mis'har, Tel Aviv" [A report on my visit to the High School of Commerce, Tel Aviv], 9–11 February 1937, CZA J17/429.

124. *Bet sefer Safra*, 24–25.

125. Y. Azaryahu, *Dokh mi-bikuri be-vet ha-sefer le-mis'har "Safra" be-Tel Aviv.*

126. Eliezer Rieger, "Pirte-kol mi-yeshivat ha-mo'atzah ha-pedagogit" [Protocol from the meeting of the Pedagogical Council], 11 February 1937, Bet Sefer Ha-tikhoni le-mis'har [High School of Commerce], CZA J17/429.

127. Statement from Dina Pugatzki, *Tzeror mikhtavim*, 24.

128. Statement from Shulamit Yerushavski, ibid., 28.

129. Allan Drinkwater, Longmans, Green to J. S. Bentwich, Education Department, Jerusalem, Palestine, 20 February 1939, CZA J17/6645.

130. J. S. Bentwich to Allan Drinkwater, Longmans, Green, 7 March 1939, CZA J17/6645.

131. The Berlitz Schools were British institutions that taught primarily in English; see ISA, M 170/36.

132. Bentwich to Drinkwater, 7 March 1939.

133. C. A. F. Dundas, Istanbul, to Lord Lloyd, extract, 25 January 1941, TNA, BW 47/1.

134. Director, Tel Aviv School of English, to Miss Yellin, n.d. [1941?], CZA A580/22.

135. "Statistics of Students, May/June/July/November 1943," British Institute, Tel Aviv, TNA, BW 47/10.

136. Correspondence between Kvutzat Rodges (later Yavneh), a religious Zionist community, and the Kibbutz Ha-Me'uhad, En Harod, June–August 1937, CZA S24/91.

137. New liaison officer to the Zionist Commission, Jaffa, to the British Foreign Office, 13 October 1918, CZA L4/25.

138. Samuel, *Unholy Memories of the Holy Land*, 20.

139. G. Sh., "Andralamusiyah leshonit" [Linguistic chaos], *Ha-Mashkif*, 25 September 1945.

140. Likhovski, *Law and Identity*, 154.

141. Strassman, *'Ote ha-gelimah*, 55.

142. P. Azai, "Ha-sefer ha-Angli kavash et ha-shuk ha-Eretz Yisre'eli" [The English book conquered the Palestine market], *Haaretz*, 31 October 1944, CZA S71/2154.

143. M. M., " 'Al ha-hayalim lashuv le-'Ivrit" [Soldiers must return to Hebrew], *Hegeh*, 20 August 1945.

144. P. Azai, "Ha-sefer ha-Angli kavash et ha-shuk ha-Eretz Yisre'eli."

Chapter 4. Zion in Babel

Epigraph: Cited in Caplan, "The Yishuv, Sir Herbert Samuel, and the Arab Question in Palestine, 1921–1925," 20.

1. Yehoash, *The Feet of the Messenger*, 194. This translation, by the well-known translator Isaac Goldberg, reads "Eretz Yisroel," using the Yiddish pronunciation of the name. Yehoash, a poet and translator proficient in several languages, had moved to Rehovot with his family and begun the study of classical Arabic and the Qur'an. The original Yiddish reads "one of the sickest points of" the Yishuv; see Yehoash, *Fun New York biz Rehovos un tsurik*, 44.

2. Moshe Smilansky, "Ba-moledet" ("In the Homeland"), *Ha-'Olam*, 16 January 1914, 6. Smilansky also criticized the denigrating attitude of Zionist colonists in Palestine, claiming that before their immigration they had considered the land "as an abandoned wasteland waiting for its redeemer and had not revised their views even after coming to Palestine and finding that it was not a virgin landscape."

3. Josef Klausner expressed this position in his 1907 article "Foreboding," in which he warned of the danger of Jewish assimilation into Arab culture, which he saw evidenced by young people taking on Arab clothing and cultural forms. He phrased the danger as a retreat from a cultured position that Jews had acquired in Europe into an uncultured position. This was the overall concern among a group of thinkers, including Ze'ev Smilansky and Ze'ev Barzilai, who recommended the maximum distance from Arabs in general; see Gorny, *Ha-she'elah ha-'Arvit veha-be'ayah ha-Yehudit*, 56–64.

4. After 1948 the state took on a far more active project of "administrative toponomy," overlaying Arab space with Jewish space not only in human habitation but also in language, giving ancient biblical names to sites that had long been called by Arab names; see Benvenisti, *Sacred Landscape*, 45, 65, 67.

5. Eyal points out the more symbolic connotations of Arabic speaking as part of a larger dynamic of cultural imitation among pre–World War I immigrants to Palestine, arguing that imitative gestures served in general to "purify the hybrids" and redraw a bright line between the categories of Jew and Arab by enabling Jews to penetrate Arab space but then withdraw again, reasserting their separation from that space. The bulk of the book, however, concerns those "virtuosi" who maintained an intensive knowledge of Arabic, penetrated the space, and thus proved the impossibility of "purifying the hybrids." His analysis of Arabic shifts toward the cultivation of "Oriental expertise" as his study progresses toward the mandate and post-1948 periods; see Eyal, *Disenchantment of the Orient*, 33–47.

6. Almog, *Sabra*, 196.

7. Lockman, *Comrades and Enemies*; LeVine, *Overthrowing Geography*.

8. Yodfat, "Yahase Yehudim ve-'Arvim be-reshitah shel Tel-Aviv (1909–1929)," 521. Arab kindness to Jews emerged in part from collaboration, born of opposition by some to the Arab national movement in general and the Husayni family leadership in particular; see Hillel Cohen, *Army of Shadows*, 66–92.

9. See, for example, the 1921 protocols on the subject of Arab workers in the city, repro-duced in Yodfat, "Yahase Yehudim ve-'Arvim be-reshitah shel Tel-Aviv (1909–1929)," 532–35.

10. Ibid., 520.

11. Mark LeVine writes of "a desire to segregate the new immigrants geographically from Arabs in a place where they could nurture their national values by speaking Hebrew, developing Hebrew educational and cultural institutions, engaging in national activities, and the like" (*Overthrowing Geography*, 61–63).

12. Ibid., 71, 95–96.

13. The collection of Tel Aviv–related interviews at the Oral History Division of the Institute for Contemporary Jewry in Jerusalem provides a rich stock of sources, which are explored in other social contexts in other chapters.

14. Rivka Rabinovitz interview, 20 Febuary 2003, 3, OHD 47(240).

15. Tzvi Elpeleg interview, 23 July 1998, 5, OHD 31(240).

16. The "good Arab," generally described as an Arab who helps Jews or is congenial to the Zionist project, has had an important resonance in the Hebrew literary imagination; see Bar-Tal and Teichman, *Stereotypes and Prejudice in Conflict*, 195–96.

17. Tzipora Brenner interview, 2001, 5, OHD 39(240).

18. Asher's last name was formerly Asherov. He explains in the interview that his father dropped the suffix, saying, "I'll leave the 'ov' to the Bulgarians"; see Asher Asher inter-view, 7 January 2011, 15, OHD 44(240).

19. Ibid., 6. This expression, which means "Slaughter the Jews!" was a standard battle cry of Arab rioters during this period, though violence was targeted toward British forces as well; see Van Creveld, *The Sword and the Olive*, 26–27. This cry apparently persisted dur-ing the First Intifada, in 1987; see Friedman, *From Beirut to Jerusalem*, 371–72.

20. Yehoash spoke of a colonist in Rehovot, S., who published sketches of the new set-tlement in both Hebrew and Arabic under the name Khawaja Musa, or "Mr. Musa." Yehoash explained that the man's Arab employees called him Khawaja Musa, whence his pen name (*Feet of the Messenger*, 80). Moshe Goldenberg, the Jewish National Fund repre-sentative in the Bet She'an Valley, also remembered being addressed in this way; see Hillel Cohen, *Army of Shadows*, 87.

21. Shoshana Kirstein, 26 August 2011, 6–7, OHD 37(240).

22. Zimra Livneh interview, 1 November 1999, 5, OHD 25(240). Trachoma is a type of bacterial conjunctivitis.

23. Eye disease was perceived as not only an Arab problem, to be treated by beneficent Jews, but also a potential threat to the Jewish population itself and thus a reason for Jews to maintain their distance from Arabs; see Shapira, *Land and Power*, 59. Theodor Herzl in fact included two ophthalmologist characters in *Altneuland*, with the suggestion that Jewish self-transformation would require medical intervention, for trachoma was characteristic not only of Palestine but also of impoverished Jewish communities in eastern Europe; see the discussion in Sufian, *Healing the Land and the Nation*, 46–47.

24. Zimra Livneh interview, 1 November 1999, 4, OHD 25(240).

25. Rivka Rabinovitz interview, 20 Febuary 2003, 3–4, OHD 47(240).

26. Chelouche, cited in Gavron, *Holy Land Mosaic*, 90. On lack of contact as a cause of stereotypes, see Shapira, *Land and Power*, 61, and Baruch Kimmerling, "A Model for Analyzing Reciprocal Relations between the Jewish and Arab Communities in Mandatory Palestine," 14. On Sephardi Jewish concerns about Jewish-Arab conflict, see Jacobson's discussion of Sephardi Jews' attempts to promote a Zionism compatible with Ottoman loyalty and positive relations with Palestinian Arabs, in "Sephardim, Ashkenazim and the Arab Question in pre–First World War Palestine."

27. "Ha-'Arvit be-vet ha-sefer ha-'amami," *Ha-Boker*, 2 July 1946.

28. Yehoash, *Feet of the Messenger*, 194.

29. Reichel argues that the kibbutz ethos was at the forefront of a rejection of European languages, the same ethos that recommended Arabic study: "This idea of the 'sabra' was juxtaposed against the idea of the educated, enlightened European Jew who studied in two or more European languages, either in a formal context or by himself, and whose thirst for knowledge was unquenchable. Although these two self-images did not actually reflect reality in a totally accurate way, the projections of these self-images limited the sons' generation by its frequent contradiction with reality" ("Ben 'kartanut' le-'ofke-tarbut,' " 1–2). At the same time, she identifies a particular type, "enlightened farmers," who, as opposed to "national farmers," were not opposed to the study of European languages, though they were not among the promoters of Arabic.

30. Cited in Assaf, *Ha-yehasim ben 'Arvim vi-Yehudim be-Eretz Yisra'el (1860–1948)*, 91.

31. Letter to Moshe Shertok, 14 April 1938, CZA S23/3021. According to this document, the Histadrut gathered after the 1929 riots to discuss ways to create ties with Arabs.

32. In keeping with the promise of eventual statehood conveyed in the 1917 Balfour Declaration, the Jewish Agency was entrusted with the task of "advising and cooperating with the [British] Administration of Palestine in such economic, social, and other matters as may affect the establishment of the Jewish National Home and the interests of the Jewish population of Palestine"; see Naomi Cohen, "An Uneasy Alliance," 107.

33. Yoav Gelber, "Maga'im diplomatiyim terem hitnagedut tzeva'it"; Shlaim, *Collusion across the Jordan*.

34. From the perspective of the settlers during that period (1936–39), "Shertok was the central address and their loyal representative in the administration of the Jewish agency" (Golani, "Moshe Shertok," 58).

35. Eliyahu Sasson [on Jewish Agency letterhead], n.d., CZA S23/3021.

36. Michael Assaf to Moshe Shertok, 12 January 1941, CZA S23/3021.

37. Eliyahu Sasson, Political Department of the Jewish Agency, Arab Division, n.d., CZA S23/3021.

38. Yitzhak Mark to Miriam Glickson, Safed, 25 March 1944, CZA S25/9395.

39. Menachem Na'or to Moshe Shertok, 19 February 1936, LA IV-208-1-1287.

40. The CZA holds more than thirty-five folders with the title "Arabic Instruction and Neighborly Relations," containing hundreds of pages of correspondence between local

leaders and educators with Moshe Shertok, Eliyahu Sasson, and Miriam Glickson at the Jewish Agency.

41. CZA S25—Jewish Agency, Political Department, 1921–1948. This is not to suggest that earlier correspondence did not come to the Jewish National Council or the Zionist Commission. Evidence suggests that it did, but I was not able to find its archival location.

42. Kevutzat Shiller to Arab Department, Jewish Agency, 2 May 1944, CZA S25/9395. Kevutzat Shiller, also known as Gan Shlomo, was founded in 1927 by a small group of immigrants from Poland and named for Shlomo Shiller, among the early Zionist Hebrew teachers in Palestine.

43. Gi'vat Brenner to Arab Department, Jewish Agency, 7 May 1944, CZA S25/9395.

44. David Sonenfeld, "Activities for Cultivating Neighborly Relations: Reports Received at the Political Department of the Jewish Agency" [in Hebrew], 13 November 1942, CZA S25/1571.

45. Y. Y. Kurstein to kibbutz members, on behalf of the Committee for Studying and Clarifying the Arab Problem, 10 February 1944, BB 2-2-1944-27-A.

46. Rosenstein, comments included in "Meeting of the Education Committee," 12 January 1948, 16–19, BB 2-7-1948-2 (Central Committee of the Party, Education Committee, protocols).

47. Yaffe's statement about his birth implies that he immigrated to Palestine from Europe at a young age; see "On the Educational Problems in the Country, Protocol, Session of the Committee for Educational Problems in the Country, Second Session," Tel Aviv, 12 January 1948, 10, BB 2-7-1948-3 (Central Committee of the Party, Educational Problems in the Country).

48. "From the Words of the Members in the Assembly of Members at the Party's Jerusalem Branch," 4 September 1943; on the agenda: activity of the party in researching the Arab problem, 1, BB 2-926-1943-1 (Arab Division, Committee for Studying and Clarifying the Arab Problem, incoming and outgoing correspondence). Speaker: Y. Burstein; emphasis in the original.

49. Joel Beinin shows that the consolidation of this commitment in 1940 was a means of demonstrating the feasibility of a binational solution in the early 1940s, when the consensus in the Zionist community was moving toward a two-state, partition model; see Beinin, "Knowing Your Enemy."

50. Kibbutz Masaryk, *Ba-Kibbutz*, May 1936, 1, YYA.

51. Kibbutz Mishmar Ha-'Emek, *'Iton penimi*, April 1937, 13.

52. "Sihot be-'Arvit" [Conversations in Arabic], *Ba-ma'aleh*, 27 January 1933, 9, YYA. The sample conversation contains a mix of formal and colloquial Arabic.

53. Kibbutz Masaryk, *Ba-Kibbutz*, May 1936, 10.

54. Ibid., 12.

55. Beinin, "Knowing Your Enemy," 104–8. Both Cohen and Bentov wrote memoirs that provide insights into their upbringing and involvement with Ha-Shomer Ha-Tza'ir; see Bentov, *Yamim mesaperim*; Aharon Cohen *Guf rishon, guf shelishi*.

56. Eliezer Be'eri, memorandum concerning the Department for Arab Activities, Kibbutz Ha-Zore'a, 20 March 1940, YYA (3)4.21.95.

57. Eliezer Bauer (Be'eri) to Eliyahu Sasson, Political Division, Jewish Agency, from Kibbutz Ha-Zore'a, 26 June 1942, YYA (2)7.10.95.

58. Zionists had particularly positive relations with the Druze, members of an esoteric religion with its origins in the Ismaili sect of Islam. These positive relations continued during and after the 1948 war, with the Hagana conducting training in Ussefiya as well; see Parsons "The Druze and the Birth of Israel"; Parsons, *The Druze between Palestine and Israel*.

59. Eliezer Bauer (Be'eri), memorandum, to members participating in the seminar for learning Arabic, Kibbutz Ha-Zore'a, 10 June 1941, YYA (2)7.10.95.

60. Reuven Mass, publisher and bookseller, to Moshe Shertok (suggesting that the Jewish Agency should purchase copies of the new series), 12 November 1940; included the first issue of the series, CZA S23/3021.

61. Miriam Glickson to Moshe Shertok, memorandum concerning the conference of Arabic teachers in the communities (which took place on 25–26 August 1942), 3 September 1942, CZA J17/322. The conference included the heads of the Department of Education as well as candidates for teaching in the communities.

62. The KZA contains Be'eri's *Studienbuch* (transcript) from the University of Berlin, which lists courses he took in Arabic language and grammar, the Qur'an, philosophy, and history; see Elizer Be'eri Personal Archive, KZA. I am thankful to Ruti Herman at Kibbutz Ha-Zore'a for making these materials available to me.

63. Be'eri, memorandum concerning Department of Arab Activities.

64. Be'eri, "Work Plan for the Seminar on Arabs and the Jewish-Arab Question, in Twenty Lectures," 28 May 1946, YYA, (1)2.21.95; the plan includes a bibliography for each topic.

65. Eliezer Bauer (Be'eri), *Ha-ʿArvim*, 11.

66. Be'eri, "The Arab Question in Youth Education," YYA (1)2.21.95.

67. Eliezer Bauer (Be'eri), *Ha-ʿArvim*, 11.

68. Eliyahu Sasson to B. Yosef, 13 February 1940, CZA S23/3021.

69. Philip Taylor discusses this phenomenon with respect to Britain and France; see Taylor, *The Projection of Britain*.

70. The phenomenon of informants was well described by Bernard Cohn, though informants were as liable to be involved in the project of "informing" their own populations as writers and voices for colonial publications or radio stations as to be informing colonial powers of goings on in their own communities; see Cohn, "Command of Language and the Language of Command."

71. For examples of propaganda newspapers in languages foreign to their producers, see Cull et al., *Propaganda and Mass Persuasion*, which documents both open propaganda efforts and what is known as "black propaganda," newspapers and other media that purport to be from a source other than the true source. These efforts were particularly active

during World War II, when radio allowed for overseas broadcasts, such as in the BBC's foreign-language broadcasts; see Taylor, *Projection of Britain*, 181–215.

72. Bromber, "Do Not Destroy Our Honour," 89–91.

73. These texts not only were journalistic but also included explanatory material about Jewish history and traditions. Jonathan Gribetz has nicely explicated the importance of one such text, a translation of the Talmud into Arabic by Shimon Moyal; see Gribetz, "An Arabic-Zionist Talmud."

74. Jewish communities of the late Ottoman period, both Ashkenazi and Sephardi, were delimited by religious tradition and ethnic origin but tended to engage in commercial and other social relations across community lines, activities that resulted in language acquisition. According to Margalit Shilo, women who worked in shops often engaged in negotiation with Arabs, and some learned to speak Arabic; see Shilo, *Princess or Prisoner?*, 115. Mordecai Kosover has shown, moreover, the influence of Arabic on Palestinian Yiddish, a linguistic indication of these contacts over generations; see Kosover, *Arabic Elements in Palestinian Yiddish*.

75. This is not to say that Sephardim were not Zionists; many were among the strongest proponents of Hebrew and Hebrew education; see Bezalel, *Noladetem tziyonim*.

76. Jacobson, "Sephardim, Ashkenazim and the Arab Question," 106.

77. Abraham Elmaliah, "Elmaliah Interview A," 17 December 1963, 18–19, OHD 2(28).

78. Moyal was one of the founding members of the Jaffa Jewish community, a doctor, and a journalist. His wife, Esther, was a writer and journalist in her own right. On the Moyals, Esther in particular, see Levy, "Partitioned Pasts."

79. Chelouche conveys that those present at the 1913 gathering were, besides himself, Abraham Elmaliah, Nissim Malul, David Moyal, Moshe Matalon, and Yaakov Chelouche; see Chelouche, *Parashat hayai*, 166–69.

80. Elmaliah, "Elmaliah Interview A," 18.

81. Rubenstein, "Ha-diyunim 'al hotza'at 'iton "Tziyoni"-'Arvi bi-shenot ha-'esrim veha-sheloshim."

82. Khalidi, *Palestinian Identity*, 123–24. Khalidi points out that with few exceptions, Palestinian newspapers were anti-Zionist.

83. Quoted in Chelouche, *Parashat hayai*, 150.

84. Abraham Elmaliah, "Elmaliah Interview D," 30 June 1964, 24–25, OHD 2(28).

85. Elmaliah, "Elmaliah Interview A," 18–19.

86. Ibid., 5.

87. Eyal, *Disenchantment of the Orient*, 49–50. Sephardim in Palestine normally knew Arabic from growing up or living in the Arab context of Palestine. While Sephardim are associated as much with Ladino as with Arabic (many did not come from or through Arabic-speaking countries), Sephardi intellectuals themselves favored the conflation of Sephardi and Arabic speaking, and it proved a lasting rhetorical feature of Ashkenazi Zionist discourse.

88. Jacobson, "Sephardim, Ashkenazim and the Arab Question," 120. Yosef Gorny describes Malul as a culmination of the late Ottoman "integrative approach" regarding Jewish-Arab relations; see Gorny, *Zionism and the Arabs*, 48.

89. Michael Assaf, "Tzorekh bashel" [A pressing need], *Kuntres* 2 (1928–29); cited in Rubenstein, "Ha-diyunim 'al hotza'at 'iton "Tziyoni"-'Arvi bi-shenot ha-'esrim veha-sheloshim."

90. 29 September 1929, CZA J1/102; cited in ibid.

91. Meyuhas quoted in ibid., 51.

92. For histories of Jewish perceptions of the revolt, see Habas, *Me'ora'ot Tartzav* [The events of 1936]; Elpeleg, *Me'ora'ot 1936–1939*; Haim, *Abandonment of Illusions*; see also Abboushi, "The Road to Rebellion," and Swedenburg, *Memories of Revolt*.

93. They included Moshe Shertok, the head of the Jewish Agency's political department; Berl Katznelson and Moshe Beilinson, editors of the labor newspaper *Davar*; Michael Assaf and Eliyahu Agassi, writers on Arab affairs (Assaf eventually became the editor of *Haqiqat al-Amr*); Yosef Shprinzak, leader of Mapai; Eliyahu Golumb and Shaul Meirov (Avigdor), leaders in the Hagana; Berl Loker, political adviser to the Jewish Agency; David Remez, secretary general of the Histadrut; Yitzhak Ben-Zvi, active in Mapai and the Jerusalem Municipality; Abba Hushi, secretary of the Haifa Workers' Council; and Reuven Zaslani (Shiloah), an informer on activities in Arab countries and eventually the founder of the Mossad intelligence services.

94. Moshe Shertok's comments, "Hitya'atzut 'al devar hotza'at 'iton ba-'Arvit," 20–22 July 1936, BB 2-023-1936-14.

95. Reuven Zaslani's comments, in ibid.

96. Yeshivat Va'ad ha-ne'emanim 'al keren ha-'iton ha-'Arvi shel ha-Histadrut, 31 December 1936, LA IV-208-1-1287.

97. "Meeting of the Arabic Committee of the Histadrut Executive Committee," 17 March 1937, LA IV-208-1-1287.

98. Yehudah Gotthelf, "Zaken ha-tze'irim ve-tza'ir ha-zekenim: Michael Assaf z"l," in *Sefer ha-shanah shel ha-'itona'im 1984*, 344.

99. Expense sheet, *Haqiqat al-Amr*, May 1937, LA IV-208-1-1287.

100. "Asmā' al-ashkhās alladhīna mushtarikūn fī jarīdat haqīqat al-amr," *Haqiqat al-Amr*, 1949, LA IV-219-240.

101. *Haqiqat al-Amr*, 24 March 1937, and Hebrew contents of first volume, LA IV-205-8.

102. *Haqiqat al-Amr*, first issue, 24 March 1937, 1.

103. Ibid.

104. *Haqiqat al-Amr*, 24 March 1937, and a list in Hebrew of the contents of the first volume, LA IV-205-8.

105. "Tamtzit ha-'inyanim" [Summary of topics], *Haqiqat al-Amr*, 10 December 1940, LA IV-104-87-369.

106. Gilbert Achcar has emphasized the range of opinions within Palestine regarding the Nazis, ranging from clear pro-Nazi views among a certain sector of pan-Islamists (the

most famous of whom was al-Haj Amin al-Huseyni) to decisively anti-Nazi positions; see Achcar, *The Arabs and the Holocaust.*

107. "Tamtzit ha-'inyanim," *Haqiqat al-Amr,* 7 January 1941, LA IV-104-87-369.

108. Michael Assaf to Y. Mereminsky, New York, 17 July 1941, LA IV-104-87-369.

109. Session of the Board of Trustees, Arabic newspaper fund of the Histadrut, Jerusalem, 31 January 1937, 1–2, LA IV-2081-1-1287.

110. This concept of *hasbara* first referred to internal educational campaigns, for both Jews and Arabs, and has persisted in contemporary Israeli discourse, often in references to overseas promotional campaigns; see Eyal, *Disenchantment of the Orient,* 66–67. The contemporary literature on *hasbara* is an overwhelmingly politicized, insider literature that is primarily interested in how Israel can best defend its own actions and why current *hasbara* efforts are not effective; see Schleifer, "Jewish and Contemporary Origins of Israeli 'Hasbara.' "

111. Assaf, *Ha-yehasim ben 'Arvim yi-Yehudim be-Eretz Yisra'el,* 104.

112. Assaf to Mereminsky, 17 July 1941. It should be noted that propaganda in this context does not have the pejorative sense it does in contemporary English, though in Assaf's analysis it consists merely of assertions rather than solid data.

113. "De'ot ha-kore'im ha-'Arviyim 'al Haqiqat al-Amr" [Arab readers' opinions about *Haqiqat al-Amr*], 1, Brit Po'ale Eretz Yisra'el 1936–1937, LA IV-205-8.

114. Ibid., 2. The feedback from Gedera and Kfar Giladi are in the same source.

115. T. Shamosh, administrator, memorandum, n.d., LA IV-104-87-369.

116. Gotthelf, "Zaken ha-tze'irim ve-tza'ir ha-zekenim," 344.

117. Assaf, *Ha-Tziyonut veha-sotzializm veha-be'ayah ha-'Arvit,* 28–29.

118. Michael Assaf to Executive Committee, Histadrut, 5 May 1947, LA IV-247-1. The letter cites both the al-Najada leader and Landeman.

119. Hillel Cohen, *Army of Shadows,* 6–8.

120. Lockman, "Arab Workers and Arab Nationalism in Palestine," 253.

121. Moshe Cohen, *Labor Zionist Handbook,* 145–54.

122. Israel Mereminsky to Dr. A. K. Epstein, Chicago, 29 September 1944, LA IV-104-87-369.

123. Elias Brown, Los Angeles, to Israel Mereminsky, National Labor Committee for Palestine, 25 March 1941 [English], LA IV-104-87-369.

124. Israel Mereminsky to G. Levinson, Va'ad Ha-Po'el of the Histadrut, Tel Aviv, 11 December 1944, LA IV-104-87-369.

125. Elmaliah, "Elmaliah Interview A," 20.

126. Horowitz and Lissak, "Mobilization and Institution Building in the Yishuv," 202–3; Goldstein, "MAPAI and the Seventeenth Zionist Congress (1931)," 19.

127. Shapira, *Land and Power,* 222–23.

128. Interview with Yehoshua Palmon, AHH 168.14 2224.

129. Interview with Yaakov Eini, 27 March 1955, AHH 192.14; additional interviews at 149.23, 193.14, 43.2.

130. During the prestate period, "the production of Orientalist knowledge was strictly split between academics and non-academics," who . . . "did not communicate with one another"; see Eyal, "Dangerous Liasons between Military Intelligence and Middle Eastern Studies in Israel," 660–61.

131. Gamliel Cohen, *Ha-mista'arvim ha-rishonim*, 11–13; interview with Yehoshua Palmon, AHH 168.14 2224.

132. Jabotinsky, "Shulhan 'agol 'im ha-'Arvim," 245–49. Eran Kaplan argues that the Revisionists sought a "Mediterranean" identity influenced by both Europe and the East, but separate from each. On Revisionist ideology, see Kaplan, "Between East and West"; Jabotinsky to John Hubbard, 10 January 1919 [English], Jabotinsky, *Letters*, 3:18; G. Binyamin to the branches of the Sneh, 18 February 1948, JA, Etzel Collection 20/4, folder 1/7/31.

133. Gamliel Cohen, *Ha-mista'arvim ha-rishonim*, 35.

134. *Haaretz*, 15 January 2004, 10, AHH, 25/19.

135. Levi Billig, "Notes for a Memorandum on the School of Oriental Studies" [typed on Hebrew University letterhead], n.d. [1927?], CAHU, Institute of Oriental Studies, folder #91, 1925–1927 (included in multiple folders).

136. Klausner, cited in Eyal, *Disenchantment of the Orient*, 49; Buber quoted in Simon, *Kav ha-tihum*, 16–17.

137. The local defense organization, Ha-Shomer, in existence from 1909 until just after the end of World War I, tended to adopt Arab language, dress, and mannerisms, speaking a distinctive pidgin language consisting of Yiddish and Arabic, and idealizing Arabs, particularly Bedouins, as strong warriors close to the land; see Shapira, *Land and Power*, 72.

138. "Ha-'Arvit be-vet ha-sefer ha-'amami" [Arabic in the national schools], *Ha-Boker*, 2 July 1946, 2.

139. Muhammad Amara, "The Place of Arabic in Israel," *International Journal of the Sociology of Language* 158 (2002): 57.

140. There was little Hebrew learning among Arabs, though a very few Arab students did enroll in Jewish schools (a government report from 1923 said that sixty-eight Muslim children and twenty-eight Christian children had enrolled). Michael Assaf writes that most of the learners were government clerks and police officers, though evidence provided in chapter 3 indicates that this was not common either; see Assaf, *Ha-yehasim ben 'Arvim vi-Yehudim be-Eretz Yisra'el*, 91.

Chapter 5. Hebrew Education between East and West

Epigraph: Menahem Ussishkin, "Ha-protokol shel ha-asefah ha-kelalit shel morim be-zikhron Yaakov" (1903), in *Sefer ha-yovel alef*, 392, cited in Reichel, "Ben 'kartanut' le-'ofke-tarbut,' " 33.

1. Following actions against the French missionary schools, the decisive move to bar European language instruction occurred at the Haifa Technikum, whose governing board had proposed teaching scientific courses in German. The pressure of several Zionists on

the board of the proposed technical school, combined with advocacy across the Yishuv, led the institution to retract the proposal and acquiesce in Hebrew-only instruction; see Saposnik, *Becoming Hebrew*, 213–32; Shilo, "Milhemet ha-safot ki-tenu'ah 'amamit"; Ben-Yosef, *Milhemet ha-safot*; Rinott, "Capitulations"; Tamir, *Seminaristim be-ma'avak-'am*.

2. Ne'eman, "Hesegim ve-hasagot," 436–37.

3. The French influence on Yishuv schools was important among elites in the decades preceding World War I but paled in influence after. Hayim Arieh Zuta wrote in 1938: "Nowadays French is thought of as the language of the small number of French in Palestine and of the Jewish aristocrats" (Zuta, *Darko shel moreh*, 178). But as Moshe Catane and Adam Richter write in the introduction to their 1953 French textbook: "The place of French in the new state of Israel is dismal, owing to the small number of French speakers who immigrated and the English conquest during the mandate years" (*Ha-safah Ha-Tzorfatit ve-dikdukah*, introduction).

4. Existing sources on Arabic include two collections of primary sources: Landau, *Hora'at ha-'Arvit ke-lashon zarah*, and Yonai, *'Arvit be-vate sefer 'Ivriyim*. There are also several works on Hebrew University, including Lazarus-Yafeh, "Transplantation of Islamic Studies," and Milson, "Arabic and Islamic Studies"; Kramer, "Introduction"; and Eyal, *Disenchantment of the Orient*. On English study, see Sitton, "Zionist Education in an Encounter between the British Colonial and the Hebrew Cultures," and Elboim-Dror, "British Educational Policies in Palestine."

5. Shohamy and Spolsky, *Languages of Israel*, 139.

6. Reshef and Dror, *Ha-hinukh ha-'Ivri bi-yeme ha-bayit ha-le'umi*, 57, 63–65.

7. "Programa le-khol shenot ha-limud, hotza'ah revi'it (1910–1911)," Ha-gimnasyah ha-'Ivrit be-Yafo, AYA 8.105/1.

8. Ibid.

9. Abraham Elmaliah, "Interview with Abraham Elmaliah," 17 December 1963, 6–7, OHD 2 (28).

10. Luria, *Ha-hinukh be-Eretz Yisra'el*, 18.

11. Ibid., 14.

12. Six students to Doresh Zion School, Jerusalem, 14 December 1919, CZA S2/620.

13. Ha-Cohen, "Eretz-Yisra'el tahat shilton ha-tzava ha-Briti," 41, 47.

14. *Tokhnit bate ha-sefer ha-'amamiyim ha-'ironiyim*, vol. 3.

15. *Tokhnit ha-limudim ha-nehugah be-vate sefer ha-'amamiyim shel ha-mizrahi*, 9:26.

16. *Hatza'ot le-tokhnit limudim shel bet ha-sefer ha-tikhoni*, Re'ali School, Haifa, Sivan 1930, AYA 8.103/22.

17. *Tokhnit limudim*, Bet sefer ha-tikhoni le-mis'har, 1946–47. The 1932–33 curriculum indicates instead that students in the ninth grade used a special "commercial reader" in their regular English class; see AYA 8.103/4.

18. The number of students in Alliance schools did not grow significantly over the course of the mandate, while the number of students in the Zionist school system grew exponentially. Thus, there were five times as many students in the Zionist schools as in the

Alliance schools in 1926, but nearly twenty times as many in 1945; see Reshef and Dror, *Ha-hinukh ha-'Ivri bi-yeme ha-bayit ha-le'umi*, 49, 53.

19. Tamar Nahshon interview, 12 November 2000, 9, OHD 29 (240).

20. Menahem Rogelski interview, 10 September 1998, 19, OHD 2 (240).

21. *Sefer ha-hinukh veha-tarbut*, 100; Reshef and Dror, *Ha-hinukh ha-'Ivri bi-yeme ha-bayit ha-le'umi*, 53.

22. *Tokhnit*, Ha-gimnasyah ha-'Ivrit bi-Yerushalayim (1924–1925), AYA 8.120/3.

23. It appears that the Jewish Agency was involved in funding some of these courses. A memorandum describing these courses stated, "Today direct contact between Jews and Arabs, such as existed in the first colonies, is lacking. . . . On the other hand, we imparted to some of the people in rural settlements, thanks to methodical study, an important thing that was lacking in the early settlements, an elementary knowledge of the literary language, of the Arab Question, and of Arab folkways"; see Miriam Glickson to Moshe Shertok, memorandum concerning conference of Arabic teachers in the agricultural settlements, 3 September 1942, CZA J17/322.

24. Reichel, "Ben 'kartanut' le-'ofke-tarbut,' " 33.

25. Noting that opinions were divided on the necessity of learning Arabic, Y. Shamosh, a professor at Hebrew University, suggested that, ideally, Arabic study would begin in elementary schools; see Y. Shamosh, "Memo: On the Study of Arabic in the Hebrew schools in Eretz Israel," presented to the Department of Education of "Knesset Yisra'el" and to the Political Division of the Jewish Agency, 30 September 1942, CZA J17.322; see also Zerubavel Haviv, "Ha-'Arvit be-vet ha-sefer ha-'amami," *Ha-Boker*, 2 July 1946, 5.

26. Luria, *Ha-hinukh be-Eretz Yisra'el*, 33.

27. This transfer did not occur completely in 1932. But leaders of the Labor stream were reluctant to subordinate their Labor ideology to an organization that claimed apoliticism. Debates continued until 1938, when the majority of educational functions of the Labor stream came under the control of the Jewish National Council; see Reshef and Dror, *Ha-hinukh ha-'Ivri bi-yeme ha-bayit ha-le'umi*, 30.

28. Reshef and Dror, *Ha-hinukh ha-'Ivri bi-yeme ha-bayit ha-le'umi*, 17–24.

29. *Notes on the Nature of the Beth Hasefer Haklali (General School)*, General Council (Va'ad Leumi) of the Jewish Community of Palestine, Department of Education, Supervising Board of the General Schools, n.d. [probably 1945–46; English], CZA J17/5853.

30. Reshef and Dror, *Ha-hinukh ha-'Ivri bi-yeme ha-bayit ha-le'umi*, 53.

31. These included D. H. Baneth and Josef Joel Rivlin. Several of the Hebrew University faculty members who sat on the committee had been teachers of Arabic in secondary schools, and several of the textbooks used by secondary-school students were written by Levi Billig and Rivlin, both part of the School of Oriental Studies.

32. Trimbur and Yaakobi, "Ha-ma'atzamot ha-eropeyot ve-hora'at safot zarot baUniversitah ha-'Ivrit bi-tekufat ha-mandat," 18.

33. "Report on the Activities of the Committee for English Studies Set up by the Jewish Agency," n.d. [1940?], CZA J17/8691.

34. It appears that the British Council was directly funding the Jewish National Council to promote English among the Jews of Palestine, offering £75 to the Jewish Agency's Committee on English in exchange for evidence that Jews were promoting English in Palestine. A grant was received in 1939–40, though at the time it was not known whether it would be renewed or whether the council would give money mainly in the form of scholarships; see Protocol of the Jewish National Council English Committee, 8 January 1939, CZA J17/320. Thereafter there were regular joint meetings between the British Council and the Jewish Agency's Committee on English; see A. A. Mendilow to J. Davison, British Institute, 4 October 1945, CZA J17/6645. For records on some of the teacher-training courses corun by the British Council and the Jewish National Council, see AYA, Aba Oren (Livington), box 5.11, folder 2298.

35. "The British Council," *Palestine Post*, 22 September 1940.

36. "English Culture," *Palestine Post*, 12 August 1940, 6.

37. Cited in *Et-Mol* 8, no. 4 (March 1983): 16.

38. Ahad Ha-'Am, " 'Al Parashat Derakhim" [At the crossroads], in *Kol kitve Ahad Ha-'Am* [Collected works of Ahad Ha-'Am], 2d ed. (Tel Aviv: Devir, 1949), and Ahad Ha-'Am,"Bet ha-sefer be-yafo" [The school in Jaffa], in *Kol kitve Ahad Ha-'Am* [Collected works of Ahad Ha-'Am] (Jerusalem: Hotza'ah 'Ivrit, 1965), both cited in Reichel, "Ben 'kartanut' le-'ofke-tarbut,' " 2.

39. Tzvi Elpeleg interview, 23 July 1998, 1, OHD 31 (240).

40. Quoted in Pennycook, *The Cultural Politics of English as an International Language*, 84–85.

41. See Adejunmobi, *Vernacular Palaver*, 9.

42. Almog, *Sabra*, 140.

43. Epstein, "Ha-hitrakezut ha-milulit be-hora'at ha-leshonot ha-zarot," pt. 1, 87.

44. Ibid., 92–93.

45. Epstein, "Ha-hitrakezut ha-milulit be-hora'at ha-leshonot ha-zarot," pt. 4, 168–69.

46. Zaydman, "Morim," 86.

47. Schneerson, *La-psikhologyah shel du ha-leshoniyut ba-aretz*, 2–3.

48. Ha-Cohen, "Eretz Yisra'el tahat shilton ha-tzava ha-Briti," 231.

49. M. Schiller, 1927, cited in Sitton, "Zionist Education," 110; Klausner, "Possibilities," in *Ha-Shiloah* 31 (1915): 481–86, cited in Sitton, "Zionist Education," 111.

50. *Tohknit limudim be-tzeruf hashkafah kelalit 'al ha-mosad ve-'al bet ha-talmid*, Herzliyah Gymnasium, 1936–37, AYA 8.103/10.

51. Koller, *Gimnasiya Realit "Balfour," Tel Aviv Gimnasya "Ohel Shem," Ramat Gan*, 17–18.

52. "Mikhtav la-horim: Li-she'elat limud ha-safot ha-zarot be-vet sifrenu," Ein Harod Bulletin 45, 3, YTA 2-13/54/1.

53. "Be-kinus ha-lashon: ha-zilzul be-'Ivrit totza'at tevusanut ve-ashlayot galutiyot," *Ha-Mashkif*, 29 September 1942, CZA S71/1828.

54. Reichel, "Ben 'kartanut' le-'ofke-tarbut,' " 3.

55. Interestingly, Zohar also recommended teaching basic Yiddish so that children would have familiarity with "diasporic life"; see Tzvi Zohar, " 'Al ha-haskalah ha-kelalit

le-dorenu ha-tza'ir" [On educating our younger generation], speech given at Kibbutz Mishmar Ha-'Emek, 20 December 1936, Shomria Institute Archives, Kibbutz Mishmar Ha-'Emek, PAED X 15792/14.

56. Luria, *Ha-hinukh be-Eretz Yisra'el*, 14.

57. Morris and Morris, *Second Year English for Palestine Schools*, introduction.

58. Diengott and Bender, *First Steps in English*, i.

59. J. S. Bentwich, "The Teaching of English in Hebrew Secondary Schools," 4, CZA J17/317; see also other grammar books: Bentwich, *English Syntax for Hebrew-Speaking Students*; Bentwich, *English Composition and Grammar for Hebrew Speaking Students*, 1:iii; Diengott, *Sefer dikduk angli le-mathilim*, 4th ed. (first edition in 1930, no changes in 1932, 1934, or 1936).

60. Bentwich, "English in Hebrew Secondary Schools," 7.

61. W. J. Farrell's remarks, "Minutes of interview with representatives of the Jewish Agency English Committee on 17 January 1938," CZA J17/8691.

62. Moshe Shertok's comments in ibid.

63. Luria, *Ha-hinukh be-Eretz Yisra'el*, 16.

64. Bentwich, "English in Hebrew Secondary Schools," 4, 7.

65. Richard Smith, *Teaching English as a Foreign Language, 1912–1936*, 3:ix–xix.

66. Bentwich, *English for Beginners*.

67. Ben-Zeev's father's family had arrived from Vilnius in 1809; his mother came toward the end of the century. The name Ben-Zeev, which he likely adopted in his early adulthood, is the exact Hebrew translation of his original name, Wolfenson.

68. "Details on the Life History of Dr. Israel Ben-Zeev (Formerly Wolfenzon, in Arabic Literature Israil Abu Zuaib)," n.d. [probably after Word War II], CZA A435/32.

69. Elhanani, "Dr. Yisra'el Ben-Ze'ev."

70. "Report from the Committee of Arabic Teachers in June/July 1939," 19–20, CZA, J17/7236.

71. Israel Ben-Zeev, *Ha-'Arvit ha-meduberet*.

72. Kapliwatzky wrote a series of manifestos about the dire situation of Arabic at the universities and in the schools, the most scathing of which was *Shevitat ra'av: Mikhtav galui*; see also *Ha-zo hi ha-derekh?* and *Mikhtavim 'al ha-matzav ba-universitah uve-vate ha-sefer ha-'Ivriyim ba-aretz*. He also wrote several textbooks displaying his teaching philosophy, including *Palestinian Colloquial Arabic*.

73. Shamosh, "Tazkir."

74. See Bezalel, *Noladetem Tziyonim*; Campos, "Between 'Beloved Ottomania' and 'The Land of Israel' "; Jacobson, "Sephardim, Ashkenazim and the Arab Question."

75. Elmaliah, *Ha-moreh ha-'Arvi/Al-mu'alim al-'Arabī*, xiii. Elmaliah, a Jew of Moroccan descent who came from an illustrious line of rabbis, was the editor of *Ha-Herut* (Freedom), a nonpolitical newspaper of the Sephardi community in Jerusalem that was published between 1900 and 1917. On the newspaper *Ha-Herut*, see Jacobson, "The Sephardi Jewish Community in pre–World War I Jerusalem."

76. This group was composed mainly of the staff of the School of Oriental Studies at Hebrew University: David Yellin, Levi Billig, D. H. Baneth, Noah Braun, Shlomo Dov Goitein, and Josef Joel Rivlin, in addition to Eliyahu Habuba, a Syrian-born teacher of Arabic at the Re'ali School in Haifa, and Yosef Mani from the Jewish Agency.

77. "Protocol of the Meeting of the Committee for Arabic Study in the Hebrew Schools," 22 March 1931, Jerusalem, CZA J17/249; David Yellin (chairman) to Josef Luria, Department of Education, Jewish Agency, 16 March 1922, CZA J17/249.

78. Avinoam Yellin, "On Teaching Arabic in the Hebrew Gymnasium," in Landau, *Hora'at ha-'Arvit ke-lashon zarah*, 75.

79. Yellin and Billig, *Mukhtarat al-qira'ah*, preface.

80. Ibid., 76–77.

81. Eyal, *Disenchantment of the Orient*.

82. Helman, "Even the Dogs in the Street," 360.

83. James P. Lantolf and Gretchen Sunderman surveyed eighty years worth of language-teaching-related articles in the *Modern Language Journal* and identified a range of arguments used in the United States to justify language learning, including greater cultural understanding, diminished provincialism, and the appreciation of beauty. Their findings discuss educators' responses to an interwar trend (also evident, it seems, in Europe) to strip away from the curriculum subjects not deemed practical, like arts and languages; see Lantolf and Sunderman, "The Struggle for a Place in the Sun." For a defense of the humanistic value of language knowledge, see Peyre, "On the Humanistic Value of Foreign-Language Study."

84. The survey of Arabic study published by the Israeli Department of Education begins with an acknowledgment of this long-standing interest; see *Sefer ha-hinukh veha-tarbut*, 100.

85. Eliezer Ben-Yehuda, letter to the editor, *Ha-Hinukh* 1 (1910): 165–67.

86. Plesner, *Torat ha-dikduk ha-'Arvi: sefer 'ezrah le-vate sefer 'Ivriyim*, introduction.

87. Plessner, *Haaretz*, 10 August 1945.

88. Michael Assaf, review of Jochanan Kapliwatzky, *Ha-safah ha-'Arvit ve-dikdukah*, *Davar*, 25 January 1942, 2.

89. This attention to the deep structure of language recalls the work of nineteenth-century comparative philologists, who held that the surface elements of a language were meaningless and even misleading, whereas close analysis could reveal the language's true structure. The American philologist Benjamin W. Dwight wrote in 1859: "Comparative etymology, like the solar spectrum, presents in separate order, and in all the harmony of their mutual connection, the different rays that combine to form what seems the single and simple light of each distinct language" (Dwight, *Modern Philology*, 308).

90. "Protokol: Ha-yeshivah le-shem yisud fakultah le-mada'e ha-mizrah shel ha-universitah ha 'Ivrit be-Eretz Yisra'el," 10 April 1922, CZA S2/390.

91. Zerubavel Haviv, "Ha-'Arvit ba-vet ha-sefer ha-'amami," *Ha-Boker*, 2 July 1946, 5.

92. Levi Billig, "Memorandum on Research," n.d. [1925–27], 3 [English], CAHU, folder 91, 1925–27.

93. Kinus ha-morim la-'Arvit, notes, n.d., CZA J17/319.

94. Y. M., "Anahnu u-shekhenenu," 101.

95. Berlin, "Ha-mizrah veha-hinukh," 340.

96. See Lipschuetz, *Torat ha-hora'ah la-lashon ha-'Ivrit*.

97. Goitein, "Ha-she'elah shel hora'at ha-'Arvit: le-hakhra'ah," 92–93; emphasis in the original.

98. Theodor Nöldeke, cited in Kramer, "Introduction," 14.

99. Goitein wrote in 1946: "This question about Arabic instruction has continued to occupy not only professionals but also the general public" (*'Al hora'at ha-'Arvit*, 8).

100. Avinoam Yellin, " 'Al hora'at ha-'Arvit ba-gimnasyah ha-'Ivrit," in Landau, *Hora'at ha-'Arvit ke-lashon zarah*, 75; also published in *Ha-hinukh* 1 (1938–39): 89–100.

101. Ibid., 76–77.

102. Josef Joel Rivlin, *Sefer limud 'Arvit*, vol. 2.

103. Y. S., "Li-she'elat anahnu u-shekhenenu," *Hed Ha-Hinukh* 1, nos. 10–12 (April 3, 1927): 169.

104. At the Eighth Zionist Congress, President David Wolfsohn stressed "the civilizing and peaceful character of our movement . . . the civilizing and peaceful significance of our undertaking"; see *Jewish Chronicle*, 16 August 1907, 16; cited in Gottheil, *Zionism*, 163.

105. Sitton, "Zionist Education," 110–12, 120.

106. "Rov ha-'olim ha-hadashim mi-Polin mehanekhim yaldehem be-vet sefer Polani," *Ha-Mashkif*, 18 January 1944, CZA S71/2142.

107. Ben-Zion Dinaburg, principal of the Hebrew Teachers' Training College, to Joseph Azaryahu, head of the Jewish National Council Department of Education, 15 November 1939, CZA J17/320.

108. Adejunmobi, *Vernacular Palaver*, 24.

109. Ha-Cohen, "Eretz Yisra'el tahat shilton ha-tzava ha-Briti," 231.

110. Bentwich, *English in Hebrew Secondary Schools*, 2.

111. *Bet sefer le-mis'har Safra, mosad tikhoni le-haskalah kelalit re'alit u-mis'harit*, 1940(?), CZA DD1/3085.

112. Bentwich, *English in Hebrew Secondary Schools*, 18.

113. *Here and There in the British Empire, With Illustrations*, 2–3.

114. Partha Chatterjee writes of the "moral privilege" of the West, saying that even when anticolonial movements challenge the West's supremacy, they maintain the perception that it encompasses theories of progress: "It is the epistemic privilege which has become the last bastion of global supremacy for the cultural values of Western industrial societies" (Chatterjee, *Nationalist Thought and the Colonial World*, 16–17). Prasenjit Duara writes that postcolonial nations are caught in a discursive framework that denies a history to postcolonial peoples, and thus denies them the prerequisites of nationalism and of freedom; see Duara, *Rescuing History from the Nation*.

115. Other selections, not discussed here, outline British scientific advances; see, for example, Marion Florence Lansing, *Science through the Ages* (1927), and R. J. Harvey-Gibson,

The Master Thinkers: Vignettes in the History of Science (1928), "List of Books Recommended for English, 1935–1936," CZA J17/320.

116. Boehmer, *Scouting for Boys*, xii.

117. Sitton, "Zionist Education," 113–15.

118. Baden-Powell, *Scouting for Boys*, 13.

119. Higham, *The Good Citizen.*

120. Mentioned in "The Jewish Agency Committee for English Studies, Draft Report for 1938–39, to be Submitted to the British Council," CZA J17/8691.

121. "Letter to High Schools," Jewish National Council English Committee, 3 October 1935, CZA J17/320.

122. "Books: Albion—England The Unknown Isle," *Time*, 13 July 1931, www.time.com/time/magazine/article/0,9171,742036-2,00.html.

123. Cohen-Portheim, *England, the Unknown Isle*, 7–8, 147.

124. H. Y. Roth, " 'Al ha-kivun ha-ratzui shel limude ha-Anglit," 143.

125. Ibid., 145–46.

126. Ibid., 146–47.

127. H. E. Palmer, "Foreign Language Teaching: Past, Present, and Future," *Oversea Education* 13, no. 3 (April 1942), in Smith, *Teaching English as a Foreign Language.*

128. K. V. Olsen, "English Language Studies in Denmark"; see also I. Morris, *The Art of Teaching English as a Living Language*, 1.

129. Howatt, *A History of English Language Teaching*, 156.

130. Quoted in ibid., 233.

131. The first edition of Berlitz's *Methode Berlitz pour l'enseignment des langues modernes*, published in 1887, was quickly translated into several major European languages (German, Italian, Spanish, English). The 1926 edition of the "English Part" (first published in 1893, it went through hundreds of printings afterward) is in the collection of AYA, one indication that the book was known by educators in Palestine; see Berlitz, *Method for Teaching Modern Languages: English Part.*

132. I did locate one defense of Latin teaching from 1962: Virshovsky, "Latinit ba-vet ha-sefer ha-'Ivri."

133. European proponents of Latin instruction, from the early modern period into the twentieth century, emphasized Latin's universal qualities and grammatical precision; see Françoise Waquet, *Latin, or the Empire of a Sign*, 257–67.

134. Bet Sefer Ha-Reali, "Din Ve-heshbon ha-menahal la-yeshivat mo'etzet ha-menahalim [to be held on] 26 December 1940," 22 December 1940, Re'ali School Archives, Directors Reports, 1933–46.

135. Cohn, *Colonialism and Its Forms of Knowledge*, 16–57.

136. Testimony of Professor Edward Granville Brown, Sir Thomas Adams Professor of Arabic and Fellow of Pembroke College, University of Cambridge, *Minutes of Evidence Taken by the Committee Appointed by the Lords Commissioners of His Majesty's Treasury to Consider the Organisation of Oriental Studies in London with List of Witnesses Examined and Index*, Treasury

Committee on the Organisation of Oriental Studies in London (London: Eyre and Spottiswoode, 1909), School of Oriental and African Studies Archive, Pam #3, 61.

137. *School of Oriental Studies*, 14–15.

138. "Report of the Interdepartmental Commission of Enquiry on Oriental, Slavonic, East European and African Studies," 1947, cited in Arberry, *The Cambridge School of Arabic*, 14.

139. M. A., "The School of Oriental Studies," *Davar*, 30 March 1933, 3, CAHU 226, "School of Oriental Studies, 1933" folder.

140. "Reply by Professor L. A. Mayer to the Statements on the School of Oriental Studies of the Hebrew University Made by the Survey Committee in Their Report," 27 June 1934, CAHU 226, "School of Oriental Studies, 1934."

141. Penslar, "Zionism, Colonialism and Postcolonialism."

Conclusion

1. A. Shekhtman "Sakanat Bavel," *Davar*, 3 March 1949, CZA S71/365.

2. United Nations Educational, Scientific and Cultural Organization, "International Seminar on the Contribution of the Teaching of Modern Languages toward Education for Living in a World Community," Nuwara Eliya, Ceylon, 3–28 August 1953, prepared through the Israel National Commission for UNESCO, UN Archives, UNESCO/ED/Sem/53/18.

3. Avraham Sharon, "Filogalutismus," *Davar*, 16 February 1949, 2.

4. A. Nahor, "Ha-halom 'al otonomyah le-Yiddish be-Eretz Yisra'el," *Ha-Mashkif*, 18 March 1949.

5. Some of the important works on language in the period immediately after the creation of the state are Rojanski, "Yiddish in Israel"; Rojanski, "Ha-umnam 'safah zarah ve-tzoremet'?"

6. E. Zusman, " 'Migdal Bavel' ba-Matate," *Davar*, 7 July 1951, 3. The playbill from the Matate Theater includes an exerpt from the script, which includes a parody of a new immigrant from Iraq; see Mossinsohn and Wolf, *Migdal Bavel*.

7. Shekhtman "Sakanat Bavel."

8. B. Elitzedek, "Yidish hi sakanah," *Haaretz*, 11 March 1949, CZA S71/365.

9. "Darush hok le-haganat ha-'Ivrit ba-medinah," *Ha-Mashkif*, 16 December 1948, CZA S71/365.

10. "Le-vi'ur ha-la'az mi-tokhenu," *Ha-Tzofeh*, 13 September 1948, CZA S71/365.

11. Shohamy and Spolsky, *Languages of Israel*, 26.

12. "Ban on German Follows Public's 'Many Objections,' " *Palestine Post*, 13 December 1950, CZA S71/365.

13. Sh. Tzemah, "Leshon 'ilegim," *Haaretz*, 13 January 1950. Among other articles, see E. Gerstein, "Sakanat ha-la'az," *Ha-Dor*, 8 February 1949; "Le'age safah," *Herut*, 5 May 1951, all in CZA S71/365.

14. Moshe Sharett, "Umah ve-lashon," speech delivered at a banquet of the Histadrut ha-'Ivrit, 30 December 1949, CZA A245/99; translated into English as "Hebrew—Basis of World Jewish Unity," from Histadrut Ivrith of America, Hebrew Language and Culture Association, *Ivrit Feature Service* 1, no.1, January 6, 1950.

15. "Perihatah shel ha-Yiddish bi-medinat Yisra'el," *Ha-Mashkif*, 8 December 1948.

16. David Sentor, "Hahramat ha-safah ha-Germanit be-hofa'ot tarbutiyot," *Haaretz*, 21 December 1950.

17. M. Brachin, "Hod malkhutah ha-safah ha-Germanit," *Herut*, 22 December 1950, CZA S71/365.

18. 'Ofri 'Ilani, "Ba-Technion yelamedu minhal 'asakim rak be-Anglit," *Haaretz*, 18 August 2008.

19. Shimon Buzaglo (Bat Yam), "Ba-teguvah la-katavah, 'Ba-Technion yelamdu minhal 'asakim rak be-Anglit," *Haaretz* (online), 18 August 2008, http://www.haaretz.co.il/captain/objects/ResponseDetails.jhtml?resNo=3841563&itemno=1012645&cont=2.

20. Gindin and Rosenbaum, "Kelitat ha-'aliyah be-Yisra'el," 40.

21. Aharon Ne'eman, writing for the Hebrew Teachers' Federation's fiftieth-anniversary volume, recalled the great achievements of the first generations of teachers, but added: "We have become lenient about language today, and what are the results? Dozens of foreign-language newspapers, cheap foreign literature filling the marketplace and weakening our own literature, movies in foreign languages, and no demand for Hebrew dailies. Our radio is full of songs and jazz in every language and the Zionist Congress, which met in Jerusalem after 54 years since its foundation, had the appearance of the generation that followed the Tower of Babel"; see Ne'eman, "Hesegim ve-hasagot," 436.

BIBLIOGRAPHY

Archival Sources

Aviezer Yellin Archives of Jewish Education in Israel and the Diaspora, Tel Aviv

Beit Berl, Moshe Sharett Israel Labor Party Archives, Kfar Saba

British National Archives, London, Colonial Office Records

Central Archives of the Hebrew University, Jerusalem

Central Zionist Archives, Jerusalem

Eliasaf Robinson Tel Aviv Collection, M1522, Department of Special Collections, Stanford University Libraries

Hagana Archive, Tel Aviv

Haifa Municipality Archive

Israel Film Archives, Jerusalem Cinematheque

Israel State Archives, Jerusalem

Jabotinsky Institute in Israel, Archives, Tel Aviv

Jerusalem Municipality Archive, Jerusalem

Lavon Institute, Tel Aviv

Middle East Centre Archive, University of Oxford

Oral History Division, Institute for Contemporary Jewry, Hebrew University of Jerusalem

Tel Aviv Municipality Archive, Tel Aviv
Yad Tabenkin Archives of the United Kibbutz Movement, Ramat Ef'al
Yad Ya'ari Archives, Ha-Shomer Ha-Tza'ir Archives, Givat Haviva

Newspapers and Periodicals

Haaretz
Ba-Ma'aleh
Ha-Boker
Davar
Ha-Dor
Hed Ha-Hinukh
Herut
Ha-Hinukh
Leshonenu
Ha-Mashkif
Mi-Bifnim
Ha-Or
Palestine Post
Ha-Po'el Ha-Tza'ir
Ha-Shomer Ha-Tza'ir
Ha-Tzofeh
Yedi'ot 'Iriyat Tel Aviv

Books, Articles, and Papers

Aaron, David H. "The Doctrine of Hebrew Language Usage." In *The Blackwell Companion to Judaism*, edited by Jacob Neusner and Alan J. Avery-Peck, 268–87. Oxford: Blackwell, 2002.

Abbady, Isaac. *Benenu le-ven ha-Anglim: nisayon le-nituah ma'arekhet ha-yehasim she-ben Anglim la-Yehudim u-ven Yehudim la-Anglim.* Jerusalem: Kiryat Sefer, 1947.

Abboushi, W. F. "The Road to Rebellion: Arab Palestine in the 1930's." *Journal of Palestine Studies* 6, no. 3 (1 April 1977): 23–46.

Abu-Rabia, Salim. "The Learning of Arabic by Israeli Jewish Children." *Journal of Social Psychology* 138, no. 2 (1998): 165–71.

Abusch, Tzvi. "Notes on Two Passages in the Biblical Account of Prehistory." In *Studies in Arabic and Hebrew Letters: In Honor of Raymond P. Scheindlin*, edited by Jonathan P. Decter and Michael Rand, 1–6. Piscataway, N.J.: Gorgias, 2007.

Achcar, Gilbert. *The Arabs and the Holocaust: The Arab-Israeli War of Narratives.* New York: Metropolitan, 2010.

Adejunmobi, Moradewun. *Vernacular Palaver: Imaginations of the Local and Non-Native Languages in West Africa.* Languages for Intercultural Communication and Education 9. Clevedon, UK: Multilingual Matters, 2004.

Aitchison, Cara. *Gender and Leisure: Social and Cultural Perspectives.* London: Routledge, 2003.

Akyeampong, Emmanuel, and Charles Ambler. "Leisure in African History: An Introduction." *International Journal of African Historical Studies* 35, no. 1 (2002): 1–16.

Almog, Oz. *The Sabra: The Creation of the New Jew.* Berkeley and Los Angeles: University of California Press, 2000.

Alter, Robert. *Hebrew and Modernity.* Bloomington: Indiana University Press, 1994.

———. *The Invention of Hebrew Prose: Modern Fiction and the Language of Realism.* Seattle: University of Washington Press, 1988.

Alterman, Nathan. *'Ir ha-yonah: shirim* [The city of the dove: Poems]. Tel Aviv: Mahbarot le-safrut, 1957.

Ambler, Charles. "Popular Films and Colonial Audiences: The Movies in Northern Rhodesia." *American Historical Review* 106, no. 1 (February 2001): 81–105.

Anderson, Benedict R. *Imagined Communities: Reflections on the Origin and Spread of Nationalism,* Rev. ed. London: Verso, 1991.

Antonius, George. "The Machinery of Government in Palestine." *Annals of the American Academy of Political and Social Science* 164 (November 1932): 55–61.

Arberry, Arthur J. *The Cambridge School of Arabic.* Lecture delivered 30 October 1947. Cambridge: Cambridge University Press, 1948.

Arlosoroff, Hayim. *Kitve Hayim Arlosoroff.* 7 vols. Tel Aviv: Stybel, 1934.

Arnon, Avraham. "Ha-moreh be-misparim" [The teacher by the numbers]. In *Sefer ha-yovel shel histadrut ha-morim* [Anniversary volume of the Teachers' Federation], 302–17. Jerusalem: Ha-Sefer, 1929.

Aschheim, Steven E. *Brothers and Strangers: The East European Jew in German and German Jewish Consciousness, 1800–1923.* Madison: University of Wisconsin Press, 1999.

Assaf, Michael. *Ha-Tziyonut veha-sotzializm veha-be'ayah ha-'Arvit* [Zionism and socialism and the Arab question]. Tel Aviv: Ha-po'el ha-tza'ir hotza'ah meyuhedet, 1938.

———. *Ha-yehasim ben 'Arvim yi-Yehudim be-Eretz Yisra'el (1860–1948)* [Relations between Arabs and Jews in the Land of Israel, 1860–1948]. Tel Aviv: Mif'ale tarbut ve-hinukh, 1970.

Azaryahu, Maoz. *Tel-Aviv ha-ʿir ha-amitit: mitografyah historit.* Beer Sheva: Ben Gurion University, Mekhon Ben Guryon le-heker Yisraʾel, 2005.

———. *Tel Aviv: Mythography of a City.* Syracuse, N.Y.: Syracuse University Press, 2006.

Bachi, Roberto. *A Statistical Analysis of the Revival of Hebrew in Israel.* Jerusalem: Eliezer Kaplan School of Economics and Social Sciences, Hebrew University of Jerusalem, 1955.

Baden-Powell, Robert. *Scouting for Boys: A Handbook for Instruction in Good Citizenship.* Edited by Elleke Boehmer. Oxford: Oxford University Press, 2004.

Bailey, Richard W. *Images of English: A Cultural History of the Language.* Ann Arbor: University of Michigan Press, 1991.

Bailony, Reem. "Transnationalism and the Syrian Migrant Community: The Case of the 1925 Syrian Revolt." *Mashriq and Mahjar* 1, no. 1 (Spring 2013): 8–29.

Baker, Colin. *Foundations of Bilingual Education and Bilingualism.* 4th ed. Clevedon, UK: Multilingual Matters, 2006.

Bar-Gal, Yoram. *Propaganda and Zionist Education: The Jewish National Fund, 1924–1947.* Rochester, N.Y.: University of Rochester Press, 2003.

Bar-Tal, Daniel, and Yona Teichman. *Stereotypes and Prejudice in Conflict: Representations of Arabs in Israeli Jewish Society.* Cambridge: Cambridge University Press, 2005.

Bartal, Israel, ed. *Ha-ʿagalah ha-meleʾah: meʾah ve-ʿesrim shenot tarbut Yisraʾel* [The full wagon: 120 years of Jewish culture]. Jerusalem: Magnes, 2002.

Bauer, Eliezer. *Ha-ʿArvim: yalkut bibliyografi* [The Arabs: A bibliographic anthology]. Jerusalem: Vaʿad ha-irgun shel ha-madrikhim, Bureau of Child and Youth Aliyah, 1944.

Bauer, Yehuda. *Jews for Sale? Nazi-Jewish Negotiations, 1933–1945.* New Haven, Conn.: Yale University Press, 1994.

Bein, Alex. *Kan en mevarkhim le-shalom: zikhronot* [Here they don't greet you: Memoirs]. Jerusalem: Bialik, 1992.

———. *Toldot ha-hityashvut ha-Tziyonit mi-tekufat Herzl ve-ʿad yamenu* [History of Zionist settlement from Herzl's period until our days]. 3rd ed. Tel Aviv: Masadah, 1953.

Beinin, Joel. "Knowing Your Enemy, Knowing Your Ally: The Arabists of Hashomer Hatzaʿir (MAPAM)." *Social Text*, no. 28 (1 January 1991): 100–121.

Ben-Hayyim, Zeʾev. *Be-milhamtah shel lashon* [The struggle for a language]. Jerusalem: Academy of the Hebrew Language, 1992.

Ben-Porat, Amir. *Between Class and Nation: The Formation of the Jewish Working Class in the Period before Israel's Statehood.* Contributions in Labor Studies 20. New York: Greenwood, 1986.

Bentov, Mordekhai. *Yamim mesaprim: Zikhronot meha-me'ah ha-mukhra'at* [The days tell my story: Memories from the decisive past century]. Tel Aviv: Sifriyat po'alim, 1984.

Bentwich, J. S. *English Composition and Grammar for Hebrew Speaking Students.* Vol. 1. Tel Aviv: Mizpah, n.d.

———. *English for Beginners*, Part 2. 1938. London: Longmans, Green, 1950.

———. *English Syntax for Hebrew-Speaking Students.* Haifa: Beth-Sefer Reali, 1928.

Benvenisti, Meron. *Sacred Landscape: The Buried History of the Holy Land since 1948.* Berkeley and Los Angeles: University of California Press, 2000.

Ben-Yehuda, Barukh. *Sipurah shel ha-Gimnasyah "Herzliyah"* [The story of the Gymnasium Herzliya]. Tel Aviv: Gimnasyah Herzliya, 1970.

Ben-Yehuda, Eliezer. *A Dream Come True.* Edited by George Mandel. Translated by T. Muraoka. Boulder, Colo.: Westview, 1993.

———. *He-halom ve-shivro* [A dream come true]. Edited by Reuven Sivan. Jerusalem: Bialik Institute, 1978.

Ben-Yosef, Yaakov. *Milhemet ha-safot: Ha-ma'avak le-'Ivrit, 1914* [The language war: The struggle for Hebrew, 1914]. Tel Aviv: Otzar ha-moreh, 1984.

Ben-Zeev, Aharon, and Avinoam Ben-Zeev, eds. *Rekhilut.* Sidrat Oranim. Tel Aviv: Ha-Kibbutz Ha-Me'uhad, 1993.

Ben-Zeev, Israel. *Ha-'Arvit ha-meduberet* [Spoken Arabic]. Jerusalem: Ahi'asaf, 1949.

Berend, T. Ivan. *Decades of Crisis: Central and Eastern Europe before World War II.* Berkeley and Los Angeles: University of California Press, 1998.

Berg, Nancy E. *Exile from Exile: Israeli Writers from Iraq.* Albany: State University of New York Press, 1996.

Berlin, Yosef Y. "Ha-mizrah veha-hinukh." *Hed Ha-Hinukh* 1, nos. 18–20 (1927).

Berlitz, M. D. *Method for Teaching Modern Languages: English Part.* 1st book. London: Berlitz School, 1925.

Bernstein, Deborah S. "Human Being or Housewife? The Status of Women in the Jewish Working Class Family in Palestine in the 1920s and 1930s." In *Pioneers and Homemakers: Jewish Women in Pre-State Israel*, edited by Deborah Bernstein, 235–60. Albany: State University of New York Press, 1992.

Bernstein, Deborah S., and Musia Lipman. "Fragments of Life: From the Diaries of Two Young Women." In Bernstein, *Pioneers and Homemakers*, 145–64.

Bet sefer Safra: Likrat shenat ha-limudim 5694 [1933–34]. Bet ha-sefer Safra, 1933.

Bezalel, Itzhak. *Noladetem tziyonim: Ha-Sefaradim be-Eretz Yisra'el ba-tziyonut uve-tehiyah ha-'Ivrit ba-tekufah ha-'Otmanit* [You were born Zionists: Sephardim in Eretz Israel in Zionism and the Hebrew revival during the Ottoman period]. Jerusalem: Ben-Zvi Institute, 2007.

Bialik, Hayim Nachman. *Devarim she-be-'al peh* [Oral works]. 2 vols. Tel Aviv: Devir, 1935.

Birnbaum, Pierre. *Jewish Destinies: Citizenship, State, and Community in Modern France.* New York: Hill and Wang: 2000.

Blau, Joshua, ed. *Ha-lashon ha-'Ivrit be-hitpathutah uve-hithadshutah: Hartsa'ot le-regel melot me'ah shanah li-yesod va'ad ha-lashon ha-'Ivrit* [Evolution and renewal: Trends in the development of the Hebrew language]. Jerusalem: Israeli Academy of Sciences, 1996.

Blommaert, Jan. *Sociolinguistics of Globalization.* Cambridge: Cambridge University Press, 2010.

Boehmer, Elleke. Introduction to Baden-Powell, *Scouting for Boys: A Handbook for Instruction in Good Citizenship.* Oxford: Oxford University Press, 2004.

Boneh, Alfred. *Eretz Yisra'el: Ha-aretz veha-kalkalah* [The Land of Israel: The land and the economy]. Tel Aviv: Devir, 1937–38.

Borsay, Peter. *A History of Leisure: The British Experience since 1500.* Basingstoke, UK: Palgrave Macmillan, 2006.

Boskin, Joseph. *Rebellious Laughter: People's Humor in American Culture.* Syracuse, N.Y: Syracuse University Press, 1997.

Bromber, Katrin. "Do Not Destroy Our Honour: Wartime Propaganda Directed at East African Soldiers in Ceylon (1943–44)." In *The Limits of British Colonial Control in South Asia: Spaces of Disorder in the Indian Ocean Region*, edited by Ashwini Tambe and Harald Fischer-Tiné, 84–101. London: Routledge, 2009.

Brown, Michael. *The Israeli-American Connection: Its Roots in the Yishuv, 1914–1945.* America–Holy Land Monographs. Detroit: Wayne State University Press, 1996.

Burke, Peter. *Languages and Communities in Early Modern Europe.* Cambridge: Cambridge University Press, 2004.

———. *Towards a Social History of Early Modern Dutch.* Amsterdam: Amsterdam University Press, 2005.

———. *What Is Cultural History?* Cambridge: Polity, 2004.

Buruma, Ian, and Avishai Margalit. *Occidentalism: The West in the Eyes of Its Enemies.* New York: Penguin, 2004.

Calvet, Louis Jean. *Towards an Ecology of World Languages.* Cambridge: Polity, 2006.

Campos, Michelle U. "Between 'Beloved Ottomania' and 'The Land of Israel': The Struggle over Ottomanism and Zionism among Palestine's Sephardi Jews, 1908–1913." *International Journal of Middle East Studies* 37, no. 4 (2005): 461–83.

Caplan, Neil. "The Yishuv, Sir Herbert Samuel, and the Arab Question in Palestine, 1921–1925." In *Zionism and Arabism in Palestine and Israel*, edited by Sylvia Kedourie and Elie Kedourie, 1–52. London: Cass, 1982.

Carmichael, Cathie. " 'A People Exists and That People Has Its Language': Language and Nationalism in the Balkans." In *Language and Nationalism in Europe*, edited by Stephen Barbour and Cathie Carmichael, 221–39. New York: Oxford University Press, 2000.

Carmiel, Batia. *Bate ha-kafeh shel Tel-Aviv, 1920–1980* [Coffeehouses of Tel Aviv, 1920–1980]. Tel Aviv: Eretz Israel Museum, 2007.

———. *Bet-kafeh: Makom katan koh! bet-kafeh, davar adir: kafeh Retzki, kafeh sifruti be-Tel Aviv, 1932–1935* [A coffeehouse, such a small place! A coffeehouse, a marvelous thing! Café Retzki, a literary café in Tel Aviv, 1932–1935]. Ben Shemen: Modan, 2007.

Carr, Elizabeth Montgomery. *A Land Divided*. London: Hutchinson, 1938.

Catane, Moshe, and Adam Richter. *Ha-safah Ha-Tzorfatit ve-dikdukah* [The French language and its grammar]. Jerusalem: Achiasaf, 1964.

Chatterjee, Partha. *Nationalist Thought and the Colonial World: A Derivative Discourse?* London: Zed Books for the United Nations University, 1986.

Chaver, Yael. *What Must Be Forgotten: The Survival of Yiddish in Zionist Palestine.* Judaic Traditions in Literature, Music, and Art. Syracuse, N.Y.: Syracuse University Press, 2004.

Chelouche, Yosef Eliyahu. *Parashat hayai (1870–1930)* [My life, 1870–1930]. Tel Aviv: Bavel, 2005.

Clifford, James. *Routes: Travel and Translation in the Late Twentieth Century.* Cambridge, Mass.: Harvard University Press, 1997.

Codo, Eva. *Immigration and Bureaucratic Control: Language Practices in Public Administration*. Berlin: Mouton de Gruyter, 2008.

Cohen, Adir, ed. *Sefer ha-humor ha-Yehudi ha-gadol: Otzar ha-bedihah ha-Yehudit veha-Yisre'elit le-doroteha* [The big book of Jewish humor: The Jewish and Israeli joke through the generations]. Or Yehudah: Kineret, 2004.

Cohen, Aharon. *Guf rishon, guf shelishi* [First person, third person]. Tel Aviv: Ha-Kibbutz Ha-Artzi, 1990.

Cohen, Ayelet. "Reshit ha-kolno'a ha-Eretzyisre'elit ke-meshakef ra'ayonot ha-tekufah" [The beginnings of Eretz Israeli cinema as a reflection of contemporary ideas]. *Katedrah* 61 (September 1991): 141–55.

Cohen, Erik. *The City in the Zionist Ideology.* Jerusalem: Hebrew University, Institute of Urban and Regional Studies, 1970.

Cohen, Gamliel. *Ha-mista'arvim ha-rishonim: Sipurah shel ha-mahlakkah ha-'Arvit shel ha-Palmach* [The first *mista'arvim:* The story of the Arab Department of the Palmach]. Tel Aviv: Ministry of Defense, Galili Center for Defence Studies, 2002.

Cohen, Hillel. *Army of Shadows: Palestinian Collaboration with Zionism, 1917–1948.* Berkeley and Los Angeles: University of California Press, 2008.

Cohen, Jeremy. *The Friars and the Jews: The Evolution of Medieval Anti-Judaism.* Ithaca, N.Y.: Cornell University Press, 1984.

Cohen, Moshe. *Labor Zionist Handbook: The Aims, Activities, and History of the Labor Zionist Movement in America.* New York: Poale Zion Zeire Zion of America, 1939.

Cohen, Naomi W. "An Uneasy Alliance: The First Days of the Jewish Agency." In *A Bicentennial Festschrift for Jacob Rader Marcus*, edited by Bertram Wallace Korn, 107–20. New York: Ktav, 1976.

Cohen-Hatav, Jacob. "Yazmut, tikhnun u-fituach merhavi: Hakamat shuk Mahane-Yehudah bi-Yerushalayim ve-hitpathuto bi-tekufat ha-shilton ha-Briti (1917–1948)" [Entrepreneurship, planning, and spatial development: The establishment of the Mahane Yehudah Market in Jerusalem and its development during the period of British rule, 1917–1948]. In *Yazamut yehudit ba-'et ha-hadashah: Mizrah eropah ve-Eretz Yisra'el* [Jewish entrepreneurship in modern times: Eastern Europe and the Land of Israel], edited by Ran Aharonson and Shaul Stampfer, 137–63. Jerusalem: Magnes, 2000.

Cohen-Portheim, Paul. *England, the Unknown Isle.* New York: Dutton, 1931.

Cohn, Bernard. *Colonialism and Its Forms of Knowledge: The British in India.* Princeton Studies in Culture/Power/History. Princeton, N.J.: Princeton University Press, 1996.

———. "Command of Language and the Language of Command." *Subaltern Studies* 4 (1985): 276–329.

Conrick, Maeve. "Legislating for Language: The Canadian Experience of Language Policy and Linguistic Duality." In *Language Issues in Canada: Multidisciplinary Perspectives*, edited by Martin Howard, 24–39. Newcastle, UK: Cambridge Scholars, 2007.

Conrick, Maeve, and Vera Regan. *French in Canada: Language Issues.* Modern French Identities 28. Bern, Switzerland: Peter Lang, 2007.

Crystal, David. *English as a Global Language.* Cambridge: Cambridge University Press, 2003.

Cull, Nicholas John, David Holbrook Culbert, and David Welch, eds. *Propaganda and Mass Persuasion: A Historical Encyclopedia, 1500 to the Present.* Santa Barbara, Calif.: ABC-CLIO, 2003.

Curran, James, and Myung-Jin Park. "Beyond Globalization Theory." In *De-Westernizing Media Studies*, edited by James Curran and Myung-Jin Park, 3–18. London: Routledge, 2000.

Cutter, William. "Translation and the Project of Culture: Transferring Western Literature into Hebrew, 1893–1930." In *Bits of Honey: Essays for Samson H. Levey*, edited by Stanley F. Chyet and David H. Ellenson, 209–28. Atlanta: Scholars Press, 1993.

Darnton, Robert. *The Great Cat Massacre and Other Episodes in French Cultural History.* New York: Basic Books, 2009.

Deem, Rosemary. *All Work and No Play? A Study of Women and Leisure.* Milton Keynes, UK: Open University Press, 1986.

De Vries, David. "National Construction of Occupational Identity: Jewish Clerks in British-Ruled Palestine." *Comparative Studies in Society and History* 39, no. 2 (April 1997): 373–400.

Diengott, Meir. *Sefer dikduk angli le-mathilim* [English grammar book for beginners]. 4th ed. Haifa: Beth Sefer Reali Ivri, 1936.

Diengott, Meir, and Samuel M. Bender. *First Steps in English.* Haifa: Beth Sefer Reali Ivri, 1937.

Divine, Donna Robinson. *Exiled in the Homeland: Zionism and the Return to Mandate Palestine.* Jewish History, Life, and Culture. Austin: University of Texas Press, 2009.

Dohm, Christian Wilhelm von. "Concerning the Amelioration of the Civil Status of the Jews" (1781). In *The Jew in the Modern World: A Documentary History*, edited by Jehuda Reinharz and Paul Mendes-Flohr, 28–36. New York: Oxford University Press, 1995.

Duara, Prasenjit. *Rescuing History from the Nation: Questioning Narratives of Modern China.* Chicago: University of Chicago Press, 1995.

Dwight, B. *Modern Philology: Its Discoveries, History, and Influence.* New York: Barnes and Burr, 1859.

Edensor, Tim. *National Identity, Popular Culture, and Everyday Life.* Oxford: Berg, 2002.

Efrati, Natan. *Mi-leshon yehidim le-leshon umah: Ha-dibur ha-'Ivri be-Eretz Yisra'el ba-shanim 1882–1922* [From a Language of individuals to the language of a nation: Hebrew speech in the Land of Israel, 1882–1922]. Jerusalem: Academy of the Hebrew Language, 2004.

Elboim-Dror, Rachel. "British Educational Policies in Palestine." *Middle Eastern Studies* 36, no. 2 (April 2000): 28–47.

Elhanani, Avraham Hayim. "Dr. Israel Ben-Ze'ev: Aharon ha-mizrahanim she-henivah admat Yerushalayim" [Dr. Israel Ben-Zeev: The last orientalist that Jerusalem produced]. *Ba-Ma'arakhah* 237 (1980): 25, 32.

Elmaliah, Abraham. *Ha-moreh ha-'Arvi/ Al-mu'alim al-'Arabī* [The Arab teacher]. Jerusalem: Mizpah, 1928–29.

Elpeleg, Z. *Me'ora'ot 1936–1939, pera'ut o mered* [The events of 1936–1939: Savagery or rebellion?]. Tel Aviv: Mekhon Shiloah le-heker ha-mizrah ha-tikhon ve-Afrikah, Universitat Tel Aviv, 1977.

Endelman, Todd M. *The Jews of Britain, 1656 to 2000.* Jewish Communities in the Modern World 3. Berkeley and Los Angeles: University of California Press, 2002.

Epstein, Izhac. "Ha-hitrakezut ha-milulit be-hora'at ha-leshonot ha-zarot," pt. 1. *Ha-Hinukh* 1, no. 2 (1911).

———. "Ha-hitrakezut ha-milulit be-hora'at ha-leshonot ha-zarot," pt. 4. *Ha-Hinukh* 1, no. 3 (1911).

Even Zohar, Itamar. "Ha-tzemihah veha-hitgabshut shel tarbut 'Ivrit mekomit ve-yelidit be-Eretz Yisra'el, 1882–1948" [The growth and consolidation of a local and native Hebrew culture in the Land of Israel, 1882–1948]. *Katedrah* 16 (1980): 165–89.

Eyal, Gil. "Dangerous Liaisons between Military Intelligence and Middle Eastern Studies in Israel." *Theory and Society* 31, no. 5 (October 2002): 653–93.

———. *The Disenchantment of the Orient: Expertise in Arab Affairs and the Israeli State.* Stanford, Calif.: Stanford University Press, 2006.

Fahrenthold, Stacy. "Transnational Modes and Media: The Syrian Press in the Mahjar and Emigrant Activism during World War I." *Mashriq and Mahjar* 1, no. 1 (Spring 2013): 30–54.

Fairclough, Norman. *Language and Globalization.* London: Routledge, 2006.

Falls, Cyril. *Armageddon, 1918: The Final Palestinian Campaign of World War I.* 1964. Reprint, Philadelphia: University of Pennsylvania Press, 2003.

Federbusch, Simon. *Ha-lashon ha-'Ivrit be-Yisra'el uva-'amim* [The Hebrew language among Jews and among the nations]. Jerusalem: Mosad ha-Rav Kook, 1967.

Feldestein, Ariel Lionard. *Halutz, 'avodah, matzlemah: Ha-kolno'a ha-eretzyisre'eli veha-ra'ayon ha-Tziyoni* [Pioneer, labor, camera: Eretz Israeli cinema and the Zionist idea]. Sifriyat Sapir. Tel Aviv: 'Am 'Oved, 2009.

Fishman, Joshua A. "Interwar Eastern European Jewish Parties and the Language Issue." *International Journal of the Sociology of Language* 151 (2001): 175–89.

Frankel, Jonathan. *Prophecy and Politics: Socialism, Nationalism, and the Russian Jews, 1862–1917.* Cambridge: Cambridge University Press, 1981.

Friedman, Thomas L. *From Beirut to Jerusalem.* New York: Macmillan, 1991.

Gal, Sari. *Bracha Fuld.* Tel Aviv: Sifriyat po'alim, 1999.

Gallagher, Catherine, and Stephen Greenblatt. *Practicing New Historicism.* Chicago: University of Chicago Press, 2000.

Gavron, Daniel. *Holy Land Mosaic: Stories of Cooperation and Coexistence between Israelis and Palestinians.* Lanham, Md.: Rowman and Littlefield, 2008.

Gelber, Sylvia M. *No Balm in Gilead: A Personal Retrospective of Mandate Days in Palestine.* Ottawa: Carleton University Press, 1989.

Gelber, Yoav. "Maga'im diplomatiyim terem hitnagdut tzeva'it: Ha-masa u-matan ben ha-sokhnut ha-Yehudit le-Mitzrayim ve-Yarden (1946–1948)" [Diplomatic contacts before military confrontation: The negotiations between the Jewish Agency and Egypt and Jordan, 1946–1948]. *Katedrah* 35 (1985): 125–62.

Gilman, Sander L. *Jewish Self-Hatred: Anti-Semitism and the Hidden Language of the Jews.* Baltimore: Johns Hopkins University Press, 1986.

Gindin, Rachel, and Yehudit Rosenbaum. "Kelitat ha-aliyah be-Yisra'el: Taksirei mehkarim" [Immigrant absorption in Israel: Research abstracts]. Jerusalem: Ministry of Immigrant Absorption, 2008. http://www.moia.gov.il/Hebrew/InformationAndAdvertising/Studies/Documents/mehkarim_book1.pdf.

Gluzman, Michael. *The Politics of Canonicity: Lines of Resistance in Modernist Hebrew Poetry.* Stanford, Calif.: Stanford University Press, 2003.

Goffman, Erving. *The Presentation of Self in Everyday Life.* New York: Doubleday, 1959.

Goitein, S. D. *'Al hora'at ha-'Arvit* [On the teaching of Arabic]. Tel Aviv: Yavneh, 1946.

———. "Ha-she'elah shel hora'at ha-'Arvit: Le-hakhra'ah" [The question of Arabic instruction: Toward a decision]. *Shevile ha-hinukh* 19, no. 2 (1946).

Golani, Moti. "Moshe Shertok: Hamedina'i shel 'homa u-migdal'" [Moshe Shertok: The politician of "wall and tower"]. In *Yemei homah u-migdal, 1936–1939: Mekorot, sikumim, parshiyot nivcharot, vechomer 'ezer* [The days of wall and tower, 1936–1939: Sources, summaries, selected episodes, and supplementary material], edited by Mordechai Naor, 51–60. Jerusalem: Ben-Zvi Institute, 1987.

Goldstein, Yaacov N. "MAPAI and the Seventeenth Zionist Congress (1931)." *Studies in Zionism* 10, no. 1 (1989): 19–30.

Gorny, Yosef. *Ha-she'elah ha-'Arvit veha-be'ayah ha-Yehudit: Zeramim mediniyim-ide'ologiyim ba-Tziyonut be-yahasam el ha-yeshut ha-'Arvit be-Eretz Yisra'el ba-shanim 1882–1948* [The Arab question and the Jewish problem: Political-ideological currents in Zionism in its relation to the Arab entity in the Land of Israel, 1882–1948]. Tel Aviv: 'Am 'Oved, 1985.

————. *Zionism and the Arabs, 1882–1948: A Study of Ideology.* Oxford: Clarendon, 1987.

Gottheil, Richard J. H. *Zionism.* Philadelphia: Jewish Publication Society of America, 1914.

Grainger, John D. *The Battle for Palestine, 1917.* Woodbridge, UK: Boydell, 2006.

Green, Eileen, *Women's Leisure, What Leisure?* Basingstoke, UK: Macmillan, 1990.

Gribetz, Jonathan. "An Arabic-Zionist Talmud: Shimon Moyal's At-Talmud." *Jewish Social Studies: History, Culture, Society,* n.s., 17, no. 1 (Fall 2010): 1–30.

Groman, Yaakov, ed. *Ha-mishar ha-kim'oni be-Eretz Yisra'el* [Retail commerce in the Land of Israel]. Tel Aviv: General Union of Merchants in Tel Aviv–Yafo, 1946.

Gross, Nahum. "Ha-mediniyut ha-kalkalit shel ha-mimshal ha-Briti ha-mandatori be-Eretz Yisra'el" [The economic politics of the British mandate regime in Palestine]. *Katedrah* 24 (July 1982): 163–67.

Gurevich, David ed. *Statistical Abstract of Palestine, 1929.* Jerusalem: Keren Ha-Yesod, 1930.

Habas, Bracha. *Me'ora'ot Tartzav* [The events of 1936]. Tel Aviv: Devir, 1936–37.

Ha-Cohen, Mordecai Ben-Hillel, "Eretz Yisra'el tahat shilton ha-tzava ha-Briti" [Palestine under British military rule]. *Ha-Shiloah* 41 (1923–24): 41–50, 141–48, 227–36, 335–41, 436–42.

Haim, Yehoyada. *Abandonment of Illusions: Zionist Political Attitudes toward Palestinian Arab Nationalism, 1936–1939.* Boulder, Colo.: Westview, 1983.

Haramati, Shlomo. *Leviyim be-mikdash ha-'Ivrit: or hadash 'al zikat shemonah anshe-shem Yehudiyim la-'Ivrit ha-mithayah, bi-khtav uva-dibur* [Levites in the temple of Hebrew: A new light on the affinity of eight prominent Jews to the revival of Hebrew, in writing and speech]. Tel Aviv: Yaron Golan, 1996.

————. *Sheloshah she-kadmu le-Ben-Yehuda* [Three who came before Ben-Yehuda]. Jerusalem: Ben-Zvi Institute, 1978.

Harshav, Benjmain. *Language in Time of Revolution.* Berkeley and Los Angeles: University of California Press, 1993.

Heller, Monica. "Language Choice, Social Institutions, and Symbolic Domination." *Language in Society* 24, no. 3 (September 1995): 373–405.

————. *Paths to Post-Nationalism: A Critical Ethnography of Language and Identity.* New York: Oxford University Press, 2011.

Helman, Anat. "Even the Dogs in the Street Bark in Hebrew: National Ideology and Everyday Culture in Tel Aviv." *Jewish Quarterly Review,* n.s., 92, nos. 3–4 (January–April 2002): 359–82.

———. *Or ve-yam hekifuha: tarbut Tel Avivit bi-tekufat ha-mandat* [Light and sea surrounded her: Tel Aviv culture during the mandate period]. Haifa: Haifa University Press, 2007.

———. "Tzerikhat kolno'a ba-Yishuv uvi-medinat Yisra'el bi-shenotehah harishonot" [Cinema consumption in the Yishuv and the State of Israel in its early years]. In *Kolno'a ve-zikaron: yehasim mesukanim?* [Cinema and memory: Dangerous relations?], edited by Hayim Bereshi et al., 73–98. Jerusalem: Zalmar Shazar Center for Jewish History, 2004.

———. *Young Tel Aviv: A Tale of Two Studies.* Hanover, N.H.: Brandeis University Press, 2010.

Henderson, Karla A., ed. *Both Gains and Gaps: Feminist Perspectives on Women's Leisure.* State College, Pa.: Venture, 1996.

———, ed. *A Leisure of One's Own: A Feminist Perspective on Women's Leisure.* State College, Pa.: Venture, 1989.

Here and There in the British Empire, with Illustrations. London: Macmillan, 1902.

Herzl, Theodor. *A Jewish State: An Attempt at a Modern Solution of the Jewish Question.* Edited by Jacob De Haas. Translated by Sylvie D'Avigdor. New York: Maccabean, 1904.

Higham, Charles. *The Good Citizen: An Introduction to Civics.* London: Longmans, Green, 1931.

Hinitz, Nahum. *Gedole Yisra'el bi-vedihah* [Great Jews in humor]. Jerusalem: Kiryat sefer, 1980.

Hochberg, Gil Z. *In Spite of Partition: Jews, Arabs, and the Limits of Separatist Imagination.* Translation/Transnation. Princeton, N.J.: Princeton University Press, 2007.

———. "'Permanent Immigration': Jacqueline Kahanoff, Ronit Matalon, and the Impetus of Levantinism." *Boundary* 31, no. 2 (2004): 219–43.

Horowitz, Dan, and Moshe Lissak. "Mobilization and Institution Building in the Yishuv." In *Essential Papers on Jews and the Left*, edited by Ezra Mendelsohn, 198–235. New York: New York University Press, 1997.

Hourani, Albert Habib. *The Emergence of the Modern Middle East.* Berkeley and Los Angeles: University of California Press, 1981.

Howatt, Anthony P. R. *A History of English Language Teaching.* 2d ed. Oxford: Oxford University Press, 2004.

Hroch, Miroslav. "From National Movement to the Fully Formed Nation: The Nation-Building Process in Europe." *New Left Review*, no. 198 (March–April 1993): 81–84.

Jabotinsky, Ze'ev (Vladimir). *Igrot* [Letters]. Eds. Daniel Carpi and Moshe Halevi (Jerusalem: Jabotinsky Institute in Israel, 1992).

———. "Shulhan 'agol 'im ha-'Arvim" [Roundtable with the Arabs]. In *Ba-derekh la-medinah* [On the path to a state], 243–55. Jerusalem: Eri Jabotinsky, 1952–53.

Jacobson, Abigail. "Sephardim, Ashkenazim, and the Arab Question in Pre–First World War Palestine: A Reading of Three Zionist Newspapers." *Middle Eastern Studies* 39, no. 2 (2003): 105–30.

———. "The Sephardi Jewish Community in Pre–World War I Jerusalem: Debates in the Hebrew Press." *Jerusalem Quarterly File* 14 (2001). http://www.jqf-jerusalem.org/2001/jqf14/sephardi.html.

Joseph, B. D. *When Languages Collide: Perspectives on Language Conflict, Language Competition, and Language Co-Existence.* Columbus: Ohio State University Press, 2003.

Joseph II. "Edict of Toleration" (1782). In *The Jew in the Modern World: A Documentary History*, edited by Paul Mendes-Flohr and Jehuda Reinharz, 36–40. New York: Oxford University Press, 1995.

Kalif, Carmella, and Adina Rinat-Benbenishti. "Rega'im gedolim be-'ir keta-nah" [Big moments in a small city]. *Et-mol* 204 (2009): 16–18.

Kaplan, Eran. "Between East and West: Zionist Revisionism as a Mediterranean Ideology." In *Orientalism and the Jews*, edited by Ivan Davidson Kalmar and Derek J. Penslar, 125–41. Waltham, Mass.: Brandeis University Press, 2005.

Kapliwatzky, Jochanan. *Mikhtavim 'al ha-matzav ba-universitah uve-vate ha-sefer ha-'Ivriyim ba-aretz* [Letters on the situation in the university and the Hebrew schools in the country]. Jersualem: Defus ha-ma'arav, 1944.

———. *Palestinian Colloquial Arabic.* Jerusalem: Kiryat Sefer, 1939; 2nd ed., 1944.

———. *Shevitat ra'av: mikhtav galui* [Hunger strike: An open letter]. Jerusalem, 1939.

———. *Ha-zo hi ha-derekh?* [Is this the way?]. Tel Aviv: Ha-Makhon Ha-Shemi, 1939.

Karlinsky, Nahum. *California Dreaming: Ideology, Technology, and Society in the Citrus Industry of Palestine, 1890–1939.* Albany: State University of New York Press, 2005.

Karmi, Shlomo. *'Am ehad ve-safah ahat tehiyat ha-lashon ha-'Ivrit bi-re'iyah ben-tehumit* [One people, one language: The Hebrew revival in interdisciplinary perspective]. Tel Aviv: Ministry of Defense, 1997.

Karni'eli, Israel. *Hoterim tahat kiyum sefatenu* [Those who undermine the existence of our language]. Tel Aviv: Igud le-hashlatat ha-safah ha-'Ivrit, 1938.

———. *'Al kipuah zekhuyot sefatenu* [On the suppression of our language rights]. Tel Aviv: Ha-agudah le-hashlatat ha-'Ivrit, 1933.

Karp, Jonathan. *The Politics of Jewish Commerce: Economic Thought and Emancipation in Europe, 1638–1848.* Cambridge: Cambridge University Press, 2008.

Katz, Elihu, and George Wedell. *Broadcasting in the Third World: Promise and Performance.* Cambridge, Mass.: Harvard University Press, 1977.

Katz, Jacob, R. Bachi, and Dan Patinkin. *'Al Prof. Alfred Boneh.* Jerusalem: Magnes Press, 1960.

Khalidi, Rashid. *Palestinian Identity: The Construction of Modern National Consciousness.* New York: Columbia University Press, 2009.

Kimche, Dov, ed. *Sefer ha-yovel shel histadrut ha-morim* [Anniversary volume of the Teacher's Federation]. Jerusalem: Teachers' Federation, 1929.

Kimmerling, Baruch. "A Model for Analyzing Reciprocal Relations between the Jewish and Arab Communities in Mandatory Palestine." In *Clash of Identities: Explorations in Israeli and Palestinian Societies,* 1–24. New York: Columbia University Press, 2008.

Kolatt, Israel. "Religion, Society, and State during the Period of the National Home." In *Zionism and Religion,* edited by Shmuel Almog et al., 273–301. Hanover, N.H.: University Press of New England, 1998.

Koller, Dov. *Gimnasiya Realit "Balfour," Tel Aviv Gimnasya "Ohel Shem" Ramat Gan* [The Balfour Realgymnasium in Tel Aviv and the Ohel Shem Gymnasium, Ramat Gan]. Jerusalem: Akademon, 2003.

Koshar, Rudy. "Seeing, Travelling, and Consuming: An Introduction." In *Histories of Leisure,* edited by Rudy Koshar, 1–24. Oxford: Berg, 2002.

Kosover, Mordecai. *Arabic Elements in Palestinian Yiddish: The Old Ashkenazic Jewish Community in Palestine, Its History, and Its Language.* Jerusalem: Mass, 1966.

Kotkin, Stephen. *Magnetic Mountain: Stalinism as a Civilization.* Berkeley and Los Angeles: University of California Press, 1995.

Kramer, Martin. Introduction to *The Jewish Discovery of Islam.* Tel Aviv: Moshe Dayan Center for Middle Eastern and African Studies, 1999.

Kuzar, Ron. "Linguistic and Political Attitudes towards Israeli Hebrew: Ongoing Revival versus Normalcy." In *Language Ideological Debates,* edited by Jan Blommaert, 267–306. The Hague: Mouton de Gruyter, 1999.

Landau, Jacob M. *Hora'at ha-'Arvit ke-lashon zarah* [Teaching Arabic as a foreign language]. Ahvah, 1961.

Lantolf, James P., and Gretchen Sunderman. "The Struggle for a Place in the Sun: Rationalizing Foreign Language Study in the Twentieth Century." *Modern Language Journal* 85, no. 1 (Spring 2001): 5–25.

Lavsky, Hagit. "Ha-umnam kayam kesher 'mahuti' ben Yehudim ve-kapitalizm? Ha-mikreh ha-Eretz Yisre'eli" [Is there really an "essential" connection between

Jews and capitalism?]. In *Dat ve-khalkalah: yahase gomlin: Kovets ma'amarim* [Religion and economy: Mutual relations; A collection of articles], edited by Menahem Ben-Sasson, 387–99. Jerusalem: Zalman Shazar Center for Jewish History, 1995.

Lawrance, Benjamin N., Emily Lynn Osborn, and Richard L. Roberts. "Introduction: African Intermediaries and the 'Bargain' of Collaboration." In *Intermediaries, Interpreters, and Clerks: African Employees in the Making of Colonial Africa*, edited by Benjamin N. Lawrance, Emily Lynn Osborn, and Richard L. Roberts, 3–34. Madison: University of Wisconsin Press, 2006.

Lazarus-Yafeh, Hava. "The Transplantation of Islamic Studies from Europe to the Yishuv and Israel." In *The Jewish Discovery of Islam*, edited by Martin Kramer, 249–60. Tel Aviv: Moshe Dayan Center for Middle Eastern and African Studies, 1999.

"Le-ahar ha-ta'arukhah" [After the exhibition]. *Mishar ve-ta'asiyah* 2, no. 7 (13 May 1924): 1.

Leheny, David Richard. *The Rules of Play: National Identity and the Shaping of Japanese Leisure.* Cornell Studies in Political Economy. Ithaca, N.Y.: Cornell University Press, 2003.

LeVine, Mark. *Overthrowing Geography: Jaffa, Tel Aviv, and the Struggle for Palestine, 1880–1948.* Berkeley and Los Angeles: University of California Press, 2005.

Levy, Lital. "Partitioned Pasts: Arab Jewish Intellectuals and the Case of Esther Azhari Moyal (1873–1948)." In *The Making of the Arab Intellectual: Empire, Public Sphere, and the Colonial Coordinates of Selfhood*, edited by Dyala Hamzah, 128–63. London: Routledge, 2009.

———. *Poetic Trespass: Writing between Hebrew and Arabic in Israel/Palestine.* Princeton, N.J.: Princeton University Press, 2014.

Liberles, Robert. "On the Threshold of Modernity: 1618–1780." In *Jewish Daily Life in Germany, 1618–1945*, edited by Marion A. Kaplan, 9–92. Oxford: Oxford University Press, 2005.

Lichtenstein, Tatjana. "Making Jews at Home: Zionism and the Construction of Jewish Nationalism in Inter-war Czechoslovakia." *East European Jewish Studies* 36, no. 1 (June 2006): 49–71.

Likhovski, Assaf. *Law and Identity in Mandate Palestine.* Chapel Hill: University of North Carolina Press, 2006.

Lipschuetz, Eliezer Meir. *Torat ha-hora'ah la-lashon ha-'Ivrit: 'Al pi hartza'ot bet ha-midrash le-morim Mizrahi* [Theory of Hebrew language instruction: According to lectures of the Mizrahi Teacher Training School]. Jerusalem: Defus ha-'Ivrit Y. Verker, 1929.

Little, Lester K. *Religious Poverty and the Profit Economy in Medieval Europe.* Ithaca, N.Y.: Cornell University Press, 1983.

Livni, Meir. *Ha-ma'avak she-nishkah: Ha-igud lema'an totzeret ha-aretz, ha-mahlakah ha-hakla'it, 1936–1949* [The forgotten struggle: The Union for Local Products, the Agricultural Department, 1936–1949]. Netanyah: Express, 1990.

Lockman, Zachary. "Arab Workers and Arab Nationalism in Palestine." In *Rethinking Nationalism in the Arab Middle East,* edited by Israel Gershoni and James Jankowski, 249–72. New York: Columbia University Press, 1997.

———. *Comrades and Enemies: Arab and Jewish Workers in Palestine, 1906–1948.* Berkeley and Los Angeles: University of California Press, 1996.

Lowenstein, Steven. "The Beginning of Integration, 1780–1880." In *Jewish Daily Life in Germany, 1618–1945,* edited by Marion A. Kaplan, 93–172. New York: Oxford University Press, 2005.

Luria, Yosef. *Ha-hinukh be-Eretz Yisra'el* [Education in Palestine]. Tel Aviv: Mahleket ha-hinukh be-Eretz Yisra'el, 1921.

MacLean, Lauren M. *Informal Institutions and Citizenship in Rural Africa: Risk and Reciprocity in Ghana and Côte d'Ivoire.* Cambridge: Cambridge University Press, 2010.

Margalit-Stern, Bat-Sheva. "'Imahot ba-hazit': Ha-ma'avak lema'an 'totzeret ha-aretz' veha-'emut ben interesim migdariyim la-interesim le'umiyim" [Women on the front lines: The struggle for local products and the conflict between gender interests and national interests]. *Yisra'el* 11 (2007): 91–120.

Marx, Karl. "On the Jewish Question" (1843). In *The Marx-Engels Reader,* 2nd ed., edited by Robert C. Tucker, 26–52. New York: Norton, 1978.

Mazrui, Ali A., and Alamin M. Mazrui. *The Power of Babel: Language and Governance in the African Experience.* Oxford: Currey, 1998.

Menard-Warwick, Julia. *Gendered Identities and Immigrant Language Learning.* Bristol: Multilingual Matters, 2009.

Michaely, Michael. *Sehar ha-hutz vi-yevu ha-hon be-Yisra'el* [Foreign trade and capital inflow in Israel]. Tel Aviv: 'Am 'Oved, 1963.

Milson, Menachem. "The Beginnings of Arabic and Islamic Studies at the Hebrew University of Jerusalem." *Judaism* 45, no. 2 (1996): 169–83.

Mir, Farina. *The Social Space of Language: Vernacular Culture in British Colonial Punjab.* Berkeley and Los Angeles: University of California Press, 2010.

Miron, Dan, and Hana Wirth-Nesher. "Modern Hebrew Literature: Zionist Perspectives and Israeli Realities." In *What Is Jewish Literature?,* edited by Hana Wirth-Nesher, 95–115. Philadelphia: Jewish Publication Society, 1994.

Miron, Guy. "From Bourgeois Germany to Palestine: Memoirs of German Jewish Women in Israel." *Nashim: A Journal of Jewish Women's Studies and Gender Issues* 17 (2009): 116–40.

Mitchell, Lisa. *Language, Emotion, and Politics in South India: The Making of a Mother Tongue.* Bloomington: Indiana University Press, 2009.

Morag, Shlomo. "Ha-'Ivrit ha-hadashah be-hitgabshutah: Lashon ba-askpeklaryah shel hevrah" [The new Hebrew in its consolidation: Language in social perspective]. *Katedrah* 56 (1990): 70–92.

Morris, I. *The Art of Teaching English as a Living Language.* London: Macmillan, 1959.

Morris, Isaac, and Rachel Morris. *Second Year English for Palestine Schools.* Jerusalem: Tarbuth, 1932.

Moss, Kenneth. "Arnold in Aysheshok, Schiller in Shnipishok: Imperatives of 'Culture' in East European Jewish Nationalism and Socialism." *Journal of Modern History* 81, no. 3 (September 2009): 537–78.

———. "Unchosen Peoplehood." Conference paper presented in Los Angeles, 30 January 2011.

Mossinsohn, Yigal, and A. A. Wolf. *Migdal Bavel: komedyah me-haye ha-aretz be-3 ma'arakhot* [The Tower of Babel: A comedy from the life of the land in 3 acts]. Tel Aviv: Matate Theater, 1951.

Myers, David N. *Re-Inventing the Jewish Past: European Jewish Intellectuals and the Zionist Return to History.* New York: Oxford University Press, 1995.

Nahir, Moshe. "Micro Language Planning and the Revival of Hebrew: A Schematic Framework." *Language in Society* 27, no. 3 (1998): 335–57.

Naor, Chava, and Jacob Shavit. *Staging and Stagers in Modern Jewish Palestine: The Creation of Festive Lore in a New Culture, 1882–1948.* Raphael Patai Series in Jewish Folklore and Anthropology. Detroit: Wayne State University Press, 2004.

Ne'eman, Aharon. "Hesegim ve-hasagot" [Accomplishments and achievements]. In *Sefer ha-yovel shel histadrut ha-morim 5663–5713* [*Anniversary volume of the Teachers' Federation, 1903–1953*], 435–51. Tel Aviv: Histadrut ha-morim be-Yisra'el, 1956.

Neumann, Boaz. *Land and Desire in Early Zionism.* Waltham, Mass.: Brandeis University Press, 2011.

Nir, Rafa'el. "Ma'amadah shel ha-lashon ha-'Ivrit be-tahalikh ha-tehiyah ha-le'umit" [The status of the Hebrew language in the process of national revival]. In *Toldot ha-Yishuv Ha-Yehudi Be-Eretz Yisra'el me-az ha-'aliyah ha-rishonah* [History of the Jewish yishuv in Palestine since the First Aliyah], edited by

Moshe Lissak and Zohar Shavit, 31–39. Jerusalem: Akademyah ha-le'umit ha-Yisre'elit le-mada'im, 1998.

Olsen, K. V. "English Language Studies in Denmark." *English Language Teaching* 1, no. 6 (May 1947): 157–62.

Ornan, Uzzi. "'Ivrit ke-safah zarah ve-'Ivrit le-dovre safot zarot" [Hebrew as a foreign language and Hebrew for speakers of other languages]. *Hinukh* 3–4 (January 1980): 217–23.

———. "Le-toldot tehiyat ha-lashon: ha-hizdamnut, ha-yekholet, veha-ratzon" [On the history of the language revival: The opportunity, the ability, and the will]. *Katedrah* 35 (1986): 83–94.

Parsons, Laila. "The Druze and the Birth of Israel." In *The War for Palestine: Rewriting the History of 1948*, edited by Eugene Rogan and Avi Shlaim, 60–78. Cambridge: Cambridge University Press, 2002.

———. *The Druze between Palestine and Israel, 1947–1949*. London: St. Antony's / Macmillan, 2000.

Parush, Iris. "Another Look at the Life of 'Dead' Hebrew: Intentional Ignorance of Hebrew in Nineteenth-Century Eastern European Jewish Society." *Book History* 7 (2004): 171–214.

Patai, Raphael. *Journeyman in Jerusalem: Memories and Letters, 1933–1947*. Oxford: Lexington, 2000.

Peiss, Kathy. "Gender Relations and Working-Class Leisure: New York City, 1880–1920." In *To Toil the Livelong Day: America's Women at Work, 1780–1980*, edited by Carol Groneman and Mary Beth Norton, 98–111. Ithaca, N.Y: Cornell University Press, 1987.

Pennycook, Alastair. *The Cultural Politics of English as an International Language*. Harlow, UK: Longman, 1994.

———. *English and the Discourses of Colonialism: The Politics of Language*. London: Routledge, 1998.

———. *Global Englishes and Transcultural Flows*. London: Routledge, 2007.

Penslar, Derek J. "Radio and the Shaping of Modern Israel, 1936–1973." In *Nationalism, Zionism, and Ethnic Mobilization of the Jews in 1900 and Beyond*, edited by Michael Berkowitz, 61–82. IJS Studies in Judaica 2. Leiden: Brill, 2004.

———. *Shylock's Children: Economics and Jewish Identity in Modern Europe*. Berkeley and Los Angeles: University of California Press, 2001.

———. "Zionism, Colonialism and Postcolonialism." In *Israeli Historical Revisionism from Left to Right*, 84–98. London: Cass, 2003.

Peyre, Henri. "On the Humanistic Value of Foreign Language Study." *Profession: Modern Language Association* (1980): 29–33.

Pilowsky, Arye Leyb. "Yiddish alongside the Revival of Hebrew: Public Polemics on the Status of Yiddish in Eretz Israel, 1907–1929." In *Readings in the Sociology of Jewish Languages*, edited by Joshua A. Fishman, 1:114–24. Leiden: Brill, 1985.

Pinsker, Shachar. *Literary Passports: The Making of Modernist Hebrew Fiction in Europe.* Stanford, Calif.: Stanford University Press, 2011.

———. "The Urban Literary Café and the Geography of Hebrew and Yiddish Modernism in Europe." In *The Oxford Handbook of Global Modernisms*, edited by Mark Wollaeger, 433–58. Oxford: Oxford University Press, 2012.

Piterberg, Gabriel. *The Returns of Zionism: Myths, Politics, and Scholarship in Israel.* London: Verso, 2008.

Plesner, Meir Martin. *Torat ha-dikduk ha-'Arvi: Sefer 'ezrah le-vate sefer 'Ivriyim* [The theory of Arabic grammar: A handbook for Hebrew schools]. Haifa: Bet ha-sefer ha-re'ali ha-'Ivri, 1935.

Presner, Todd Samuel. "Muscle Jews and Airplanes: Modernist Mythologies, the Great War, and the Politics of Regeneration." *Modernism/Modernity* 13, no. 4 (2006): 701–28.

Provence, Michael. "Protest, Counterinsurgency, and the League of Nations in Syria." Unpublished paper.

Rabau-Katinsky, Ziona. *Be-Tel-Aviv 'al ha-holot* [In Tel Aviv on the sands]. Ramat Gan: Masadah, 1973.

Rajagopal, Arvind. "Mediating Modernity: Theorizing Reception in a Non-Western Society." In *De-Westernizing Media Research*, 293–304. London: Routledge, 2000.

Reichel, Nirit. "Ben 'kartanut' le-'ofke-tarbut': Mekomah shel ha-haskalah ha-kelalit ba-hinukh ha-'Ivri be-eretz yisra'el 1882–1935" [Between "provincialism" and "cultural horizons": The place of general studies in Hebrew education in the Land of Israel, 1882–1935]. Doctoral diss., Tel Aviv University, 1994.

Reshef, Shimon, and Yuval Dror. *Ha-hinukh ha-'Ivri bi-yeme ha-bayit ha-le'umi* [Hebrew education in the days of the national home]. Jerusalem: Mosad Bialik, 1999.

Reuveni, Yaakov. "Ha-markiv ha-yehudi be-manganon memshelet ha-mandat: Hebetim kalkaliyim u-mediniyim" [The Jewish component in the mandate government apparatus: Economic and political aspects]. *Medinah, mimshal ve-yehasim benle'umiyim* 31 (1990): 43–75.

———. *Mimshal ha-mandat be-E. Y., 1920–1948: Nituah histori-medini* [The mandate government in Palestine, 1920–1948]. 'Iyunim ba-meshek uva-hevrah [Issues in the economy and society]. Ramat-Gan: Bar Ilan University, 1992–93.

Revusky, Abraham. *Jews in Palestine.* New York: Vanguard, 1938.

Rieger, Eliezer. "Ha-'itonut, ha-kolno'a veha-radio" [Journalism, cinema, and radio]. In *Ha-hinukh ha-'Ivri be-Eretz Yisra'el* [Hebrew education in the Land of Israel], 1:173–80. Tel Aviv: Devir, 1940.

———. "Shene piske-din." *Mishar ve-ta'asiyah* 2, no. 3 (22 February 1924).

Rinott, Moshe. "Capitulations: The Case of the German-Jewish Hilfsverein Schools in Palestine, 1901–1914." In *Palestine in the Late Ottoman Period: Political, Social, and Economic Transformation*, edited by David Kushner, 294–301. Jerusalem: Ben-Zvi Institute, 1986.

Rivkai, Israel Rubin. *'Al sefat yeladenu ba-aretz: mikhtavim le-horim 2* [On the language of our children in the land: Letters to parents 2]. Tel Aviv: Mefitz ha-sefer, 1938.

Rivlin, Yosef Yoel. *Sefer limud 'Arvit* [Arabic textbook]. Tel Aviv: Omanut, 1937.

Rojanski, Rachel. "Ha-omnam 'safah zarah ve-tzoremet'? Li-she'elat yahaso shel Ben Gurion le-Yidish le-ahar ha-sho'ah" [Really a foreign and grating language? On the question of Ben-Gurion's relationship to Yiddish after the Holocaust]. *'Iyunim be-tekumat Yisra'el* 15 (2005): 463–82.

———. "The Status of Yiddish in Israel, 1948–1951: An Overview." In *Yiddish after the Holocaust*, edited by Joseph Sherman, 46–59. Oxford: Boulevard, 2004.

Rokem, Na'ama. *Prosaic Conditions: Heinrich Heine and the Spaces of Jewish Literature.* Evanston, Ill.: Northwestern University Press, 2013.

Roth, H. Y. "'Al ha-kivun ha-ratzui shel limude ha-Anglit" [On the desired direction in the teaching of English]. *Moznayim* 16, nos. 1–6 (1943).

Rozenblit, Marsha L. *Reconstructing a National Identity: The Jews of Habsburg Austria during World War I.* Studies in Jewish History. Oxford: Oxford University Press, 2001.

Rozin, Orit. *Hovat ha-ahavah ha-kashah: Yahid u-kolektiv be-Yisra'el bi-shenot ha-hamishim* [The duty of tough love: Individual and collective in Israel in the 1950s]. Tel Aviv: 'Am 'Oved, 2008.

Rubenstein, Elyakim. "Ha-diyunim 'al hotza'at 'iton "Tziyoni"-'Arvi bi-shenot ha-'esrim veha-sheloshim" [The discussions about publishing "Zionist"-Arabic newspapers in the 1920s and 1930s]. *Kesher* 1 (May 1987): 45–54.

Samuel, Horace Barnett. *Unholy Memories of the Holy Land.* London: Leonard and Virginia Woolf, 1930.

Saposnik, Arieh Bruce. *Becoming Hebrew: The Creation of a Jewish National Culture in Ottoman Palestine.* New York: Oxford University Press, 2008.

Saraceni, Mario. *The Relocation of English: Shifting Paradigms in a Global Era.* Basingstoke, UK: Palgrave Macmillan, 2010.

Schaefer, Ursula. "Linguistics, Ideology, and the Discourse of Linguistic Nationalism: Some Preliminary Remarks." In *Linguistics, Ideology, and the*

Discourse of Linguistic Nationalism, edited by Claudia Lange et al., 1–36. Frankfurt am Main: Peter Lang, 2010.

Schleifer, Ron. "Jewish and Contemporary Origins of Israeli 'Hasbara.'" *Jewish Political Studies Review* 15, nos. 1–2 (2003): 123–53.

Schlor, Joachim. *Tel Aviv: From Dream to City.* London: Reaktion, 2007.

Schneerson, Fishel. *La-psikhologyah shel du ha-leshoniyut ba-aretz: hakirah be-vate ha-sefer ha-ironiyim be-Tel Aviv bi-shenot 1936–7, 37–38.* Tel Aviv: Seminariyon mehkar la-psikhologyah u-pedagogyah refu'it sotzialit, 1939.

School of Oriental Studies: History and Development. London: Waterlow and Sons, 1934.

Sefer ha-hinukh veha-tarbut. Tel Aviv: Misrad ha-hinukh veha-tarbut, 1951.

Sefer ha-shanah le-bogre bet ha-sefer "Safra." Tel Aviv: Bet ha-sefer Safra, 1935.

Sefer ha-shanah shel ha-'itona'im 1984. Tel Aviv: Agudat ha-'itona'im, 1984.

Segal, Miryam. *A New Sound in Hebrew Poetry: Poetics, Politics, Accent.* Bloomington: Indiana University Press, 2010.

Segal, Yerushalayim. *Zikhronot Yerushalayim Be-Tel Aviv* [Memoirs of Yerushalayim in Tel Aviv]. Tel Aviv: Moledet, 1993.

Segev, Tom. *One Palestine, Complete: Jews and Arabs under the British Mandate.* New York: Holt, 2001.

Seidman, Naomi. *A Marriage Made in Heaven: The Sexual Politics of Hebrew and Yiddish.* Berkeley and Los Angeles: University of California Press, 1997.

Selzer, Michael. *The Aryanization of the Jewish State.* New York: Black Star, 1967.

Sewell, *Work and Revolution in France: The Language of Labor from the Old Regime to 1848.* Cambridge: Cambridge University Press, 1980.

Shalit, David. *Makrinim koah: Bate ha-kolno'a, ha-seratim veha-Yisre'elim* [Screening power: The cinemas, the films, and the Israelis]. Tel Aviv: Resling, 2006.

Shamosh, Y. "Tazkir: 'Al limud ha-'Arvit be-vate ha-sefer ha-'Ivriyim be-Eretz Yisra'el." Department of Education of Knesset Yisra'el, Jewish Agency Political Division, 30 September 1942.

Shapira, Anita. *Land and Power: The Zionist Resort to Force, 1881–1948.* New York: Oxford University Press, 1992.

———. "Religious Motifs of the Labor Movement." In *Zionism and Religion*, edited by Shmuel Almog et al., 251–72. Hanover, N.H.: University Press of New England, 1998.

Shapiro, Yonathan. *'Ilit le-lo mamshikhim: Dorot manhigim ba-hevrah ha-Yisre'elit* [An elite without successors: Generations of leaders in Israeli society]. Tel Aviv: Sifriyat po'alim, 1984.

Shavit, Jacob. "Ben 'hevrah yishuvit' le-'hevrah politit': ha-Yishuv ha-Yehudi be-Eretz Yisra'el bi-tekufat ha-Mandat." *Katedrah* 14 (1979–80).

———. *Ha-historyah shel Tel-Aviv* [The history of Tel Aviv]. Tel Aviv: Ramot, Tel Aviv University, 2001.

Shavit, Zohar. "Boire un café en hébreu: Les cafés littéraires sur la scène culturelle de la Tel-Aviv de l'époque du Yishuv" [Drinking a coffee in Hebrew: Literary cafés on the Tel Aviv cultural scene during the Yishuv period]. *Yod* 13 (2008): 147–69.

———. "Le-male et ha-aretz sefarim: safrut mekorit le-'umat safrut meturgemet be-tahalikh yetzirato shel ha-merkaz ha-sifruti be-Eretz Yisra'el [To fill the land with books: Original literature versus translated literature in the creation process of the literary center in the Land of Israel]. *Ha-Safrut* 25 (1977): 45–68.

———. "Tel Aviv Language Police." In *Tel Aviv: The First Century; Visions, Designs, Actualities*, 191–211. Bloomington: Indiana University Press, 2011.

Sheffi, Na'ama. *Germanit be-'Ivrit: Targunim mi-Germanit ba-yishuv ha-'Ivri, 1882–1948* [German in Hebrew: Translations from German into Hebrew in Jewish Palestine, 1882–1948]. Jerusalem: Ben-Zvi Institute, 1998.

Shenhav, Yehouda. *The Arab Jews: A Postcolonial Reading of Nationalism, Religion, and Ethnicity.* Stanford, Calif.: Stanford University Press, 2006.

Sherman, A. J. *Mandate Days: British Lives in Palestine, 1918–1948.* New York: Thames and Hudson, 1998.

Shieffelin, Bambi B., et al., *Language Ideologies: Practice and Theory.* New York: Oxford University Press, 1998.

Shilo, Margalit. "Milhemet ha-safot ki-tenu'ah 'amamit" [The language war as a popular movement]. *Katedrah* 74 (1995): 87–119.

———. *Princess or Prisoner? Jewish Women in Jerusalem, 1840–1914.* Brandeis Series on Jewish Women. Waltham, Mass.: Brandeis University Press, 2005.

Shlaim, Avi. *Collusion across the Jordan: King Abdullah, the Zionist Movement, and the Partition of Palestine.* Oxford: Clarendon, 1988.

Shohamy, Elana Goldberg, and Bernard Spolsky. *The Languages of Israel: Policy, Ideology, and Practice.* Bilingual Education and Bilingualism 17. Clevedon, UK: Multilingual Matters, 1999.

Shohat, Ella. *Israeli Cinema: East/West and the Politics of Representation.* New ed. London: Tauris, 2010.

———. *Taboo Memories, Diasporic Voices.* Durham, N.C.: Duke University Press, 2006.

Shur, Shimon. *Gedud megine ha-safah be-Eretz Yisra'el 1923–1936* [The battalion of the defenders of the Hebrew language in Palestine, 1923–1936]. Haifa: Herzl Institute for Research of Zionism, Haifa University, 2000.

Simon, Akiba Ernst. *Kav ha-tihum: le'umiyut, Tziyonut veha-sikhsukh ha-Yehudi-'Arvi be-mishnat Mordekhai Martin Buber uvi-fe'iluto* [Line of demarcation: Nationalism, Zionism, and the Jewish-Arab conflict in the thought and action of Martin Buber]. Givat Haviva: Center for Arab Studies, 1973.

Sitton, Shoshana. "Zionist Education in an Encounter between the British Colonial and the Hebrew Cultures." *Journal of Educational Administration and History* 29, no. 2 (1997): 108–20.

Slater, Don. *Consumer Culture and Modernity.* Oxford: Polity, 1997.

Slezkine, Yuri. *The Jewish Century.* Princeton, N.J.: Princeton University Press, 2004.

Smith, Barbara J. *The Roots of Separatism in Palestine: British Economic Policy, 1920–1929.* Syracuse, N.Y.: Syracuse University Press, 1993.

Smith, Richard C., ed. *Teaching English as a Foreign Language, 1912–1936; Pioneers of ELT.* Vol. 3, *Michael West.* London: Routledge, 2003.

Sombart, Werner. *The Jews and Modern Capitalism.* Translated by M. Epstein. Social Science Classics Series. New Brunswick, N.J.: Transaction, 1982.

Sorkin, David. "Emancipation and Assimilation: Two Concepts and Their Application to German-Jewish History." *Leo Baeck Institute Yearbook* 35 (1990): 17–33.

Sovran, Tamar. "Ha-'Ivrit ki-sefat tarbut" [Hebrew as a language of culture]. In *Ha-'agalah ha-mele'ah: Me'ah ve-'esrim shenot tarbut Yisra'el* [The full wagon: One hundred twenty years of Israeli culture], edited by Israel Bartal, 52–62. Jerusalem: Magnes, 2002.

Storrs, Ronald. *The Memoirs of Sir Ronald Storrs.* New York: Putnam, 1937.

Strassman, Gabriel. *'Ote ha-gelimah: Toldot 'arikhat ha-din be-Eretz Yisra'el* [Wearers of the robe: The history of law in the Land of Israel]. Tel Aviv: Lishkat 'orkhe ha-din be-Yisra'el, 1984.

Sufian, Sandra M. *Healing the Land and the Nation: Malaria and the Zionist Project in Palestine, 1920–1947.* Chicago: University of Chicago Press, 2007.

Suleiman, Yasir. *The Arabic Language and National Identity: A Study in Ideology.* Edinburgh: Edinburgh University Press, 2003.

Swedenburg, Ted. *Memories of Revolt: The 1936–1939 Rebellion and the Palestinian National Past.* Fayetteville: University of Arkansas Press, 2003.

Taikher, M. *Hanhalat pinkasim* [Bookkeeping]. Haifa: Bet sefer tikhoni le-mishar 'Atid, 1941.

Talmon, R. "Arabic as a Minority Language in Israel." In *Arabic as a Minority Language,* edited by Jonathan Owens, 83:199–220. Berlin: Mouton de Gruyter, 1999.

Tamir, N. *Seminaristim be-ma'avak-'am: Sipur mi-yeme milhemet ha-safot be-Eretz Yisra'el* [Seminar students in battle: A story from the times of the language war in the Land of Israel]. Tel Aviv: Yavneh, 1963.

Tartakover, David, Meir Schnitzer, and Richard Flantz, eds. *Hatzagah rishonah: kerazot kolno'a Tel Aviv shenot ha-sheloshim* [First performance: Cinema posters of 1930s Tel Aviv]. Jerusalem: Arkhiyon ha-Yisre'eli li-seratim, Sinematek, 1995.

Taylor, Philip M. *The Projection of Britain: British Overseas Publicity and Propaganda, 1919–1939.* Cambridge: Cambridge University Press, 1981.

Tebbutt, Melanie. *Women's Talk? A Social History of "Gossip" in Working-Class Neighbourhoods, 1880–1960.* Aldershot, UK: Scolar, 1995.

Thompson, E. P. *The Making of the English Working Class.* London: Gollancz, 1963.

Tidhar, David. *Entziklopedyah la-halutze ha-Yishuv u-vonav* [Encyclopedia of the founders and builders of Israel]. Tel Aviv: Sifriyat Rishonim, 1947.

Tokhnit bate ha-sefer ha-'amamiyim ha-'Ironiyim [The curriculum of the urban national schools]. Vol. 3. Jerusalem: Hanhalah ha-tziyonit, Department of Education, 1923.

Tokhnit ha-limudim ha-nehugah be-vate sefer ha-amamiyim shel ha-mizrahi [The curriculum in place in the national schools of the Mizrahi movement]. Vol. 9. Jerusalem: Jewish Agency, Department of Education, 1931.

Tornquist-Plewa, Barbara. "Contrasting Ethnic Nationalisms: Eastern and Central Europe." In *Language and Nationalism in Europe.* edited by Stephen Barbour and Cathie Carmichael, 183–220. New York: Oxford University Press, 2000.

Trimbur, Dominique, and Danny Yaakobi. "Ha-ma'atzamot ha-eropeyot ve-hora'at safot zarot ba-Universitah ha-'Ivrit bi-tekufat ha-mandat" [The European powers and the instruction of Hebrew at Hebrew University during the mandate period]. In *Toldot ha-universitah ha-'Ivrit* [History of Hebrew University], 3:134–59. Jerusalem: Magnes, 2008.

Tryster, Hillel. *Israel before Israel: Silent Cinema in the Holy Land.* Jerusalem: Steven Spielberg Jewish Film Archive of the Avraham Harman Institute of Contemporary Jewry, Hebrew University of Jerusalem and the Central Zionist Archives, 1995.

Tzeror mikhtavim. Tel Aviv: Safra School of Commerce, 1945.

Ullendorf, Edward. "Hebrew in Mandatary [*sic*] Palestine." In *Hebrew Study from Ezra to Ben-Yehuda,* edited by William Horbury, 300–306. Edinburgh: Clark, 1999.

Van Creveld, Martin. *The Sword and the Olive: A Critical History of the Israeli Defense Force.* New York: Public Affairs, 2002.

Virshovsky, Hayim. "Latinit ba-vet ha-sefer ha-'Ivri" [Latin in the Hebrew school]. In *Halakhah u-ma'aseh ba-hinukh ha-tikhon: Kovetz ma'amarim mukdashim le-ve'ayot bet ha-sefer ha-tikhon ha-'iyuni* [Theory and practice in high school education: A collection of articles dedicated to the problems of the academic high school], 46–51. Jerusalem: Bet sefer tikhon le-yad ha-universitah ha-'Ivrit, 1962.

Wallach, Yair. "Readings in Conflict: Public Texts in Modern Jerusalem, 1858–1948." PhD diss., Birkbeck College, University of London, 2008.

Waquet, Francoise. *Latin, or the Empire of a Sign*. New York: Verso, 2001.

White, Anne. *De-Stalinization and the House of Culture: Declining State Control over Leisure in the USSR, Poland, and Hungary, 1953–89*. London: Routledge, 1990.

Wirth, Louis. "Urbanism as a Way of Life." *American Journal of Sociology* 44, no. 1 (July 1938): 1–24.

Wistrich, Robert. "Zionism and Its Jewish 'Assimilationist' Critics (1897–1948)." *Jewish Social Studies* 4, no. 2 (1998): 59–111.

Wrenn, C. Gilbert, and Dudley Lee Harley. *Time on Their Hands: A Report on Leisure, Recreation, and Young People*. Washington, D.C.: American Council on Education, 1941.

Yehieli, M. A. [Aharon Moshe Wizansky]. *Le-she'elat ha-safah* [On the language question]. Zurich: Mizpah, 1921.

Yehoash. *The Feet of the Messenger.* 1923. Reprint, Manchester, N.H.: Ayer, 1977.

———. *Fun New York biz Rehovos un tsurik* [From New York to Rehovot and back]. 2 vols. New York: Oyfgang, 1917.

Yellin, Avinoam, and Levi Billig. *Mukhtarat al-qira'ah* [Reading selections]. 3rd ed. Haifa: Bet ha-sefer ha-re'ali ha-'Ivri, 1944.

Y.M. "Anahnu u-shekhenenu." *Hed Ha-Hinukh* 1, nos. 18–20 (1927).

Yodfat, Arieh. "Yahase Yehudim ve-'Arvim be-reshitah shel Tel-Aviv (1909–1929)" [Jewish-Arab relations in the early days of Tel Aviv, 1909–1929]. *Ha-Tziyonut* 3 (1974): 520–47.

Yonai, Yosef. *'Arvit be-vate sefer 'Ivriyim* [Arabic in Hebrew schools]. Sidrat Te'udah. Jerusalem: Department of Education and Culture, Agaf toldot ha-hinukh veha-tarbut, 1992.

Y. S. "Li-she'elat anahnu u-shekhenenu." *Hed Ha-Hinukh* 1, nos. 10–12 (April 3, 1927).

Yuval, Ami. *Ilan natu'a be-admato* [A tree planted on its land]. Haifa: Pardes, 2005.

Zahra, Tara. *Kidnapped Souls: National Indifference and the Battle for Children in the Bohemian Lands, 1900–1948*. Ithaca, N.Y.: Cornell University Press, 2008.

Zakim, Eric. *To Build and Be Built: Landscape, Literature, and the Construction of Zionist Identity*. Philadelphia: University of Pennsylvania Press, 2006.

Zaydman, Y. A. "Morim: avot tehiyat ha-lashon." In *Sefer ha-yovel shel histadrut ha-morim 5663–5713*. Tel Aviv: Merkaz Histadrut ha-morim be-Eretz Yisra'el, 1956.

Zerubavel, Yael. *Recovered Roots: Collective Memory and the Making of Israeli National Tradition*. Chicago: University of Chicago Press, 1995.

Zimerman, Moshe. *Simane kolnoʻa: toledot ha-kolnoʻa ha-Yisre'eli ben ha-shanim 1896–1948* [Signs of cinema: The history of Israeli cinema between 1896 and 1948]. Tel Aviv: Diyonon Press, Tel Aviv University, 2001.

Zuta, H. A. *Darko shel moreh: pirke zikhronot, sekirot, u-ma'amarim me-et ehad ha-morim ba-dor ha-tehiyah* [The way of a teacher: Memoirs, surveys, and articles from one of the teachers of the revival generation]. Jerusalem: Re'uven Mass, 1937.

INDEX

Locators in italics indicate pages with illustrations.

Abbady, Isaac Abraham, 99, 104, 112–13, 120

Achebe, Chinua, 99

activism, pro-Hebrew, 44–45, 53, 61, 105–9, 113–15, 228; economic aspects, 84; legal system and, 124–25; municipal governments and, 127–28

adult education, 136–38. *See also* business schools; foreign-language instruction; languages: study/teaching of

advertisements and advertising agencies, 84–89

agriculture and agricultural settlements, 68, 189

Ahuzat Bayit society, 146

aliyah, waves of, 26–27, 65, 75, 223, 244–45n19. *See also* immigrants and immigration to Palestine

Allenby, Edmund, 119

Alliance israélite universelle schools, 184–86, 267–68n18

Almog, Oz, 191

al-Salam (newspaper), 166

Alterman, Nathan, 29

alte zakhen. See used goods

Altneuland, 74

Amara, Muhammad, 179

Amikam, Israel, 107–9, *109,* 116–17

An Anthem of Local Products, 70–71

Anderson, Benedict, 12

anecdotes, 20, 30, 44–45, 51, 77–78. *See also* memoir writing; oral histories and interviews

Arabic culture and language, 22, 142–47; clothing, 175; commerce and, 73–75, 80–81; military intelligence and, 144,

Arabic culture (*Continued*)
174–78, 200; perception of, 15–16,
151–52, 201–2; promotion of (*see* study/
teaching of); propaganda efforts and,
15–16, 162, 165–72, 200; study/teaching
of, 151–61, 177, 183, 186–88, 198–207,
218–20, 267n23; Yiddish and, 81. *See also*
Jewish-Arab relations
Arabists/orientalists, 178–79; Arabic
language/culture and, 144–45, 160–61;
education and, 188, 199–200, 203,
267n31. *See also* orientalism and
orientalists
Arab-Jewish relations. *See* Jewish-Arab
relations
Arab Jews, 37, 73–75, 238n39, 247n49
Arab labor, 146–47
Arab press, 163–72
Arab Revolt of 1936–39. *See* violence,
anti-Zionist
Arabs, Palestinian, 16, 22, 160; commerce
and, 64, 71, 80–81; Hebrew language
and, 180, 206, 265n140; Yiddish
speaking, 81; Zionism and, 15, 46, 151,
163, 172
Arendt, Hannah, 6
Arlosoroff, Hayim, 101, 105
Aschheim, Steven, 74, 246n41
Assaf (Osofsky), Michael, 153, 166, 168,
170, 172
Assaf, Simha, 125
assimilation and assimilationism, 93–95
'Atid School of Commerce, 93–94
'avodah. *See* labor, concept of (Zionist)
Azai, P. (Pinhas Elad), 140–41

Babel/Bavel metaphor, 24, 68, 98, 222–23,
225–26; economic aspects, 64, 71, 244n4;
linguistic aspects, 7, 10, 143. *See also*
language diversity
Bachi, Roberto, 11, 233n19

Baden-Powell, Robert, 213
Balfour Declaration, 100, 119
Battalion of the Defenders of the
Hebrew Language, 53, 57–59, 107–8,
115, 224
Bauer, Ernst. *See* Be'eri, Eliezer (Ernst
Bauer)
Be'eri, Eliezer (Ernst Bauer), 156–58,
160–61
Belkind, Israel, 189
Ben-Gurion, David, 68, 76
Bentwich, J. S., 136–37, 196–97
Benvenisti, Meron, 143
Ben-Yehuda, Eliezer, 6, 202
Ben-Zeev, Israel, 198–99, 269n67
Berlin, Yosef Y., 205
Berlitz, Maximilian, 217, 272n131
Bialik, Hayim Nachman, 30–32, 63, 106,
236nn8, 236nn10
Bibliographic Anthology, 161
bilingualism, 14, 17–18, 84–85, 110–11, 192,
194. *See also* Hebrew language:
hegemony of
Billig, Levi, 178, 199, 204
binationalism, 155–56, 160, 260n49. *See also*
collaboration, Jewish-Arab
Binyamin, G., 177
Blommaert, Jan, 8, 233n11
Blumgarten, Solomon. *See* Yehoash
(Solomon Blumgarten)
Boehmer, Elleke, 213
Boneh, Alfred, 75
Brawer, Avraham Yaakov, 74
Brenner, Yosef Hayim, 83
Brinker, Menahem, 49
British Council, 188–89, 268n34
British Institute, 137–38, 189
British-Jewish relations. *See* Jewish-British
relations
British mandate, 16–17; civil service, 102,
111–12, 117–18, 251n35; economic

policies, 83; legal system, 124–25; linguistic aspects, 16, 23, 100–105, 110–13, 126–29; Yishuv and, 126–27, 212–13. *See also* Balfour Declaration

Buber, Martin, 179

bureaucracies. *See* clerical workers

Burke, Peter, 18–19

business correspondence, 88–89, 92

business schools, 92–93, 95–96. *See also* English language: business education and; Safra School of Commerce; Tel Aviv School of Commerce

Central Council for the Enforcement of Hebrew (CCEH), 49, 60, 86–87, 89, 93–94, 97

Central Translation Bureau, 120–23

Chaver, Yael, 9

Chelouche, Yosef Eliyahu, 151, 163–64

cinema, 27, 50–55, 58–61

"The City Revealed" exhibition, 1–3, 25, 228

civil service, 117–18. *See also* British mandate; clerical workers

clerical workers, 111–13, 118, 251n35

Clifford, James, 24

coercion, state, 33. *See also* Hebrew language

coexistence between Jews and Muslims, 155, 173, 179–80. *See also* binationalism

coffeehouses, 27, 44–49

Cohen, Gamliel, 176–77

Cohen, Hillel, 172

Cohen-Portheim, Paul, 214–15

collaboration, Jewish-Arab, 145, 170, 172–73, 257n8

commerce, 64–67, 244n10; education for (*see* business schools); high, 83–95; international aspects, 84, 88 (*see also* imports and exports); linguistic aspects, 64–77, 84 (*see also* languages); low, 73–81

(*see also* peddlers and peddling); Tel Aviv and, 73–74, 76–80; Yishuv and, 63–69, 83

conflicts, Arab-Jewish. *See* Jewish-Arab relations

contacts between Arabs and Jews. *See* Jewish-Arab relations

court system. *See* legal system

culture, Hebrew, 27–29, 31–33, 68; the home/women and, 35–39; linguistic aspects, 41–42, 233n15 (*see also* languages); threats to, 48–50. *See also* cinema; coffeehouses; Hebrew literature

culture, Jewish, 56–57, 104. *See also* culture, Hebrew; Yiddish literature

Curran, James, 50

Danin, Ezra, 175

Delek. *See* Revisionists

Department of Arab Activities, 156–58

Departments of Education, 187–88

"The Desired Direction in the Teaching of English," 215–16

De Vries, David, 112–14

diaries and journals, 38–39

Diaspora and diasporic conditions/culture, 57; antidotes to/negation of, 15, 183–84, 204–5; commercial aspects, 21, 64, 66, 71, 82; linguistic aspects, 14, 76, 102, 191. *See also* exile and exiles

diglossia, 14

Di Goldene Keyt (literary journal), 223

Dizengoff, Meir, 50–51, 58, 76, 84

Dohm, Christian Wilhelm von, 67

A Dream Come True, 6–7

Drinkwater, Allan, 136–37

Druze, 261n58

the East. *See* Levant/Levantine/*levantini*/Levantinism

Edelshteyn, Y., 41–42

Eden Cinema, 51, 59

Eden Cinema program, 54

Edict of Toleration, 67

education. *See* adult education; business schools; Hebrew language instruction and Hebrew schools; Jewish education; languages: study/teaching of

Eini, Yaakov, 175

Elad, Pinhas. *See* Azai, P. (Pinhas Elad)

Eliash, Mordechai, 105–6, 125–26

Elitzedek, Bezalel, 224

Elmaliah, Abraham, 163–65, 174, 178, 184, 199, 269n75

Emmanuel Ha-Rusi (Emmanuel Novogrebelsky), 78–79

English language, 16, 201, 215–16, 234n31; books and newspapers, 140–41; business education and, 93, 135, 185–86; civil service and, 117, 123; demand for, 125–35, 210–12; examinations in, 117–18, 123; legal system and, 126; mandate Palestine and, 16, 22, 99–104; opposition to, 103, 135, 190–91; proficiency in, 123–24; promotion of, 189, 268n34; study/teaching of, 136–39, 183–85, 187–90

English literature, 211–12

Epstein, Izhac, 191–92

Europe: culture and values, 211–15; diaspora (*see* Diaspora and diasporic conditions/culture); languages, 209–11, 271n114 (*see also* English language; French language; German language; Italian language; Jews, Polish-speaking)

Even-Zohar, Itamar, 233n15

exile and exiles, 14–15, 24, 66, 73–74, 222. *See also* Diaspora and diasporic conditions/culture; multilingualism

exports. *See* imports and exports

Eyal, Gil, 176, 257n5

eye disease. *See* trachoma

Farrell, W. J., 196

film. *See* cinema

filogalutismus (philo-galut-ism or philo-exile-ism), 222

Fishman, Joshua, 9

foreign-language films, 52–61

foreign-language instruction, 62–63, 96–97, 152, 182, 184, 217, 221; justification for, 195–96; opposition to, 189–94; theories of, 204–8, 217–20, 270n89. *See also* business schools; *under individual languages*

foreign languages, 224–25. *See also* language diversity; *leshonot lo'aziyot* (foreign languages); *under individual languages*

French language, 97, 110–11, 182, 266n3

Frumkin, Gad, 125

fund-raising efforts, 131, 173–74

galutiyut. *See* exile and exiles

Gedud megine ha-safah. *See* Battalion of the Defenders of the Hebrew Language

German language, 46–49, 59–60, 223–25

Gimnasya Re'alit. *See* Hebrew High School for Commerce

Glickson, Miriam, 153–54, 160

Goffman, Erving, 34–35

Goitein, Shlomo Dov, 183, 205–7

Golani, Boaz, 226

Golumb, Eliyahu, 167

Gottlieb (Yedidyah), Ben-Zion, 3–4

Greenblatt, Stephen, 20

Haaretz (newspaper), 172

Ha'avarah (transfer) agreements, 71

Ha-Cohen, Mordechai Ben-Hillel, 100, 104, 131, 135, 185, 193, 211

Haganah, 175, 177

Ha-Herut (newspaper), 163–64, 269n75

halutziyut. *See* pioneering and pioneers

Hamelitz, 89–90

Hamelitz flyer, 91

Haqiqat al-Amr (newspaper), 168–73

hasbara ("explaining") projects, 170, 173–74, 264n110. *See also* propaganda

Ha-Shomer, 265n137

Ha-Shomer Ha-Tza'ir, 155–56, 177

Ha-Va'ad Ha-Le'umi. *See* Jewish National Council (Ha-Va'ad Ha-Le'umi)

Hebrew Gymnasium in Jaffa, 184

Hebrew Gymnasium of Jerusalem, 186

Hebrew High School for Commerce, 92–93

Hebrew language, 28–29; Arabic and, 202–7; challenges to hegemony, 20, 97, 194–95, 209–10, 223–26 (*see also* foreign-language instruction); commerce and, 77, 88–89, 92; discrimination against, 106, 128; enforcing/policing of, 10, 31–34, 77–78, 85–88, 93–94, 97–98, 132–33, 224 (*see also* telegraph service controversy); exclusivity of, 4, 135, 226, 265–66n1; hegemony of, 17, 20–21, 59, 76, 232n9 (*see also* monolingualism and monolingualization); Jewish nationalism and, 27, 105, 110–11, 113, 139; judiciary and, 105–6, 124–25; limitations of, 29–31, 63, 115, 183, 234n22; proficiency in, 118, 253n57; promotion of, 21, 34–37, 87, 100–101, 107–9, 131, 138–39, 176–77; revival of, 1–8, 182, 232n5; Sabbath and, 29–31, 236n6; study/teaching of, 203, 253n57 (*see also* Hebrew language instruction and Hebrew schools); Yiddish language and, 14, 56–57

Hebrew Language Committee, 6, 8

Hebrew language instruction and Hebrew schools, 181–221. *See also* Hebrew language

Hebrew literature, 19, 29, 235n33. *See also* translation and translators

"Hebrew" products. *See* products of the land (*totzeret ha-aretz*)

Hebrew Teachers' Federation, 12, 42, 57–58, 182, 239–40nn58–59

Hebrew telegraphic code. *See* telegraph service controversy

Hebrew University School of Oriental Studies, 15, 161, 178, 188, 204

Heller, Monica, 17–18

Helman, Anat, 34, 58

Herzl, Theodor, 74, 101

Hevrat Magen (Society for Protection), 163–64

Higham, Charles, 213–14

Hirsch, Frieda, 39

Histadrut, 125, 154, 167–68, 172–74, 177

history, cultural, 18–19

the home, 37–39, 238n41, 238n43. *See also* languages; leisure time and activities; women

Horesh, Shimon, 178

Hroch, Miroslav, 6

Husayni family, 172

identity, national, 17–18, 110. *See also* nationalism, Jewish

Igud le-hashlatat ha-'Ivrit. *See* Organization for the Enforcement of Hebrew

immigrants and immigration to Palestine, 11–16, 26–27, 44, 151, 258n11; Arabic language and, 142–43; economic aspects, 64–65, 78–81; German, 45–46; Hebrew language and, 20–21, 37, 238n41; languages and, 49, 134, 142–43, 222–27; media consumption and, 49–50, 58, 61. *See also* aliyah, waves of; language diversity

imports and exports, 63, 83

"informal state," 33, 61, 237n23

informants and informers, 175–78, 261n70

intelligence gathering. *See* military intelligence

international trade. *See* commerce; imports and exports

interpreters. *See* translation and translators

Irgun, 177

isolationism, economic, 69–71

Israel, prestate. *See* Palestine

Israel National Commission for UNESCO report, 222

Italian language, 193–94

Jabotinsky, Vladimir, 174, 176–77

Jacobson, Abigail, 163

Jaffa, 46–47, 75, 146

The Jazz Singer, 53

Jerusalem, 74, 131, 198

Jewish Agency, 57–58, 131, 152–54, 160, 259n32

Jewish-Arab relations, 142–80, 170, 198–200, 205, 258n16; personal contact/ encounters, 154–55, 158–61, 200; role of language, 147–49, 152–55, 165; surveillance and control, 200 (*see also* military intelligence); violence, 147, 152. *See also* binationalism; coexistence between Jews and Muslims; violence, anti-Zionist

Jewish-British relations, 104–5, 209–15, 250n12

Jewish education, 187–88. *See also* Hebrew language instruction and Hebrew schools; languages: study/teaching of; *under individual schools*

Jewish National Council (Ha-Va'ad Ha-Le'umi), 115–16, 128, 187–88, 267n27, 268n34

Jews, Arab. *See* Arab Jews

Jews, Eastern European, 74, 246n41

Jews, German-speaking. *See* German language

Jews, Libyan. *See* Jews, Tripolitanian

Jews, Polish-speaking, 65–66, 69, 210

Jews, Sephardic, 163–67, 262n75, 262n87. *See also* Levant/Levantine/*levantini*/ Levantinism; languages and culture, 47, 178–79, 262n74, 262n87; Palestinian Arabs and, 151, 199

Jews, Tripolitanian, 37

jokes. *See* anecdotes

Joseph II, 67

Judea Film Company, 57–58

Kalvarisky, Hayim, 161, 166

Kapliwatzky, Jochanan, 199, 203, 269n72

Katznelson, Rachel, 37

Kfar Masaryk (kibbutz), 155–56

Khalidi, Rashid, 164

Kisch, Frederick, 105, 115

Klausner, Josef, 178–79, 257n3

Krichevsky (movie distributor), 52

Kupferberg, Alfred, 84

Kurstein, Y. Y., 154

labor, concept of (Zionist), 29–30

Labor Zionists, 68–69; education and foreign language study, 185–86, 191, 267n27; fund-raising efforts, 173; Jewish-Arab relations and, 22, 147, 154–55; Sabbath and, 32–33. *See also* Histadrut

Ladino language, 11–12, 30, 47, 164, 225, 262n87

Land of Promise (Le-hayim hadashim), 55

language diversity, 3–5, 222–24; acceptance of, 35–38, 227–28, 274n21; Yishuv and, 14, 17, 82. *See also* Babel/Bavel metaphor; multilingualism languages, 11–12, 17–18, 21, 81, 195–97, 228–29; business education and, 93, 135 (*see also* business schools); colonial aspects, 219–20; competency, 8, 12, 143, 145, 233n11; informal acquisition of, 36, 262n74; infractions and policing of, 27, 32–34, 81, 85–86 (*see also* Hebrew language); nationalism and, 17–18, 26–27, 110; political aspects, 180; sacred vs. profane, 29–30; study/teaching of, 22–23, 95, 200–202, 217–18, 270n83 (*see also* Arabic culture and language; English language; foreign-language instruction; Hebrew language instruction and Hebrew schools). *See also* Arabic culture and language; English language; foreign-language instruction; foreign languages; French language; German language; Hebrew language; Italian language; Jews, Polish-speaking; Ladino language; Yiddish language

languages, official, 4, 100–101, 118–20, 129, 250n1. *See also under individual languages*

language services. *See* translation and translators

language surveys, 42–43, 239–40nn58–59

legal system, 124–25

leisure time and activities, 44; controlling, 32–34, 236n12; language and, 21, 26–61; media consumption, 49–50, 58, 61; reading (*see* reading and literature); technology and, 49–50. *See also* cinema; coffeehouses; reading and literature; the home; writing

leshonot lo'aziyot (foreign languages), 36, 87. *See also* Hebrew language: commerce and

letter writing, 39

Levant/Levantine/*levantini*/Levantinism, 74, 205–6, 247n49. *See also* orientalism

and orientalists; commercial and linguistic aspects, 76–77, 87–88; threat of, 93–95

Levin, Nahum, 224

Levin, Shimriyah, 70–71

LeVine, Mark, 145, 258n11

Lewald, August, 72

Lirik, A. S. (Aaron Levi Riklis), 26

literary salons. *See* coffeehouses

literature, 19, 216, 219, 235n33. *See also* Arabic culture and language; English literature; Hebrew literature; reading and literature; Yiddish literature

Lockman, Zachary, 47, 145, 172

Loewe, Heinrich, 41

Ludvipol, Abraham, 62–65

Luria, Yosef, 56, 185, 187, 196

luxury goods and stores, 84, 88

Malul, Nissim, 164–66

mandate Palestine. *See* British mandate

Mapai (consolidated labor party), 154–55

Margalit-Stern, Bat-Sheva, 88

Marx, Karl, 67

Mayer, Leo Ari, 220

Mayne yidishe mame. See *My Jewish Mother*

media consumption. *See* leisure time and activities

melakhah. See labor, concept of (Zionist)

memoir writing, 39. *See also* diaries and journals

Mendilow, Adam A., 188, 214

Mereminsky, Israel, 173–74

Meyuhas, Yosef, 166

military intelligence, 144, 174–78, 200. *See also* informants and informers

mista'arvim [undercover agents]. *See* informants and informers

Molcho, Yitzhak, 52

Money, A. W., 119

monolingualism and monolingualization, 9, 105, 110–11, 189–90. *See also* Hebrew language: hegemony of

mothers. *See* the home; women

mother tongues. *See* languages

movies. *See* cinema

movie theaters, 51–56

Moyal, David and Esther, 163–64

multilingualism, 7–13, 64, 119, 180. *See also* bilingualism; language diversity

My Jewish Mother, 57–58

nationalism, Jewish, 17–18, 110, 151, 227. *See also* culture, Hebrew; Yishuv; Zionism and Zionists

Ne'eman, Aharon, 182, 274n21

New Method Readers textbook series, 197–98

newspapers, 43, 171; Arabic, 122, 164; coffeehouses and, 48; English, 89, 138, 140, 189; Hebrew, 48, 106, 156, 166; Palestinian, 164, 262n82; promotion of Hebrew in, 88; propaganda and, 151, 162–73, 261–62n71; Sephardic, 163–65; Zionist Arabic, 144, 166–70. *See also under* individual names

Novograbelsky, Emmanuel. *See* Emmanuel Ha-Rusi

Nurock, Max, 112, 127

Occupied Enemy Territory Administration (OETA), 119

office workers. *See* clerical workers

Official Gazette (newspaper), 106, 126

oral histories and interviews, 81, 146–50, 246n47. *See also* memoir writing

Organization for the Enforcement of Hebrew, 77, 126

orientalism and orientalists, 15, 160–61, 178–79, 198, 202–7, 219–20. *See also* Arabists/orientalists

Ostjuden. See Jews, Eastern European

Ottoman period, 179, 262n74

Palestine, 21, 75, 144–45; demographics, 11, 13–15, 64–65; economic aspects (*see* commerce; products of the land (*totzeret ha-aretz*)); linguistic aspects (*see* languages); partition of (*see* binationalism). *See also* Arabs, Palestinian; British mandate; immigrants and immigration to Palestine; Yishuv; Zionism and Zionists

Palestine Post (newspaper), 138, 189

Palestine Royal Commission report of 1937, 118

Palmach, 175–76

Palmon, Yehoshua, 175–76

Park, Myung-Jin, 50

Patai, Raphael, 70

peddlers and peddling, 72–82, 245–46n31

Penslar, Derek, 74, 221

Persitz, Shoshana, 55–56, 242n108

Pinsker, Shachar, 44, 47

pioneering and pioneers, 26–27

Plenius (newspaper), 89

Plessner, Martin, 202–4, 207

police, 117, 118, 128, 253n57

Polish language. *See* Jews, Polish-speaking

Post and Telegraph Office, 114–15. *See also* telegraph service controversy

Poston, Ralph, 104

private versus public spheres. *See* the home; leisure time and activities

products of the land (*totzeret ha-aretz*), 69–71, 79–80, 87, 97, 244–45n19, 245n24

propaganda: Arab, 169–72; British, 162–63; fund-raising for, 173–74; newspapers and (*see* newspapers); Zionist, 151, 162–72. *See also hasbara* ("explaining") projects

Purim holiday, 3, 232n3

"The Question of Arabic Study: Toward a Decision," 206

Rabau-Katinsky, Ziona, 78, 80
radio broadcasts, 82, 216, 261–62n71
Railways Department and railway union, 121–22
reading and literature, 40–44, 140–41, 239–40nn58–59. *See also* literature
Re'ali School in Haifa, 184–85, 218
Reichel, Nirit, 152, 195, 259n29
Reuveni, Yaakov, 113
Reuven Mass publishing house, 158–60
Revisionists, 174–77
Rieger, Eliezer, 53, 69, 136
riots, Arab. *See* Jewish-Arab relations
Rivkai, Israel Rubin, 38, 238n41
Rivlin, Josef, 58–59, 208
Rivoli (store), 84
Rokach, Israel, 85, 133
Rokach, Shimon, 88
Rosenstein (Even-Shoshan), Zvi, 155
Roth, Hayim Yehuda (Leon), 183, 215–16

the Sabbath, 29–33
Safra, Yosef, 92
Safra School of Commerce, 92–93, 96, 135–36, 211
Samuel, Herbert, 142
Saposnik, Arieh, 7, 9
Sasson, Eliyahu, 152–53, 161
Schneerson, Fishel, 192–93
schools. *See* Alliance israélite universelle schools; business schools; foreign-language instruction; Hebrew language instruction and Hebrew schools; Jewish education; languages: study/teaching of; *under individual names of schools and universities*
Schurr, Shlomo, 95
Segal, Miryam, 31

Segal, Yerushalayim, 52–53, 60
Seidman, Naomi, 38, 232n5
Semitism. *See* Levant/Levantine/*levantini*/Levantinism
Senator, Werner, 57
Shahar (unit of Shai intelligence division), 175–77
Shai intelligence division, 175
Shamosh, Yitzhak, 199
Shapira, Anita, 175
Shapiro, Yonathan, 12, 234n22
Sharon, Avraham, 222
Shavit, Zohar, 7, 10
Shekhtman, Aharon, 222–24
Shenker, Arieh, 85
Sherman, A. J., 104
Shertok (Sharett), Moshe, 152, 196, 225
Shmurak, Menahem (Emil), 98
Shohamy, Elana, 182
Shuckburgh, John, 116
Sitton, Shoshana, 209–10
Slezkine, Yuri, 102
Smilansky, Moshe, 142–43, 257n2
social control and expectations, 32–34
sociolinguistics and sociolinguists, 8, 17–19
Sokolov, Nahum, 123
Sombart, Werner, 67
Somekh, Shimon, 177
Spolsky, Bernard, 182
Storrs, Ronald, 118–20
Strassman, Gabriel, 139–40
Sutker, Paula Gottlieb, 1–4, 24–25, 228

Tabenkin, Yitzhak, 32
Tammuz, Binyamin, 46–47
Tartakover, David, 61
teachers, 42–43, 137; of Arabic, 160; promotion of Hebrew and, 182, 189; training of, 188. *See also* Hebrew Teachers' Federation; languages: study/teaching of

Tebbutt, Melanie, 73
Technion, 9, 226
technology and leisure activities, 49–50
Tel Aviv, 1–2, 28, 75; commerce and, 73, 77; languages and, 10, 76–77, 235n33; linguistic policies, 127–29, 132–33, 224
"Tel Aviv Language Police," 10
Tel Aviv School of Commerce, 95–96, 136
telegraph service controversy, 107–9, 114–17
The Theory of Arabic Grammar: A Guidebook for Hebrew Schools, 202–3
totzeret ha-aretz. *See* products of the land (*totzeret ha-aretz*)
Tower of Babel. *See* Babel/Bavel metaphor
The Tower of Babel (play), 223
trachoma, 148–49, 258n23
trade. *See* commerce
translation and translators, 40–43, 119–23, 239n52; British mandate and, 127; historical aspects, 232n3; municipal governments and, 130; services, 89–90, 90

Ullendorff, Edward, 44, 104
undercover agents. *See* informants and informers
universities. *See* foreign-language instruction; Hebrew language instruction and Hebrew schools; languages: study/teaching of; *under individual names of universities*
urban centers and life, 28, 65, 244n6
used goods, 82. *See also* peddlers and peddling
Ussefiya Arabic seminar, 158, 159
Ussishkin, Menahem, 181

Vidra, Naftali, 89
Viëtor, Wilhelm, 217–18

violence, anti-Zionist, 46, 145–48, 169, 258n19
violence against Jews. *See* Jewish-Arab relations

Wallach, Yair, 106
Wauchope, Arthur, 108, 118
Weller's jam advertisement, 85, 86
the West. *See* Europe
West, Michael, 197–98
Wirth, Louis, 28
Wizansky, Aharon Moshe, 27
women, 88, 232n5. *See also* the home
writing, 39. *See also* diaries and journals

Yaffe, Aryeh, 155
Yaffe, Bezalel, 105
Yedidyah, Ben-Zion. *See* Gottlieb (Yedidyah), Ben-Zion
Yehoash (Solomon Blumgarten), 34, 142, 151, 257n1
Yeivin, Shmuel, 106, 120
Yellin, Aviezer, 57–58
Yellin, Avinoam, 199–200, 207–8
Yellin, David, 204
Yiddish films, 56–59
Yiddish language, 17, 75; Arabic and, 81; Hebrew language and, 14, 56–57; opposition to, 56–59, 73, 223–24; rejection of, 27
Yiddish literature, 40
Yishuv, 8–9, 13; British mandate and, 126–27, 212–13; demographics, 11, 121; economic aspects, 21, 63–68, 71–72, 97, 245n25, 247n73; linguistic history and policies, 11–16, 19–22, 121, 131–32, 233n20; media consumption and, 50; Palestinian Arabs and, 151–52; political aspects, 111

Zahra, Tara, 17

Zaslani (Shiloah), Reuven, 167

Zhokhovitzky (Zakif), Gedalyahu, 90–92

Zionism and Zionists, 11–14, 26, 177–78, 263n93; cinema and, 51–52, 61; economic aspects, 21, 64, 68–69; Europe and, 209–13; linguistic history or policies, 4–6, 10, 14, 24, 130–31, 204, 209; propaganda efforts (*see* propaganda); Sabbath and, 32–33. *See also* Arabs, Palestinian; culture, Hebrew; Labor Zionists; Revisionists; violence, anti-Zionist

Zionist Organization, 115

Zohar, Zvi, 195